SCHOOL OF ORIENTAL AND
AFRICAN STUDIES

BROTHERS IN INDIA

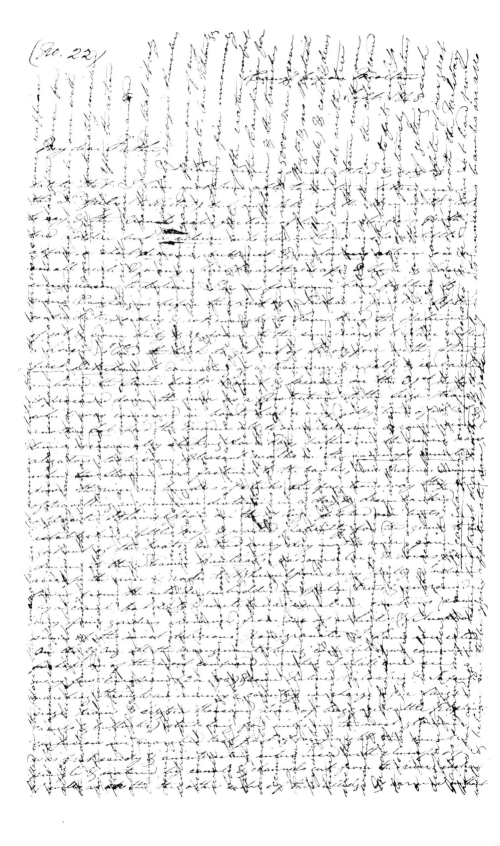

BROTHERS IN INDIA

The Correspondence of
Tom, Alfred and Christopher Bassano

1841-75

Selected, Edited and Introduced
by
MARY DOREEN WAINWRIGHT

SCHOOL OF ORIENTAL AND AFRICAN STUDIES
UNIVERSITY OF LONDON
Malet Street, London WC1E 7HP
1979

This edition © M.D. Wainwright, 1979

  British Library Cataloguing in Publication Data

Bassano, Thomas
  Brothers in India.
  1. India - Social life and customs - Sources
  2. India - History - 19th century - Sources
  I. Title II. Bassano, Alfred
  III. Bassano, Christopher IV. Wainwright,
  Mary Doreen V. University of London.
  School of Oriental and African Studies
  954.03'08   DS421

  ISBN 0-7286-0056-0

Printed in Great Britain by
Redwood Burn Limited
Trowbridge & Esher

FOREWORD

The letters printed in this volume are from the private
collection of Miss Valentine Bassano, grand-daughter of Walter
Waterfield Bassano, and great-niece of the three brothers who
went to India in the 1840s.

Miss Bassano wrote to the Director of the School of Oriental
and African Studies, London, in November 1970 about the
possibility of having some family letters edited for publication. As some of the correspondence related to India, the
letter was passed to the present editor, who visited Miss
Bassano in her home early in 1971, and there saw a bundle of
letters written mainly by her great-uncle Thomas Bromsall
Bassano, a coffee planter in South India. During subsequent
visits over a period of two or three years, numerous other
letters and papers came to light. They were not sorted or in
any particular order, but mixed up with other family letters
and papers, as they had been put away over the years. Detached
sheets had frequently been misplaced, so that many of the
letters seemed at first sight to be incomplete. However, the
missing portion of a seemingly incomplete letter usually turned
up somewhere in the end. Miss Bassano kindly allowed all the
papers which were found to be temporarily housed at SOAS for
examination.

Reading, identification, and sorting of the letters took a
long time, and the making of working copies much longer, as
many of the letters were difficult to read, partly because of
the practice of writing small and "crossing" to make the most
of limited space,* and partly because of faded and difficult
handwriting and absence of punctuation, and in one case, of
idiosyncratic spelling – and also because the work had to be
done in the time which could be spared from other duties, and
between research visits to India. However, it became clear
that here were some family letters – not generally available –
which both from the interest of their contents and the vividness of their style, deserved to be made known to all those
interested in the personal lives and actions of the minor, as
well as the major, actors in the fascinating drama of British
India. Miss Bassano's collection is not limited to letters of
Indian interest, and certain letters written from the Crimea
and from Australia are also included here for the light they
throw on the characters or careers of the three "India"
brothers.

The Bassanos were a Derby family, of Venetian extraction,
who had moved to London near the beginning of the nineteenth

---

* See Frontispiece

century, and who for forty or fifty years played minor roles in some of the great events of the day. Francis Matthias was a dispenser of medicines at the medical depot of the army during the battle of Waterloo, and thereafter for forty years a member of that department – the Army Medical Department – which was to be held responsible for the miseries of the troops during the Crimean War; Thomas Bromsall carried opium from India to China for Jardine & Matheson, as Second Mate of their crack clipper *Lanrick*, and later was one of the pioneer European coffee planters in South India; Alfred served with the 32nd Regiment for twenty-six years, taking part in the siege of Multan during the Second Sikh War, and later during the Indian Mutiny was wounded at the battle of Chinhat and besieged in Lucknow; Christopher Bakewell, one of the early medical students of King's College, London, served in India with the 70th Regiment and died in the Crimea; Philip Henry, for many years a clerk in the War Office, went to the Crimea with the commission of inquiry into the supplies for the British army; while Charlotte Ellen took part in the great emigration movement of the period, was an observer of the Australian gold rush and later married one of the pioneer settlers of Ballarat. Walter Waterfield was one of the Special Constables sworn in at the time of the Chartist agitation, as well as being a clerk in the Army Medical Department, so even he, the most stay-at-home member of the family, was touched by "history".

As I was editing this volume Dr. A.L. Rowse identified Shakespeare's Dark Lady of the Sonnets as an earlier member of the Bassano family, initiating much correspondence in *The Times* and other journals.** Here again perhaps a Bassano played a minor role in history, and it is pleasant to speculate that the Venetian court musician from whom the "Brothers in India" were directly descended – Antonio Bassano – was the source of the names Antonio and Bassanio in *The Merchant of Venice*.

I am grateful to Miss Bassano for her help, hospitality, and patience over a period of several years, to the School of Oriental and African Studies for financing the publication of this volume, and to Mr. Martin Daly, Publications Officer of the School, who has supervised the production of the volume. Mrs. Ella Whitehead prepared the final typescript – I am much indebted to her for her care and skill.

School of Oriental & African Studies   M.D. Wainwright
October 1977

** A.L. Rowse, *Shakespeare the Man* (Macmillan, 1973)

CONTENTS

ILLUSTRATIONS

Simplified family tree

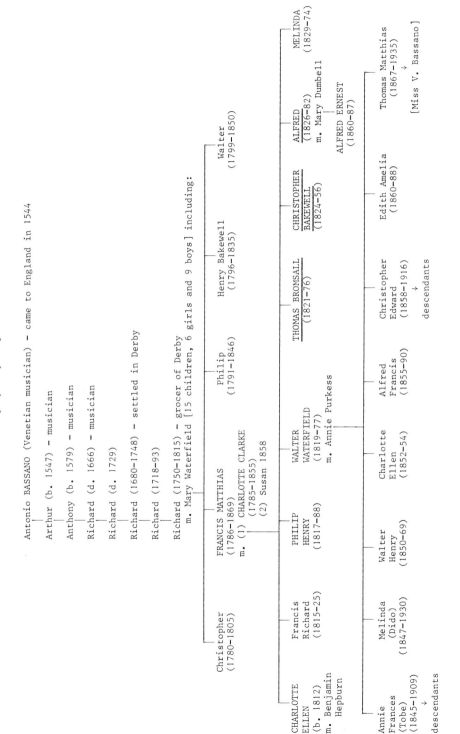

Antonio BASSANO (Venetian musician) – came to England in 1544

Arthur (b. 1547) – musician

Anthony (b. 1579) – musician

Richard (d. 1666) – musician

Richard (d. 1729)

Richard (1680-1748) – settled in Derby

Richard (1718-93)

Richard (1750-1815) – grocer of Derby
m. Mary Waterfield [15 children, 6 girls and 9 boys] including:

Christopher
(1780-1805)

Francis
Richard
(1815-25)

FRANCIS MATTHIAS
(1786-1869)
m. (1) CHARLOTTE CLARKE
(1785-1855)
(2) Susan 1858

PHILIP
HENRY
(1817-88)

WALTER
WATERFIELD
(1819-77)
m. Annie Purkess

Philip
(1791-1846)

THOMAS BROMSALL
(1821-76)

Henry Bakewell
(1796-1835)

CHRISTOPHER
BAKEWELL
(1824-56)

Walter
(1799-1850)

ALFRED
(1826-82)
m. Mary Dumbell

ALFRED ERNEST
(1860-87)

MELINDA
(1829-74)

CHARLOTTE
ELLEN
(b. 1812)
m. Benjamin
Hepburn

Melinda
(Dido)
(1847-1930)

Walter
Henry
(1850-69)

Charlotte
Ellen
(1852-54)

Alfred
Francis
(1855-90)

Christopher
Edward
(1858-1916)
↓
descendants

Edith Amelia
(1860-88)

Thomas Matthias
(1867-1935)
↓
[Miss V. Bassano]

Annie
Frances
(Tobe)
(1845-1909)
↓
descendants

x

"You can have a splendid *spider preserve* of a *very
large* and *superior* breed, and there is *no climate* like
this for the *growth* of WHISKERS. Now *don't* get
excited ... Ye Gods & little fishes: an extensive pair
of whiskers & a spider preserve! If this don't bring
you to India I'll swallow the first Bengal tiger I
catch without salt." [36]

It was November 1846, and Alfred Bassano, Ensign in the 32nd
Regiment, twenty years old and newly arrived in India, was
writing to his brother Christopher, a medical student at King's
College, London, tempting him to follow him "immediately (if not
sooner) to the beautiful East" - "this land of cholera & enlarged
livers" - as an "Army Sawbones". Alfred was the youngest of the
five surviving Bassano brothers, and the second to look for his
livelihood in India. His sailor brother Tom, five years his
senior, who had left his ship at Calcutta over two years before
(in June 1844), was at present sailing out of Bombay carrying
opium to China, as second mate of the crack Jardine & Matheson
brig *Lanrick*. The spider-loving, luxuriantly-whiskered
Christopher (born in 1824) was eventually to reach India in June
1849, as Assistant Surgeon with the 70th Regiment.

These three young men were the "B[assano]s in India", as Tom
called them. Alfred served there with his regiment until 1859,
Christopher left for the Crimea in 1855, while Tom, who abandoned
the sea late in 1847, spent twenty years in South India (until
his retirement in 1868) first as a coffee planter in the Wynaad
and later as an agent at Tellicherry.

Of the many English families which came to have members
scattered round the world during the nineteenth century, the
Bassanos, though of exotic origin, were typical. England in the
nineteenth century had become a young country, with a much
greater proportion of young people in the population than ever
before, following the great decline in infant mortality, without
any corresponding decline in the birth rate. The father of the
young Bassanos was himself one of fifteen children, of whom only
five reached manhood. But his own eight children all survived -
although the eldest died young - while the only one of his sons
to lead a normal married life also had a family of eight children. As Alfred Bassano remarked of this brother, Walter, "If
he goes on at this rate he will give them some trouble to make

1

out the next population tables", for Walter, who married in 1844, was "going ahead once a year". All these extra children had to be provided for, and their great numbers meant that, rather than stay at home, they had to go out into the world to earn their livings. An unusually large number of them either never married at all, or had very small, or no, families themselves, and this helped to re-adjust the balance in the population. But it was emigration which provided the great safety valve. Had all the children who swarmed in "every street and blind alley" - as Charles Lamb noted in his "Bachelor's Complaint" - grown up to have families of the usual size, the population would have increased between 1801 and 1851 by far more than the hundred per cent which was in fact the case. The unusually high pro- portion of single people helped, but much more so the fact that the world was wide open to young people with their ways to make - and they took their opportunities. Whether they went West to seek their fortunes in the newly opened lands of North America, or South following the discovery of gold in Australia, or East to India now under British control, or whether they sought their opportunities in the extensive new developments in Britain itself, was largely a matter of accident and of personal circum- stance. But wherever they went they were moved by economic motives, leaving home to seek a livelihood, neither looking for adventure (though they often found it), nor burdened by a sense of mission.

* * * * * * * * *

THE BASSANO FAMILY

The Bassanos were descended from Venetian court musicians introduced into England by King Henry VIII in 1544. There were five brothers, Alois, Antony, Jasper, John, and John Baptist, and they were first lodged, with some of their children, in the Charterhouse. This was in the year 1544-5. A few years ago Dr. A.L. Rowse identified Emilia Bassano Lanier, daughter of John Baptist, as Shakespeare's Dark Lady of the Sonnets. Shakespeare must certainly have known the family, as they remained court musicians throughout the century and up to the Civil War, when they left London. Some members returned to London after the Restoration to play at the court of Charles II, but others who had moved to Stone in Staffordshire, remained in the midland counties of England, inter-marrying with local families, moving first to Lichfield, and then to Derby.

The first of the Derbyshire Bassanos, descended from Antony (or Antonio), was Richard (1680-1748). His grandson, another Richard (1750-1815), was the grandfather of the brothers who went to India. He was a prosperous grocer and wine merchant of St. Mary's Gate in the town of Derby, who on his death left property valued at about £2000. He had married Mary Waterfield, a local beauty, whose portrait as Maria in Sterne's *Sentimental Journey*, was later to hang in the Derby Art Gallery, and who died in 1834. They had fifteen children, of whom only five sons survived infancy or early childhood: Christopher (1780-1805), solicitor of Derby; Francis Matthias (1786-1869), Apothecary to the Forces; Philip (1791-1846), provision dealer of Derby; Henry Bakewell (1796-1835); and Walter (1799-1850), tea merchant of London. These family names re-appear to cause some confusion in the next and succeeding generations.

It was Francis Matthias, the fifth child and second son, who was the father of the Bassanos in India. He was born on the 24th February 1786, at a quarter past three in the morning, and spent much of his childhood at the village of Woodeaves, near Ashbourne, where his uncle Waterfield was one of three partners owning a cotton mill, and where he developed that love of the countryside and of flowers and plants which remained a lifelong obsession, and which perhaps influenced his choice of occupation – that of druggist. "This is a country", his son Philip was to write of the Crimea in May 1855, "that father would glory in, it being covered with wild flowers ... the most beautiful Country imaginable ..." [136]. Nevertheless, Francis Matthias was to spend all his adult life in the rapidly expanding metropolis of London. He lived to see the population there nearly trebled, and the whole shape and character of the city transformed, especially after the coming of the railways in the early 1830s. Then houses were demolished to make way for railway lines and stations, and their inhabitants crowded into the remaining dwellings, adding to the appalling squalor and conges- tion of the slums of central London and of the East End, while on the other hand suburbs were developing with increasing rapidity.

Francis Matthias moved to London in 1809 or 1810 after completing his apprenticeship with Henry Bronne, chemist of Derby. He had been apprenticed for the customary seven years, at a premium of £70, on the 20th April 1801, and had later spent two years as a dispensing assistant with a firm of druggists, but in 1811 he opened his own shop in Chiswell Street, near Finsbury Square, London. The same year, on Saturday, 27th July, he married Charlotte Clarke (1785-1855) at St. Luke's, Old Street. She was the daughter of Thomas Clarke of Bermondsey, and their first child, a daughter, was born in June 1812. A large sum (£550) had been invested in the shop, but the venture failed within the next two years (1814), and Francis Matthias had to give up any idea of acting as druggist and apothecary on his own account. His father lent him a further £200 to tide him over the next year or two, and the small family went to live in Bermondsey with the Clarkes.

It was in 1815 that Francis Matthias's long connection with the Army Medical Board began. He took and passed the examination for Dispenser of Medicines, and was appointed on the 8th April

1815, just before the birth of his second child, Francis Richard. His son was born on the 2nd May and a few days later Francis Matthias left England for his first posting, to the medical depot of the Duke of Wellington's "Grand Army" at Antwerp. He remained there from the end of May 1815 until February 1816, when the station was broken up. He was then responsible for removing forty wagon loads of stores to the Valenciennes depot, where he stayed until May 1816. Some time during this period his wife and two children joined him, as they are included on his passport for the return journey. He was said to be twenty-nine years old (it should have been thirty), five feet six inches in height, with fair hair, blue eyes, and an oval face. In November 1816 he began his long service at the office of the Board, remaining a Dispenser of Medicines until 1825, when he was appointed Apothecary to the Forces, an office which he retained for over thirty years. The Director-General of the Army Medical Board (later Department) during most of this time - from 1815 to 1851 - was [Sir] James McGrigor, with whom F.M. Bassano occasionally dined, and whose portrait in later years hung in the Bassano drawing room [97]. When he heard of Sir James's retirement Christopher Bassano, in Meerut with the 29th Regiment, remarked that he now looked forward to some changes in the Medical Department "better adapted for the times we live in and the advancements lately made in science". Perhaps, he added, medical officers would now be able to get modern instruments and new and valuable medicines, and "perhaps also a few newly discovered diseases and medicines will be added to the list, and the vast number of old & useless ones erased" [80]. His hopes were not to be fulfilled, as this was the department which was to be so bitterly attacked for incompetence during the Crimean War a few years later.

During these years the family lived at a variety of addresses in Bermondsey, Westminster, Marylebone, Kensington, and Fulham. The father's pay during his first fifteen years' service - while his family was growing - averaged £125 a year: by 1830 it had reached £173 a year. By then Francis Matthias and Charlotte had completed their family of eight children: Charlotte Ellen, born 1 June 1812; Francis Richard, born 2 May 1815; Philip Henry, born 18 March 1817; Walter Waterfield, born 25 June 1819; Thomas Bromsall, born 8 September 1821; Christopher Bakewell, born 10 April 1824; Alfred, born 25 June 1826; and Melinda, born 21 September 1829. The eldest son died when he was ten years old, but the rest, growing up in this robust age of extraordinary and rapid change, were never to become what is usually thought of by the word "Victorian". They grew up when London was expanding rapidly, when cholera first appeared - they knew the London of Edwin Chadwick's great reports, of Dickens's *Bleak House*, of Henry Mayhew's *London Life and the London Poor*. They grew up in an England experiencing a period of unprecedented change and upheaval, culminating in the "Hungry Forties", a decade of social distress which saw rick burnings, Chartist riots, agitation for improved conditions in the factories, agitation for the repeal of the corn laws and for free trade. The true Victorian age, with its stability and recognisable social manifestations, could only flower in that era of prosperity, beginning in mid-century, which saw England at the height of its power. By then the Bassano children were grown up and out in the world, except for the youngest, Melinda, the only one to fit somewhat into the Victorian pattern, of which her habit of calling her parents "Papa" and "Mama", rather than "Mother" and "Father" (or even sometimes "Dad") as did the older children, is perhaps a symbol.

The boys were educated at The Philological School (later St. Marylebone Grammar School), at Gloucester Place, an institution "to educate the sons of Clergymen, Naval and Military Officers, Professional Men, Merchants, Manufacturers, Clerks in Public Offices, the higher order of Tradesmen, and other persons of an equally respectable class of society, whose families have been in better circumstances, and are reduced by accident or misfortune, whereby they are rendered incapable of affording their children a suitable education".

The two eldest surviving sons then followed their father into government service. Philip Henry, born in March 1817 at Pump Court, Long Lane, Bermondsey, was appointed a clerk in the War Office in 1837, and remained there until "axed" in 1865. "How dose Philop and the Torey ministry get on?" his brother Tom was to enquire in 1841. "And", referring to his struggles with the new science of statistics, "the dead tactics – what the deavle name again? th'Slack Slicks?" [5]   Philip travelled frequently in the course of his duties, and letters have survived written from Dublin, from Scotland, and most interestingly from the Crimea [135-140], where he went in 1855 with the commission of inquiry into the supplies for the British army in the Crimea – the Tulloch and McNeill commission. Some years after his retirement, in 1872, he went on one of the early Cook's tours to Italy – his journal survives – and a few years later he visited his sister in Australia (1876-7). He never married, and helped all his family financially from time to time – Alfred and Christopher with their outfits, Tom in his ventures in coffee planting, his sister Ellen on her emigration to Australia, and his sister Melinda at home, contributing to her expenses, and also paying for some of her luxuries – her piano, for example. "What a kind brother Philip has been to us all, has he not", exclaimed Ellen [129]. His salary gradually increased until in 1858, when he was one of the seventy-eight clerks in the second class at the War Office, he was earning £345 a year. On retirement in 1865 his pension was fixed at £277 10s. However, he lived well, with a house at Laleham on the Thames, where he could enjoy his favourite recreations of boating and fishing, and on his death he left assets valued at almost £4000. He was more prudent financially than his brothers. As young Tom

Bassano remarked in 1841: "I can't [h]elp laughfing at Philop loosing 10 shillings, for I thought he always maid his bets so that he could not loose, but if he wins he get a good deal."

Walter Waterfield, the next son, born in June 1819, at Great Smith Street, Westminster, was first appointed a temporary clerk (at £90 a year) at the Army Medical Board in July 1839, and remained there as a clerk until he too was "axed", in 1871, when his post was abolished. Walter was the only family man among the brothers, and in later years the centre of family life. He married Annie Purkess (1822-91), daughter of a music seller, on 30 May 1844, at St. Marylebone Parish Church, and had eight children, constantly teased by his brothers: "You will be obliged to emigrate or amputate if you go on at this rate for England can never stand such a rapid increase ...", wrote Alfred in 1847. And, "Fancy the little imps ... calling you *Pa*. What a *Pa*! Why, an aligator would make as good a one." [26] He was nicknamed "Mopsticks", and he and his two eldest daughters, Annie Frances (1845-1909), known as Fan, Frank, Tobe or Taube, and Melinda (1847-1930), known as Dido, figure frequently in the correspondence. Christopher and Tom in particular become fond uncles, and even the "facetious" Alfred, flattered by the attentions of the latest baby when home on leave, called her "a *jovial* baby" [97].

Most of the letters printed here were addressed - to save postage - either to Francis Matthias or Walter at the Army Medical Board, or to Philip at the War Office.

The two girls of the family were also expected to earn their own livings. Ellen, the eldest, born at Chiswell Street, in June 1812, taught for a time at a girls' boarding school, Cedar House, Hillingdon, and later tried to establish her own, without much success, in spite of her brother Tom's advice to "keep the plate well polished and then the people won't be able to pass it without seaing it and when I come home it will take me 3 dog watches to tally them all [the pupils]" [5]. She was very unsettled right through the 1840s, and she also thought of going to India, at first to open a school, but, wrote Tom in alarm: "tell [Ellen] not to come to India upon any account ... I am sure there's nothing to be done in the school line." [15] Her second plan, of joining Tom on his coffee plantation, was no better received, for Tom, he wrote, was "always living in mud houses, 15 feet square, tents, and sometimes no house over me at all" [54]. Ellen determined, therefore, to emigrate to Australia, sailing alone from Gravesend in November 1850, on board the *Anglia*, and nearly dying from seasickness during the voyage. She landed at Adelaide, which she did not like, and soon moved to Melbourne, staying first at a hotel "where she was eaten up by mosckettos bugs &c" before moving into private lodgings. "She does not seem in good spirits and I don't wonder at it poor girl", reported her brother Christopher from Meerut

[83]. Ellen, who was in her thirty-ninth year, gave up the idea of opening a school, and got a job as a governess in the family of one of the leading citizens of Geelong, Mr. Strachan, a merchant. Nearly a year later she took a position as governess to five of the nine children of Captain Hepburn, who had a big cattle and sheep station "110 miles up the bush" at Smeaton, twenty miles from the Ballarat. Both employers paid her £50 a year and her keep, a salary which in real terms compared favourably with those of her brothers in India at the same period, for after paying their expenses they found themselves with little or nothing left, while Ellen was soon remitting gold home, and having goods sent out to her in exchange.

On the journey to Smeaton Ellen was thrown out of the chaise into a waterhole, where "all that was to be seen of me was my bonnet just emerging from the water ... I had to walk a mile with the water dripping out of me before we came to a house". [91] Other adventures followed which she took in her stride, but nevertheless she remained very unsettled. Australia, she wrote in October 1852, "is fit for no one who cannot work like a horse, endure as much as the houseless beasts of the field, and be ready to take advantage of everybody" [92]. This was the period of the gold rush. [90 & 91] Ellen still hoped to go to India, and wrote to her brother Tom in the Wynaad in South India the same year, once again asking to join him. He again put her off, but later asked her to go after all, sending detailed instructions for the journey. Her brother Christopher sent her the money for her journey, while her brother Philip offered to pay her passage, not to India, but home to England. However, in January 1854, she took a step "which sealed my future happiness or inextricable misery" and married her employer's younger brother, Benjamin Hepburn, a young man nearly fourteen years her junior. [108] The couple moved to Glen Donald Station, then to Forest Hill, and finally to Ballarat. She corresponded regularly with her brothers in India and they with her, and both Tom and Christopher, who were very unhappy in India in the 1850s, often spoke of selling up and going to Australia to join her, but in the event neither did. Ellen never re-visited England, though both Tom and Philip went to see her later in life, and she outlived both her husband and all her brothers and her younger sister in England.

Melinda, the youngest child, born in Foley Street, in 1829, was more in the later Victorian tradition, staying at home until her mother died and her father married again, working as a governess and companion from time to time, when she could not avoid it, but mainly enjoying the responsibilities and pleasures of being an Aunt to her nieces and nephews and paying long visits to friends and relations. Her father was by this time, the end of 1854, earning nineteen shillings a day, with allowances for servant, fuel, and forage for one horse. And now that all the children except Melinda had gone out into the world the family moved into a smaller house, which is described in detail in a letter to Christopher written by Melinda in 1853. The house was No. 6, Elysium Row, Fulham, "a very large *looking* old fashioned house, two kitchens downstairs, two sitting rooms one on each side of the door, which we call the oak room & the dining room. For the oak room Papa has bought a new set of chairs, & a new carpet, & with my handsome piano it makes a pretty neat room. He has also had three of my chalk drawings framed, & Uncle Walter's large portrait & that of Sir James regilded. They are hung up in the dining room & look very well. Mama's and Alfred's bedrooms are over these rooms [Alfred was home on leave]. Alf's is a very pretty room, panelled green, & my room is at the top of the house and the servant's also. They are all wainscoted, the hall & staircase as well, not a bit of paper hanging about the house. Each of the bed & sitting rooms has two windows, which with the kitchen windows makes fourteen and all of exactly the same dimensions. We have a small piece of garden in front, a moderately sized piece at the back, and a stable. There is nothing but a nursery ground in front, and the omnibuses pass our door to & from town every ten minutes." In the hall were arranged a "group of Sikh & Afghan arms" taken home by Alfred, and in the oak room a case of Indian butterflies. [97] There is no mention of washing or toilet facilities, though Alfred when taking rooms later, after his final return from India, was to insist on "plenty of *water* for a bath daily" [Letter of 25 Nov. 1859 - not printed].

This London home might be compared with Alfred's bungalow at Meerut [26], with its accommodation for fourteen servants; Christopher's "nice little bungalo" at the same station, with equally extensive servants' quarters [82]; Tom's "splendid Bungalow" at Manantoddy, "the dining hall being 35 foot by 24, one sitting room, & 3 bedrooms, quite in Europe stile, beautifully furnished &c." [94]; and Ellen's home in the bush, with "two parlors, 3 bedrooms, a storeroom, and a kitchen, all on the ground floor, and a verandah nearly all round the house, with outhouses consisting of stable, coach house, and servant's room", [160].

Melinda too had several opportunities of becoming a Bassano in India. "I will then bring you out to India and get you married to that young fellow you used to be spoony upon in Pick[er]ing Terrace", wrote Christopher in May 1853 [93]. Five years later her brother Tom was promising her that "a month's residence in the Wynaad would find you a husband" [175]. And yet again a few years later, when he was living in Tellicherry, he remarked that he could get her and his two eldest nieces "married in a week" [183]. "A good looking girl like her ought to have kidded on some chap to have spliced her long ago", he complained [185]. But Melinda, who seemed to enjoy life at home - and was indeed suspected of extravagance - was not tempted - wisely, no doubt. Though by the 1840s the whole of

India had come under British control the number of Europeans
living in India outside the army and civil service was very small.
European settlement was not encouraged, and the labour necessary
at all levels, except the very top, was provided by Indians.
"I don't want to get you to come out here", Tom had written to
his brother Philip, "as clarcks are not used, as the blackeys
they have taught to write accounts so nicely, and so cheap" [13].
The women shipped out to relatives in India might find husbands
easily, but for most of them the life compared unfavourably with
life at home, or, for the independent minded, with life in those
rapidly developing parts of the world where women were at a
premium, and opportunities for an independent life correspond-
ingly greater.

These then, with Tom, Christopher and Alfred in India, are
the chief characters in the ensuing correspondence, supported by
numerous aunts, uncles and cousins, all drawn from that large
class of English society which formed the raw material for the
great nineteenth century novelists, but seen here undistorted by
the eye of genius, and the comic, or tragic, vision. The Bassano
children were contemporaries of all the great novelists of the
age, and it is salutary to have as a comparison with their works
of genius, a picture of the age as it appeared to more matter-of-
fact people, who belonged to a happy, stable and united family.

In their surviving letters they live again - Ellen, that
robust and enterprising spinster, lost in the Australian bush,
taking refuge in a hollow tree and coming out to "dance the
polka occasionally to keep myself warm" [91]; Philip, a "good
tempered meerchaum smoking convivial party giving *Bachelor*" [23]
with his love of the river and fishing; Walter ("Mopsticks"),
the family man, his wife Annie, and "the kids"; Melinda, the
rather spoilt young sister and favourite aunt; and above all the
brothers in India - Tom, the volatile and impulsive, hard-working
and full of schemes; Christopher, everyone's favourite, rather
vain, but kind, and in his profession conscientious and competent;
and Alfred, a cheerful wag and brave soldier, gradually falling
into the "blues" under the pressures of debt, slow promotion, and
the boredom of military life in peacetime. The earliest surviving letters - written under the stimulus of an exciting life in a
strange new land - are the most vivid: Tom at sea, and in his
first attempts at coffee planting; Alfred marching across
northern India, and at the siege of Multan; Christopher confident
of curing all ills before the never-ending epidemics of India
made him for a time "hate the sight of a sick man". We know
more about them than about their friends and contemporaries who
stayed at home, for in a society freed from all the minor
activities which fill the spare moments in a normal home
environment, and in a climate which for long periods makes any
physical exertion impossible, the writing of long letters and
journals filled many an empty hour. Not only were more letters
and journals written, but more were preserved, because they

came from far away and described exciting events. Such letters serve as illuminating footnotes to the official records, and are useful checks on reminiscences and memoirs written after the event. They add much not only to the history of the British in India, but also to the history of the British people in general, and if they add little to the history of Indian society and people they illuminate some of the lives caught up in the web of that society, even if only temporarily, and contain much incidental information about the face of the country. The chief characters in the drama of British India are well documented in print, the more obscure much less so.

The letters which are printed here are only a fraction of those which were written. Only those written, or sent, home have survived, and not all of those. Of the extensive correspondence between the brothers themselves while in India hardly anything remains. Because Christopher kept a record, which has been found, of all the letters which he posted during his stay in India, and for a time of the letters which he received, it is possible to get some idea of the total volume of the correspondence which has been lost. Between 1849 and 1855 he wrote some forty letters to his brothers Tom and Alfred, all of which are lost, and received many in return, of which only a couple survive. Alfred and Tom also corresponded regularly off and on, but all that remains are the few letters relating to their one meeting in 1858. Even many of the letters sent home have been lost - thirteen of the thirty written by Christopher, ten of the first twenty-seven written by Alfred, and many written by Tom and also by Ellen in Australia.

The only changes made in the letters as printed has been the division into paragraphs and the addition of punctuation: the spelling is unchanged. Tom's spelling was always eccentric and his punctuation non-existent; Alfred's major idiosyncracy was the spelling of "ennemy", while Christopher had some difficulty with the "ie" rule and a tendency to spell his brother Walter's name "Water". Tom's early letters with their lack of punctuation and phonetic spelling have a breathless vividness from which the addition of punctuation - though essential in the interest of intelligibility - rather detracts. Many of the letters were written across the page twice, to make the best use of the available space. This makes for difficult reading, the worst example being a family letter - printed as Letters 8 to 14 - which was written on one and a half sheets, folded to give six sides, each side written across three or four times, in two inks, black and red. It is so difficult to decipher that one wonders whether the recipients bothered to do so - it was, however, kept, though not all together in one place, when found. There was a mail once a month, and from the postmarks it can be seen that these letters, by the overland mail, took about six weeks to arrive, though sometimes as little as four weeks - in contrast to the three or four months by sea. The letters

travelled overland to Bombay, by steamer to Suez, overland to
Alexandria, by steamer to Marseilles, and then overland and across
the Channel to Southampton. Christopher said he looked forward to
the day when there would be a *railroad* all the way home [65].

Though in private letters there may be a temptation – the
writers not being on oath – to exaggerate for dramatic effect, or
for amusement, or out of a naturally ebullient nature, yet the
Bassano brothers, remembering that they were writing to employees
of the War Office and Army Medical Board made sure that important
details were correct, and their accuracy where it can be checked
can be confirmed.

* * * * * * * * *

THE BROTHERS IN INDIA

I. THOMAS BROMSALL BASSANO (1821-76)

Tom Bassano was the third of the five surviving sons of
Francis Matthias, born on the 8th September 1821 at North End,
Fulham. He was a "poor scholar" as he never ceased to lament,
but after "30 years hard work, a many years as a mean labourer"
[194], he became a successful businessman, cutting a dash in
Tellicherry in South India, where, he boasted "the fellows all
look upon me as immensely rich, nothing like mystyfying people".
[183] In his letters he can be seen to develop from a love-sick
and unsophisticated nineteen-year-old apprentice sailor to a
rather testy, liverish and gouty middle-aged bachelor living in
retirement in France – but still impulsive and full of impractical
schemes.

He was the one brother of the true pioneering type, making his
own way in India by hard work. Perhaps, as his sister Ellen
believed, he would have done better and been happier in a
pioneering country like Australia – or the United States – where
he might have ended his days as a rich and respected first
settler, as did his brother-in-law, Benjamin Hepburn of Ballarat.
"He would have made his fortune twice over had he come to this
country", Ellen wrote. "I wish he would sell his plantations and
come to us. He's just the sort of man for this place, rough and
ready" [162]. As it was, he spent ten years at sea, and twenty
in India, and then "having worked many a year to get a Xmas at
home" [196] found that in fact he enjoyed "any place except
England, for English people as a rule are such false, backbiting
humbugs", [202], and that he had felt much more himself in India
than he did in England [183].

His career began when at the age of sixteen, in February 1838,
he was apprenticed for five years to ship-owner William Tindall,
at a yearly wage of £3, rising gradually to £8 in the last year

11

of his apprenticeship. During these five years he made five long
voyages to the East, and the first five letters printed here,
written in 1841 at the beginning of, and during, his fourth
voyage, give a vivid picture of life at sea and of Tom himself,
aged nineteen and twenty.

While ashore he had fallen in love with the daughter of a
neighbour, a girl called Eleanor (whose name he never learned to
spell), but when he approached her father, he was told that she
could marry "any one but a salor", leaving them both "broken-
harted". "I would not of caired had I been told when first I
caim home", wrote poor Tom in a despondent letter to his brother
Walter - ending "If I never see you any more" - "but after father
laying out such a deal of money upon me, and then such a thought
to have to leave of[f] going to sea!" [2]. He was writing from
the Downs just before setting sail on his fourth voyage. Soon
after they set sail the ship was caught in a gale and Tom fell
over the yard while trying to secure a sail, but managed to save
himself. "Their were two men triing to sequre the sail", he
wrote, "but they did not like to go down before the sail so the
captain asked me "For god's sake go and get it done Tomey", so I
maid answer Yes. So hanging over the yard to get them rove I
fell over the yard. 'He gone over board', they all cried, but I
caught hold of the buntline as I fell ...". [3]

The ship returned once more to the Downs, and Tom who was
waiting for a letter from Eleanor, did his best to delay the next
attempt at sailing. When the wind changed during his watch he
refrained from calling the skipper, and when the Second Mate
called him later and all hands were called, Tom moved "like a
snail" instead of his usual quickness. He was called upon to
give the song "A Fair Wind", but said that he only wished the
wind would change again. His wish was granted and it became
impossible to set sail, and then he cried out, "What a lark! Har
Har Har! Blow great guns!", and then he began to laugh and sing
out to everything he took hold of. [4] He got his reward, and
the letter came before they finally got under way.

The voyage continued a hard one, and writing from Madeira,
where he spent his twentieth birthday, he wrote of a later gale,
"By Jorge my boy I thought we should of capsised". After the
gale the wind dropped, so that they had to tow the ship into
anchorage, which took about "8 howers" rowing - "such a jolly
pull it gave me a jolly good swetting". "I whish", he remarked,
"we had of had Cris and Alfred to of pulled and then they would
of got their belley full, I know I had". [5] He had passed the
watches away in thinking about "Ellenor" and was also trying to
study navigation to improve his prospects, though "it is
preshash hard to work all day and then draw afterwards", he
complained.

After his return from the last of his long voyages, at the

end of 1843, and being now out of his apprenticeship, Tom
determined that on the next voyage he would leave his ship at
Calcutta, and seek his fortune there, convinced that he would
never rise to be captain as he was such a poor scholar. [7]
Certainly his early letters in particular boast neither punctuation nor conventional spelling - but they are lively and
vigorous, giving vivid pictures of himself, and his life, while
his uncertain use of aitches and sometimes phonetic spelling
give some indication of his mode of speech.

It was in June 1844 that he left his ship after "a fine and
pleasant passage out - plenty of fun, dancin, singin, jimnastics,
etc. etc." - at Calcutta "a butiful, stately place", in spite of
the dead bodies filling the river at low tide, and set about
looking for a new berth. Having received a family letter from
home, he replied to each member separately [8-14]: to his father,
describing his search for a berth and the situation in Calcutta
where it was "rather unhealthy" with the "colorha raging a
little"; to his mother and younger sister, then fourteen years
old, hoping that she was keeping up what she had "larnt", "for
you see what a searious looss to me it is being such a bad
scolhar", and telling them he would send for Eleanor when he was
settled; to his elder sister wishing her luck with her school,
and describing the "punkers" in the church; to his brother
Christopher just entered medical college, suggesting that "as
dead bodies are scarce and dear at home you would like me to
bring you two or 3 home, as this river is full of them at low
water", adding "for all that, we bathe in this river, and have
to drink the water"; to his young brother Alfred, just eighteen
and a "grate favourite with the girls", complaining that he
hadn't contributed to the family letter with his "ready stock of
wit"; to his brother Walter, just married, with a description of
Calcutta; while he reassured his eldest brother, Philip, about
the climate and opportunities, for Philip had written urging him
not to "cut", but to return home. There were as many grey-headed
old men in India as at home, reported Tom, and in any case, he
believed "a man does not die without it was intended for him to
die ther when he was first born, and so [there is] a sertain
destiney raining over us to carry us to that very spot, to the
exact time certified for us to kick the buckit".

Tom found his berth in Calcutta and made several voyages
during the next two years - including one to the Sandwich
Islands (Hawaii) - and by April 1846 he was sailing as chief
mate. But while in China he got the chance to join one of the
crack clippers owned by the firm Jardine and Matheson, which was
making immense profits out of the opium trade. He joined the
Lanrick as second mate, with the promise that he would be made
chief when the opportunity should occur. Though he stayed with
the *Lanrick* for nineteen months - the first officer to stay more
than six months as the captain was a very difficult man to serve
under - he never achieved his ambition. When the berth became

13

vacant it was given to a nominee of "Mr. Matherson", for "every thing goes by intrest out here not merit". But the *Lanrick* was a "splendid brig", so he stayed on, sailing out of Bombay. Because it was the fastest of the clippers he spent only a short time at sea and a long time in harbour, which used up all his savings, as he had to pay his own expenses in harbour. He was earning one hundred rupees a month, and paying twelve rupees a month for a servant. However, there was plenty of fun in Bombay – the theatre with "devilish good performers" – horse races, shooting, and sightseeing, and especially the yatch regatta, where he won the cup for his captain though "dam the present did he make me". Later he won the race for gigs. When in China there was fun "dancing polkers" at Wampoa. And for the rest, amusement at the antics of a pet monkey. [15 & 16]

Tom Bassano was a fine practical sailor, reporting with pride the opinion of one chief mate that "it was punishment to me to see any body go aloft before me, and likewise punishment to keep me from working" [8], and he was later presented with a "splendid pair of boarding pistols" for "his zeal in drilling the crew to the use of arms" [22]. But the clippers were being displaced by steam boats, and fearing that he was "totally jamed" by his poor education, Tom decided to leave the sea and seek his fortune ashore.

His opportunity came on a voyage from Bombay to Calcutta at the end of 1847. The brig carried as passenger a man going to Cananore to open up a coffee estate near Manantoddy in the Wynaad for his brother, a captain in the Artillery. The passenger had just missed the P. & O. steamer and so had been forced to take the slower brig. During chats on deck during his watch Tom remarked that he too would like to turn coffee planter. When he arrived at Calcutta, Captain Smyth, brother of his passenger, went on board and offered him a job helping to get the plantation started, at £100 a year with house and horse found. The captain of the *Lanrick* was "so enraged" that he refused to pay his wages until Tom got a "lawer's letter". He stayed in Calcutta for a short time, learning surveying and cutting a dash driving on the Esplanade. "In fact, master Ensign", he wrote to his brother Alfred, "if you were to see me you'ld think me Lord High Admaral of Great Britain instead of a 2nd dickey." [17-19]

Europeans had begun to plant coffee in South India in the 1820s, and the first estate near Manantoddy had been opened just under twenty years before, in 1828. "I can just picture to myself", wrote Tom, "how happy I shall be – plenty of shooting, tigers by the hundreds and wild elephants by scores." He travelled round to Tellicherry by sea, practising his shooting at a bottle "so that when I get to Manantoddy should a tiger be about to make a spring at me I can depend upon my eye to bring him up all standing in time to save my life". [19] His girl

Eleanor had by now grown tired of waiting, so Tom asked his
brother Christopher "a good judge in those matters" to recommend
a nice girl for a wife.

He began his new life in the jungles of the Wynaad at the
beginning of 1848, when he was twenty-six years old, and after
ten years at sea.

Coffee planting

The reality of coffee planting proved to be very different
from his imaginings, and for the next year he was working hard
"living in mud houses, 15 feet square, tents, and sometimes no
house ... at all", cutting jungle, planting coffee bushes,
"scrambling over slippery steeps and high hills", and building a
bungalow for his employer. [54] In this first year he cut the
jungle and planted 160,000 bushes, that is 160 acres, and was
too busy to write home.

He then went to work on the coast, from November 1848 to
April 1849, for another master, John Wells of Calicut, scraping
ginger, and again living in tents. In April 1849 he went back
into the Wynaad jungle to work on another coffee estate for his
master, Mr. Wells, living in a little place about ten feet
square, while building another bungalow of sixty feet long, and
planting 280,000 coffee plants. "He seems", wrote his brother
Christopher, "in excellent spirits and signs himself the *Jangle
Wallah*." [61]

However, he was less pleased when he was again sent down to
the coast as soon as the fine weather came in the hills in
August, while his master's family moved up to take advantage of
it. At the end of his twelve month agreement, in November 1849,
he insisted on a new agreement paying him this time two hundred
rupees a month, with the usual expenses. He then went back to
ginger scraping, at three different stations. As he was to
write: "I have gained more experience of the manner of the world
amongst shore people in the last 12 months than the whole of my
life before." By late 1850 he had been working hard for three
years without achieving anything for himself. His family had
been worried about him, "fully persuaded he was dead", as he had
been writing neither home nor to his brothers in India.
Christopher, in Meerut, though rather unsympathetic, made
enquiries of the postmaster at Calicut "about your hide & seek
son Tom". Had he died, he remarked, they would have heard about
it. [80] Tom, it seems, had again changed masters at the end of
his second twelvemonth agreement with Mr. Wells, and at the end
of 1850 had begun to work for the Morris family. He was again
unfortunate, as his new master soon died. However, the heirs in
London asked Tom to continue as manager of the estates. The
London Bassanos then stepped in and made better terms for him
than Tom had made for himself. He was to continue to manage the

coffee estates of this family for almost five more years, until mid-1855.

He was now able to begin to open an estate on his own account, with financial help from his family, especially Philip, who advanced £300. [210] And by the middle of 1853 he was able to report that he had one hundred acres of land cleared, but only twenty planted, that is, 20,000 plants. He also had a "splendid Bungalow", twenty-four head of cattle, and fifteen hundred rupees in the bank. Later in the year he bought another forty acres, making sixty acres planted, which he expected to give Rs.3000 of coffee the next year. [106] This was a typically over-optimistic estimate, as he in fact harvested two tons, about Rs.800 worth. [128] He was also now keeping a "splendid little girl of 15 year old".

Throughout these years however, Tom was very lonely and unsettled, sometimes talking of going home, sometimes of selling up and joining his sister Ellen in Australia, or conversely asking her to go out and join him as housekeeper, sending detailed instructions for the journey. He begged his brother Christopher to visit him, or transfer into a regiment stationed in South India, and cure him of "jungle fever", tempting him with tales of a planter's life. On the plantation he had five hundred hands at work, with twenty headmen and two European supervisors, he said, and "a large and splendid mansion to live in à la Neybob" with lots of horses to ride, and an immense tusker for Christopher to shoot. At Tellicherry on the coast there were one thousand women garbling coffee, of whom he could take his pick. "It is now 9 years since I saw any of you", he cried. *"Do come."* [102 & 106] To Ellen he promised a "batchelor of about 44 rolling in wealth". [110 & 117] But Christopher too was wretched and hating everybody [109], while Ellen had taken the step which was to seal "her future happiness or inextricable misery" and got married. [108]

Ellen and her new husband, Benjamin Hepburn, wanted Tom to join them as "just the sort of man for this place, rough and ready" but did not like to persuade him "in case it might not turn out as we expect". [162] One of his friends however while on a visit to Australia called on the Hepburns and on his return advised Tom to stop "wasting life in an out of the way place amongst wild beasts, savages & jungle fever". "With roughing it at first", he said, "and assistance such as yr brother-in-law has promised, you could be sure to get on, I should think - far better than sticking plants into holes, pruning branches, pulling berries ..." [163] Ellen too wrote with detailed instructions on how to reach their sheep station and what to take [159 & 161], but by the time these letters reached Tom in mid-1856 he had "given up all idea of coming to this colony". [165] "I am very sorry I did not persuade Tom to come here three years since", wrote Ellen in July 1857, "He would have

been a richer man than he is had he done so, but I was afraid of
the responsibility in case he might find things different to what
he expected. Benjamin wished it very much." [165] Benjamin had
made about £6,000 in the first year of their married life. On
hearing this news Tom immediately asked for a loan of £1,000,
without success, though Ellen was "very grieved to have to
refuse". [165]

However, by the end of 1854 things had begun to look up for
him, and his estate was progressing rapidly. [118] A few months
later he left the Morrises to concentrate on his own estate,
which had given ten tons of coffee, worth Rs.4000, he told
Christopher. He had been offered Rs.7000 for the estate, "so
you see I am worth 1000£ old boy", he boasted. [125] He told
Philip however that he had got eight tons, worth Rs.3400,
probably the truer estimate. [128] He still talked of selling
up and going home, or to Australia, but finally decided to stick
it out in India. "Dear Lin", he wrote to his younger sister,
"where was I to turn to put myself so well off in the world
again", though "your poor brother ... lives a dull life in a
jungle with wild elephants for neighbours, and cheeters & tigers
taking my cattle out of my cattle pens of a night." [127] He
could not go home, he said, without ruining himself. During
these years Tom, as Ellen remarked, "often changed his mind".
[132]

Mrs. Charlotte Bassano, the mother of the family, died in
1855, and Christopher in 1856, so Tom, after thirteen years
without seeing any of his family, at last decided to go home for
a visit. The "run home" did him a "world of good" [166] and
after his return to India in late September 1857 he settled down
happily to deal with the "monstrous pile up of business"
awaiting him [167]. There is no more talk of selling up and
starting afresh in another part of the globe, until his final
retirement more than ten years later. He brought back with him
a box of medicines which he sold at a good profit, and an agreement to open up another fifty acres for his brother Philip. [170]
Philip had not only advanced money to open the original estate,
but sent gifts of hoes and other implements. [128 & 135]

About a year after his return from England Tom at last met
his youngest brother Alfred whom he had not seen since he was a
boy of seventeen. Alfred had been besieged in Lucknow with his
regiment and then given six months sick leave. He decided he
"might as well take a run over to see Tom". "Not a bad idea
going eighteen hundred miles to see a fellow, but Tom is always
writing to me to come & see him, having about as much knowledge
of geography as a Tom Cat ..." Alfred made a leisurely trip of
it, while Tom waited on tenterhooks to receive him, posting
horses in May 1858, but not actually seeing his brother until
August. "I have had my horses posted for him ever so long", he
wrote, "one 80 miles away since 11th [May], the other since the

15th, and a borrow[ed] one also since the 15th. Kept cooking no
end of grub, expecting to see him ride in every minute, and by
jove, he has not come. I never passed such an anxious fortnight
in my life." [169] At the end of July he was still writing:
"Fancy dear Alfred being on the Hills and I not yet seen him ...
Hope to see him heer in a few days." [174] When they had last
met Alfred had been seventeen and Tom twenty-two, now Alfred at
thirty-two was looking "care worn" and nearer forty-five,
according to his sister Ellen's comment on his photograph [letter
of 22 Oct. 1860 - not printed], while Tom's likeness sent home a
few years before had not been "recognized by any of them" [159]
as he had got "beastly fat" as Alfred unkindly put it [157].

It was about this time, when he was thirty-seven, that Tom
made his last attempt at matrimony. His father, widowed three
years before, had decided to marry again. Alfred considered
this a huge joke, but Tom rushed off a letter to his sister
Melinda, who was being displaced as her father's housekeeper,
telling her to go out and join him, taking with her "the eldest
Miss King" as a bride for him. [175] Melinda replied coolly,
advising him to think it over. [176] She had no intention, one
feels, of emulating her elder sister, and was not tempted by "a
dull life in a jungle" with wild elephants for neighbours and
tigers and cheetahs stealing the cattle at night, with or without
the promised husband.

Tom stayed on in India for another ten years after Alfred had
left, with one more trip home in 1862. He prospered reasonably
well, getting out of coffee before the disastrous year of 1866,
when the plantations in South India were destroyed by the
depredations of the coffee borer. As early as 1863 he was
reporting that he now had an interest in only one estate which
he was expecting to sell soon. Of coffee planting he wrote: "I
don't think much of it now. Labour is deer and the fellows from
the superintendants to the dog boy do nothing - all getting too
big for their work." He set up as an agent in Tellicherry,
buying "a splendid house in a park of several acres and looking
over the coconut trees to the sea". He had had his eye on the
house for several years and got it for six thousand rupees. He
was able to repay Philip with interest, lend money to Alfred
(which was repaid in 1872 [204]) and put by enough capital for
his own retirement. He suggested that "the girls" (Melinda and
his two eldest nieces) should go out and he would get them
married in a week, though he would have to act "the swell" for a
bit "& make a bit of a dash". They were not, as ever it would
seem, tempted. [183] Few letters survive from this period and
those mostly to his young nieces, full of an uncharacteristic
moralising, but overdone as usual: "Don't neglect going to church
under any pretext whatever, once a day at least", he wrote. [181]

In 1867 or 1868 he at last went to Australia to visit his
sister Ellen, with some idea of settling there, but in the end

decided to go home for good. He was then forty-seven years old, and had been in India for twenty-four of them. He got home before his father died - in 1869 at the age of eighty-three - and embarked on a period of riotous living in London. "A man from India", he complained, "is expected to be a gordous swell and to live with a woman seems to [be] simply ruin, as nothing seems to controul them in their eagerness to have everything they see." In the end he "bolted" to Paris with a "young person" "the best little thing that could be" leaving his brother Walter to placate his outraged, and unpaid, landlady. "I should have gone to the bad if I had not left", he said. [191]

He lived in France until his death seven years later - first in Paris, then in Boulogne, and finally at Le Havre - at the same time keeping up his business interests in India, and frequently visiting his family in England and being visited by them. A glimpse of his life in Le Havre is given in a letter written by his nephew Alfred, then a boy of thirteen. This was in October 1873 when Tom was fifty-two years old. He had chartered a small yatch of sixty tons with a crew of two men and a boy "which crew he bullies like mad". His livestock consisted of "16 fowls ... 9 canaries, 2 goldfinches, 2 linnets, 2 dogs, 14 pigeons, and an Alderney cow". He frequently sailed across the Channel to visit the family, including Melinda at Eastbourne, and according to young Alfred made a cruise to New York - however young Alfred like his father was a wag, and this may be no more than a family joke. [212] When Melinda became seriously ill in July 1874 her brother Walter went over to Le Havre to collect Tom, but they returned too late, and Melinda died on the 31st July, aged forty-five. [213] Neither Tom nor Walter long survived her, Tom dying on 9th February 1876 at the age of fifty-four, and Walter (the "Mopsticks" of the early letters) the next year.

II. ALFRED BASSANO (1826-82)

Alfred Bassano was the youngest son of Francis Matthias, born at 32 Foley Street (Army Medical Depot) on the 25th June 1826. He was commissioned Ensign in the 32nd Regiment on 3rd April 1846, "a protegé of Mr. Coleman's & Mr. Fergusson's" [56], both of the War Office. He retired on half pay with the rank of Major General in 1872, was made a C.B. the next year, and later served as Assistant Military Secretary at Hong Kong. He died on 12th September 1882 at his home in Inverness Place, Bayswater. He had married Mary (Minnie) Dumbell of Belmont, Isle of Man, in November 1859, but she had died less than a year later soon after the birth of their son, "Young Alfred" (1860-87), and he had never re-married.

It was natural that a young officer without private means should look to a regiment about to serve in India, and the 32nd

Regiment had received orders to proceed to that country on the 19th March 1846, while stationed at Dublin. In India there was some chance of seeing action, with the consequent possibility of promotion without purchase, and although young officers almost invariably got into debt, this did not inconvenience them too much, as long as they stayed in the country. It was in fact the only country, as Alfred was later to write, where a poor man could "preserve his independence and pay his Tailor's bills, without considering very carefully what he is about ..." [151] Alfred moreover had heard his brother Tom's traveller's tales since boyhood, and was familiar with the idea of going to India - though he was later to express forcibly his opinion of such tales, as well as of the accuracy of books about India. "Pay no attention", he was to write, "to any hints you may receive from buffers who have already sufficiently fried their tripes in India, or read in books on this country, as the authors must in most cases be people of no observation, impaired upper stories, or never been here at all ... they are only calculated to mislead ..." [36]

The regiment, nicknamed "The Lilies", embarked at Fermoy on the 29th May 1846, in five detachments, on board the transports *British Sovereign, Duchess of Northumberland, Edinburgh, General Palmer,* and *Aboukir.* All reached Calcutta safely during the first two weeks of September, and the men immediately went by water to Chinsura, twenty-four miles above Calcutta, en route for Agra. Their destination was later changed to Meerut, fifty miles north-west of Delhi. They set out on the three months' march on the 20th November 1846, after having spent two months at Chinsura. They arrived at Meerut on the 19th February 1847, and remained there for twelve months.

While stationed at Chinsura Alfred Bassano began a series of long letters home, which he numbered. Over a period of two and a half years he wrote twenty-seven, seventeen of which have been found, the series being almost complete from No. 10. Thereafter he "lost the character of a good correspondent", remarking "do not be annoyed at my scarcely ever writing home as nothing but ... being engaged in another War is likely to enable me ... to be a good correspondent again." [151] And later, "I seem to have lost all idea of writing and get so disgusted at my own miserable productions that I expect before long I shall cease to write altogether." [152] Of the letters which he did write during the nine years 1850-59 thirteen (no longer numbered) have survived. During two of these years he was home on leave, and seven of the letters were written in the one year 1858, after the siege of Lucknow. A dozen letters written during his later life, after his return from India for good in 1859, have also survived.

Only one letter (No. 5) survived from the batch sent home from Chinsura, and that is the letter to his brother Christopher, already quoted from, advising him to follow his brothers to India. [36]

The march to Meerut, which was a matter of great expense for a newly arrived subaltern with no cash, as he had to buy a tent and pay for the conveyance of his baggage and was "cheated and chiselled ... in consequence of not being able to pay ready money" [26], was described in great detail in three letters written after his arrival at Meerut, based on diary jottings – the first (No. 8) has not been found, but the other two (Nos. 10 & 11), describing the march from the 12th December 1846 are printed here [20 & 21], and are full of vivid description. At the crossing of the River Son the heavy baggage in five hundred hackeries (ox carts) needed the "united efforts of the entire regiment" to get them across, officers and men up to their knees in water all day. The river was three miles broad and with five streams, four fordable and one having to be crossed in boats. A drummer boy was drowned, Alfred's horse nearly lost its footing, and a major and subaltern crossing on an elephant laden with gunny bags fell off to the sand and water below "well *bonneted* by the gunny bags in their descent."

Christmas Day 1846 was spent at Sasseram and New Year's Day at Benares, after crossing the Ganges in thirty large boats. Here they stayed two days, playing cricket, looking round the city, watching "a great native festival, immense temples carried on men's shoulders ... bands of music, the firing of guns, juggling, sham fighting, nautch dancing, and elephants, camels & horses, superbly caparisoned ...", and watching a review of native troops "fine soldierlike looking chaps". The regiment continued to Allahabad, camping in mango groves on the way, then on to Cawnpore for three days, the camp at night being "a scene of the most riotous & ludicrous confusion" as drunken officers went round loosing tent ropes, toppling over the tents, and "exposing the scenes of the interior", including in one tent a party of officers and nautch girls. At Mohan Ke Serai there were more high jinks, a "glorious spree" in which about twenty officers and nearly one thousand men engaged in a mock battle, using unripe fruit as weapons, "comp[an]y attacking & pursuing comp[an]y with the most furious determination". As a result of the battering they all got "the great difficulty the next day was to know Jenkins from Tomkins". The march continued to Aligarh, with capital shooting on the way, then in heavy rain to Hauper, and on to Meerut.

Life in Meerut [21-27]

The 32nd Regiment was stationed at Meerut for twelve months from 19 February 1847 to 14 February 1848, but "as for giving a long description of Meerut, the Devil himself could not fill a sheet about it", wrote Alfred, "... a collection of dirty mud huts, open at the front to expose their wares, principally all

kinds of beastliness which they feed upon ... with a population
of about ten men & women to a pig sty". Fortunately for their
own comfort the barracks and officers' bungalows were "clear of
all this collection of stinks ... capital buildings arranged in
rows ... ending in a common of great extent ... with a distant
view of the Himalaya mountains". [22] Here the officers led "an
indolent life" with "rather less than nothing to do". There was
a parade at 4 or 5 a.m. for about half an hour, three or four
days a week in the hot season, and every day in the cold, and
thereafter nothing to do, except for occasional duties as orderly
officer or sitting on courts martial "drawing pen & ink cartoons
& caricatures of field officers, coinciding or differing with
what the president says, according ... to your inclination to
delay or bother the proceedings". The days passed in reading,
sleeping, lounging and larking about the bungalow, reading
newspapers and playing billiards in the mess, eating, smoking,
chatting, and riding to the Mall in the evening, to listen to the
band. Death was common, drunkenness universal. The men of the
32nd celebrated St. Patrick's Day 1847 with the men of the 80th,
and "had they been required the answer would have been 'the whole
of the Garrison are drunk' ..." Several deaths followed. [21]
In the officers' mess there were many "ludicrous scenes", but
according to Alfred the officers of the 9th Lancers and of the
80th Regiment were even more drunken than those of the 32nd:
"They think us very slow because we have only three or four
drunken chaps in the reg[imen]t and we don't think their manners
at all improved by their being always ... three sheets in the
wind."

There were other scandals to enliven the monotony: "Capt
Robyn coolly walking off with Major Cumberland's wife" [23], who
however proved "very expensive in her habits" [24], and soon
Robyns "over head & ears in debt" had to sell out [26].
Matrimony "a case of late occurrence" was only "entered into for
a spree to supply the mess with a fund of jokes ... without much
regard to decency". [23]

In the cold season there were more healthy pursuits – athletic
sports and lots of cricket matches, and, for the officers,
hunting. Alfred founded the "Jackal & Jackass Club", and by
"exchanging & selling" ended up with an excellent pony in his
stable, after having kept two horses for some months "all for
nothing and without any risk". "So", he remarked, "I succeeded
in making some use of my sharpness at last". [26] In January
there were the Meerut races, three times a week for a fortnight,
the only source of income for many officers, for "A great many
men in this country are dependent entirely on their bets, their
pay being all stopped to defray debts for former extravagances".

There were too station balls, farewell dinners, theatrical
performances and Indian shows, including a Madras juggler "who
performed the most astounding feats of dexterity" which "would

22

rather astonish the English jugglers". In fact, "he performed so many wonderful tricks that if this was not a very enlightened age he would be scragged to a certainty for having dealings with the devil". [26]

There were also occasional field days, and plenty of drill in the cold season *"fortunately* with *imaginary bullets"*, said Alfred, for "you would be much safer as an ennemy than a friend", and at ball practice the men perpetually missed even the butt, which was "as large as a haystack". [24]

But there was a more tragic occurrence. "The papers here are blackguarding us right & left", reported Alfred in November 1847, "& say that Meerut was the only station in India where courts of supposed honorable men were found so subservient to the commander-in-chief as to answer his call for blood". The commander-in-chief had resolved to confirm the death sentences on men found guilty of striking superior officers, instead of commuting them to transportation for life, as had long been the custom. The first three executions were carried out at Meerut, and one of these was a man of the 32nd, for striking a sergeant. "All the garrison were had out in full dress. The culprits are then marched round the square, preceded by the Provost Marshal, the execution party, and their coffin, the band playing the Dead March, and the prisoner accompanied by the clergymen. After this, he kneels on his coffin, is blindfolded, and quietly shot, if inefficiently, as in the first case, where the poor wretch continued in an upright posture on his coffin after the discharge, only two balls striking him, not mortally, when the Provost stepped up and blew all the upper part of his head off. The corpse is then laid at the side of his coffin, and the troops marched in subdivisions past the body. They all died very pluckily ...", reported Alfred. The Lancer private "fell pierced by seven balls in places where any body would think he must die on the instant, yet he kicked for a moment or two till shot by the Provost. But our learned Bones say it is almost impossible to kill a man instantaneously, but that they have lost all feeling & it was a muscular vibration." [24] Though sympathetic to the men, Alfred's views were conventional, believing that the commander-in-chief should have confirmed the courts martial long ago, and so nipped violence to superior officers in the bud. "We are seriously thinking", he wrote, "of calling out two or three editors, & if they won't come, horse whipping them to stop their mouths in future." [24]

The 32nd Regiment left Meerut for Ambala at 4 a.m. on the 14th February 1848, marching via Delhi "the finest appearance of any Indian town I have yet seen", reported Alfred. He gave "two horses a pretty hard day's work", visiting the Qtub Minar "the most beautiful & the highest tower in the world", Hindoo Rao's house, the cantonment, and the Mall. He continued his sight-seeing for a second day, admiring the beauty of a city unobscured

by smoke, and "the King's palace [Red Fort] containing some of
the most beautiful workmanship I ever saw ... [but] unappreciated
by the present generation, who build up mud huts against, & cover
with filth, & allow to fall into ruins the most durable & beautiful carvings in the world". [27]

They reached Ambala on the 1st March, but in six weeks were
off again to Ferozepore. "I had scarcely got settled in my
bungalow", complained Alfred, "... & arranged my plans of
amusement – out with the hounds three times a week ... tamed a
wolf ... buried a general – drank the promotion wine of the last
batch of lucky fellows – enjoyed the blaze of some Artillery
stables being burnt down & had an offer of a room at Simla ...
than we were cooly told on evening parade that we were to march
that same night at 12 o'clock ... to march with an army to
Mooltan to lick Moolraj, the rajah, who ... has had the audacity
to murder two British officers." [28] This was the beginning of
the Second Sikh War.

There was the greatest confusion on leaving Ambala, and on
the march to Ferozepore the "Lilies" became "a disorderly rabble".
All the officers and men suffered badly from the heat. During
one stage of twelve and a half miles, from Wadnee to Bhaga
Poorana, the left wing got lost in a dust storm, and there were
seven deaths, while many men fell out sick. The dead men "were
all sewed up in their bedding & buried side by side in a separate
hole before their bodies were cold ... forked & sheet lightning
... flashing on the drawn swords & fixed bayonets of off[ice]rs
& men ..." [28] They reached Ferozepore on the 27th May 1848,
and then suffered from dust storms almost every day [28 & 29],
"but as we are certain of quitting ... we have not found it
necessary to cut our throats or take laudanum at present" [29],
and in fact were "all very merry on the thoughts of an approaching campaign" [28], enjoying their hunting, races, and supper
parties.

The siege of Multan [30-33]

The 32nd Regiment marched from Ferozepore to join the Multan
field force on the 10th August 1848. They again suffered
terribly from the heat on the way, with many casualties. Alfred
Bassano had the good fortune to miss the march, going ahead with
the first detachment to protect the siege train, "after contradictory orders & rot enough to have tried the patience of Job,
& severe duty, & exposure to the sun enough to have killed a
horse". The detachment went down river to Bhawulpore on two
steam boats, Alfred and another subaltern travelling on the
Meanee. They arrived at Bhawulpore on the 17th August and
waited for the guns to be got out of the boats. On the 29th
August began "perhaps one of the most confused marches I shall
ever see – a very few Europeans (2 or 300) & some native cavalry
& infantry marching through an ennemy's country in charge of a

24

large siege train & sixteen thousand head of baggage cattle
(elephants, camels & bullocks) stretching for miles in the most
glorious confusion." They joined the rest of the regiment before
Multan on the 4th September 1848.

Multan was surrounded by a wall of burnt brick, forty feet
high and surmounted by thirty towers and covered by a ditch with
masonry scarp and counterscarp. "The town & fort", wrote Alfred,
"are very strong & surrounded by gardens, topes of trees, & brick
buildings & temples capable of being defended with great disadvantage to the besiegers. The town is very large & has a very
pretty appearance from the outside. The white domes of the
numerous temples & one bright blue one peeping from the palm
trees & glittering in the sun has a very pretty effect."

On the 6th September they all got ready for action "with an
immense deal of joking & facetiousness", squaring accounts,
sharpening their swords, and loading pistols. But it proved to
be a false alarm, and it was on the next day, while working in
the trenches, that Alfred came for the first time under fire.
He was then twenty-two years old. On the 9th September Colonel
Pattoun of the 32nd led a detachment of the 10th Regiment and
49th Native Infantry to attack some advance posts of the enemy,
but was driven back with considerable loss - fourteen killed and
seventy-one wounded.

A major attack on the enemy's advanced position was launched
on the 12th September by a force consisting of six companies of
the 10th Regiment, six companies of the 32nd, three regiments of
Native Infantry, three squadrons of irregular horse, and a troop
of horse artillery. Alfred Bassano was with the first company
of the 32nd Regiment. "The men", he wrote, "lost all order &
regularity, 10th & 32nd men all mixed up together." The buildings in the grove of trees which they had failed to capture on
the 9th were "speedily carried, shooting & bayonetting every man
in the place ... heaps of slain piled up in every room ... & had
not the bugle sounded the halt, their trenches & batteries right
up to the walls of the town would have been speedily captured,
but ... we were obliged to content ourselves with occupying what
we had carried". The 32nd lost two officers killed, four
wounded, with two men killed and thirty-one wounded. One of the
officers killed was Colonel Pattoun, who, as in the previous
attack on the 9th, attacked gallantly, but according to Alfred
foolishly, and was cut to pieces. "He forgot that he commanded
the force & rushed about like a mad man & ultimately fell ...
attempting to enter the building with ladders at its strongest
point, when there was an entrance in the rear, not barricaded &
perfectly undefended, which anybody might have known, who was
not in such a ridiculously excited state as to be unable to use
his eyes." The men were as "brave as lions", but the "damndest
fools in Christendom, firing away their powder & shot without
any aim".

During the attack Alfred himself seeing men running out of the back of the same building "made the inference that wherever they got out was the easiest place for us to get in", and ran round, where he had an encounter with a "huge Seikh, armed to the teeth", and was only saved by several of his own men coming up behind him and shooting the Sikh, who fell down "a corpse". All the people inside the building were massacred, shot down through the doors and windows - "just like a slaughter house", wrote Alfred. And all for no purpose, for on the 14th September the siege was raised and the British troops withdrawn a few miles to await reinforcements. Their Indian ally, Sher Singh, with his five thousand Sikhs, had gone over to Mulraj.

For the next few months the English camp was constantly being put on the alert by false rumours that Mulraj had moved out of the town and was about to attack. On one occasion Alfred rode out of camp to check such a rumour "perfectly unarmed, but knowing that a good pair of spurs were worth fifty brace of pistols" and that "not a man in Moolraj's wretchedly mounted cavalry" could have come near him in a race to the camp. Having proved the rumour false he was "laughingly reproved" by his colonel [Markham] "for his breach of military discipline".

On another occasion however he was fortunate not to be captured or killed. On the 30th October he and another officer who were out riding were saved from capture by some villagers who warned them that twenty of Mulraj's cavalry were near by. The horsemen tried to cut the two officers off from their camp but "we soon found out the superiority of our steeds" and beat them in the race to the camp. But, wrote Alfred, "had it not been for the devotion of the villagers ... we should have crossed the nullah & been made prisoners or mincemeat of".

Towards the end of December reinforcements arrived from Bombay, and the siege was resumed. The army under General Whish now consisted of 32,000 men and 150 guns, and on the 27th December 1848 the army advanced in four columns. Three companies of the 32nd Regiment under Major Case, who was severely wounded, made part of the advance. The enemy abandoned the suburbs and retired into the city. The houses in the suburbs were ransacked and looted, and the next day a general bombardment began.

On the 2nd January two columns were ordered to the assault and the town was carried. Mulraj now retired into the citadel. Alfred Bassano was part of the storming party of the right column led by Captain Smyth, which found their wall unbreached and had to retire, the town being carried by the left column through a breach "like a carriage road". The city was sacked "& immense quantities of spoil collected by the men amidst scenes of facetiousness & barbarity beyond description". The attack on the citadel then began, and Mulraj finally surrendered at 7 a.m. on the 22nd January 1849. Alfred's company was sent

to occupy Mulraj's house "where we kicked up the Devil's delight".
The great quantities of port, sherry and beer which were found
were spilt on the ground to prevent the men getting drunk, while
gold coins and bars of gold were found to the value of £50,000,
with pearls and other valuables. "My company boned something
considerable amongst them, in spite of the precautions taken",
reported Alfred. "The sufferings of the garrison must have been
dreadful." "War", he was to comment later, "has made fearful
ruffians of us all."

After the fall of Multan, General Whish's troops were ordered
to join Lord Gough's army "to extricate him from his difficulties".
Gough had won a doubtful victory at Chillianwallah on the 13th
January during which the 24th Foot had been almost cut to pieces,
with thirteen officers killed, ten wounded, and half the men
either killed or wounded. The 9th Lancers and 14th Dragoons had
run away, riding over their own artillery. "The loss on our side
is so great & the advantages gained little or nothing", wrote
Alfred, "that it appears to all here that he is rather in a
pickle."

On the way they captured the fort and garrison of Cheniote
[34], and joined Lord Gough in time to take part in the battle of
Gujrat on the 21st February. It was "a beautifully managed
affair, more like a parade than an action", wrote Alfred, though
he "had great difficulty in preventing them [his company] from
breaking their line and charging the Ennemy against orders".
This victory was the end of the war. "Their dead are lying about
the country in all directions, wherever they made a stand being
marked by rows of them ... the jackals, pariah dogs, kites &
vultures appear to be the greatest gainers by war in this
country".

After the war the 32nd Regiment marched to Lahore where
during a stay of eight days the regiment indulged in an orgy of
drunkenness. The men, Alfred reported, were "doing their best
to assist the climate by getting drunk every day by hundreds, &
as by dint of robbing houses, cutting throats & plundering dead
bodies for the last six months there is no lack of tin amongst
them this delay before a large town is giving us endless trouble
& filling the hospital". [35]

From Lahore the regiment marched to Jullundur, arriving on the
18th April 1849.

On the frontier, 1849-56

The regiment was stationed at Jullundur until the end of 1851,
then at Peshawar during the years 1852 and 1853, and then from
the beginning of 1854 until the Autumn of 1856, at Kussowlie and
Sabathu. Alfred Bassano's activities are not well documented
during these years as he wrote few letters. For four months of

the winter of 1850/51 he was on escort duty with the Governor-General, Lord Dalhousie, who was making a tour of inspection of the Punjab. At Amritsar Alfred and some other "lively Subs" behaved in a way unlikely to endear themselves to the Great Man, "knocking the turbans off dignified looking natives & smashing the lamps of oil ... and many other eccentric proceedings", while on their way by elephant to see "the most magnificent illumination I have or ever shall see". He was also present while Dr. Dunlop was making the portrait of Gholab Singh for the Governor-General. [58]

Two years later Alfred went on leave, sailing from Karachi in February 1853, in the *Earl of Balcarres*, "an old crazy bark and totally unseaworthy" according to his brother Christopher [93], but according to his brother Tom "the finest and quickest in the merchant service" [94]. He reached home in June 1853, having been away for seven years. "He is altered & yet he is *not* altered", wrote his sister Melinda. "When I rushed to meet him at the door it struck me he looked so like Tom, & I think he has grown like what Tom was when he left home ... I think he looks more like a seafaring, than a military man." He made a great hit with his brother Walter's youngest child, calling her a *jovial* baby, and spent his time visiting friends, going on trips up the Thames with his brother Philip, and suffering unspecified disappointments in affairs of the heart – *too fast*, said Tom – which made him resolve never to return home again, "but his spirits are very elastic", remarked Melinda, and "he will change his mind I hope". [116]

He had a pleasant voyage back to India, arriving in February 1855. "We jumped overboard several times and bathed in the sea, shaved our heads, played ecarte, backgammon, & whist all day, eat dolphin & flying fish, caught sharks and talked sentiment, arrived at Bombay, stayed at a hotel for a fortnight, visited the cave of Elephanta, took a steamer to Kurachee, stayed about a week, eating oysters, riding, & driving about, then again by steamer to Mooltan, a pleasant journey of about a month up a river ... thence by mail cart to Lahore, 208 miles in 18 hours, drove myself ... stayed one day, thence again by mail cart to Jullundur, came an awful smash into a banyan's shop on the road ... picked myself up and off again to Umballa, where I arrived just in time for dinner at my own mess about a week before the expiration of my leave." [150]

During these years of peace-time soldiering Alfred's preoccupations were with promotion and with his debts. He considered applying for a company in a regiment in the Crimea, writing to his brother Philip at the War Office: "Now if you think this war will last and can afford to give me a chance of distinction, for I am really just in the state of mind to storm a breach or do anything desperate, try and get me *promoted*." But, he added, "You must not attempt to get me promoted unless

28

you feel convinced I shall be in plenty of time to come in for
lots of fighting ... for I am getting to the top of the
L[ieutenan]ts in the 32nd ..." And he later decided that the
expense would be too great, and "I have come to the conclusion
that I must not think of quitting this country until I am out of
debt." [151 & 152] For the rest he led a "very quiet retired
life studying Persian, Hindustanee & Arabic, and breeding
foxhounds", his temper slightly soured, but with plenty of leave
which he spent travelling in the hills.

The siege of Lucknow [150, 154-158]

In the Autumn of 1856 the 32nd Regiment was ordered to Lucknow
to relieve the 52nd Light Infantry. During the march they
suffered from cholera, losing upwards of forty men. One company,
which was later massacred in the Mutiny, was left at Cawnpore to
form a depot, while the rest arrived at Lucknow on the 27th
December 1856, "where we had splendid quarters", wrote Alfred,
"given to us gratis in a palace on the banks of the 'river
Goomtee'". There he hoped "to pass a very pleasant time of it
hunting, rowing, riding & driving, not to mention lots of balls,
parties, private theatricals & archery meetings". The reality
was to be very different, months "in a st\te of filth & misery
in a dark sort of store room" unable to move from his bed while
bullets, round shot and shell fell all around, fortunate to be
alive at all.

Early in 1857 the unrest which was to culminate in the Mutiny
and massacre at Meerut on the 10th May, had already begun to make
itself felt. A mutiny at Lucknow itself was prevented on the 3rd
May by disarming the 7th Oudh Infantry during the night. From
the 16th May the men of 32nd Regiment were constantly on duty,
sleeping in their clothes, arms by their side, until the evacuation of the Residency on the 22nd November. On the 14th June
Alfred Bassano led a party of the 32nd with two guns and some
cavalry in pursuit of members of the police battalion who had
deserted after plundering some houses. The deserters were
overtaken and about forty killed, and others taken prisoner.
The 32nd lost one soldier, who died of heat stroke.

Then on the 30th June came "that disastrous business at
Chinhut". [157] Three hundred men of the 32nd Regiment,
commanded by Colonel Case, with eleven guns and some native
infantry and cavalry left the city at 6 a.m. under Sir Henry
Lawrence, Chief Commissioner for Oudh, to meet the mutineers who
were reported to be within eight miles of Lucknow. They came
upon the enemy in overwhelming numbers at Chinhut, concealed
behind a line of trees. The men of the Oudh Artillery with the
British force overturned their guns and abandoned them, while
the 32nd, led by Col. Case, tried to capture the village of
Ishmaelgunge but were forced to retreat by overwhelming numbers.
Col. Case was shot down, Alfred Bassano went to his assistance,

29

and was then himself wounded in the foot "rather a bad smash, a grape shot slap through the foot, in on one side & out on the other cutting my boot right off my foot". [157] Retreat became a rout - the 32nd Regiment lost four officers and 111 men killed or died of heat stroke, their bodies, arms and equipment marking the whole line of retreat, while the rest got back to the Residency as best they could, some of the wounded carried by native infantrymen. Alfred himself was rescued and carried on his back by a sepoy of the 13th Native Infantry for some distance, according to an independent witness, although he does not mention the incident himself, and then "managed to walk about 4 miles & ride two, and do a little fighting besides on the way home". [157] Numbers of the wounded later died.

The siege of Lucknow began the next day, 1 July 1857. Before the siege began the 32nd Regiment had twenty-three officers present, of whom thirteen were killed or died of wounds or disease, eight were wounded, one laid up with cholera most of the time, and only one, Captain Lawrence, went through the whole siege untouched. Four of the officers were killed at Chinhut, including Col. Case, and three during the massacre at Cawnpore, the remainder died during the siege itself. The regiment also lost the 111 non-commissioned officers and men killed at Chinhut, 82 killed at Cawnpore, and 174 who were killed or died during the siege - 185 were wounded, of whom 55 died soon afterwards. Forty-three women and fifty-four children were killed at Cawnpore as well as the wives and families of the three officers, and three wives and six children died during the siege.

Alfred Bassano having been so severely wounded at Chinhut was unable to take any part in the defence of the Residency until September, but on the 26 September he headed a sortie which captured seven guns from the enemy. The next day he succeeded to the command of the regiment, taking over from Major Lowe who had been severely wounded, for although low on the list, by 27th September he was the only surviving captain. Major Lowe had succeeded to the command of the regiment when Colonel Inglis became commander of the garrison on the death of Sir Henry Lawrence on the 4th July. Alfred commanded the regiment for two months, and when the Residency was finally evacuated on the night of 22nd November, it marched out under his command. He was then engaged in the defeat of the Gwalior rebels at Cawnpore (6 December 1857) and in part of the campaign in Oudh, before going on six months' sick leave.

Alfred was mentioned in dispatches, but considered himself "very hardly used" [173] as no honour was conferred upon him. "What rot appears in the papers about the operations in India", he exclaimed. [158] "A few unpleasant truths could be told by first rate officers", he said [158], but "these war stories are very long winded ones & cannot be told in letters, besides there are so many imbecile old fools of high rank generally implicated

in all disasters which makes it dangerous to express opinions
for fear of your friends showing the letters". [173] However,
he managed to clear off his Indian debts and his major debts at
home [158] out of his extra pay and allowances, and to pay the
expenses of his visit to his brother Tom in South India, for as
he remarked to his brother Philip, "there is nothing like a
bloody war for a poor man. You are either shot, or shot up to
the upper grades with great rapidity." [173]

The 32nd Regiment set sail for England on the 24th April 1859,
and disembarked at Portsmouth on the 26th August, where at
11 a.m., in the dockyard, they were inspected by Queen Victoria.
The same day they went by rail to Dover, and on the 13th September
the survivors of the siege were entertained to a banquet by the
people of Dover. Alfred had returned home in advance of the
regiment but was present at the banquet. He had been up to the
Isle of Man to arrange his marriage to Mary Dumbell, which took
place in November. His son Alfred was born on the 10th October
1860, but his wife died ten days later - she was twenty-three
years old, Alfred thirty-four.

The regiment was stationed at Dover until August 1860, where
Alfred enjoyed lots of exercise and fun, a bathe in the sea every
day, fruit before breakfast and a fresh water bath every day, and
"the devil's own work" getting the regiment into shape again.
He continued to serve with the regiment, in England until 1863,
Ireland 1863-5, Gibraltar, 1865-6, Mauritius 1866-8, and South
Africa from 1868, retiring on half-pay in 1872, when he was
forty-six years old. His great interest remained, as in India,
hunting, but he was never again to be the letter writer of his
first two or three years in India. "You complain about my
father's letter writing", wrote his fifteen year old son in
March 1876, "well I am sure I can't tell you any thing about him.
The last news I had of him was a cheque to buy a bicycle with,
which I received about the middle of the Xmas holidays and never
a word have I heard from that time to this ... It is very queer
..." [26 March 1876 - not printed]. Alfred died in 1882, and his
son, who had followed him into the regiment, survived him by only
five years, dying in 1887, while stationed in Malta.

III. CHRISTOPHER BAKEWELL BASSANO (1824-56)

Christopher Bassano, the fourth of the five surviving sons of
Francis Matthias, was born on the 10th April 1824, at High Street,
Fulham. From the beginning of 1844 until 1848 he was a medical
student at King's College, London, and was admitted a Member of
the Royal College of Surgeons on the 18th August 1848. For six
months, from 1st May to 1st November he acted as the physicians'
clinical clerk for the in-patients at King's College Hospital,
and then went to Chatham to await his posting as Assistant
Surgeon in the Queen's Service, "an anxious time" for him, he

remarked. "Who is to have the 12th Lancers?", he asked his
father in the Army Medical Department, "of course it is too
expensive for me." Finally on the 22nd December 1848 he was
gazetted Assistant Surgeon with the 70th Regiment, under orders
for India. [37-40]

He bought his uniform from George Linney, the military tailor
[41], and early in January sailed for Cork, to embark with his
regiment. At Cork they were delayed by gales [42 & 43], but he
finally sailed on the 20th January, on board the *Diana* [44], with
a detachment consisting of one captain, four subalterns, one
staff officer, seven sergeants, seven corporals, one drummer,
one hundred and forty-five privates, nineteen women, and twenty-
five children [47]. After a week of blowing about the Channel
they put in at Milford Haven, having been in great danger, "but",
he remarked, "I am glad to say I was not aware of it". [45]
With three of the other officers he went on shore to attend
divine service and offer up prayers for their safety. [46] It
was discovered that the cargo had been damaged, so they all had
to disembark and stay in Milford Haven for a fortnight. One of
the soldiers deserted, but was captured and brought back, and
the sailors went on strike - six of them were taken before the
magistrates and sentenced to two months imprisonment, and the
captain had to find fresh hands.

The officers were billeted at the Nelson Hotel during their
time ashore, and spent an agreeable time riding about the
countryside, and making the money fly, so that on re-embarking
Christopher found himself £11 poorer than when he had landed.
[49] In the evenings they sang glees with the three daughters
of their hostess. [48] Christopher said that he regretted there
was no railroad to London, then he could have got home for a
week. They set sail again on the 25th February 1849.

The voyage to India lasted almost four months, from 25th
February to 19th June, and in addition to treating the sick and
delivering three babies, Christopher passed his time in the
usual manner - dancing, gymnastics, shooting at bottles, catching
sharks and albatrosses, bathing in the sea, playing chess,
backgammon and whist - during one game of whist during a gale
"the ship was tossing about so much ... we were obliged to hold
our cards while they were being dealt". At St. Nicholas (Cape
Verde Is.) he and other officers went ashore with the captain
in the ship's boat and when ready to return to the ship found
that it was out of sight. They had to pull for three hours
before they caught sight of it again, for it had been drifting
away from the shore at the rate of three miles an hour and was
then fifteen miles away. [51]

They landed at Calcutta on the 19th June 1849 and the whole
detachment of about two hundred men, women and children were
immediately taken to the barracks at Dum Dum, some ten miles

away, Christopher following the same evening after first calling
at the Medical Board. At Dum Dum, where he was stationed for
four months, he shared a bungalow with two former college friends,
now serving with the East India Company. "A medical man in the
H.C.'s service", he complained, "is treated as he should be. He
has that assistance which converts his office into what as a
Surgeon or M.D. he has only a right to be troubled with" [60],
whereas "appointments are only coveted in the Queen's service
from their necessity" [80]. In his letters from India Christopher oftens appears as rather humourless and complaining, yet
he was a general favourite, both in the family and in the
regiment, where he was regarded as kind, cheerful, and conscien-
tous, "a hard working sole", as his Surgeon's widow later put it
[114], who, wrote his colonel, as a medical officer showed "a
zeal and devotion seldom surpassed" [115]. Later, when he was
serving in the Crimea, he was again reported to be "a great
favourite", of whom it was said that in his treatment of the sick
"no one could be kinder". But in India, though apparently
outwardly cheerful, he was the least happy of the brothers,
constantly, after less than two years in the country, trying to
get home on leave in charge of the invalids, and after his sister
Ellen had settled in Australia frequently speaking of selling out
and joining her to try his luck as a doctor in "Australia Felix".
He at last got a year's leave, in late 1854, and sailed with the
invalids from Calcutta in March 1855, after almost six years in
India. On arrival in England at the end of July, he decided to
accept immediate promotion for service in the Crimea, and he left
for Scutari in September 1855. After about four months looking
after the sick, he died of fever in the General Hospital,
Balaklava, on the 1st February 1856. He was in his thirty-
second year.

While in India Christopher kept a note of the letters which
he posted. In the six years he wrote seventy-one letters to the
family, of which fifteen were to Alfred, twenty-one to Tom, five
to Ellen in Australia, and thirty to members of the family at
home. Only seventeen of these letters have been found, seventeen
out of the thirty written home - none of the letters to his
brothers in India survive. He also kept a rather scrappy diary,
which is also still in existence. Of the letters home twenty
were written in the first two years, none at all in the next two,
and the remainder in the last eighteen months, before sailing
for England in 1855.

Dum Dum and Calcutta [60-76]

Christopher spent his first eighteen months in India at Dum
Dum and Calcutta - at Dum Dum until October 1849 and then at
Calcutta until the 20th December 1850. He soon discovered that
medical officers in India - unlike the regimental officers -
were kept very busy, and the more competent and conscientious
they were, the more work they had to do, and the less leave they

could obtain. Those who carried out their profession with
"great assiduity and activity", he was to complain, "place themselves in a worse position than if they did only what they were
obliged to ... [and] the more value attached to a medical officer
the less chance he has of the slightest recreation". "As long
as medical officers are considered as unfit to be recommended for
leave of absence on the same ground as other officers", he asked,
"how are they to recruit their strength except by having recourse
to malingering ...? It surely requires no great amount of brains
to see that med[ica]l officers, who are never for a moment at
rest or free from calls, are the men who require the most
indulgence." [80]

At Dum Dum where eighty-four men died from cholera and
dysentery in the regiment's first three months in India,
Christopher spent up to four hours each morning, from 5 a.m. to
9 a.m., at the hospital, and then after breakfast was kept busy
answering calls. He attributed the deaths to the "crouded state
of the barracks". He was always a great advocate of fruit as a
means of keeping healthy - it should, he said, be part of the
daily diet of the men - and in his treatment he considered lime
juice and fruit to be "the sheet anchor in dysentery", and fruit
an excellent remedy for vomiting in the case of cholera. [63]

When he moved to Calcutta in October 1849 he first lived in
the General Hospital and then was on permanent duty at the Fort.
There he was at two different periods in charge of the opthalmic
cases, most of whom he cured, attributing his success to the
same treatment. "My sheet anchor in this disease", he wrote
after two years experience, "as well as nearly all others in this
country, is lime juice or fruit; without administering this in
nearly every case of ophthalmia & dysentery in this country, other
judicious treatment becomes perfectly useless, and in many cases
absolutely injurious. I have been preaching this ever since I
was in the country, and I am now glad to find others are of the
same opinion. But until soldiers in hot climates are recommended
to eat fruit by medical men, or until that article is served out
to them as a portion of their rations, they will continue to die
of dysentery and become the victims of cholera; and ophthalmia
will still be at the top of the list." [80]

As well as being hard worked, he also soon discovered that
"even with great economy the expenses are frightful" [61] and he
managed to live under his pay of Rs.225 a month during his first
year only "because I have from being on duty at the hospital
escaped going to mess". [69] The mess expenses could equal or
exceed the total pay of a subaltern and so drove most of them
"into the Agra Bank". [65] This was because they included the
expense of paying the share of every mess guest "of whom there
are not a few, as we are obliged to invite every officer to mess
who leaves his card" which "causes our wine a/c [to] be very
large, and ... I cannot get mine below Rs.50 per month, although

I generally take beer." "These expenses", he maintained, "which an individual officer cannot avoid, are disgraceful to the service." Another unavoidable expense, deducted from their pay, was that of keeping up the band, and another bringing out a billiard table. In fact, after paying all expenses he had been left with "only 30R. a month to buy furniture, pay palenkins and in fact anything connected with domestic arrangements, and save up money to buy tents and horses." [69]

His various complaints about conditions annoyed his father who replied that he could not condescend "to answer the graceless and ill-judged complaints ... and surely I had a right to expect better things from one in whose behalf I have done more than for any two of my children." [70]

However, Christopher enjoyed Calcutta and left "by no means tired of it". [77] In spite of the frightful expenses he managed to buy first a pony in Dum Dum, for 100 rupees, and later in Calcutta a buggy and horse, for 470 rupees, and which he re-sold for 400 when he left Calcutta. [74] The first few months in Calcutta were "most delightfully spent" with innumerable parties, magnificent weather, and many acquaintances and friends to visit. [67] He attended several grand balls. "You can form no idea", he told his sister Melinda, "of a ballroom in India - one room is equal to half a dozen in England and instead of, as you might suppose, being warm they are much cooler than those in England, even in the warm weather." At one fancy dress ball "on a most magnificent scale" "the amusements of the evening were excellent". He also went to a ball at the town hall every fortnight in the cool season. [64] But by April 1850 he was asking his brother Walter for "the composition of that sticky stuff they put on paper to catch flies" to help clear "our rooms of musquetoes". [69]

One unpleasant duty for the medical officers, for which he blamed his brother in the Army Medical Department, was preparing a report on old records. "Don't send any more of your humbuging letters, like that of the 30th April 1850", he begged. "The four presses full of dirty dry drafts and returns in a godown which had not been opened for years, soon produced in our hearts that peculiar depression of spirits, accompanied with languor and lassitude which at my suggestion and Harvey's expense, was only removed by a few bottles of Bass Pale Ale and a mild Manilla cheroot." [73]

Before leaving Calcutta Christopher sent presents home with a brother officer who was travelling overland, including a daguerrotype of himself, which still survives. He is shown with a cropped head instead of his usual luxuriant curls, following an attack of acute rheumatism which had caused it all to drop out. [76, 78 & 79] "Mark what a disagreeable fellow I look but how profoundly intellectual. I long to hear Walter's abuse about

35

it", he commented later. [82] However a few months later he was able to report that his hair had grown very thick and curly again, and that he had added "a large stack of whiskers". [83] He had begun to go grey before leaving home [75] but was now able to report "I am however not so gray as I used to be, which is remarkable and very gratifying". At the same time, as it was his birthday, he asked to be sent the year of his birth "for I have not the least idea of my age. I expect I am damned old". It was in fact his 27th birthday. [81]

Cawnpore and Meerut

The left wing of the 70th Regiment started for Allahabad en route for Meerut on the 19th October 1850. They travelled by river in two flats and an accommodation boat for the officers, each of the three pulled by a steamer. [74] The steamers returned to Calcutta to collect the second wing, which embarked for Allahabad on the 20th December, Christopher with them. He travelled in the *Nerbudda* steamer which was towing a troop boat. [77] The destination had by now been changed from Meerut to Cawnpore. The *Nerbudda* was "a very comfortable steamer" and Christopher enjoyed himself "to the utmost" admiring the scenery, shooting crocodiles, and enjoying Christmas and New Year. Of the towns which they passed only Benares, where he got lost in the narrow streets for several hours, impressed him. From the river it had, he said, "a most splendid appearance". They arrived at Allahabad on the 19th January, and, after three days rest, began their march to Cawnpore. They averaged thirteen miles a day, the officers as well as the men walking most of the way, as it was cold, "but the Col[onel] not knowing much about the country insisted on all the officers remaining with the men". [77 & 78]

On arriving at Cawnpore they found that an assistant surgeon was required to do duty with the 29th Regiment at Meerut, and Christopher got the job. From Cawnpore to Meerut was a twenty-seven days march, but Christopher went via Agra to see the Taj Mahal, travelling in his new buggy drawn by coolies. He left on the 12th February 1851 and enjoyed the journey "amazingly". In Agra he met an old friend with whom he stayed three days, and arrived at Meerut on the 10th March, where he shared a bungalow with a friend, Assistant Surgeon Miles, doing duty with the 1st Bengal Fusiliers. He sent home a description of their bungalow and a plan [82], and said that his only regret was "that there are few fruit trees in the garden, for I am still as great advocate for fruit as ever, and make it a portion of my daily meal". [80] The surgeon of the 29th, Dr. Dane "a queer fellow and not much liked, I fancy, by the officers", handed over to his charge all the opthalmic patients, about twenty-eight, "having heard of my success in that department". Christopher had made up his mind to live quietly in Meerut to save expense, for he was already thinking of applying to get home in charge of the invalids, after less than two years in India, "and then I might volunteer for Africa, and get my promotion". [80]

Nevertheless he found Meerut "an excellent station", the roads plentiful and good, and the fruit better than in any other part of India which he had visited [84], and he managed to enjoy himself with balls and hunting. The officers' wives were "a rum lot of females", but the soldiers' wives were not at all the same persons as at home, many of them, he reported, were very elegantly dressed. He refused to take part in the scandal spoken against the ladies. Replying to his brother Walter's request for some gossip, he said: "Why, if I were to write about the scandal against the ladies of one Reg[imen]t in India, it would fill a volume. Nobody who has never been in India can form any idea what a rum lot of females are married to officers in India, and how freely all their faults are conversed and canvassed at the mess table. No matter whether good or bad, mention anybody's name at the table and I defy you hear a word in favour of him or her from the moment they were born. For my part ... I take no part in such conversation, and never retail what I hear against the ladies." [80]

In September Christopher tried to get a month's leave to go to visit his brother Alfred at Jullundur, but his application was refused and he was recalled to serve with his own regiment at Cawnpore. He spent the rest of 1851 at Cawnpore, and all of 1852, with a month's leave at Lucknow. He wrote no letters home, and only one short diary entry at the end of the year. The year 1853 was also spent in Cawnpore. "Nobody", he complained in May 1853, "cares a bit about the health of doctors, and they care duced little for one another so that any poor devil is kept at work until he is nearly dead." [93] He wrote to his sister Ellen in Australia about the possibility of setting up practice in that country [96 & 102]. His brother Tom, who was feeling equally miserable in the jungles of Manantoddy, begged him to take leave or exchange into a regiment stationed in South India: "And as for the expence in coming what is that to you? You are provided for life, sick or well ... Come and see the stunning fair girls of this coast ... Write sharp about exchange or leave as this solitude in the jungle will kill me". [94] Six months later he wrote again: "I wish to God you would come down and see me ... I have desese of the hart which may carry me off at a moment's worning." [106]

The 70th Regiment however had been hit by an exceptionally bad cholera epidemic, which carried off the Surgeon. He died on the 1st August 1853 leaving Christopher, the junior Assistant Surgeon, in medical charge of the regiment. He was later officially commended for his "cheerful and unvaried exertions" [115] during the epidemic. "Altho' young in the service [he] conducted the medical duties in a way which would have done credit to the most experienced Surgeon." [112] The only other

37

medical officer present was a doctor in the East India Company's service, and "they were both overworked and nothing but the most determined resolution could have carried them on till help arrived". [112] Being in medical charge more than doubled his pay, "but I would willingly give it up", he wrote, "if I could get the invalids and go home". [101]

The regiment marched to Ferozepore, and there at the beginning of 1854 Christopher handed over charge to the new Surgeon, Dr. Currie. However cheerful his exertions, he was now feeling extremely miserable - he complained that his family had quite forgotten him - he hated everybody - and he especially hated the sight of a sick man. [109] However, as a reward for his exertions during the epidemic he was at last put in charge of the invalids going to Calcutta, and then home, with a year's leave. He first spent a month's leave in Kashmir, in October 1854, where he was "most disappointed with the women who are by no means pretty, although better looking than the women of Bengal". [111]

He left Ferozepore in November 1854, but did not sail from Calcutta until March 1855. His brother Tom again asked him to visit him, while he was waiting to embark, recommending him to sail to Madras "in any small country boat" then take a bullock transit coach to Bangalore where he would be met. [125] However, Tom was now in good spirits, doing well, and working on his own account at last, so he did not press him. And Christopher sailed in medical charge of the *Marlborough* on the 29th March 1855. He had a four month voyage home, the chief excitement of the voyage being caused by the madness of one of the passengers, who had to be restrained from interfering with the sailing of the ship. [126]

Christopher reached England at the end of July, with one year's leave due to him. However he decided to go out to the Crimea, because of the better promotion prospects, and sailed after only a month at home. He went first to Scutari and then to Sebastopol with the troops employed in destroying the docks. Later he served as medical officer on the transport *Gibraltar*, which carried the sick from Balaklava to Scutari, as well as in the General Hospital. And there, having survived all the fevers and epidemics of India, he succumbed to those destroying the British army in the Crimea, dying on the 1st February 1856. He left all his effects to his sister Melinda, who received about £400 from the proceeds. [141-149]

* * * * * * * *

During the decades when the Bassano brothers were in India, and especially in the 1840s and 1850s, India as well as Britain itself was going through a period of great expansion, upheaval and change, but we hear of public events only when the corre-

spondents were personally involved, as in the case of Alfred at
the siege of Multan and later when besieged in Lucknow, and of
social change, nothing. The brothers show no interest in Indian
society and customs - they were matter-of-fact young men, who
accepted society and conditions as they found them, sharing
current values, assumptions and prejudices. Though Christopher
remarked: "It is astonishing how soon one gets over the prejudice
against the blacks. They are a much handsomer class of people
than I have yet seen ..." [62], yet only Tom, the planter, would
seem to have had friendly relations with Indians. He went to
considerable lengths to get a clock repaired belonging "to a very
swell native friend of mine" because he had "a great respect for
the owner". [183 & 184] Tom, with his "splendid little girl"
and Alfred "obliged to lavish my affections on black Venuses
generally smelling most confoundedly of beetle nut ..." had the
usual relations with Indian women, although Christopher, the
doctor, seems to have restricted himself to admiring Indian
women from afar, and to have confined his attentions to regimental wives and daughters. He enjoyed visiting and tea parties,
musical evenings and balls, and was a great favourite with his
colonel's family, and with the other ladies.

They were accustomed to rapid change. They were also, as
Londoners born and bred, accustomed to the dirt and squalor of
a city with a totally inadequate drainage system and a water
supply coming mainly from that open sewer, the Thames. Brought
up in Bermondsey, Westminster and Marylebone they could not have
avoided some familiarity with dirt, poverty and wretchedness -
and yet they invariably comment on the dirt and squalor of
India - and Philip on that of Istanbul - even when admiring the
external appearance of Eastern cities. We must believe that the
filth and wretchedness of Indian towns and cities was infinitely
worse, or at least more pervasive, than anything they had known
at home. The streets of Multan, remarked Alfred "are very
narrow & beastly dirty as usual in all Indian towns", while
"Ramnuggur contains nothing of interest except filth to an
astounding extent". Bhawulpore too, though "a very pretty
Indian town from the outside" was "dirty & wretched as usual
in". The quotations could be multiplied. Even when describing
cities which were much admired, such as Delhi and Lahore, the
same comments about dirt and wretchedness are made. Delhi,
surrounded by a high wall, with its lofty towers and minarets
presented "the finest appearance of any Indian town I have yet
seen". From the top of the minarets of the "Jumma Musjeed, a
splendid mosque in the heart of the city" could be had "a very
fine view of the city, the flat white roofs of the houses ...
not being obscured by smoky chimneys, had a very pretty effect
... The streets are wide & the shops well stocked & many of the
houses well built, but the goods heaped together - everything
presenting the appearance of dirt, wretchedness, & cheap &
gaudy splendour peculiar to this country". [17] While of Lahore,
"the prettiest & most interesting town in India I have yet seen

(barring Delhi)", Alfred also remarked that "you cannot get at any of the interesting without going through a great deal of the disgusting". [35]

Nevertheless, and in spite of being London children, they all took to the pioneering or frontier life, with its rural amusements - Alfred with his hunting and love of variety and "great taste for knocking about foreign countries"; Tom in the jungle; and Ellen in the Australian bush with her garden and domestic animals. "I hope", she wrote to her brother Tom, "you do not dislike dogs and cats and turkeys and fowls and duck, because we have swarms, and do not bring me a monkey or a parrot, for sometimes I am almost mad with those I have." [159] Christopher alone seemed to miss the more urban entertainments, as well as the skating of which he was so fond, and he alone retained any great interest in events at home - the Great Exhibition of 1851 for example, and the Regatta. But they all kept up their musical interests, though so many generations removed from the family origins as professional musicians. Tom led the shanties at sea, and wrote home to ask "Walter to be kind enough to send me that song of the monks of old and Christopher if he will send me the song of the jolly Rose, the bright rubies that garnish thy lip". [16] While Christopher himself, who was "considered a first rate vocalist and musician" was also to write home "perhaps you will send me a copy of Old King Cole ... and any other song you think would suit my sweet voice". [73] Melinda also was a first rate singer, and had her piano, as did Ellen in Australia. Among the family friends at home were music sellers and publishers. Alfred was perhaps the one exception, his dislike of that favourite musical piece of the day "The Battle of Prague", being almost the only musical comment in his correspondence.

The brothers were addicted to puns and riddles sending each other examples of each, had strong family attachments and complained constantly about short or infrequent letters, but having gone to India to gain a livelihood, they were content to carry out their duties with more or less competence, and for the rest to live their lives as agreeably as possible. In this they were typical of all but a few of the British in India. And life could be agreeable enough for officers, civil servants and merchants. Though they complained of the discomforts and boredom of India, they enjoyed an aristocratic style of life as "sahibs" unknown to the middling classes of the rapidly industrialising society from which they came, and in later life looked back on their Indian service with nostalgia. "I ... would give anything for a quiet tent and a gun in an Indian jungle", wrote Alfred Bassano six years after he had left India for good. And, "In England, I don't know how it is, I don't feel myself so much as I do out here", complained Tom after a spell of leave at home. Or, as Surgeon Harvey's widow put it, "I am verry comfortable in Ingland, but still every thing is verry dull." [114]

The Writers

Upper left: Thomas Bromsall
Upper right: Alfred
Lower left:
       Christopher Bakewell
Lower right: Charlotte Ellen

The Recipients

Upper right: The Father, Francis Matthias

Lower right: Walter Waterfield

Lower left: Melinda

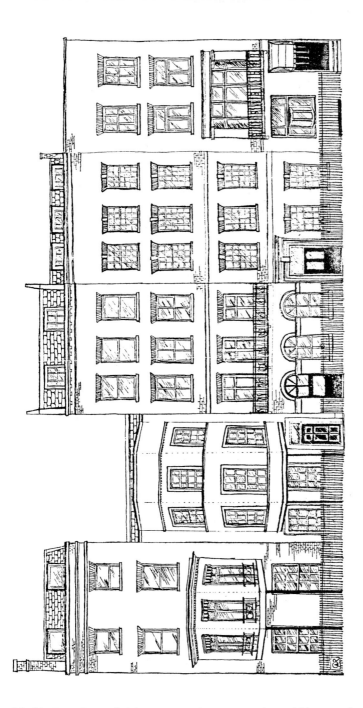

12-14 St. James' Place, London, now the offices of the
publishers William Collins. Number 13 housed the Army
Medical Department, the address to which many of the
letters were sent.

"Maharajah's Boat on the Dhul Canal, Cashmere"
See item 111.

CHAPTER ONE

"Nothing like a roving life ... here
there and eaverywher"

In November 1830 Francis Matthias Bassano,
Apothecary to the Forces, with a salary of £173 per
annum, applied to the Governors of the Philological
School in Gloucester Place, New Road, near Lisson
Grove, for a free place for Thomas Bromsall, the
third of his five surviving sons, at that time nine
years old. Optimistically he stated that his situation in the Army would make it possible to educate
the boy for the medical profession. But Tom, as he
was never to cease to lament in later life, was a
"bad scholar", and a few years later he ran away to
sea. His father then agreed that he should be
allowed to make the sea his career, and on 15
February 1838, when he was sixteen years old, he was
apprenticed for five years to William Tindall, at a
yearly wage of three pounds for the first year,
rising to eight pounds during the last year.[1]

During the next three years he made three voyages
to the Cape and Ceylon, sending home long "spirited"
letters,[2] and between voyages entertaining his
family with his travellers' tales.[3] Before setting
out on his fourth voyage in the summer of 1841 his
father equipped him with paper, pencils, books and
navigational instruments – in addition to the usual
supplies such as clothes, shoes and soap – so that
he could study during the voyage and so advance his
career.[4] But Tom, now aged nineteen, had fallen in
love during his time ashore, and while in dock,
waiting to set sail, he continued to visit his "dear

---

1. Application form for a free place, copy of indenture, and
   memoranda by F.M.B. – among the Bassano papers.
2. None have survived, but they are mentioned e.g. in a letter
   from Charlotte Ellen, the eldest of the family, to her
   brother Walter, 7 March 1840.
3. See for example the end of Letter 23 for a comment from
   Alfred, the youngest brother, after his arrival in India.
4. Memoranda by F.M.B.

Eleanor",[5] but at their last meeting just before he
sailed, he was told by her father, to his distress,
that unless he gave up the sea he would never be
allowed to marry her.

I

"ANY ONE BUT A SALOR"

(Voyage to Ceylon
1841-2)

1. *Waiting to sail: a visit aboard*[6]

Tom Bassano to Walter Bassano[7]   5 Spread Eagle Street
                                                     [London]
                                                     10 July 1841

Dear Walter
    I recieved your letter this eav[en]ing. When you come, if
you don't get their and out of the dock before 5 o'clock you will
be shut in, so that he must leave the gig at the Blue Posts at
the end of the Commercial Road, close at the dock gate. I am
not quite sure of them having a bait Stables, but I can't go to
see tonight as I have to go out. But if they have not, their is
one opposite that has, next door to the butcher's. But I don't
know what you want to put the horse up at all for. If he gets
down to the docks between ½ past 3 and 4 he can drive right to
the ship and then he would catch the captain and he would crack
a bottle of wine with you. But you can neather get in or out
after 5 o'clock with gig. I have made a track on other side[8]
for gig at stated times, but if you come later than 5 you must
put the horse up, and then all the chance for you would be the
mate asking you to take tea which is at 10 minutes past 6 o'clock,
which he most likeley will. So take your choise. I have likewise made you a track if after 5 o'clock, putting gig up at the

---

5. Whose name he never learned to spell correctly.
6. This letter, and the rest in this chapter are written without
   punctuation. Throughout this volume punctuation has been
   added for ease of reading, but the original spelling is
   retained.
7. Clerk in the Army Medical Board office, aged 22 years.
8. On the back of the letter is a sketch map of the docks,
   showing routes to the ship *Sumatra*.

Blue Post — which is, round dock wall, in wicker gate, round
bason, ditto export dock, to ship.

I remain your[s] truly
T. Bassano

2. *"My dear Ellenor"*

Tom Bassano to Walter Bassano   Downs
                                                       8 August 1841

Dear Walter
    I hope you will not forget to go to my dear Ellenor whilst I
am away. But I am afraid it will be to no purpose for me to
offer my hand as the secret was opened to me after I left you on
Sunday. Her father had told her any one but a salor and told me
that unless I knock of[f] going to sea and anchor on shore it is
of no use to go to that quarter again. But I requested a year
more, which was granted. Ellen is as broken harted as I am
about it, but I told her to keep up her spirits as well as I
could, and sead I would. But I cannot, for every thing seem to
go against me. Don't tell her so. Say I am in good spirits.
But I would not of caired had I been told when first I caim home.
But after father laying out such a deal of money upon me and
then such a thought to have to leave of[f] going to sea! But
then I could not get anything without being apprenticed again to
some business and that is such a waist of 5 years, but it is more
for what other people would think. As for my self I don't care
twopence about the 5 years for I would learn any business I set
my mind too. But I am afraid their is no chance of stoping
ashore: as I have made my bed so I must lay in it. I shall push
forward as much as I can this voy[a]ge and see how things turn
out whe[n] I come home again, but I am afraid it will be to no
purpose if I don't leave of[f] going to sea. And if I continue
going I shall go to America and sail out of their and then I
shall be out of the frowns of every body — at least that is my
way of thinking, but my thought[s] wander about so that I am
quite sick, weeak and tottery. With writing this scrawl every
thing has been uppermost and nothing at hand and it has maid my
head ac[h]e I can hardley see. Don't say anything to Ellinor
about how I am for it will wear of[f] during the voyage I hope,
nor yet to anybody else. Write me a letter to the Downs if the
wind is between SW and NW and then I shall recieve it, but if
when you get this it — the wind — is shifted it is of no use to
send one. Send me one to Ceylon in 2 months time. I think the
mail leaves every 6 weeks but Philop will tell you. We shall
be in Ceylon in the begining of December till about the 25. I
will send you a letter from Madera if their is any ships their.

So good buy dear Walter if

I never see you any more
I remain your affectionate
Brother T. Bassano

I have given them a hint about leaving of[f] going to sea as
you can sea in the leaf for father.

[On the cover] The ship sailed. Don't write.

3. *A gale at sea*

Tom Bassano to Walter Bassano   Downs
                                                 Thursday [11 August 1841]

Dear Walter
    W[e] are now snug in the Downs once more, the Wind at SW
blowing a gail. I wrote to you on Sunday last and sent it on
Monday morning. I wrote in the side of it "the ship is gone,
don't write" because we were heaving the anchor up whe[n] the
boat caim. We got under wey by 10 o'clock but as soon as we got
round the foreland the wind hauled into the same quarter again.
However, we did not feel inclined to go back again so we tacked,
but maid very little progress it begining to blow again.
However we got as far as Dungerness by 2 o'clock Monday night,
let go the anchor under the Ness, got sails furled, got below by
3 o'clock, roused out at 6 o'clock again to haul up more chain,
humbuged about the decks till tea time. At 8 o'clock night the
wind hauled more to the Sout[h] so their was no shelter their,
and having every appearance of a gail we were obliged to heave
the anchor up and get out of that as soon as we could. We had
hardley got the anchor up before it caim on. We set two double
reafed topsails and tried to stand of[f] the land, but the ship
would neather stay nor ware being so light. The wind had such
power on the broard side so their was nothing in sight but to go
ashore. The captain orde[re]d the fore sail and main sail to be
loosed, which we did, and mizen also, and in the midst of
setting those sails she broke some of her fore topsals reafe
points. Their were two men triing to sequre the sail but they
did not like to go down before the sail so the captain asked me,
"For God's sake go and get it done Tomey", so I maid answer
"Yes". So hanging over the yard to get them rove I fell over
the yard. "He gone over board", they all cried, but I caught
hold of the buntline as I fell and cam[e] wack on the frore stay,
grabed them and saived myself. The nigh[t] was so dark that
nobody could see, so out bauled I, "I am all right". Then their
was a chear. The ship drifting ashore all the time with the
extra sail we wore round and stood off clear, exceptain just
puting our jib boom into a schooner's fore top and shuving him
along without dooing any damage. So we box hauled about their,
going 1 mile to windward, 3 to leward, all hands so tired their

44

legs bending under them. So at day brake we run for the Downs
again and anchored their with both anchors and 100 fathom of
chain out to each, got our breakfast, and turned in all day, not
before we wanted it. We shall not make another attempt till we
get a fair wind, so if you will send me a letter by return of
post I would be very thankfull. Excuse me paying for the letters
as we are obliged to trust to the boatmen and if you give them
the money they keep it, and we have to give them 6d for taking
them ashore. If I had some of those quean's head to stick on [9]
I would, but I have not, so write to me as soon as possable.
With kind love to all I remain your affectionate brother

                         T. Bassano

4. *Waiting for a letter about Eleanor*

Tom Bassano to Walter Bassano   [The Downs]
                                                 15 August 1841

Dear Walter
    I recieved your letter of the 13 on Saturday, but let me tell
you my sicking yarn before I got it. Friday, Wind SW, light
breaze, appearance of a shift; 8 o'clock p.m. wind hauling more
to Southard; 10 p.m. wind S by-W to 12 p.m. - my watch. I was
in such a funck, my heart in my mouth. I ought to have call'd
the skipper, but would not, for I knew he would of got the ship
under wey directley if he knew it. So I kept a sharp look out
at his cabin door for fear he should wake and come on deck. So
I thought I would meet him flat in his face and say I was going
to call him to tell him there was a shift of wind, for I should
get blown up for not calling him when wind shifted. But however
he did not wake. At 12 o'clock I called Second mate, told him
it was his watch. When he caim on deck, "Holo", ses he, "the
wind has changed. Why did you not call the captain?". "Why, it
is flying about first at W. then at South", said I, "Well, what
is the use of calling him till wind is steady?". So on that I
went below. He called the captain at 1 o'clock. Up he caim -
knock out all hands, heav anchor up. O crikey, Bill, was not I
in a funck, quite down in the mouth - in[s]tead of going about
with my usual quickness, crawling along like a snail. "Come
Tome [Tommy]", said the captain, "Give us the song man 'a fair
wind'". "Yes Sir", said I, "I have a good deal to sing for".
"Why?", said he. "Because there is a letter coming for me this
morning which if I get it, it will make me happy for the voyage,
but if not, I shall be half dead all the time. For my part, I
wish it would blow from the Westward again that you would be
obliged to have a man standing by to hold the hair on your head

---

9. The penny post had been introduced in January 1840.

                         45

or it would blow away." He could not help laughfing at what I
said. "Well", said he, "if that is the case I wish it would.
But I can't stop there with a fair wind. What would Mr. Tindal
say to me for it?" Well, if you look at the map you will see
that we [had] to beat to get round the foreland, and then it
would be a long lay and a short one. However, by the time when
we had got round the foreland [the wind] had hauled to the West
again. "What a lark! Har Har Har! Blow great guns!", said I, so
that the captain might hear me. "Tome, you rascal, you have got
your wish". "Thank goodness for it", said I. Then it came on
blowing again. "Square the main yard" - "I I sir" - "Haul the
main sail up" - "Haul the fore sail up" - "Roll them up lads".
Then I began to laugh and sing out to every thing I took hold of.
"See the chain clear" - "I I sir" - "Cock bill the anchor, clue
the main topsail up, jump up, take a reaf in it and stow it" -
"Stand by the fore topsail, clue the fore topsail up" - "I I
sir" - "Brace the yard by". "Stand by the anchor - all hands
by the chain - let go the anchor". Su-----ze goes the chain.
"Give it her byos, cheerily. Check her a bit. Give it her
again - wether bit her[e]." The Anchor's gone. We safely ride.
Off comes the boat, a letter for TBB. I could not help dropping
a tear when I saw it and when I saw her name who is so dear to
me. And after reading what you say I am of the same opinion as
you now. I perfectly agree with what you say about thanking
God &c., but their is no feer of falling again. It was only in
my sickness as I wrote you in my first letter. But I am
perfectly happy now.

Well - about the washing. The captain will make it all
wright whe[n] we come home with father, if he pays for it. It
is with having two bill[s] and Mr. Tindal did not like it.

I have used my instrument today both for lattitude and
longitude, but have not worked it yet as I wanted to write to
you. It is a butifull instrument the captain and everybody
sais, and dirt cheep, so I hope father won't think Bradford is
a humbug. He altered it to my liking very nicely. My glass is
a most butiful one now and you can reed vessals' names with it
before you can with the captain's. I have not begun before
today with my nautical Instruments as it is so inconvenient to
work of an eav[en]ing. Their is so much bustle with the men
round the light. But when we get watch and watch then I will
carry on like a rast of studding sails, boom working to windward
against an ebb tide.

I can't [h]elp laughfing at Philop loosing 10 shillings, for
I thought he always maid his bets so that he could not loose,
but if he wins he get a good deal. But however he has made a
mull for once. I have got prescius little money this time, and
prescius little traffic - none at all. What I have got I will
lay out to the best advantige, segars for you, and flowers for
Ellenor, bless her, and her sister Lewezer, and Fred, for they

46

are always on my side - Charlot against me. I shan't forget
what she told me the last night I walked out with her - Sunday
it was. Have you taken Ellen to Richmond yet? You said you
would some Sunday as she did not like to go with so maney. Their
has just come along side a boat, so I must end my letter. You
may send me a nother letter if you like, and direct it as you did
the other. Excuse me paying for it as I told you the reason
before. Give my best love to my dear Ellenor next time you see
her, and three X X X - 3 kisses, as this is the way a sailor
sends them. She must kiss the letter as I have kissed it.
Don't forget.

    With best love to brother[s] and sisters, mother and father,
and beleave me, dear Walter, your affectionate brother

                    Thomas Bassano

5. *The passage to Madeira*

Tom Bassano to Walter Basssno   Madera
                                       Sunday, 5 September 1841

Dear Walter
    We have arrived safe heer at last, which is 5 Weeaks
tomorrow since we left the docks, which is no foolish passage,
which with a NE wind we would of come all the way in 9 Days.
Well, I think the last scrawl you had from me was on the 13 or
14th of August. Well, on Wednesday morning the 18th at 3 a.m.
we tossed the anchor up and beet as far as Dungeness by
6 o'clock. We did not anchor their but it fell light wind and
during the night we run on board the Duk[e] of Roxburg[h] the
ship that James - that chap that is going out to Sidnay -- is in.
But it was a calm, so we pushed them off with bote hooks and
spars and so did no damage to eather Ships - it was through the
Stubbornness of their captain. At 9 o'clock the next day
eav[en]ing we let go the kedge on a w[h]arf off Hasting[s]. It
fell quite calm and the tide began to run up so we did not want
to be drifted back again, but we had not bean their above an
hour before the Wind spring up from the eastward and blew the
ship ahead of her anchor. It was my watch so I told the captain
it was a fair wind and ship ahead of anchor. "Knock out", said
he. Up they come, "fair wind" in eavery boddys mouth. The way
sheat came up was hand over [?mitton], with the long song my
boy and studding sails - up she rises - oh hoy, chearley men,
hoy - sprad her wings - ahoy, chearley men, fair wind, oho, hoi,
chearley men - hoy, holey, ho, hoy. We soon got every thing set
and got as far as the Isle of White [Wight] next day Friday,
when at 8 o'clock at night all in a minute the wind chopt round
to the same quarter again in all studing sails, brace the yards
up, so have a beating match again, but the wind kept light while

we got as far as the start by Sunday at 12 o'clock, but it came
on to blow [so] that we were obliged to up stick[s] and run to
Torbay, and as we were going in we have to haul our wind to get
round the point. By Jorge, my boy, I thought we should of
capsised. It came down a puf[f] from the mountains over the
[?river] all down to leward. We could not let go the topsail
halyards or else we would of run on board a vessel of[f] anchor.
But it was all soon over. We made her all right and got our
suppers and turned in. Next morning heve up anchor, off she
goes, hammer away again. Well, we got as far as Ushant by
Tuesday 23 at 9 p.m., tacked ship, Ushant Light, bairing S b-W
7 leagues laid N b-W by compas[s] 2 points and $\frac{1}{2}$, vairiation
West - that is for Ellen whilst I think of it - cours[e] W b-S.
But on Friday night we got a fair wind which run us a couple of
hundred miles and then droped, left us becalmed. We picked up
a ship's spair topmast during the calm, which had been in water
3 months - had belongd to an outward bounder, as it was a new
spar - and when we came to cut the barnicles of[f] it had been
burnt half way along, right a way through, which hevidently must
have been a ship on fire, praps all hands perished. At night a
breaze spring up and we passed some more, but could not stop to
pick them up, and it continued to strengthen and bring us hear.
But just as we got under the land the wind dropt so we were
obliged to lower the boats down and tow her in, which was about
a couple or three miles & such a jolly pull it gave me a jolly
good swetting, for we were about 8 howers getting her into the
anchorage. I whish we had of had Cris and Alfred hear to of
pulled, and then they would of got their belley full. I know
I had.

I am [?starting] with my navigation like a brave fellow, for
I think as you said about Dear Ellenor. Give my Dear love to
her and maney kisses, and I think I can trust you with that
commission, dear Doct[or]. Say I said so. I wish she had some
of the butiful bunches of grapes that I have been buying and
eating - peaches, apricots, Wine, plumbs & cetera - such a jolly
blow-out - spanish onions and all. I must get her a nother
basket and flowers for her and buy a parrot from Ceylon, if I
get that far. I have begun to copey the island, but I don't
know weather I shall save time to finish it, for it is preshash
hard to work all day and then draw afterwards. But wat is the
ods if you are well as I am at present. But I often pas[s] a
watch away thinking about Ellenor. All though I think as you
say still their is a some thing that seems to stand in the way.
I often dream about it too, but always to the [w]rong. But
don't dispair, whilst you have a jurey mast to rig if your
other mast go by the board, and a yard of canvas to keep up to
the wind, with good groun[d] ta[c]kle, blue sanday bottom, and
you will ride it out till it is all blue.

I hope it is all settled about the washing, for it is a
great boar. I Expect it will be the Latter end of December

48

before we get their, but at all events before we leave Ceylon,
so you can write your letter accordingley. And when you doo
write don't forget to put a good string in about Ellenor. By the
buy, it is her birth day this month. Give her many happy
retearns for me. It is mine also[10] on Wednesday. The Cook is
going to stand two dozen of Wine that day for our mess - we live
with him - and the other apprentices, and [he is] going [to] save
some flower and make a damson pie. So I shall spend the best
birth day I have yet since I have been to sea.

I hope Ellen's school is increased since I left. home.[11] Tell
her to mind and keep the plate well polished and then the people
won't be able to pass it without seaing it, and when I come home
it will take me 3 Dog Watches to talley them all. I am boson
this voyage, which is a promotion, so will be able to pipe all
hand[s] to muster when I sea them.

I hope Mr. Lonsdale is gote quite Sober again. Tell him I
shall give him a sad repramand when I come home. I thought it
was only salors that go for a cruse once on a way. I hope the
horse that [h]appens to be a mare - but we can't help making
blunders some times - is quite well. Tell him to get the steam
up by the time I get home so as to go at the rate of 20 mile an
hour.

How dose Philop and the Torey ministry[12] get on? And the
dead tactics - what the deavle name again? th'Slack Slicks?[13]

It is just struck 6 bell[s] by the French man-of-war that is
[h]eare, which is Eleven O'clock, and the sheet is full, so
with love to all, Father, Mother, Brothers, Sisters,

> I remain, dear What,
> your affectionate brother
> T. Bassano, Boatswain.

Dear Walter, since I rote this letter, which was on Sunday
eav[en]ing, I [have] been Working away hoisting in whine and
eating fruit at an unmerseeful rate and on Tuesday night, when
we had done work, I plunged overboard in a swet, having a cargo
of wine on board me which put me in a cold swet, and then I got
drinking again, and turned in, but could not sleep. I was in a
perspiration and my head was like being boiled. I bathed it two
hours in arac[k] which did me a little good, but I could not
sleep all night. So today, as you may expect, I am laid up,

---

10. His 20th.
11. His sister, not Eleanor. See Letter 10, Chapter Five (IV).
12. Peel's Conservative ministry came into office on 30 August
    1841. Philip was a clerk in the War Office.
13. Statistics.

spiting blood, and such a pain cross my chest and throat that I
can [h]ardley stand. I have bought a bucket or two and some
flowers for Ellenor. Give my happy returns to Ellinor on her
birth day, and as you sea it is a preshious birthday to me.
Instead of regailing myself I am laid up, so it is like a dead
day. I don't know how this letter will get to you, but their is
a man-of-war that is going to Brest, so I spose it will go by
him. Good buy. I can't sit up to write any more.

> I remain your affectionate
> Brother T. Bassano.

We are going away this afternoon.

After returning from his fourth voyage to Ceylon
in 1842 Tom Bassano went on a short coaling voyage
to Middlesbrough. His apprenticeship ended in
February of the next year.

6. *The sea coal trade*

Tom Bassano to Walter Bassano   Sunday, 9 July 1842

Dear Walter
    We left the pooll on Monday eav[e]ning and sailed down to
Purfleet and their took in ballast. Left their on Tuesday
eavening and after a fair passage we arrived off Middlesboro on
Friday morning. A steam boat towed us in to the port. It is a
very pretty place, but small. The country is so butyful. All
round the land rises and the different coloured fields slopeing
away to the water's edge has such a butiful appearance - you
have no Highdear. Whe are to load coales on Tuesday or Wednesday,
so I suppose it will be Thursday before we leave here, so paraps
I shall be home again on Sunday or Monday. Talk about the coal
trade being [a] hard life and dirty: I neaver had such times
since I was at sea, for all I have done is to eat, drink, and
sleep - work I have had none. Such lazey times nobody had. If
you see Ellenor give my kind love to her and say I am quite
well and I hope she is the same. I think I shall take a salley
over the fields tomorrow to have a look at some larg[e] farm
house as their is plenty in sight - for their [is] nothing like
a roving life, happy go luckey, here there and eavery wher.
Withe best love to all at home I remain your affectionate
Brother

> Tom

"I HAVE FICKSED MY MIND ON DOING THE BEST OUT HERE AND I WILL DO IT"

Having returned from another long voyage at the
end of 1843 Tom Bassano decided that he had no chance
of ever becoming a ship's captain and that on his
next voyage to the East he would leave his ship at
Calcutta, look for a berth there, and make a fresh
beginning in the China trade. He was now twenty-
two years of age. His father provided him with
letters of introduction, and the whole family wrote
letters to await his arrival in Calcutta. He was
still hoping to be able to marry Eleanor.

7. *"Poor fellow, I pity him"*

Philip Bassano to Melinda Bassano   Dublin
                                                 19 February 1844

My Dear Melinda
    ... I have had a letter from Tom somewhere off Portsmouth.
Poor fellow, I pity him on account of an idea he has got in his
head that he is *"not adequate to the situation of a Captain as
he is such a bad scholar"* - those are his words, poor fellow.
He says *he feels his incompetency* on that account. I differ
with him on that point as there are very few Captains half so
good scholars as he is, besides it is good seamanship that is
principally required in a Captain. I regret the step he seems
bent upon taking, of leaving the ship when he arrives at
Calcutta, because of the many and great dangers he is liable to
get into out there, and which I have heard personally from two
young men who did much the same sort of rash act. I shall write
to him by the Overland Mail.[14] When does Father write, and how
is he to be addressed? I suppose it is of no use directing to
the Ship. He tells me that Father has bought a lot of cigars of
him for me. Tell him I am very much obliged to him for it, and
tell him not to let himself be bamboozled out of them before I
get some ...

---

14. See Letter 14 below for Tom's reply.

8.¹⁵ *Looking for a berth in Calcutta*

Tom Bassano to F.M. Bassano

Calcutta
Sunday, 30 June 1844

Dear Father

I received your kind letter on my arrival here, and on the
Sunday following I delivered the 3 letters of recomendation.
The one at Howrah dock, Cap [?Travers] told me he had a captain
inquiring the other day, but was unfortunately su[i]ted now.
But he often has inquirers made and he should bear me in mind.
He said the worst of it was I could not talk the language, but
at all events he should let me know. Mr Fraser inquired of me
how Cap Henderson's eye was, so I told him I was not personally
acquainted with him, but you were, as I had been so little a[t]
home since I had been at sea. He had a long chat with me about
ships &c. and said the best thing that I could do was to go with
Cap Reynills in the Waterwitch, as I should be able to learn the
language – never mind what, as he will take you for nothing, and
when you get to China their will be sure to be something. But
however when I took Captain Reynnels letter he told me to call
in the morning and he would se[e] me, as he could not see me
now. I went in the morning to the hotel. He had gone. I went
and told Mr. Fraser that, but he said he had not gone, as he was
going to call upon him before he went. And he sent me to
inquire at the agents, and they told me he had got his ship
droped down the river, past our ship, as far as Garden Reach,
which is past all the shipping, on the Saturday. But he had not
left their when I left our ship on the Monday morning to go to
town. However I did not see him, but he got the letter. I
have not seen any thing nor heard from any of them since, as
they said they would send to me when any thing turns up. I
heard that Cap Darley was here. He was serving the last of his
time in the Achilles when I joined her, so I knew he was the
best chap to apply to. Accordingly I found out where he lives
and went and asked for him. "Alloo, I know your face somewhere,
but don't know wher." I then made myself known to hime. He
told me to come upstairs, and their I told him how I had come
out. He said he had a ship in view which he was going to have,
but it might be that the mate has been a long time in her and
does not want to leave, and he could not turn him away without
cause. But at all events, if he did not get a birth for me
before he got his own ship I should sertanly go with him. He
had the ship Warrior last voyage at the China Expedition, along
with this ship and all her officers, and so he knows the Chief

---

15. Letters 8-14 were all sent home together. Letters 8-12
were written on the same sheet, each page crossed three or
four times, and both black and red ink used. Letters 13
and 14 were written on a separate sheet. These letters
are extremely difficult to read.

Mate and Cap Cribble. But the Captain is nothing - the mate has
all to do with the ship. And he told me to tell Mr. Consitt,
the mate, he should come and pay him a visit on board. And
Consett gave me a good caracter and said I might leave, but their
was no need untill I had the other birth to walk into, as we
should be here another month yet. I am a regular favourite of
Consitt's. I don't want to boast, but I know it always pleases
a father to hear good of his sone, and I may say I have made a
fresh begining in a new world. He said at the cabin table that
it was punishment to me to see any body go aloft before me, and
likewise punishment to keep me from working, and that if he did
not do something for me in Calcutta he should make me second
mate of this ship when I got home, as he is going to be captain
after this voyage.

   I am sorry to say that Doctor Stewart is dangerously ill and
not expected to live. It is rather unhealthy here. The colorha
[cholera] is raging a little. We have lost one of our men, a
Strong healthy fellow. He went ashore upon the Wednesday well
and harty, got drinking at thease raskally punch houses, was
taken ill, carried to the hospital as quick as possible, and
died before the morning. Their is another one been drinking
and walking in the sun the same way, but he is not dead, but in
the hospital. He was better today. I had a sunstroke myself.
I went as I told you to sea Cap Darly, and walked about a good
deal before I could find him out, and when I cam[e] on board I
had such a dreadful headhake I was all most mad, which terminated
on the second day with pains in my bowels. The 3 day I turned to
again and am as right as rain again. Their is not the least
occasion to walk in the sun her[e] if you know wher[e] you are
going, but I did not, I had to hunt for the place - for there
are palakeen bearers who will carry you about all day for 2
shilling, and they are all about the town for hire. They are a
long box to lounge down in, with a door on each side, a pole at
each end, and a black fellow will carry you 5 miles in less than
an hour for 4 anners, which is 6 pence. It is like our omnibus
for conv[en]ience, but better, as they take you to the door and
wait till you come out again, and then trot off with you again.
And whilst you are in one of thies things their is a chap will
runn after you with book[s], hand them into you, and their you
may read all the time and buy the book, give him a farthing, or
nothing, according to the disposition of the Person inside.
[Here there is a small drawing] Palankeen barer, with chap along
side giving you book, going 5 knot before the wind.

   I shall conclude, dear Father, and I remain your affectionate
son Tom.

9. *"It is my intention to stop here a good spell"*

Tom Bassano to Charlotte Bassano   Calcutta
                                              Sunday, 30 June 1844

Dearest Mother
    I was desired by Elleanor to write to you from here as she
told me that you said I never wrote to you at all – which is very
true, but I pray don't think that you are forgotten – far from
it. But young men have got nothing particular or amusing to send
their parents except their best wishes and love – which is as
strong as ever it was, even to the time we could just call your
name and prattle to your delight. And that I never neglected in
all my letters sending my love to you, and I trust that Ealenor
did not forget to give it you. We are parted now, but I trust
it is not for ever. But it is my intention to stop here a good
spell, and as soon as I am able to keep a wife I shall either
send for Ealenor or come and fetch her. She has told me she
went to bid her mother good buy which as you and I have told her
in her letter to continue to, which I trust she will do. After
I am settled and am able to tell you w[h]ere to write to I hope
to here you have left Ellen in good Sercumstances and got some
pretty secluded spot on the banks of the Teams [Thames], so that
if I come home with a ship of my howne I shall be able to say
"man the boat" and with as much ease pull and sea you happy and
comfortable, with little Melinaka to wait upon you. (If you
read this letter for Mama don't think I mean hard work, but
pick up a neadle, hook her gown &c.) I cannot write to Melinda
as it will be too much postage, and I can't afford it. Tell
Elleanor I have written to you as she said. And beleave me,
dear Sister, your affectionate brother T. Bassano. I hope you
are keeping up what you have larnt, for you see what a searious
looss to me it is being such a bad scolhar. – Well, dear Mother,
in the next writing watch their is to me you must write without
fail, and beleave me, my dear Mother, your affectionate son,
T. Bassano.

10. *The church at Calcutta*

Tom Bassano to Ellen Bassano   30 June 1844

Dear Ellen
    I am sorry you could not send me better news than you have
regarding the school, but I am glad it is no worse, and I hope
it will be soon better. I think that boy is to[o] big for you,
as I said before I went. But it is a great acquisition, the
writing master. Are [Ah], you will succeed at last. Give my
rememberance to Aunt Ryle and cousan Jo[h]n, also to A[u]nt
Tompson and cousans. I am very greaved to hear A[u]nt has been
so ill again, but the Lord's will must be done I suppose.

I went to church the other Sunday eavening, just to see the
people, and you cannot think what a pretty sight it was. It was
a butiful church, but the large space in the middle of the church
is all (black ink[16]) filled up with what they call punkers, that
is, long frames about 6 foot long by 3 foot, covered with white
linnen, at the lower corner a bunch of roses and on them in gold
a cupid, and thease are hung above all the people's heads 4 foot
apart all along the church, with strings from one to the other
and then led outside the church, and their is a black fellow
pulling away. And so their they go, fan fan away, so you all
get fanned all the time you are in church, which makes you quite
cooll.

I remain your affectionate brother Tom.

11. *The river at Calcutta*

Tom Bassano to Christopher Bassano   30 June 1844

Dear Cristopher
    I received a few lines from you telling me that you have just
entered collage, and I hope that you may like it, and turn out
a first rate docter.[17] I think that you will make a very good
one, and when you enter the army you may be like me to come and
see the butiful sights of the east. You won't have much time to
study, but I expect you will give your mind to it and turn out
to delight us all with your dipluma at the end of the term.

It is not of much use to describe any of the beauties of the
place, but perhaps as dead bodies are scarce and dear at home
you would like me to bring you two or 3 home, as this river is
full of them at low water, and when the tide flows it flotes
them away, so their they flote, up and down by the tide, till
they get out to sea. Still, for all that, we bathe in this
river, and have to drink the water. I thought it was beastly
at first untill thirst made me drink it, and now I think it
butiful water. Well, if I stop out here I shall have the
pleasur[e] of se[e]ing you before the rest of the family. Well,
good buy docter. I remain your affectionate bro[ther] Tom.

---

16. This letter is so far written in red ink diagonally across
    a page already written across twice. The writer now goes
    back and fills the spaces between these red lines with
    lines written in black ink.
17. See Chapter Four.

55

12. *About Eleanor*

Tom Bassano to Alfred Bassano   30 June 1844

Dear Alfred
    I received a letter from Eleanor telling me of some of your
and Master Jim's sprees togather. And do you realy consider
yourselfs fools to what you will be if you do. I think you are
going the right way to work to be double fools and donkies, for
bilard [billiard] tables are not the resorts of wise men, as I
used to put you down as the making of one, but you have banished
my expectations.

    I am very much obliged to you, you rum little dog,[18] for
taking Elleanor into your peternal charge, and I hope you will
be particularly attentive to her. I suppose you have had plenty
of fun at picknic parties, and I suppose you are as grate a
favourite with the girls as you used to be. Jim, I suppose, you
sufer as when I was at home, and I doubt not that you will turn
him out of hands compleat. You may tell Charlot that Walter
tells me that she is thick with [*illeg.*] again, which I am
extreamly sorry for. And tell her she must cut him, for when
Ellen comes out to me here, or I come for her, she is to come
with us, so she must not form any connection with such a scamp
as he. Not only that. I have a very nice young man here, a
friend of mine, a mate of a ship, which I intend for her. In
fact I have all most settled it, and I am sure she will approve
of my choice.

    You neglected writing to me in the family letter, which I
rather am inclined to think was unkind, for you could have
amused me with your ready stock of wit, and their was plenty of
room on the first sheet – rather you could have crossed it two
wayes – but next time that they all write don't neglect. I
remain your affection[at]e brother Tom. Give my love to Jim as
a brother.

13.[19] *The passage out. Description of Calcutta*

Tom Bassano to Walter Bassano   Calcutta
                                                   5 July 1844

Dear Walter
    I received your letters on the 22 of June, and this is the
first male from here, on the 6 or 15th, I am not sure which, but

---

18. Alfred was five years his junior – just 18 years old.
19. Letters 13 & 14 are written on one sheet, now torn into
    2 pieces.

shall see tonight. The way I intend sending them, as their is a
good deal, I thought it would be cheaper to send them in a
bundle - and a young chap that has been middeys' servant has left
us and got into the Beatic, the male packet between here and
Sues, so he is going to take them with him as far as Sues, and
there put them in the post. So you will have to pay nothing, or
else me.

We had a fine and pleasant passage out - plenty of fun,
dancing, singin[g], jimnastics &c. &c., also a gazette embelished
with [?jokes] and full of fun. I used to get a read at them in
the middies birth, and kept a good look out to try one or two of
the numbers, but could not suckseed. The mate is, and has been,
a great favourite of mine since - I mean, I have of his, and am
so still. He sais that I am welcome to my discharge when I have
a birth, and he will have to pay a man [?£3] for another man in
my place, as that is the cost of seaman's wages shipping in this
port, so I must consider it a great favour. So, you se[e] their
is no occasion for me to cut.

I cannot write to tell you what a butiful cheap and nice place
this is. The ship is not 6 yards of the river side. Then
another 6 yards of field. Then the carriage drive. Then a
level field ½ a mile across backed by splendid mansions and
palises. Right - Sepoys barracks and jungle behind. Left -
Fort William, whith its telegraph tower and butiful Cathedral
or church rising above the ramparts, mote, palasades, [*illeg.*].
This stands in the middle of the plaine, or park. Farther along,
and going on the first discribed background, is the butiful
Governor's palace, which they call House, and merchants' palaces,
and hotell, &c. A little to the left of where we lay is a
butiful piece of artechere [architecture], light, open and grand,
with steps and landings right down to the water, called a guat
[ghat], or landing place. It is also used by the natives to
pray, thro[w] the water in, and marry in. Here they marry the
children at 4 or 5 year old. Their is a fus[s] at it every day[20]
with the natives. It is built in the honour of James Princeps,
a very clever man that was here. The town is a butiful, stately
place, full of grand churches and monuments, statutes which the
East India Company send out. Their is as much fus[s] here with
the Governer as their is with the Quean at home. The Aukland
steamer has come in here. He - Governer - has been up in the
country, and he came down to her[e] on business. I saw him.
He embarked in his boat - like the Lord Mare's barge - as he got
by the ship. He came down in a carrage and 4, with sepoy
outriders, and was saluted by the steamer and the yards man[ned]
for him. It was a pretty sight.

You may go ashore here and get white shirt, trousers, jacket,

---

20. James Prinsep (1799-1840).

waistcoat, and socks, for a rupee, and butiful well made things to[o]. But the most laughable things here are the danbd [damned] great adjatents, or scavengers. They are perched upon all the most out of the way places – top of church steaples, governer['s] [?palace] &c. &c. – and thear they walk about the streets alongside you as unconserned as possible, and pick up everything that otherwise would stink. So their is a heavy fine for any one that hurts or kills them. The park I spoke of is the favourite drive of all Calcutta of a night, and you never saw such a butiful variety of poneys, horses, and turns out, upon every day. Well, with jolly good luck to the wedding of poor Aney[21] [words deleted] your affection[at]e brother Tom.

14. *Opportunities in India*

Tom Bassano to Philip Bassano[22]   5 July 1844

Dear Phillop
    I thought it very good of you sending me so much good advice, and your kind fears of the unhealthiness of the climate. But my way of thinking is this – if a man goes to ever such an unhealthy place he does not die without it was intended for him to die there when he was first born, and so a sertain destiney raining over us to carry us to that very spot, to the exact time certified for us to kick the buckit. And, dear Phillop, I have seen as healthy gray headed old men here as ever I saw in England. But wher[e] the great mortality lies is with drinking, and then it was intended for that chap to die a drunked & so on, so don't be alarmed upon that score. Upon the other hand I assure you you are mistaken about men flying their country. It is the reverse. It is steadey saving coves who see that a captain with a small craft can make t[w]o or 3 thousand a year, come out and make their fortune, and then go home and live at pease. For instance, look a[t] Docter Gordon's friends, the Master Henderson, he made his money in the opium line, and I am sure it would not do to say to Dr. Gorden that he had to cut for some thing, do you thing it would? But then you may say that is only one instance. But here is another – my friend Darley – again, my friend John Brown, brother to that black rouge [rogue] William Brown, he was steward of our ship. When he got to Ceylon he learnt what money could be made her[e], so he came out and got a birth out here. He is at Calcutta now in the Sidey schooner, a opium clipper, and he told me he was making at least 7 hundred a year, and could make more if he had more money in hand. And I am sure a more steadey, prudant and cleaver fellow could not bee. Walter knows him. So

---

21. Walter, a clerk in the Army Medical Department, married Annie Purkess, in 1844.
22. Clerk in the War Office, aged 27 years.

excuse me if I don't profit by your intreatis to come back again, for I have ficksed my mind on doing the best out here and I will do it.

I wish you had sent me some newes about the disturbance in Ireland and dam O'Connall &c. &c.[23]

I hope you will like your segars that Dad bought for you. This is the place for segars - you can by 100 imitat[i]on minoulas [Manilas] or havanors [Havanas] for 6^d, and I am sure more butiful segars never were in people's mouthes.

This is the place for young men in any ragula business to get births. A young chap - a printer by trade, one of the readers that read the tipe backards - he has seen every thing almost - he is the son of a clergyman and of a good education, but had thrown himself away assorting with bad company, and came by us a middy servant, and has been it for 3 years in Green's ship - but got tired of a disipated life, so looked for a birth here, first as one thing, then as another - tried the printing and has got a birth to go to Delli up the country, as editor, or something, of the Gazette there - 200 rupees a month, 6 servants, a house and grounds. It is no puff, as I have seen the agreement. But I don't want to get you to come out here, as clarcks are not used as the Blackeys they have taught to write accounts so nicely and so cheap.

You must tack - give one another your news, so put all togather you may form some idear of the mart of the east. I remain your affection brother Tom.

III

"I HAD SET MY AFFECTIONS UPON BEING CHEIF
OF THIS BRIG"

Tom Bassano found his berth in Calcutta, and made several voyages - including one to the Sandwich Islands [Hawaii] - during the next two years, but no letters survive from this period. In April 1846, he joined one of the crack clippers owned by Jardine & Matheson, as second mate although he had been chief mate on his previous vessel, in the hope that he

---

23. Philip wrote from Dublin where his War Office duties had taken him during the winter of 1843-4. Daniel O'Connell had been agitating for repeal of the Union and was arrested in October 1843 and sent to prison after trial.

would soon be appointed chief mate in this ship
also. He stayed with the *Lanrick* for nineteen
months without achieving his ambition. Convinced
that he was "totally jamed" because of his poor
education, and moreover seeing that the clippers
would soon be superseded by steamboats, he determined
to leave the sea and seek his fortune ashore.
Eleanor had become tired of waiting.

15. *The brig Lanrick. Bombay yacht races.*

Tom Bassano to Walter Bassano   Bombay
                                             16 February 1847

Dear Walter
    It is so long since I last wrote that I am afraid you'll be
thinking that I have kicked the buckit. The fact is I have been
putting it off in hopes that I might be able to write and tell
you that I was cheif-mate once more, but no such luck, which has
made me quite down in the mouth. The state of the case is this
(I will pitch you a long yarn as it eases my mind to be able to
tell my misfortunes to you, and then it gains me points, as I
may expect a long yarn in return from you). I told you when I
joined the Brig I left a cheif mates-ship and expected to get
cheif here, but did not. This time when in China the House told
the Captain that when he got to Bombay our Cheif was to be made
Opium inspecter there, and so of Course I thought that under the
curcomstances in which I joined that I of course should be made
Cheif at the same time. I could have joined one of the Schooners
in China, but as it is always bad Weather in China, and much a
sameness, I thought I would stick to the Brig. I was so cocksure
of being Promoted, and she being such a splendid Brig I would not
leave her. So we left Hongkong for Bombay Dec. 7th, arrived at
Singapore on the 14th, left on 15th, arrived in Bombay on the
8th January. The Brig makes the quickest passages of any of the
clippers, as you may see by the inclosed articles out of the
Singapore Press, so you cannot wonder at my Being fond of such a
Noble vessel.[24]

---

24. "The *Lanrick* has made an extraordinary passage for this
    season of the year. Between Bombay and Singapore she was
    seventeen days and from Singapore to Hongkong another
    seventeen; thus making the whole run in 34 days exclusive
    of stoppages at Singapore. We are told that this passage,
    during the strength of the monsoon, is unprecedented in
    the history of the clippers."

    Tom Bassano joined the brig in China and made all told six
    voyages in her.

After Arriving here I thought I would wait and see what was to
be done, as I was so sick of still having to say that I was only
2nd mate. The cheif mate from our first arrivel has been
Surveying opium on tryal untill the other day it was finally
settled that he should stop on shore all together. In the mean
time there were any quantity of applications for the birth, but
I used to tell them not to tear their shirts, not supposing for
a moment that Capt. White would give it to any one but me, and
so I never applied for it as he knew full well under what promise
I joined his ship at his own request. At last it seamed generaly
understood that a young fellow named Crockit was coming for
sertain. All the time the captain used to come on board and
speak very kindly to me and tell me to do this and that, so I
think it was bosh until the Cheif came off and told me Crockit
was shiped. A Capt. Frances was on board at the time, who had
known me in Calcutta when in the Audax, and he told me to appley
to White if I had not spoke before. I said I had not, as after
Capt. White['s] promis I thought there was no necessaty for it.
So next morning I went to his house and told him in a polite way
what claim I considered I had to the birth, but he told me it
was not his doing but that Mr. Mathersons had requested that in
event of Beaumont stoping in Bombay Mr. Crockit was to have the
birth as he had known Crocket's father and had promised to
forward his son's prospects, but that he (Capt. White) had
mentioned my name and he had said he would promote me to one of
the coast Scho[o]ners when we came back, and that I had better
stop wher[e] I was, as he thought (I supposed) that I should have
leaft his brig in disgust, which I fulley intended to do had he
not told me it was not his doings. He said he had spoken to the
House to rais[e] my wages, but the pay is a poor recompence to
the loss of the name of Cheif (and, after all, perhaps he will
only give me 110 instead of 100 rupees per month) for I am sick
and tired of still calling myself 2nd mate. But I suppose I must
bear it as roling stone gather no moss. I could have joined a
barque here as Cheif - Capt. Frances ship - but then I should
have been out of an employ which is considered a good one, and
the other ship is the only ship which a House in Singapore has
got. But the fact of the matter is that every thing goes by
intrest out here, not merit. The Captains cannot take any body
they chuse. I should think that Father can surely command a
little intrest. It is the same firm as Jardine Mamacks in
England. Could amongst our numerious medical acquaintainces at
the office[25] you mite get a letter from that House - would be of
great service. Otherwise I must drop it all togather and take
to the disgusting English traid wher[e] a fellow must be always
up to his Eyes in tar.

I have received Letters from Father & Cristopher of June 2nd

25. Army Medical Department. William Jardine had begun life as
    a Surgeon.

and will write to him next mail: Ellen's July 21st, and tell her
not to come to India upon any account without she has a house
and friends to go to at her landing, and I am sure there's
nothing to be done in India in the school line:[26] Melinda June
1st and am glad to here she is getting on so well: yours of June
2nd and am sorry to here Anny is unwell and hope before this she
is quite recovered. The description of that nice house of yours
almost tempted me to come home and your dear little child[27]
togather. In fact, had I known as much as I do now I would have
come home when I came up from the Sandwich Islands, more than
60£ coming to me. But this Brig has taken it all, for she sails
so fast so is only a short time at sea and a long time in
harbour. I have been in her 10 months and out of that time she
has only been 3 months & 17 days at Sea, all the rest she has
been in harbour, and we have to find ourselves in harbour, mess
& Servants, so instead of being in pockit by her I have not a
Shellick to my name.

I have received no letter from Alfred since the one in which
he tells me of his procuring his Commission Dated April 5th
1846.[28] His regiment is up the Country, but I don't know the
name of the place. I have written to him nevertheless. Phillop
I hope is well, but have not received a letter from him lately,
the same complaint you have been making I suppose of me. But
know I cannot find amusement in writing to you all as I used
when I was Cheif mate, besides I have been very much cut up about
[it] as I had set my affections upon being Cheif of this Brig.
Not only that. I have been so attentive to Capt. White, tryin[g]
to please him in every way, especialy since I have been here.

Now I made a great [mis]take knowing the irritable disposition
he is. It was this. You shall have the yarn throughout - as I
have sat down to write I may as well carry on whilst I am in the
humer. The Gents of Bombay are getting up a Yatch Club, and all
ready have several fine Yatchs here and [a] regatta every year.
Capt. White Brought a very fine yatch round from China in place
of our longboat, for Which he gave 900 dollars, for making sure
that he would beat all the Yatchs here. And all he wanted was
to run one race and get the Cup, and then he would sell her.
But imagine his rage - after he came here he found he could lick
none of them. I used to go out with him every night and I
could see that he did not sail her properly, and every body used
to run her down, and so of course he got ragelor disgusted with
her and used to try all sorts of plans and get in a stink and
make her worse. He cannot sail her properly. The same way last
voyage he used to sail the ship's longboat and every Boat used
to lick her, and when the old Cheif sailed her she used to lick

---

26. See Chapter Five (IV).
27. Annie Frances, b. 1845.
28. See Chapter Two.

the other Boats. Well, I would have it I would sail the boat
and lick them all, and offer[e]d to bet 100 rupees I would.
Well, it so happened that a bet was made between the fines[t]
boat in Bombay, which has taken several Cups and was the first
boat the man built that built Capt. White's Boat, and another
new boat that a Capt. had built here in Bombay. It was to come
off one afternoon, and Capt. White told me to bring the boat to
him at the usual place as he wanted to go round the course with
them and see what the boat rearly would do. She was rigged as
a schooner at this time. So in the morning of the day I took
the schooner's mast out and rigged her as a cutter (we had both
rigs on board and had tried her as a cutter before, but thought
she did not do so well) but I was determined to get the boat's
maine up ore make the skipper in a fit for doing it. The Cheif
was on shore, so I had it all to myself. At the appointed hour
I took the boat down to the rendezvous and cruised about untill
the Captain came, but I pretended not to see him, and when the
boats started I started with them (and in the mean time the
captain got a dingey and pulled on board the rendezvou[s] boat)
and went round the course & came in first. They all *hoorayed*
the little boat, and Capt. White was well pleased. I went
alongside for him, and he asked why I had rigged her as a cutter,
so I told him that as I had sprung a little of the schooner's
masts I thought it might[carry away, and he would be an[n]oyed.
I very innocently asked hime wher[e] he was when the boats
started, and he said he was on the pear [pier], so I said I
could not see him and thought he was not coming. He said he was
glad of it as the boat had done so well. And after that he was
going to play the deavel with all the boats and win the cup, but
on an Evening sailing her he could manage her with no better
success. So on the regatta day he asked me if I would run her.
I said I would, and so accordingly I did, and came in 15 seconds
before the other boats, 15 in all. I then went alongside the
winning steamer w[h]ere he was and all the gents, and White was
as pleased as a dog with two tailes as the Prize was a 50 Guiney
cup. Well, I was every thing for the next month, untill the
next regatta when the Challenge cup was to be run for a 70 Guiney
cup, and he wanted me to run her again. But the new cheif had
joined and so I preaviously had been getting up a crew to pull
in his new gig, which he brought from China, in the pulling
match, and training every morning and evening, and so on the
morning of the race I went and told him that if he had no
objection I wanted to pull instead of sailing his boat, and he
of course could not refuse. And while he was sailing his boat
we pulled the gig and won the prize, 100 rupees, and when I
went on board the steamboat the gents all began at me because
I was not sailing the Cutter. The boats had been round once
and Capt. White was the 4th Boat, and I waited on board untill
he came round again and then he was 3rd Boat in, and the gents
who had been betting in favour of our (Capt. White's) boat, said
to White that they would not have bet if they hade known that I
was not going to sail her, and he was infernally savage because

63

I did not. He had Capt. Frances in the boat, my friend, and he
told me afterwards that he could not sail a boat a bit. Above
all things he pitched a lot of ballast overboard to make he[r]
go faster, but instead of that it only made her lay over the
more. I could not make it out during the race to see he[r] so
crank. A race is coming off again next month, but I won't have
anything to do with her, as it is more profitable work to pull
the gig, for dam the present did he make me after winning the
Cup for him.

We have plenty of fun here at this seson of the year. The
theater is open twice a weak and devilish good performers they
have got. Wee had the horse races off the last weak. I went to
see them and plenty of fun they had there - a donkey race,
Greasy pole, Treakled buns, &c. One race - the best of the lot
- was 20 untrained Arabs horses & Arabs to ride, no saddles.
And to see those fellows fly along was beautiful. I went in to
the caves of Elephanta last eavening - a splendid place to see -
a tremendous high mounting compleatly hollowed out. We are
going to make up a party to go shooting next week. Their is
plenty of sport to be had about 20 miles from Bombay on the
main land.

Mr. Matherson is coming out by the next mail and is to go
with us to China, which will be a good thing for us, as it will
bring us all into notice. But I suppose he will discover my
parah [poor] education - thanks to myself for it though - and
that will dam me. I shall turn Jack one of thease days, and
then I can go happy go lucky all over the world and nobody know
anything about me, for I am totally Jamed - what with the
examinations to pass at home, and so much letter writing to
skipper out here - the name of it Jams me up in a heap. But,
Olor, dam the odds - it will be all the same 100 years hence.

I here enclose an article out of the Singapore press just
showing you how fast we sail - but I think I mentioned it before,
but it is too much trouble to look. Well, I don't know what
more to write about at present. Remember me with best wishes
and love to all brother[s] & sisters, and to dear Anney. I
should so like to see her and the dear Little Girl - but I
suppose I am out of my rec[k]oning. There will be two I
suppose - tempus fugit, this being 47. It will be getting on
for 4 years since I left home, but I hardly know, time goes so
quickly. I hope Father is in good health and happiness, and
Poor dear Mother - it is my only prayr that I shall see her
again, dear, dear soul, God bless her. I suppose you, Anney
and Child must be a great comfort to look upon, and also dear
Melinda will be a great stay to her. Don't show her this letter,
as I am sure it will make her fret, as the upper part of it I
am afraid I have been wandring. But read it to her, and leave
out the worst parts. I should like to see a few lines from her
in your next letter. Get her to write, will you. Ther[e] is

one thing I should like to ask you, but keep it to yourself. In your next letter tell me how Ellenor is and if she is married &c. for people always paint the deavel blacker than he is. It [is] 11 o'clock. Tell dear Dad I shoul[d] like to hear from him as it is a long while since I received any letters at all. The mail has come in tonight, so perhaps I shall have some letter[s] in the morning, so I will hold on a bit. Their has no letters arrived by the mail, so I shall conclude by saying Good by, dear Walter, I remain your ever affectionate brother

T.B. Bassano

16. *Concerning a recent voyage to China on the* Lanrick

Tom Bassano to Melinda Bassano   Bombay
                                                  8 September 1847

Dear Melinda
    I received your long letter in China just before we left for Bombay, and must return my sincere thanks to little Linney for such a long and amusing letter. I am glad to here that you are still so comfortably situated and hope you may continue so. I am also Glad to here that Ellen's school is getting on well. Christopher from what you say is very happy, and I suppose he will soon be one of the B[assanos] in India. Walter and Phillop I shall write to next mail. I had a letter from Alfred by the same mail I got your letter, but it was a very short one and very little newes in it, because I read your letter first which gave me such a long account of him, and the principal thing that he told me was the same thing. He has, it appears, been sticking into you all at home his house and 8 servants. Now, a house up the country, where he is, is [a] mud shead very similar to a cow shead in England, but not half so good - a few holes with bars & shutters in for windows, a mud partition in the middle to make the shead in two halves, called rooms. The roof is thatched and their is no cealing to hide the rafters, so accordingly when you look up you may see a w[h]ip snake crawling alon[g] the rafters, lizards by the dozens cralwling about the walls catching the muskitoes by thousands. And the house is, I suppose, surrounded by jungle, or els[e] a bog or swamp, as most houses in India are generally on such *capital sites*. As for the 8 servants he can get them cheaper than I can and make his 125 rupees go further than I can, as my one servant cost[s] me 12 rupees a month.[29] I wrote him a very long letter from this a few days since[30] and gave him a severe riperamand for not sending me a longer letter with the account of his voyage out. Phillop has only written

---

29. See Chapter Two, Letter 27 for Alfred's comment.
30. See Chapter Two, Letter 22 for a description of this letter.

me one letter since I have been in India by the buy. You might
as well ask him to write to me as we shall be in Bombay 3 or 4
month, or else go to Calcutta, an[d] in that case I should get
the letter all the same if he Addresses the Letter to care of
M. Pestonjee, Merine Lane, Bombay. You all paint Walter's little
child as such a dear little thing. I should very much like to
se[e] her. Tell Walter to write to me also, as I shall get all
letters addressed as above, weather in Bombay or China, as
Pestonjee will forward them as he understands the shipping
Pigeon. I am sorry to here of dear Mother loosing all her teeth,
and no wonder she is distressed about it. Give my love to her
and tell her not to scold me about not having written for so long
a time, but the fact is I am always going to write and keep
putting it off untill the last minute and then ther[e] [happens]
something to stop me untill to[o] late.

I am still in the Lanrick and this voyage with our new cheif
mate we have been very comfortable as he is very gentlemanly and
amiable man. He has a mother and two sisters living close to the
Queen's Road,³¹ as his last letter states that they have just
moved to Victoria Road, Kensington. I suppose it must be some
of the new streets just built about our place. Captain White
has behaved very well this last trip. He has seamed to think he
could not be kind enough to us. I was rather unwell coming from
China and the ship struck on a rock in the China Sea, but being
a very strong vessel she went over it without doing her much
damage. It was in the middle of the night and whilst I was
unwell, but I ran on deck thinly clothed and got a violent fever
& ague and have only just began to mend from the effects of it.
The fine weather just coming on in Bombay it will soon enable me
to gain my strength again, but on the whole the Climate agrees
with me very well.

I am very much afraid the clippers will soon die a natural
death as the steamboats are begining to run to China and
caperble of carrying 5000 Chest of opium, to leave China &
Bombay every month. China is in a very dull state - no traid
going on as [Sir John] Davies³² has been up to Canton Blowing
up the poor Chineas Forts and spiking 8 or 9 hundred guns, that
the Chineas are frightened out of their wits and in consequence
no traid is being carried on. The opium is less in China at
present than in Bombay. I dare say you will say what a dry
letter this is, writing about opium speculations & such nonsense,
nothing interesting to a young ladies ear. But you see the fact
is that we sailors have nothing to write about but what we are
engaged in. I used to take a delight in writing to you all when
I could describe the new and beautiful seans that I was seing,

---

31. The Bassanos were living at 76 Queen's Road, Bayswater.
32. Sir John Davis, Superintendent of Trade and Governor of
    Hongkong, 1844-8.

ut once told it is all stail and the same thing over and over again.

We went to Wampoa about half way up the river to Canton this last time in China and had a very pleasant time of it. There was a French Frigate lying in the reach and the Officers used to come on board and admire our beautiful trim vessel and used to invite all the English officers on board the French Frigate on Sunday eavening to see French plays that they got up. The sailors Performed and very excellently too. They had a splendid Brass band - it was a treat to heare them. After the Perform-ances were over the decks were cleared and we all used to stand up to dance - such fun - French and English officers dancing Polkers &c. on one side and the sailors dancing upon the other, the vessel hung all round with light. It had such a merry and lively appearance and the Frenchmen so exceadingly polite to us in particular as they thought so much of our vessel. In return we gave them a nice little Cold colation on board of us one eavening, and mustered a band - 2 Fiddlers we always have in the ship, and the rest we got from others ships. The French men quite enjoyed it and got so merry, danced quardrills & Polkes, any quantity. The Frigate was a Crack vessel and she certainly was a most beautiful vessel. I went all over her one day, the first Frigate I have ever been on board of, and to me a sailor it was a most beautiful sight to see every thin[g] so beautiful arranged & so clean - such a quantity of men, 4 deck, and not a speck of dirt to be seen. Some of thease fine days, dearest Melinda, when I come home, I must take you over some English man-of-War, but I doubt weather I could find such a moddle of this Identical one.

Tell Dear Father & Mother I shall write to them next mail, and Walter & Phillop the mail after, also Cristopher, and so tell them to be sure to write to me so that I may get their letters in Bombay before we leave, as I shall be her[e], as the last time, 3 or 4 months, as I said before. And ask Walter to be kind enough to send me that song of the Monks of old and Cristopher if he will send me the song of Jolly Rose, the Bright Rubies that garnish thy lip. By the buy, I think I have to apoligise to Cristopher for not answering the letter he sent me some time ago. If I did I don't remember it. And tell him when he writes to me to send me a good long letter, as he must have such long yarns to spin that I shall be glad to read as he is always on the move with his fellow students. To conclude, remember me to my good Godmother, for I dare say she often says I never send her a chit and so am very undutiful. With love to Dear Mother & Father and Brother[s] & Sister Believe me, Dear Linney, your very affectionate Brother

T.B. Bassano, Lanrick.

P.S. This day was my Birth day[33] so I suppose you wished me a very many happy returns.

I have just turned over the letter to dry it and find that I have got another half sheet not filled cross wise, so for want of something better I will tell you of a most laughable monkey we have on board. We have taught him all sorts of tricks. He stands on his head upon being told, chases the Boys on board and bites their heals, goes through the Muskit exercise and is particulilly fond of throwing pieces of wood down the hatches upon your head when he sees you underneath. At dinner times he comes down into the cabin and sits on a box placed for him close to the captain and quietly sits and takes any little bit of meat &c. which is put in his plate and neaver attempt to tuch anything else. He drinks grog & wine as much as he can get, taking the glass in his hand and tossing it off so naturally, and it is such fun to see him drunk. He tries to stand on his head and roles over, staggers along and tumbles about. Today he has been amusing himself in a Flower cask he found open and so he is just like a miller. The reason I thought of him for a subject is he has just come in my cabin as white as can be, and is sitting along side me, looking at me writing, every now and then pulling my arm and chattering. He is the talk of Bombay. Every body that comes on board is delighted with him and the first thing is to make him drunk. Last night he got so drunk that he Fell over board. He is up to all sorts of fun and mischief all day.

Well, dear Melinda, the yarn of the monkey has spun my letter out into a very long one and as it is getting late I must once more, dear Linney, bid you adue, remaining your ever affectionate Brother, Tom.

IV

"I HAVE LEFT THE SEA AS A PROFFESION & I HOPE FOR EVER"

At the age of 26 and after ten years at sea Tom Bassano now took the first opportunity that offered to seek his fortune ashore. This was to go and work for a coffee planter in the Wynaad, the largest coffee-planting district in India, and so to exchange one hard life for another.

---

33. His 26th.

68

FROM SAILOR TO COFFEE PLANTER

17. Tom Bassano to Alfred Bassano[34]   Parke Street, Calcutta
                                              8 December 1847

Dear Alfred
    You will be rather surprised to here that I have left the sea
as a proffesion & I hope for ever. I have entered into an
engagement to Coffee Plant. The way it came about is this. A
passanger missed the P. & O. Steamer, just before we left
Bombay, and so was obliged to take a passage with us, or wait in
Bombay a month. This passanger turned out to be a Smyth, brother
to the one I am now stopping with, and he was to go to Cannanore
to coffey plant, and he used to genarally stop up during my night
watches with me, and I having been a good while in the Ceylon
traid I could give him a many useful hints about the Coffee
Business. So after [illeg.] a few days I said I would very
much like to turn coffee planter myself, so he then told me it
was not his consern but that it was his brother's in Calcutta,
but that he would mention the subject to him, and that I should
here from him in Calcutta when I arrived there. Whe were then
bound from Bombay to Calcutta as I told you in my last letter.
So consequently, a week agoe I had this Capt. Smyth come on
Board the Lanrick to me, and Capt. White's permission he had
obtained previous, and so all I had to do was to make up my mind
and pack up my traps and walk, which you may depend I did in
double quick time, and I am now living at the above address,
happy and Comfortable. And all I am doin[g] is waiting to find
a ship to take me round to Cannanore. And my agreement runs
thus - all expences paid from the time of my leaving the ship
untill I arrive on the estate, and a standing income of 100 a
year for two years and then it is to be increased as agreed by
both parties, house & horse to be found also. So here I am
leading a dashing life untill such times as I go, driving out in
the carrage with Capt. Smyth & Mrs. Smyth round the Esplanade,
cutting such a dash. In fact, master Ensign, if you were to see
me you'ld think me Lord High Admaral of Great Briton instead of
a 2nd dickey. You were talking to me about cutting a dash if I
came to see you - it would *doo* your hart good to see me now.
Capt. White, after giving his consent to my leaving, refused to
pay me the whole of my pay, so I just went and got a Lawer's
letter written and he sent me such a polite letter in return and
my pay, saying that it was a mistake.

    I have not heard from home for an age and am not likely [to],
so dear Alf, you must give me all the news untill my letter[s]
get into the proper channell again. So when you write to me
address to care of William Smyth, Esqr., Manantoddy, Joyhuad

---

34. In Meerut. See Chapter Two, Letter 25.

[Wynaad], Madras Presidency, and believe me to remain yours
truly

T.B. Bassano.

18. Tom Bassano to Philip Bassano   76 Parke Street, Calcutta
                                        [December 1847]

Dear Phillop
    You will all be surprised at home to here that I am about to
turn coffee planter. I write to tell you of it according to my
promis[e] at Bombay. I said in Melinda's letter I would go
round the family, and tell Father I will write to him & Ellen
when I arrive at my new abode. The way in which it came about
was we brought a passanger from Bombay to Cannanore who was
going to commence coffee planting. His brother, being a
Capt[ain] in Artillery and worth money, finds the cash and he
carries on the estate in his own name as officers in the
Comp[any's] Army are not allowed to be land holders. So during
the passage to Cannanore I said I would like to turn coffee
planter and offerd my survices, and he told me he should write
to me in Calcutta, as we were bound from Bombay to Calcutta.
Accordingly the brother came on board to me and said he wanted
me to go round, previously asking Capt. White if he could spare
me, and he said "of course". So I packed up my traps and
walked, as he offered me a room at his house untill I could get
a passage round, he to pay all expences untill I got on the
estate. So I have been living at his house the last fortnight
like a prince, riding out on horse back of a morning, and in the
carrage round the Esplanade in the eavening with Mrs. Smyth, as
he is a married man. He also during my stay here has been
teaching me surveying, as he at present holds the appointment of
survayer to the district as well as his Capt[ain's] appointment.
And he tells me that they have not survayers where the plantations are and so when he buys land he wants me to survay it for
him, to see that he has got the actual quantity, as the way the
planters measure the land is - they know how many coffee trees
they can plant in an acre, but it takes them 3 or 4 years to
clear the jungle before they plant, so it would be a deavle of
a goe to find at the end of that time that you have only got 400
acres instead of 600. So I am to be survayer of the district
there and am now quite a profess[ional] hand as it is very simple
to a person who knows Navigation, as it [is] noe more than land
sailing instead of sea sailing - at sea using the Log for the
distance, and on shore using the Chain for distance and spirit
leavel for the rise and fall of the ground.

70

I wrote to Alfred a few days since,[35] but shall not be here long enough to have an answer as it takes 20 days. I hope after this trouble I [have] taken in writing you such a long letter that you will answer it, as I think that during the four years I have been from home you have only written to me once. The other half sheet is for Cristopher. Be kind enough to give it him, and *when you write* address to Care of William Smyth Esqr., Manantoddy, Madras Presidency, and I remain your affectionate Brother

T.B. Bassano.

19. Tom Bassano to Cristopher Bassano

39[36] Parke Street, Calcutta
[December 1847]

Dear Cristopher

It is so long since I heard from home that before you receive this letter you will have passed your Examination and [be] on your way out to India.[37] You must read Phillop's letter and see what I am about. As regards coffee planting, I had a deal of trouble with Capt. White, blast him. He has been the worst man to me that ever I was with, and yet I stoped with him the last 19 months and am the first officer which sailed with him for more than 6 month. He advised me not to leave, saying every thing against the step I was about to make, and [h]olding out the same old promise that I should be cheif mate in China, but to no purpose, as my resolution was fixed. And so T left him, and he was so enraged at my going that he refused to pay my wages due to me and so I told Mr. Smyth, and he said "O[h], just go to my lawyer and tell him how you stand". So accordingly I went, and he sent him a lawyer's letter and so he wrote me such a polite note saying he had made a mistake, and the sum within by the berar [bearer].

I have not heard from home since I was last in China and I suppose I shall not for the next 6 months, as all the volley of letters will have to go through a new channel.

I think eventually this will be a very wise undertaking. I am to be found in house, horse & 100 a year at my new abode, and the Gent. who is now begining the plantation has a wife and children in England and is only going to get the plantation in

---

35. Letter 17. The letter took 12 days at the most as Alfred sent it home on 21 December.
36. The number is so written.
37. See Chapter Four.

a state of foordwardness and then he will leave me in command
and he will go home to his family.[38] I can just picture to
myself how happy I shall be - plenty of shooting, tigers by the
hundreds, and wild Elephants by scores. And Smyth is sending
round by me 5 Double Barrell rifles and Five Fowling piece
double Barrels for the good of the estate, so I shall have 2 of
them in my possession. I sail from here on the 23rd, the
Exmouth, for Telcherry, and hope to be round there by the middle
of January. I intend to practice shooting at [a] Bottle going
round, so that when I get to Manantoddy should a tiger be about
to make a spring at me I can depend upon my eye to bring him up
all standing in time to save my life.

I shall not write again untill I reach my house. Be kind
enough to pass this letter round the family and tell Phil to do
the same. The only thing that will be wanting at my new house
will be a wife. Now, if Ellenor had waited a little she could
have come out, but no such luck. At all events perhaps you can
recomend me a nice girl of your own acquaintance, as I thing you
are a good judge in those matters. I wonder if Eliza Allen is
single now, or Miss Treaderway. You chaps never tell us any
news about old Flames. The fact is, I suspect, you are all
getting such Burra Adamies[39] that thease sort of things are
beneath your notice. Well, dear Cris, write to me as soon as
possible, and tell me some thing to make me laugh. But to
conclude, as your sheet is full and I am encroaching on Phillop's
and beleave me to remain your affectionate Brother

TBB

---

38. See Chapter Five (I).
39. great men.

CHAPTER TWO

"One of the Queen's loyal butchers"

At about the same time that Tom Bassano was joining the crack opium clipper *Lanrick* in China, his youngest brother, Alfred, was commissioned in the 32nd Regiment, which had received orders to proceed to India. He was then nineteen years old. His Ensign's commission was dated 8 April 1846, and on the 29 May the regiment embarked on board five transports at Fermoy in Ireland.[1] After a three month voyage all reached Calcutta in the first two weeks of September, and went straightway by water to Chinsura, 24 miles above Calcutta, where they stayed for two months, before setting out on the three month march to Meerut (fifty miles North-West of Delhi) where the regiment was to be stationed.

While at Chinsura Alfred wrote a batch of at least five letters home, the first of a long series of twenty-seven which he wrote regularly by almost every mail during the next two and a half years. Only one of the first nine has survived[2] but from No. 10 onwards the series is almost complete.

The regiment left Chinsura on 20 November 1846 and arrived at Meerut on 19 February 1847 remaining there for twelve months.

---

1. *British Sovereign, Duchess of Northumberland, Edinburgh, General Palmer,* and *Aboukir.* See G.C. Swiney, *Historical Records of the 32nd (Cornwall) Light Infantry* (London, 1893).
2. No. 5 to his brother Christopher, advising him to go to India. See Chapter Four, Letter 36.

FROM CHINSURA TO MEERUT
(1846-7)

20. *Crossing the River Son - Benares - Allahabad - Cawnpore -*
Mokun Ke Serai

Alfred Bassano to Philip Bassano   Meerut
(No. 10)   14 August 1847

Dear Phil
    My letter to Walter (dated 20 April) conveyed the news of the
march to the 11 Dec[ember]. I shall now - if you are not getting
sick of my long yarns & the difficulty of reading them -
continue my account.

    On the 12th I was introduced to two of the Ameers of Scinde,
encamped here, & invited to our Mess, oily looking cut throats
elegantly dressed. Towards the end of this week we bid adieu to
the beautiful hills covered with foliage & enlivened with
peacocks finding a great increase in the temperature as we
descended to the plains again. Nothing out of the way occurred
till we reached the banks of the Soane & encamped; where we
found a Reg[imen]t of Nat[ive] Inf[antry] occupying part of the
ground & invited the Off[ice]rs to dinner. The muffs had been
three days getting their baggage over, altho' their Reg[imen]t
was very strong & only possessed three hundred hackeries.[3] But
I don't wonder at it if those who dined at our Mess were a
specimen of the rest of the Off[ice]rs - such sinking ducks, the
questions they asked, & the hints & information they obtained
from the facetious 32nd would have put the most serious man in
the United Kingdom into such a fit of laughter that I should
doubt his recovery.

    The morning of our arrival on the right bank of the River the
left wing was employed on the burning sands half the day passing
the heavy baggage over (which always preceded the Reg[imen]t a
day) till relieved by the Right Wing. This *first* day *three*
hundred hackeries were passed over to the opposite bank & on the
following one the *remainder, 500* in *number*, by the United efforts
of the entire Regiment arrived at Dharie on the opposite bank.
The River is three miles broad, but at this season of the year
that breadth is composed of soft sand intersected with five
streams, four of which were forded & one crossed in boats. The
latter also is *fordable*, but *dangerous*. Both Off[ice]rs & Men
had their meals brought to them & were exposed to the burning
Sun & up to their knees in water all day, our laborious duty not

---

3. Ox-carts.

being completed till *ten* at *night*. A Drummer was carried down
by the stream & drowned & I very nearly had a swim for it, my
duty that Morning being to see the Colours safe into Camp, which
having done I rode back to take my share of the fatigues of the
day & in crossing the deep I got out of the ford & the water
within 3 inches of the top of the saddle my frisky steed "Smoker"
being scarcely able to keep his footing. However, I gained the
opposite sand without the assistance of the boats & joined a
jovial party of Off[ice]rs headed by old "Blood an 'ounds", alias
Maj. Brooke,[4] who had succeeded in breaking open a case of claret
off one of the hackeries & were refreshing the inner men to a
jolly extent. In fact the above Major sometimes also called
"gabber & guts" never loses an opportunity of moistening his
lips, & on this occasion there was no want of assistance to
finish the case. While this was going forward at our quarter of
the River, our other Major, "Brikfast",[5] & a Light Comp[an]y
Sub[altern], in their endeavours to get through the duties of
the day *dry*, had mounted an Elephant laden with gunny bags, but
while congratulating themselves on their elevated position, the
burden not being properly secured slipped, & *down* came the Major
& Flanker to the sand & water below, being well *bonneted* by the
gunny bags in their descent.

But I must proceed, for if I allow my hand to write all the
facetious remembrances of that day both this & my next chit will
contain nothing else. So here goes for the next event worth
recording, our arrival at the ancient town of Sasseram, which is
large & thickly populated, containing some old & very fine ruins
of the places of interment of former Mahommedans of distinction,
from the top of one of which – surrounded by water & only
approached by a boat – you may look down on the surrounding huts
comprising the town. Here we halted & spent our Christmas day
with the Ther[mometer] 85 in the shade.

Time flies: two or three halts in mango groves & we arrive
at the holy River Ganges, broad & deep even at this period of
the year & crossed in about thirty large boats, marched through
the city of Benares & anchored in a plain two or three miles
beyond it. Here we stayed two days – got licked at cri[c]ket
by the Station Club – examined the town – found the streets
narrow & crowded & containing nothing of interest excepting the
Minarets & *Sardines*, the *former* a large building with two lofty
towers commanding a most extensive & beautiful view, the latter
nice little fishes which had become scarce at Mess. Here we
witnessed a great native festival, immense temples carried about
on men's shoulders, glittering with tinsel & gold, bands of
music, the firing of guns, juggling, sham fighting, nautch
dancing, and Elephants, Camels, & Horses, superbly caparisoned,

---

4. Henry Vaughan Brooke, commanded the regiment, 1848-9.
5. Major George Browne.

making altogether such a noise & glare as would astonish the
weak intellects of "you gentlemen of England that sit at home at
ease". A review of the Native Troops also took place here. They
are fine Soldierlike looking chaps only wanting pluck to rival
any troops in the World.

After quitting Benares till our arrival at Allahabad the
country was flat and uninteresting but relieved by both ancient
& modern native Temples, small but remarkably tasty in their
architecture – our Encampments generally in *mango groves*. At
Okey-Chokey old Joseph of ours had his tent burnt down at
12 o'clock at night, obliging him to practise a Light Inf[antr]y
movement in a light & airy costume. There was very little
damage beyond the loss of the tent. Crossed the River Ganges by
a bridge of boats & encamped at Allahabad. In the town and
vicinity are many *burra*[6] Bungalows & *boat achcha*[7] Temples. Here
we were invited to a picnic, *Camp fashion*, every man bringing
his own chair and eating & drinking utensils – the Fort &
Armoury well worth seeing. The road for some time past thronged
with Natives with vessels suspended from a bamboo stick across
their shoulders, journeying to the River Ganges to obtain the
water, which is considered holy and they get a living by selling.
Their bamboos are generally decorated with little red flags.
Very amusing horse and pony races weekly. Arrived at Cawnpore
where we stayed three days – got licked at Cricket by 15 runs.
The town is very large & every description of European goods may
be obtained – the Barracks good, and pretty buildings. A
Reg[imen]t of Irregular Cavalry stationed here, their picturesque
& varied dresses, thigh boots, &c. contrasting beautifully with
the strict uniformity of the Regulars. It wants very little
imagination to carry you back to the days of chivalry, their
costumes and warlike forms well justifying the delusion that you
are beholding an assembly of the renowned Knights of old – the
only Reg[imen]t I have seen superior to this are the Life
G[uar]ds & Blues. The Camp here was a scene of the most riotous
& ludicrous confusion. At night a mischievous party well screwed
paraded the Camp, casting adrift the tent ropes, letting them
topple over & exposing the scenes of the interior. In one tent
there was a party of four or five fellows and about a dozen
Nautch girls – the fun & confusion caused by the fall thereof
beyond description – tumblers & milk punch swept off the table
& but for one of our fellows cleverly dowsing the glims[8] it
would have ended by a blaze in Camp. In another tent an ass
belonging to the 61st, marching up with us, walked up & down
his tent with a drawn sword, vowing destruction to his per-
secutors outside, but his cold steel & threats that we should
hear more from him in the morning only increased his persecu-

---

6. big
7. very good
8. putting out the lights

tion & in the morning his courage had cooled down to such an
extent that he thought it better to swallow his affronts.

We left Cawnpore with regret & [a] few days after had our
first march attended with *heavy wet*, in consequence of which we
stayed three days at Mokun Ke Serai, a delightful encampment
bearing a close resemblance for miles round to an immense &
beautifully wooded park. The air was cool & the weather fine
after the rains. We passed the time playin[g] cricket, visiting
the magnificent ruins of a Mahommedan town, frisking in the
tombs & on the terraces & towers of departed princes – but they
are now surrounded by mud huts & wretched poverty has succeeded
former grandeur – "sic transit gloria mundi". Here too we had
a glorious spree. A lot of Soldiers perched themselves on the
branches of the Shaddock trees & knocked down the unripe fruit
by hundreds, those below pelting one another. The fray soon
became general & being sanctioned by the Colonel, who joined in
it for a short time, about 20 Off[ice]rs & nearly a thousand
Men were soon engaged & a rash L[ieutenan]t in an endeavour to
distinguish himself by leading about a hundred Men to flank the
opposite party, a movement which did not at all pay, for his
ammunition failing he suffered the *fruits* of his rashness,
anything but *mellow*, one *sour* customer about the size of a
cricket ball, & quite as hard, nearly extinguished a luminary,
& other more unpoetical parts of his body suffered severely
during a disorderly retreat. The better part of valour was soon
found by the Off[ice]rs to be discretion & accordingly most of
us took up positions behind hackeries or trees, making effectual
sallies every now & then with a good supply of shots. The Men
continued the sport nearly all day, Comp[an]y attacking &
pursuing Comp[an]y with the most furious determination. The
combat did anything but improve the beauty of the Corps, & the
great difficulty next day was to know Jenkins from Tomkins.

For a continuation of my adventures on the march, with an
account of what I *did* & what I *didn't*, see my next chit. My
last letter to Father (No. 9) posted 8th July, was despatched
just four days too soon to acknowledge the receipt of Melinda's
containing a few lines from Father & *a slight effervescence*
from Chris, in which the latter worthy bothers my dull compre-
hension by some allusions to *Adam*, but I cannot understand what
the *first Mail* had to do with depriving me of a previous letter.
The former young Lin demands an explanation of a *doosra* & as
she has written more than any of you this time, for which she
may expect a return before long, I must proceed to explain –
accordingly "*doosra*" in the language of the East means "*another
or the other*". Remember me to all & believe me to be

    Your affectionate brother the sanguinary Ensign
                Alfred.

Lt. Ackland's papers for the sale of his Commission have

been sent in which will make me 2nd Ensign in less than a Month.
There are also other sells & exchanges expected shortly. Captain
Walter Kirby, 29th Reg[imen]t *died* at Kussowlie on the 4th of
this month (son of Mr. Kirby, W.O.).

A doosra *chit* will come by the same mail.

21. *Continuation of the march to Meerut − St. Patrick's day
    celebration − hunting − various items of news*

Alfred Bassano to Christopher Bassano   Meerut
(No. 11)   15 August 1847

Dear Chris
    This letter will complete my adventures on the march. My
last by the same Mail to Phil left me at Mokun Ke Serai. The
weather during the nights, until sunrise in the morning, were
bitterly cold. Our coats & cloaks did double duty, being placed
on our beds at night & used to march in in the morning. I was
rather disgusted at the idea of my perishing with cold when I
came out here to be fried. The villages until our arrival at
Secundra Rao were all alike "built of mud instead of bricks",
& little or no variety in the scenery. The shooting, however,
was capital & my expeditions in that line not at all unproduc-
tive. There were some antique ruins at Secundra Rao, which
appears to have been formerly a place of some importance. At
Allygarh, which is a good sized, well stocked, & bustling little
town, there is rather a strong fort which I inspected, & a
monument to the Off[ice]rs of the 76th who fell taking it in
1803.[9] But I should say it was principally famous for its
monkeys, for I never saw such a swarm as are congregated in the
trees round a tank there & appear to be on terms of easy
familiarity with the Natives, who treat them with great
reverence & looked carving knives at me because I caught one a
crack with my riding whip for setting my horse rearing & then
sitting on a wall & grinning at the performance − but I don't
think his facetiousness will extend to Europeans for the future.

    On Sunday, the 14 Feb[ruary], I went on with the first
Comp[any] in advance − at 2 o'clock came on to rain very heavily
before we were two miles from the Camp and continued long after
our arrival at Golauttee, a distance of 14 miles − found no
tents pitched, the encamping ground a complete swamp & our
Servants quite helpless from the cold − had to put them up
ourselves, wet to the skin & perishing − & with great difficulty
obtained a *dinner* & wound up by sleeping in wet beds. Next day
we were again hard up for our *khana* as the Reg[imen]t did not

---

9. The fort was stormed by General Lake in the Maratha wars.

:ome on for the rain, obliging us to shoot for our feed. On the following day we marched to Hauper, a good sized place where the [East India] Company have a breeding stud, & two days after arrived here & dined with the 80th - were inspected a few days after & attended a levee on the arrival of Lord H[ardinge][10] - gave a ball &c. &c.

On St. Patrick's day the men of the 32nd & 80th dined together & had they been required the answer would have been "the whole of the Garrison are drunk". The Capt[ain] of one Comp[any] signed for 240 bottles of beer & 60 gallons of rum. Numerous admissions into Hospital & several deaths occurred in consequence. Soon after, the Sergeants gave a ball to which we all went & danced and flirted with their wives & daughters - one of them was found drowned in a well in the morning. A few days after, several of us were out with dogs in full cry after a jackal, I was riding my ches[t]nut, only purchased the day before, & flattering myself on taking the lead, when a great mud wall came in sight, the jackal & dogs being very soon over, but I did not much like its appearance & consequently tried to rein in, when I was not very agreeably surprised to find there was no credit due to myself, for my horse had ran away & the devil himself could not stop him. However, he cleared it like a deer, but unfortunately there was a dry ditch on the other side which capsized him & we both rolled over together, but having sustained no damage I was quickly remounted & off again.

We were inspected by the Brigadier on the 13th May, who expressed his satisfaction at the cleanliness of the men in a most ridiculous speech, telling them he understood *they were* clean at Corunna, &c. We were formed in square & it was most amusing to see the ludicrous faces every one were making to preserve their gravity, & an Ensign nearly swallowed the Colours in the attempt.

We tried to enliven the place by a Nautch,[11] but it failed in consequence of the chaps walking off with the girls before the performance had continued long.

Two natives were bitten the other day by a snake which caused their bodies to swell to the size of giants, but their pulse[s] continued to beat for two days altho' they lay in a state of insensibility out on the common, after which decom[position][12] began to take place very rapidly. But the Natives kept watch over the bodies to keep the vultures & jackals off & would not have them buried as they had sent some distance for a wise Man of the East to charm the poison out, but the wonderful bloke

---

10. Governor-General. 1844-8.
11. Dance.
12. Letter torn.

not arriving, they were at last induced to bury them.

I expect - tell my anxious Mother - to awake some fine
morning & find myself eaten up, as a hard hearted *Doctor* insists
on keeping *a rampant* animal in the Bungalow which he bought when
it was quite young & on spoon diet, & is endeavouring to tame
it - its amiable disposition showing itself daily in a more
furious attempt to tear the hand that feeds it & break loose.
The knowledge of a furious beast indifferently fastened makes
your slumbers uncommonly pleasant, especially as you have all the
doors & windows open in consequence of the heat.

Col. Hill is about to exchange into the 21st, by which we lose
a perfect gentleman & one of the best Commanding Off[ice]rs in
the Service.

I rec[eive]d a l[ette]r from you dated 18 June, in which I
have the first mention made of Messrs. Cox & Co. dishonoring my
bill for £20, & from what you say, it appears - as I thought -
without previous reference to Father. And as soon as I have a
confirmation of the damn'd uncivil & annoying thing I shall
certainly give them a bit of my mind on the subject, for had it
not occurred [and] I had wanted a loan of money even to purchase
my Lieut[enanc]y he would I think have advanced it. For however
you explain anything of this sort it is sure to make the person
at least suspicious altho' he has mentioned it to no one nor
given me the slightest cause to think he ever doubted my
explanation.

Our principal cases of sickness have been apoplexy, but for
a Reg[imen]t just come out we have been wonderfully lucky.

I don't know whether I mentioned in that outfit list I sent
you[13] that firearms & saddles suiting the tastes & means of the
purchaser are indispensable when you arrive out here & are much
better & less expensive at home. Try if you cannot in any way
obtain a little practice in horsemanship before you come out, as
you will find these devils to begin upon. I dare say I often
mention things twice, but that is preferable to the silent
system often practised on me.

Tell Melinda I shall write to her next month & Walter that I
shall answer his letter when it arrives. So he has got an
increase to the family.[14] Congratulate Annie for me, altho' I
have already done so *on spec.*, & tell her the eldest shall have
my tiger preserves & the youngest I will settle my mango groves
on, *provided* she is christened *Mango*. If he goes on at this
rate, he will give them some trouble to make out the next

---

13. See Chapter Four, Letter 36.
14. Walter's second daughter Melinda (Dido), born 6 June 1847.

population tables.

In your last letter you take advantage of the *distance* to *bully* me. If you were out here I should request you to name your friend, but in my next letter to Walter I shall ask him to lick you & place it to my account. *Remember* me *to all* (in case my letter to Phil by the same mail does not arrive) and take the change from your affectionate brother

Alfred.

II

"I ALWAYS WAS A LAZY DEVIL & I AM NOW SURE TO
CONTINUE SO AS I AM PAID FOR IT"

(life in Meerut 1847-8)

22. *Regimental life - Meerut - officer's funeral - mess party*

Alfred Bassano to Walter Bassano   Meerut
(No. 13)   18 September 1847

Dear Mopsticks[15]
    I rec[eive]d your bullying letter on the 2nd July, but do not know whether I shall be able to make this letter long enough for you & be in time for the Mail, as I was engaged yesterday in answering a tremendously long one from Tom who has just returned again from China to Bombay and had a splendid pair of boarding pistols made a present to him for his zeal in drilling the crew to the use of arms, as one vessel in the same employ was plundered & the crew all murdered by the Chinese. He is very well & was on the point of writing to some of you when he sent off mine.[16] I am a great mind to send you his letter as it is a very jolly one, but perhaps it would be no use, as you will receive one at the same time.

    I put off writing this to the last minute to see if I got a chit, but it appears the Mail has been robbed coming from Benares here, so in all probability I have lost one. You appear to be very savage about something I said in one of mine, but 'pon my word, I do not recollect saying anything so strong as your quotation, for I very seldom read my letters over. If you send me back the obnoxious epistle I will have it curried for tiffin, which will be an economical way of eating my words.

---

15. Walter's nickname.
16. Chapter One, Letter 16.

81

Our mode of life here is a parade at 4 or 5 o'Clock in the
morning – only 3 or 4 times a week during the hot season – which
lasts about half an hour, when we ride back to our Bungalow,
read, or lay down & sleep for an hour or two, get up, have a
bath, breakfast in the verandah where we have a table & chairs,
smoke a cheroot or hookah, read, go to sleep again or lounge or
lark about the Bungalow till 12 or 1 o'Clock, go to Mess, play
at billiards or recline on sofas reading the newspapers in the
reception room with a punkah going till about 2 when we adjourn
to the Mess room, take tiffin & canvass the events of the day,
return to the billiard room, play at pool till 4 or 5 o'Clock,
return to our own or other fellows' Bungalows, amuse ourselves
variously until the sun has lost its power. About 6 the horses,
buggies & tandems come in play to ride or drive to the Mall,
where a band plays, or go round the tank – a large piece of
ornaméntal water surrounded by trees with a temple on each side,
where the Natives bathe and pray & faquirs beg. This is an
extremely pretty ride of about 2 Miles, but the only one having
any pretensions to beauty at the Station.

As for giving a long description of Meerut, the Devil himself
could not fill a sheet about it. The town itself is a collection
of dirty mud huts, open at the front to expose their wares,
principally all kinds of beastliness which they feed upon, such
as beans roasted – the same we give to our horses – dirty rice
&c. &c. with a population of about ten Men & women to a pig sty.
There is one more open place where some enterprising Native
rogues and discharged Serjeants or other Europeans keep shops
stocked with European articles. But the Barracks & Officers'
Bungalows are I am glad to say clear of all this collection of
stinks, and are capital buildings arranged in rows, intersected
by ro[a]ds & covering a space of two Miles in length, ending in
a Common of great extent with sand hills, where we hunt the
jackal or fox on a cool morning or evening, with a distant view
of the Himalaya Mountains. I will give you a rough plan of the
station in my next.

But I have been straying, for I have not yet finished my
account of what we do rot roj, or ever day. I left off at the
evening ride or drive, which we return from about 7 o'Clock,
then have another bath, put on a clean suit of white (this 2nd
or 3rd during the day) consisting of a white Jacket & waistcoat,
trowsers, &c., and go to dinner, where we dine as in England at
a table, sitting in chairs, every one his own Khitmutgar[17] at
his back, & the repast much the same as in England, fish, flesh,
& fowl, very similar to England, but not quite so good – in
fact every thing money can procure. But Chris will be able to
tell you what style we live in in the Army, as he has dined at
Chatham, but the 32nd being a cut above the common, have a

---

17. Table servant.

82

greater quantity & more splendid Mess plate, & give a better
dinner with far superior wines, to most Reg[imen]ts. I have not
yet dined with any reg[imen]t that gives as good a spread.
After dinner we return to the reception or billiard room, smoke
two or three cheroots, & drink a cup of coffee, then return to
our *virtuous* couches. This is the indolent life we lead in the
hot season, & with regard to duty very little more in the cold –
a longer *parade* in the morning and *every* day, with occasional
field days when all the Reg[imen]ts act as a Battalion. Being
Member of a Court Martial or Orderly Officer in your turn, which
does not occur very often, gives you a little extra to do, but
not much. The former duty consists of sitting at a wooden table
drawing pen & ink cartoons & caricatures of field Officers,
coinciding or differing with what the President says, according
to your taste or humour that morning, and arguing according to
your inclination to delay or bother the proceedings. The latter
duty consists of girding your belt round your loins, sticking a
cheroot in your mouth & making four mounted sallies to the
B[arrac]ks, one in the morning, one in the evening, one at
Tattoo (half past 9 at night) & the other to see that the Guards
are all right at 10 or eleven at night, none of which delay you
more than a quarter of an hour, & the rest of the day you are
just as free as any other. In fact, there is rather less than
nothing to do, which suits me amazingly, for I always was a lazy
devil & I am now sure to continue so as I am paid for it.

We lost our junior Ensign, Sullivan, on the 3rd of this Month.
Poor fellow, he died very suddenly & was buried next morning.
As senior of the rank I commanded the firing party. An Officer's
funeral is an imposing sight, the Men marching with reversed arms,
band playing the Dead March, Off[ice]rs in full dress & three on
each side of the coffin. But death in this country is treated
most philosophically. Widows are called in church to be married
again the following week & in this case every thing went on as
usual. The same night Ackland took his leave to return to
England, having sent in his papers to sell. Consequently there
was a great jollification, drinking his health & prosperity,
the champagne going like water, singing & giving him the musical
honors, with one foot on the table, many failing in the attempt,
and Batt, alias Richardson, fell into an empty wine glass on the
table, where he rolled over amidst roars of laughter. I just
took enough to make my sparkling wit boil over, but no more, for
I never make myself unable to appreciate & add to the ludicrous
scenes when an opportunity offers, which you can only do by
keeping sober.

Well, you are going ahead once a year. You will be obliged
to emigrate or amputate if you go on at this rate, for England
can never stand such a rapid increase. Remember me to Annie &
tell her I am sorry she did not know of my wish to have this
Child christened Mango in time. You had better keep the name
for the next, & call the next Rattlesnake, & after that call

them respectively, Banana, Boa Constrictor, Aligator, if this
arrives before they are all Christened - if not, why they lose
the valuable preserves which I have made a vow not to settle on
any one who is not named accordingly. But Annie can't have any
objection, as they [are] all pretty names. But delay is now
becoming dangerous. A few letters have just been deliv[ere]d
but none to me & the Meerut bag is closed immediately if not
sooner.

Remember me to all & believe me your affectionate brother

Alfred

Give the enclosed to Lin. Remember me to all my Uncles,
Aunts, Cousins, Amblin, Tipping, old Tom, & *KITTY*, & tell Uncle
Walter I will write to him by the next mail.

Remember me to Mr. Coleman & son, Mr. Ferguson, Mr. Stewart,
and all the W[ar] O[ffice] gentlemen.

If Father has not already got my *Ensign*'s Commission enquire
of Mr. Coleman about it. I do not want it sent out here, but
ask Father to *take charge* of it & put it in a dry secure place
& *not forget where*. Also all my Com[mission]s up to *Field
Marshal* request him to take charge of, as I wish to find them
safe when I return.[18]

23. *A swarm of ants - another funeral - a wedding - other
regiments - regimental gossip - reminiscences of home -
expenses in India*

Alfred Bassano to Philip Bassano   Meerut
(No. 14)   4 October 1847

Dear Phil
    I think it is high time I dropped you another line, so here
goes, as Byron says. I hope Walter & Melinda will get theirs
safely of 17th & 18th Sept[ember] & tell Ellen I owe her one.
I have not much news this time, so I must make the most of it.
There was a swarming of the white ants a few days ago, from
whose nests in the outer wall of the Bungalow there issued a
description of fly with bodies about the size of a grub & very
long wings, the verandah being instantly filled with squirrels,
lizards, sparrow[s], large *black* ants, and a mongoose, all
eagerly preying upon them, the compound being also full of
crows, kites, and minars, darting to & fro and ravenously

---

18. All were kept - up to Major General - and are now among
    the Bassano papers.

84

devouring those that escaped the former ennemies.

We have had another death, the victim this time I am sorry
to say was Lt. Kyrle, a good natured, gentlemanly fellow, and
quite a pal of mine. I met him first on the Bristol Steam boat
going over to Cork. We were in the same cabin on the voyage out,
same Company, and tented together on the march. He died of
fever on the 22nd Sept[ember] very much regretted by all of us,
altho' you will scarcely believe it in England when I tell you
how the remainder of the week was spent. On Wed[nesday] morning
the poor fellow died, several of the Reg[imen]t being present at
his death and playing billiards &c. for the remainder of the day
as usual. The next morning the funeral took place, many coming
direct from that to billiards, and at 11 o'Clock going to an
Auction of the effects of Ens[ign] Sullivan, which was conducted
with great merriment. The next day we all went to a theatrical
performance by our own Serjeants & Men, and returned to sup and
sing at Mess, the next morning (Saturday) going to the wedding
of Lt. Jeffery, and returning to a champagne tiffin, the
bridegroom disgusting his *fair* bride (a darky) & papa by getting
well screwed and indelicately facetious. And old Joey of ours,
who was married a very short time ago got beastly, chased the
Khitmutgars round the Bungalow, fell down, & made his white
trowsers all green, and someone telling him he was all over
green, put himself on the defensive & asked who dared to call
him green, then swore no one should take his wife home, & in
turning round his buggy threw the horse down twice & was
ultimately driven away by Marshal Saxe (alias Capt. Case) who
got him off by promising to drink some brandy & water with him
at his Bungalow, followed by his poor wife in a palki[19] *in
tears* - I don't mean to say the *palki* was *crying* for it bore
its *weight* of *woe manfully* altho' evidently overcome and obliged
to be carried off by *four* strong men.

The rainy season, which by the by was a decided failure, is
now over. The days are cool & the mornings & evenings quite
chilly.

The Reg[imen]ts here don't pull at all well together &
associate very little. The reason is that both the 9th Lancers
& 80th are much too drunken & coarse for the 32nd. As for the
Lancers - dining with them is great fun, but rather dangerous,
for as you are quietly sitting at table a fellow will sing out
"look out" & without further notice a plate comes scaling down
the table to the great danger of every one's head, the
individual who was favoured with the compliment immediately
returning it with a tumbler, silver salt cellar or even a
decanter of wine, for they are not at all particular, and it is
not an uncommon trick after pouring out a glass of wine or water

---

19. Palanquin

to smash the decanter or glass water jug on the table & bet that they will make a cannon with a wine glass off two of the lamps in the room. And one night some of us were dining with them and in the billiard room after Mess a fellow coolly smashed a lamp with his cue, the broken pieces and oil covering the fellow who was standing beneath it. The consequence is in many cases a challenge and apology next morning. And they get too drunk to know what they do or say so the 32nd have given up almost entirely having anything to do with them. They think us very slow because we have only three or four drunken chaps in the Reg[imen]t, and we don't think their manners at all improved by their being always, as Tom would say, three sheets in the wind. And the 80th are full of fellows who have risen from the ranks and New South Wales gentlemen who have never been in England, discipline and manners both amongst Officers & Men being at such a discount that a newly joined Ens[ign] said he did not care a dam for the commanding Officer and told a Capt[ain] to kiss his ——————, a slight apology setting all to rights again.

We have a little excitement here now with our own Off[ice]rs returning from leave after astonishing the Natives in the hills. Capt. Robyn is coolly walking off with Major Cumberland's wife and quietly writing for her clothes, and telling the husband he is ready to give him any satisfaction after ten o'Clock in the morning as he is a late riser. And one of our L[ieutenan]ts at Mussoorie is carrying on rather a close intimacy with the wife of a Capt[ain] there, which is expected to lead to a facetious result. For every thing is regarded in this country in a ludicrous light, even matrimony (a case of late occurrence) being only entered into for a spree to supply the Mess with a fund of jokes cracked by the husband at his wife's expense, without much regard to decency.

I promised in my last to write this Mail to Uncle Walter, but I now find I don't know his address - it is some Queen St., but whether Great or Little and the number, I have forgotten - so am afraid of its miscarrying. Remember me to him, and tell him this is a capital Service, and that I shall return to drink a bottle of his good old port yet, and hope to find him in the enjoyment of the same good health and spirits and able to laugh with the same hearty good will at my marvellous tales of the East as he used to in the olden time at my trumpery jokes. And I'll tell him tales over his souchong and bohea[20] of the doings of the Legalized Depopulating, or *Hon.* E[ast] I[ndia] Company, as will make his hair stand on end. And tell me in your next how Aunt Ryle is - I hope all right again - and John and Arthur, and whether there are any more little Johns or likely to be any little Arthurs, and tell the latter worthy, in case I get my legs under their mahogany again, I hope he has not forgotten how

---

20. Walter Bassano, Sr. was a wholesale tea merchant.

to lay on the ground and make that jolly punch Mother used to
say I had too great affection for. I wonder whether you will be
the same good tempered meerchaum smoking convivial party giving
Bachelor when I return a sun-dried & enlarged-livered old Indian,
and if we shall be able to get Bill Tipping and Amblin, Sawbones
& Mopsticks (if Annie will let him) to laugh Aha & quaff ha ha,
and kick up a fume as of old, when Amblin used to laugh at my
getting white in the gills. Tell him I've a stronger stomach
now and that when I return (about a century hence) I'll annoy
him by skating on the round pound, when *of course* he will *cease*
to be the *Lion*. And as for Bill Tipping, if he talks to me of
ascending the mountain, or rather molehill, at Teneriffe I'll
stick the Himalayas in his throat, and stop his quaff aha for
ever. I'll stand none of his dam'd poop or quarter deck airs,
for I know sheet anchor from a clove hitch as well as a
Battalion from a blunderbuss & no mistake. Then for a family
meet on Xmas day, Mother & Father sitting in their arm chairs
smiling at the noise and Indian yells of their sun-dried Sons,
the Field Marshal sitting as President and the Admiral as Vice,
& as the rising generation (Walter's handy works) will make such
a long table necessary, I vote that every person present shall
be provided with a speaking trumpet and telescope to see & be
able to address his conversation to any of the family who may
chance to be a quarter or half a mile off - but all this trouble
can easily be avoided if Walter will only employ Chris as his
family Doctor.

I hope you and the Governor are not seriously inconvenienced
by the want of the tin you so generously advanced and I am so
tardy in repaying, but our Colonels have no consideration for
the difference betwixt our pay & theirs, and are perpetually
letting us in for some damned subscription or other, which
cleans out the savings of my desperate economy - and are awfully
disgusted, & make your situation very unpleasant, if you don't
humour them sometimes. & my bad luck in horse flesh, and being
obliged only this Month to purchase two shell jackets & a new
blue coat has completely upset my calculations and compelled me
to break my promise of making a remittance.[21] Well, I am now
senior Ensign & if my luck befriends me and I get a speedy
lieutenancy 54 Rs. a Month will be no trifling addition to my
finances, and if the worst comes to the worst, nine out of every
ten of our Off[ice]rs are already deep in the Bank books, and I
can but fall into the prevailing fashion and touch them up for
a loan to repay you, which I am quite willing to do if Father
and you are inconvenienced or annoyed by my delay.

---

21. Philip, the eldest brother, now aged 30, and having been
    a War Office clerk for ten years, helped all his brothers
    and sisters financially from time to time. Alfred, with
    no private income, was like all young army officers in
    India finding his pay insufficient for his way of life.

Remember me to Aunt Isabella and Cameron and cousins Susan and Kate, Dick, Phil, Mark, Mary, &c. &c. Is Kate as saucy as ever, or is Mary assuming the Command and bringing her to order? I have got a lot of *precious* stones which I intend sending you all the first opportunity in a beautifully carved sandal wood box, consisting of garnets, chrystals, red and white cornelians, bloodstones and others the name of which I forget. They are all carved and polished, shaped for seals, brooches, and one (bloodstone) for a signet ring.[22] Give my love to Annie & tell her to take care of those babes, especially the one Ellen says has got a cast in her eye (I can scarcely prevent myself from writing an indelicate joke here) and to take care Mary and Lizzy don't break their precious pates, because I want to have them framed and glazed, so they had better take care for the enlightened Natives in this country lick the women like the devil and I intend to bring home a Man expert in this most useful art to thrash all the nonsense out of all the delicate minded young ladies of my acquaintance that have caused any mischief during my absence. Are Amblin & Chris still as far advanced in the favour of spiff *gals* as formerly? I'm obliged to lavish my affections on black Venuses, generally smelling most confoundedly of beetle nut. By the By, how does Dick & his *gal* get on? Is he still as profusely liberal of his valuable affections as formerly. Remember me to young Stewart & Gurney & tell the former to remember me to his Sisters & Miss Shaw - also Col. Tulloch, Mr. Croomes, Mr. Coleman & son Leonard, Mr. Ferguson, Mr. Kiddle, Mr. Drake, Mr. Borrow, Mr. Hanby, Mr. Roberts, Mr. Matthew, not forgetting Mr. Stewart and Mr. Collin, and if they enquire how I'm getting on, tell them I'm as well & happy as a young alligator (unless you can supply me with a better simile). Pon my word, I am disgustingly forgetful - I have left out some ladies now, vizt. Mrs. Coleman and daughters and my paper is nearly filled. I wish I had some means of remitting some little Eastern curiosities to shew I have not forgotten all my former friends. Give my love to Mother & Father, Ellen & Lin, and say what you like to that Collector or Prosector[23] and Mopsticks,[24] and believe me your affectionate brother

Alfred, one of the Queen's loyal butchers

Until you hear to the contrary, direct your letters Upper Provinces, Bengal (*via Bombay*), for altho' under orders to march to Umballa, it is not at all unlikely that our destination will be changed. I hope this letter will not be overweight. Walter blows me up for writing on small paper & this is no larger than his. Remember me to Mr. Hughes and Wimbridge, and ask the former if he has recovered that beating he got at

---

22. The box with some of the stones is still with the family.
23. Christopher, see Chapter Four, Introduction.
24. Walter.

cribbage the morning the Duke of Sussex was buried, and the
latter who he has taken in lately about the stone on his
mantelpiece that David killed the giant with. Tell him I'll
send him the very jawbone that Samson slew the Philistines with,
which has lately come into my possession in a way which leaves
no doubt it is the very identical bone. I have not had time to
get an answer from Tom to my last letter yet, so know no more
about him than what I told you in my letter dated a fortnight
ago. If Mr. Coleman don't know of the death of Lt. Kyrle,
communicate it to him and tell him I saw the poor fellow buried,
so there is no room for a doubt about it. The Express arrived
yesterday, but the English letters will not be delivered for a
day or two. I suppose there is one for me. Tell Walter that
the curries in this curry eating country are not at all hot.
Therefore John Bull need not torture his inside for the sake of
imagining he is eating it as it should be - John has evidently
been gulled by some facetious old Indian. The powder that is
sold in England is no more like the original than chalk is like
cheese. Smack Tom's head on my responsibility the next time he
sets you all eating & burning your throats with chili powder to
be like Indians.

24. *Regimental news - military executions - drill - hunting*

Alfred Bassano to Christopher Bassano   Meerut
(No. 15)   20 November 1847

Dear Chris
    This news being principally of a masculine interest I shall
devote the sheet to you altho' I still owe Ellen one. I hope
you receive all my letters, which you can easily see by the
numbers. My last one (No. 14) was to Phil, dated 4 Oct[ober].

    All our Off[ice]rs have rejoined & the Reg[imen]t is
becoming very sporting. King's horse came in second in the
Mussoorie races & Williams rode his own in a hurdle race at
Simla, but got a cropper and lost. Capt. Robyns has rejoined,
bringing Maj. Cumberland's wife with him. She is a very fine
woman & has left two children with her husband, but is very
expensive in her habits. Robyns is getting over head & ears in
debt & it is expected must sell out before long. There have
been several theatrical performances of late. Col. Hill & Lt.
O'Callaghan took their farewell dinner with us, the latter to
proceed to Ceylon on the Staff & both being very popular the
cheers were terrific when their healths were proposed and drank
with all the honors, one foot on the table. We shook the walls
& astonished the Natives for miles around. Col. H., who has
been twenty years in the Reg[imen]t was very much affected.
They were to start soon after dinner in palkis being carried
away by about twenty Off[ice]rs making a frightful noise.

The days are now very cool and the mornings & evenings so
chilly that we are often obliged to have fires in our Bungalows
and have them regularly at Mess.

Two parrots were brought some nights ago by a juggler & made
to sit on a pole & twirl a stick with a flame at each end round
& round in their beaks in a most extraordinary & wonderful
manner. We have lots of cricket matches now - 32nd against 9th
Lancers, gentlemen of the Station against the Men, Companies
against the H[onorable] Art[illery] &c. &c. with various success.
We pitch tents on the Common & tiffin there, and cook up a little
fun.

We have had three executions here, one of the H[onorable]
Art[illery], one of the Lancers, & one of our own Men - the
first for striking Dr. Macaulay, the second for throwing his cap
at his Major, and our own Man - a great blackguard - for striking
a .Serjeant. All the garrison were had out in full dress. The
culprits are then marched round the square, preceded by the
Provost Marshal, the execution party, and their coffin, the band
playing the Dead March, and the Prisoner accompanied by the
clergyman. After this he kneels on his coffin, is blindfolded,
and quietly shot, if inefficiently, as in the first case, where
the poor wretch continued in an upright posture on his coffin
after the discharge, only two balls striking him, not mortally,
when the Provost stepped up and blew all the upper part of his
head off. The corpse is then laid at the side of his coffin,
and the troops marched in subdivisions past the body. They all
died very pluckily, especially the Lancer Private, who had been
a midshipman in the Navy and a gentleman of fortune, which he
had dissipated away. On marching past his own Reg[imen]t he
said in a manly voice "Adieu, comrades, take warning by my fate
- drink has been the ruin of me - I have always done myself more
injury than any body has done to me" & when kneeling on his
coffin, he said "Good bye, Comrades, take a good aim" & the next
moment fell pierced by seven balls in places where any body
would think he must die on the instant, yet he kicked for a
moment or two till shot by the Provost. But our learned Bones
say it is almost impossible to kill a man instantaneously, but
that they have lost all feeling & it was only a muscular vibration. The papers here are blackguarding us right & left & say
that Meerut was the only Station in India where Courts of
supposed honorable Men were found so subservient to the Commander in Chief as to answer his call for blood, and then go on
to say we are in a state of Mutiny here. If all Her Majesty's
Troops are as well conducted & easily Commanded as the 32nd
England's not much to fear from either Mutiny or Ennemies.
There have been a great many cases lately in India of violence
to superior Off[ice]rs, the Mutiny Act obliging the Courts to
sentence to Death such Offenders, the Com[mander] in C[hief]
invariably commuting it to transportation for life, the very
thing these Scoundrels want under a delusion that they will be

able to get a ticket of leave & lead a very jolly life. Cases becoming more numerous the C[ommander] in C[hief] suddenly comes to the resolution of confirming the Courts Martial, a thing he ought to have done long ago & nipped it in the bud. This Station chanced to have three just at the time, which are all confirmed, & the 61st, a Reg[imen]t who hissed & coughed down a Court Martial while formed up in square to have it read, all their Off[ice]rs on leave being suddenly recalled in consequence of their outrageous conduct, have escaped without an example, this being our first Man sentenced to Death, and they have had several whose sentences were commuted a short time previous. The Newspapers are bullying away & telling the most awful crammers & I suppose the English Press will soon be doing the same thing. We are seriously thinking of calling out two or three Editors, & if they won't come, horse whipping them to stop their mouths for the future.

The 80th have left the Station for Dinapore – they are no loss – & we are still in doubt if we move, not having received any orders yet. We have had dear little Arthur to [stay] with us on his way down the country to join his father [letter torn].

We have plenty of drill now the cold season has commenced & cut about the Common at Light Inf[antry] like devils, forming little squares and repelling the attacks & firing into imaginary Cavalry *fortunately* with *imaginary bullets*, as these movements are conducted upon some *scientific* principle, the object of which appears to be to cause our own Men to do one another as much bodily injury as possible, by forming little squares so that they fire into one another with great coolness. In fact, you would be much safer as an ennemy than a friend, for the former would only catch the stray bullets. My own consolation is – to judge from the aim the Men take the clouds appear to be our greatest ennemies, which takes away considerably from the danger of a volley. I am convinced that this circumstance alone saves our Armies, for if we made friends with the clouds our Men would mow one another down like blazes. We had ball practice the other morning, a target being placed in front of a large mud butt as large as a haystack, the Men firing one after the other and perpetually missing even the butt, the balls you could see ducking & draking over the Common for a long distance, one nearly potting a Sepoy who was walking about a quarter of a mile off.

We shot an Adjutant the other day measuring nine feet from wing to wing. I have got the bone of his leg which makes a capital walking stick a yard long. But our greatest amusement now is hunting & a Club called the Jackal & Jackass Club, *originated* and *named* by *me*, causes immense fun. Men in this country come about with jackals, foxes, hares, honey, and anything else the jungle produces which they think they can sell. I bought on several occasions for a few annas some of these

beasts, got some other fellows to come mounted bringing their
dogs to the Common, let them out, & hunted them. It took
rapidly, insisted on my managing the affair, forming a Club &
having subscriptions. I immediately drew out a paper, made the
subscription 2 Rs. & formed the above Club which numbered 20
Members in a day. All my proposals for its management were
agreed upon & it is now in a most flourishing state. My
Compound is often quite a menagerie of wild beasts, chained or
boxed up for hunting. A furious jungle cat, as large as a good
sized spaniel, broke away. Of course there was no catching it
again altho' it ran into one of the Servants' houses, for no
one dare go near it, but we let the dogs loose and after a
furious fight numbers carried the day & it was killed. We have
already had some very good runs, but we often lose the game at
last from having no dogs which run by scent. We crossed a very
stiff country one day, five out of seven of us were spilt by
our horses, coming down at different jumps, no one being hurt in
the least except Davies who slightly sprained his wrist. I was
the last but one spilt & was laughing at the others when my
horse, a most exciteable beast, in spite of a powerful curb, ran
furiously off with me, and the ground being full of holes, he
caught his foot & pitched over. I was fortunately not a bit
hurt & jumped up & caught the reins before he had had time to
get up & run away. Another day we were out after a fox which
doubled the dogs beautifully and at last made for a sugar
plantation. Straubenzie, in trying to cut him off, rode over
the dogs & got a frightful cropper. They were fortunately his own
hounds. We lost the fox. Since then we have had several hunts
after jackals, hares, &c. with great success as far as killing
them goes, altho' we generally get a much longer & better run
with more excitement when they are lost. We can get plenty of
jackals, but foxes are scarce. However, I procured one yesterday morning & gave notice of a hunt in the afternoon. There
was a very large meet in consequence, and after a very good run
the dogs pinned him. I was first in at the death & have got
his brush nailed over the door of my room. Since then there
have been several hares & jackals hunted, producing great fun,
but I have not been able to get another fox. I have just got
a jungle cat and two hares for this afternoon, which promises
good sport.

There are lots of horse races still being got up in the
Regiment, and two or three more cricket matches for next week.
The climate is delightful, the sun shining all & every day.
However, many of the Off[ice]rs with plenty of money are getting
tired of the country, and I expect, when once the example is
set, to see lots of fellows selling, in fact there will be
plenty of promotion before long. How are you getting on? I
long to see your name in the Gazette.[25] Col. Pattoun[26] has

25. See Chapter Four.
26. Richard Tyrrell Robert Pattoun, commanding the Regiment,
1843-8.

joined and appears to be a very good fellow. I rode in a pony
race the other day, and won. I have got a capital little bull
terrier which arrived from Agra two days ago.

But I must cut this letter short, for it must be posted
before twelve. It leaves me in better health and spirits than I
ever enjoyed in my life. I hope it will find all you the same.
How is dear Mother and Father? I hope they have fewer cares and
anxiety now I am away and, I flatter myself, doing so well. Give
my love to Annie, Ellen and Melinda, not forgetting the *butchas*
(Annie's young uns), Phil, Walter. I have not had an answer to
my last letter to Tom & my salaam to all my relations and
friends, and cook up amongst you some long letters to

Your affectionate brother
Alfred.

I have no time to fill this up.

Give my salaam to my W[ar] O[ffice] & A[rmy] M[edical]
B[oard] friends.

25. *Amusements - exchanges and promotions*

Alfred Bassano to Ellen Bassano   Meerut
(No. 16)   21 December 1847

Dear Ellen
     I must make this a short letter, as I have put off writing
to the last day in expectation of the Mail, 3 days overdue, but
I enclose you a chit lately received from Tom[27] which will make
amends. I think it a most satisfactory epistle & take credit to
myself for having brought him to his senses.

     I have not a great deal to tell you. Hunting has been my
principal amusement lately & we have had some fine runs. I have
already six brushes for being in first at the death & am in
daily expectation of a wolf hunt. We have had lots of cricket
matches & horse races lately & the Meerut races commence on the
4 of next month. We have got a Camp pitched about 24 Miles off
where we go & stop a few days & shoot. It is prettily situated
in the immediate vicinity of small hills & ruined temples &
surrounded with thick jungles dotted with palm trees & interspersed with Mango topes,[28] swarming with monkies, parrots, owls,
&c. I had a magnificent view of the snowy range from the hill
in rear of the tents - the view was distinct & beautiful, a long

---

27. See Chapter One, Letter 17.
28. Groves.

line of black mountains in rear of which you saw the more lofty
peaks of the Himalayas covered with perpetual snow.

We had a Station Ball on the 8th, but it was attended by very
few ladies. We have also had a theatrical performance, but it
was not so good as usual. I received Father & Walter's letter
of the 4th Oct[ober]. It is now almost certain that we march to
Umballa the latter end of next month, or beginning of Feb[ruary],
but we have not yet got the route. The temperature is now
delightful, mild during the day, & cold enough for a blazing
wood fire in the evening.

Promotion is now all the talk. Robyns has been gazetted out
in this country, King getting the Comp[any] & Stewart the
Lieut[enanc]y. Major Brown has also sent in his papers to retire
on half pay. Capt. Kelly is also going & probably Lt. Reed, in
addition to exchanges which are being negotiated, but which will
do me no good as money is producing all the present changes,
which is very unfortunate, as I should have slipped up the
Lieut[enant]s capitally if I had been lucky enough to have got
my promotion. But the only way is to take it cooly & I am still
as well, jolly, & merry as ever. I am like Mark Tapley,[29] never
disponding, better luck next time, it's no use crying, take it
cooly, hurroo maringo, hullaloo boys. There will be another
fox hunt this evening, when I hope to win another brush, for
Fanning being in the sick report I have got the run of the
stables & am rough rider to the Bungalow & shall ride his
gallant grey, a capital leaper, this afternoon. But the Mail
bolts in 5 minutes, so give my love to Father & Mother, Lin,
Annie & brothers, relations, friends &c. &c., young 'uns, &
Believe me
                    Your affectionate brother
                              Alfred

Tell Chris to Write & tell me how he is getting on.

Ask Father to send me out a Monthly Army List - my present
one being excessively stale.

26. *Dinners - balls - races - Indian jugglers - the next march
- high jinks*

Alfred Bassano to Walter Bassano   Meerut
(No. 17)   20 January 1848

---

29. *Martin Chuzzlewit* had first been published in monthly parts
    in 1843 and 1844.

Dear Walter

Tell Ellen my last letter (No. 16) was to her, enclosing one from Tom, which I hope will be safely received. It contained my proceedings & adventures up to the 21st of last Month, from which time you must unravel the thread of my narrative.

On Christmas Eve we gave a farewell dinner to Capt. Robyns, adjourning at 12 o'Clock at night to witness the Christmas eve ceremony at the Roman Catholic Chapel, which only consisted of bad singing & ranting in Latin, no doubt to the great edification of a lot of Private soldiers. The conclusion however was a little more satisfactory, for some of our fellows, overladen with champagne, must needs mistake their own buggies & horses & lick other fellows' Servants, the proper owners coming up & saying they were no gentlemen, compliments passing, kicking one another out of the Compound, & threats of hearing more in the morning, great mind to pull more horse whip &c. made the conclusion of the ceremony uncommonly amusing.

The next day - Christmas Day - as is usual in this country, on getting up in the morning the Bungalows were found to be decorated with bunches of flowers, wreaths of flowers tied from pillar to pillar across the gates & large branches of trees stuck in the ground in all directions by your Servants, who presently after brought in their Christmas offerings of baskets of fruit and flowers, which afforded amusement for the day, pelting one another with what we could not eat. The Captains of every Company gave their men a bottle of beer each, plum pudding &c, the Col[onel] & Capt[ain] drinking some ale offered by the Men and wishing them a happy Christmas. At our own Mess bowls of bishop circulated freely after dinner & singing & smoking kept up till a late hour. I hope you all spent as jolly a Xmas day. The next day I took a long ride and visited the Elephant sheds here & was shown about 60 & several young ones, the ground being covered with meal cakes prepared and baked by an immense number of Men employed for the purpose of preparing food and attending to the elephants.

I have also been exploring the country round about and found many ancient burial places and temples, some of them showing great taste and skills in architecture, one in particular composed of red sand stone & white marble beautifully carved. The ceilings of the towers still showed their having been gilt with silver and gold & rude paintings on [?chalk]. It was evidently erected as a burial place for Mahommedans of distinc-tion, many of the tombs of white marble being still in good repair with inscription in the Native character upon them.

On the 31 Dec[ember] we gave farewell dinner to Major Brown, who has proceeded to Europe to go on half pay. After his health was drank he was hoisted up in his chair in a second and carried round the room amidst a great uproar. I don't consider him much

95

loss – he was a stingy old Scotchman.[30] The same night I went
to a ball given by the Artillery & as is always the case in India
very few ladies & most of those married. The consequence is
very few can dance & so get drunk instead, reeling away one after
the other, getting up one side of their horses and falling down
the other, driving their buggies into ditches, and awaking next
morning with headaches, and drinking soda water, and vowing they
will never go to another ball as long as they are in the country,
and breaking it the next time for the want of something else
to do.

We have had several jackal & fox hunts, hare coursing and
pigeon matches since my last letter which afford capital
amusement.

The first day of the Meerut races commenced on the 4th
Jan[uary] & lasted for a fortnight, 3 times a week. The race
course is a very good one, with a grand stand and a large tent
pitched to provide tiffin. All Meerut turned out in their best
Mufti, & no bad weather occurs in the East to spoil a day's fun.
I went every day, and the races were very good and amusing.
Old General Gilbert set a capital example by riding his own
horses in three of them, all of which he won by his superior
riding. He is one of the best jockeys in India. You meet with
some wonderful characters. Sub[altern]s without a sixpence
beyond their pay bet their fifty or a hundred gold mohurs –
(a gold mohur is sixteen rupees) – with the greatest coolness
upon anything, they don't care what it is. A Cornet in the 9th
Lancers in our billiard room a few nights ago in a billiard match
backed the losing side twice for fifty gold mohurs, a game which
he lost with the most perfect indifference, but being a cool &
plucky better he won most of it back again in subsequent matches.
However, one L[ieutenan]t in the Lancers, who has been fourteen
years in the Service, during the whole of which time he has bet
upon every subject in heavy sums, the late races have brought to
a smash. He has been forging, & is now in arrest afraid to
stand a Court Martial, & has been allowed to send in his papers.
A great many Men in this country are dependant entirely on their
bets, their pay being all stopped to defray debts for former
extravagancies. Francis of the 9th, his racing stud alone (the
best in India) costs him 500 Rs. a month, all of which he makes
by the races. My old ches[t]nut horse "Blazer" which I sold to
King, won two races, by which he bagged five times as much as he
gave me for him. And Power ran a beautiful grey arab pony,
formerly mine, in the pony race, which would have won also but
Power was not able to get a light weight to ride, his being
ridden by a Man & the others by little boys – in spite of which
he pressed the winner very close & has offered to run him fairly

---

30. Major George Browne, a Waterloo veteran, who had entered
the regiment in 1813.

weighted for what he likes. So you see my stud have been
astonishing the Natives. In fact, my horse flesh has undergone
great changes, for I have been exchanging & selling till it ends
in my having got an excellent pony in my stable, and kept two
horses for some Months, all for nothing and without any risk.
I told the fellows I could not stand my first loss, old "Smoker"
which I bought for a hundred & sold for ten, and that I intended
to make use of my experience by twisting & changing my stud till
it ended in my having one for nothing - which is now the case.
So I succeeded in making some use of my sharpness at last, which
is very fortunate for we have got the pleasant prospect of
another expensive march before we have been eighteen months in
the country, and are in daily expectation of our Route to
Umballa, the road there being up to our knees in sand & consequent comfort of paying for a lot of camels to convey our
baggage, instead of the less expensive hackeries. However, I
have got sufficiently in advance of my pay to go on this march
with much more comfortable feelings than I did the last, being
able to pay every farthing I owe & start with a little ready
money, which will prevent my being cheated and chiselled as I
was the last march in consequence of not being able to pay ready
money for things.

During the race week we had athletic sports among the Men of
the Station, running, jumping, wrestling, throwing heavy weight,
&c. for which we subscribed & gave prizes & a champagne tiffin
in our Mess tent to the Ladies who chose to come & see them.
Then came a race ball given by the 9th Lancers & 32nd in con-
junction. So what with one thing and another Meerut has been
quite enlivened during the last three weeks. Have you had many
balls? I suppose you are shivering & skating away & trying to
persuade yourselves you are jolly, while we are revelling in
perpetual sunshine & feasting our luminaries on evergreen trees,
which your fathers never possessed in your quarter of the globe,
in spite of the song.

We have had several Cabool men at the Bungalow lately, with
fruit and birds for sale, just like English - apples, pears,
blackberries, larks, goldfinches, cats &c. so I suppose if we
ever get up to Cabool we shall fancy ourselves back in England
again. One of these ferocious looking fellows brought some
pomegranates which I tasted for the first time. They are in
appearance like a very large poppy pod, and when opened contain
small pods of a transparent pink which you pull out & eat, and
demnition good they are. We had a Madras juggler yesterday in
the Mess compound, who performed the most astounding feats of
dexterity. He balanced a stick on his chin which at the upper
end had a lot of smaller sticks branching out in all directions.
He then got some wooden birds about the size of sparrows &
perfectly solid & weighty, with a round hole cut in their breast
- these he fixed at the end of the smaller sticks, then placed a
pea shooter in his mouth. You then pointed out a bird which he

shot with such force as to knock it off the stick it was placed on, never missing one, & balancing the remainder all the time. Another thing he did which was very much applauded was he had a long bamboo, about 12 feet, with a small cross piece in the centre - then he placed the end on the ground, sprang up to the cross piece, which he stood upon & jumped about the compound with the most perfect freedom. It would rather astonish the English jugglers, who think it very wonderful to see a man or woman jumping about on stilts, to see a man get up himself & perform twice as many antics on a single pole. Then, spitting flames of fire, playing with carving knives & swallowing swords is thought nothing of - no humbug about it. They are almost naked & will let you inspect their goods & push the sword down their throat yourself & see it make the skin of their stomach project out & keep hold of the hilt yourself and pull it up again. Then you get a bheestee[31] who pours water through a pipe into one nostril & out it comes in a stream from the other or mouth. Then this fellow lifted up a heavy weight with his eyelid. In fact, he performed so many wonderful tricks that if this was not a very enlightened age he would be scragged to a certainty for having dealings with the devil.

I don't know what Phil means by going down the country again. We go to Umballa next, which is farther north & from there in all probability to Lahore or some of the new hill Stations about to be formed and shan't be coming down again towards Calcutta for years. The Col[onel] has obtained leave for us to march via Delhi, so we shall see the highest tower in the world & one of the most ancient & finest towns in India & it only makes two or three marches difference. Before we turn our faces to Calcutta again I shall be as black as coal for I have already arrived at Mahogany colour.

I was very sorry to hear of Mr. Coleman's death - a better fellow never breathed. I saw it first in the newspapers on Xmas day. I hope they will allow Leonard to retain the Army List. Keep a sharp look out for my Ens[ign]s Commission or else it will be mislaid, not at all unusual, especially in the confusion by Coleman's death, & preserve it in a dry place. Thank Phil for his long letter of 23 Nov[ember] & tell him any communication from home gives me as much pleasure as mine can possibly give to any of you. But you all take every thing I say seriously. Now, I never was serious in my life & the Army [is] not the place to make you so, with a perpetual war waging in the Bungalow & first one & then another being chased about & pelted with anything that comes, first pulled out of bed, ducked &c. &c. if you chance to wish to lay late, which I fortunately very seldom do. Poker & I carried Tammy out of bed into the middle of the garden the other day & after I had been

---

31. Water carrier

98

to the balls I was obliged to place a large supply of water & a
long bamboo at my bed side with which I defended myself &
enjoyed my rest for some hours longer than I should otherwise
have been able to do. No quarrelling here, altho' we have been
together ever since we have been in the country. Tammy & Poker
are the jolliest fellows possible. We ride one another's
horses, bully one another, put salt in one another's tea at
breakfast, lick one another, and play all kinds of practical
jokes. In fact, there is not a Bungalow in the lines which
affords one half of the amusement of ours. Cahill, our fourth
fellow, however is a perfect disguster, scarcely on speaking
terms with anybody - quite a bear, without an idea above
collecting pice.[32] But he affords us amusement as a butt, for
we take rises out of him whenever he shows his face outside his
own room & make him retire growling, to our infinite enjoyment.

I am sorry to hear from Phil dear Mother is poorly. I wish
I could give her some of our clear blue sunny skies, with the
Ther[mometer] 64, which I think would assist in restoring her.
& I am sorry to hear of the smash in Barclay's house. I hope
John & Arthur will get something as good. Remember me to Mr.
Stewart & son & Gurney & tell the two latter if they have
leisure to write & wish to know anything of the land of the East
I shall be happy to communicate with them. How is Annie and
your *butchas* (young 'uns). Tell Ellen I hope she superintends
their morality, and request Aunt Lin not to teach them·to scream
at a spider & faint on the shortest notice, or any other of the
minor descriptions of *gammon* practised by the fair sex. And
tell Aunt Kate not to teach them to *wink* at every young fellow
they see, & ask Sawbones[33] to teach them to smoke in order to
endure my hookah when I return. Fancy the little imps (don't
tell Annie I called them imps) calling you *Pa*. What a Pa!
Why, an aligator would make as good a one. Now, don't get
savage or else I will write to Annie and Chris to lick you.
Remember me to Uncle Walter & my Aunts & Cousins & tell Chris
to write & tell me how he is getting on. I hope Father is
enjoying his usual health and that you play him at cribbage to
make his winter evenings pass merrily, & that you don't insist
on doubling Mother at Vingt'un.[34] But my Khitmutgar has just
placed tiffin on the table in the South verandah, my paper is
full, & the Express has just arrived, so with love to all

I remain your affectionate brother
Alfred.[35]

---

32. Small coin, 1/4 Anna or 1/64 Rupee.
33. Christopher.
34. A card game.
35. With this letter is a plan of the bungalow (thatched with
    straw) which Alfred shared with Dr. Moorhead, Birtwhistle
    & Cahill. Fourteen servants are listed, plus, in some
    cases, wives and families.

III

MEERUT TO UMBALLA TO FEROZEPORE
(February to July 1848)

The 32nd Regiment left Meerut for Ambala on 14
February 1848 and arrived there on 1 March, having
taken fifteen days for the march of 167 miles.
However, they stayed there for only six weeks, for
after the assassination of Mr. Vans Agnew,
Assistant Resident at Lahore, and Lieutenant
Anderson of the Bombay Fusiliers at Mooltan on the
20 April – the beginning of the Second Sikh War –
the regiment was moved to Ferozepore, suffering
severely from heat on the march of twelve days in
the hot season (15-27 May).

27. *Meerut gossip – Begum Somroo & Sirdhana – description of
Delhi – Delhi to Kurnaul – Kurnaul to Ambala – life at
Ambala*

Alfred Bassano to Philip Bassano   Umballa
(No. 18)   18 March 1848

Dear Phil
    Time flies merrily on & I am now seated in a comfortable
room in a comfortable Bungalow at the above place fully
prepared to astonish your weak intellects with an increased
catalogue of the wonders of the East, granted that Mopsticks
has received my last, *No. 17*, dated 20 Jan[uary] & containing a
plan of my late Bungalow.

    Well, now I'm off. For some time after that chit our chief
source of amusement was with Madocks of the 98th who used to
get screwed every night at Mess, & in that state made to perform
the most ludicrous absurdities by the wags of the Reg[imen]t.
And the next morning fictitious letters were written to him
demanding an apology for some supposed insult, the hoax always
succeeding & affording additional fun. However, he managed to
sell us all a bargain the last night of his stay in Meerut.
There was a large dinner party in one of the Bungalows and late
in the evening when the party began to wax noisy & facetious
the jests were suddenly put a stop to by Madocks falling off
his chair apparently in fits, imitating the convulsions of a
dying man to perfection. All was confusion. Dr. C. was roused
up from bed to see him & was taken in by the alarming symptoms
as well as the rest & began to prepare to bleed him, when he
jumped up and laughed in their faces to the great disgust of
the Bones & amusement of the rest of us. It will always be a
standing joke against the D[octo]r.

100

Tell Melinda I received her letter of 1st Dec[ember] in which
she appears to be bothered about Tom's & my description of a
bungalow.[36] I don't suppose he ever saw a Bungalow - there are
none in the seaport towns he sees, both Officers & Men are in
B[arrac]ks. You might as well look for a *villa* in the heart of
the city. He misapplies the word to the mud huts in which the
native population reside from one end of India to the other, the
proper Hindustani name of which is "ghur". Bungalows are
detached houses built by Europeans expressly for Europeans at
full-batta stations where the Off[ice]rs are given an allowance
in lieu of quarters, & are large houses built of brick, with
very few exceptions all the rooms on the ground floor, &
generally thatched roofs. In fact, if you took away the
verandahs you would imagine them farm houses in England.

Another Sub[altern] has cut to England to sell or exchange
(Hedley), a capital fellow. We gave him a night of it as usual,
chaired him round the room & saw him into his palki gari[37] at 3
in the morning, after dancing a hornpipe on the supper table.

On the 8th Feb[ruary] I rode over from Meerut to Sirdhana
where the Begum of Somroo, who died some years ago, held her
Court. I dare say you have seen her Son, Dyce Somroo, who
lately quitted England to come back to this country. It must
have been a flourishing place in the Begum's time. I called on
the Padre at St. John's College, a fine building containing a
printing press which was being worked, & saw a lot of nigger
students & obtained a guide who took us over the Catholic
Chapel, a most beautiful building with two lofty spires &
several small & beautiful domes peculiar to the architecture of
the East. The inside is elegantly carved and the end next the
altar tastefully inlaid with various coloured marbles. It was
built & endowed by the Begum & planned by an Italian in her
service. We afterwards visited the palace, a fine building now
uninhabited & falling into decay. Many of the rooms are hung
with large portrait paintings, some full length, of the Begum
& the European adventurers of various nations attached to her
court. There is a fine billiard table, rests & cues all rotting,
in one large room. The vapour bathrooms & plunging bath are
superbly executed in marble. We afterwards inspected some
smaller residences built for the Europeans of her Court,
elegantly fitted up with fountains, terraces, groves, vineries,
& everything likely to make exile sweet to a European. But the
fountains are choked up, the terraces are crumbling away, & the
groves, vineries, & flowers have perished in the embrace of rank
& poisonous creepers. There's sentiment for you. The Begum
was a convert to the Roman Catholic faith & died upwards of
eighty, leaving immense wealth. In fact we spent a delightful

---

36. See Chapter One, Letter 16.
37. A sort of palanquin on wheels.

day inspecting the late Begum's quarters, but altho' surrounded
by so much food for reflection we were unsentimental enough to
require food of a more substantial description & our Servants
having picquetted our horses in a grove & spread out a substantial
repast on the ground we lounged on the tombstones of some old
mussulmen & refreshed the inner man, amusing ourselves in the
meantime by giving an old faquir & his Son - who had got over the
prejudices of their caste not to be above drinking the good things
of this world - beer & brandy & cheroots, until the young chap
got most amusingly *mutwala*,[38] pitching into the Natives & singing
& dancing to a ludicrous extent, amusing us till the cool of the
evening when we rode home. A few days after we dined with the
9th Lancers, got a complimentary speech from the Brig[adier] on
parade, & at 4 o'Clock in the morning of 14 Feb[ruary] last, to
the tune of "Paddy will you now", we amputated our canes for
Umballa.

The first two days march nothing particular - country flat as
a pancake & well cultivated, interspersed with topes - villages
small mud ones, the ruins of a serai - out shooting, & bathed in
the Jumna. The third day we marched *13 Miles*, crossed the
Jumna by a bridge of boats and encamped outside the Lahore gate
of Delhi. The town is surrounded by a high wall & with its
lofty towers & minarets presenting the finest appearance of any
Indian Town I have yet seen. The principal street[39] is very
broad, with a water course running down the centre.

Rode out to see the *Cootub*[40] *11 miles off*, the most beautiful
& the highest tower in the world. It is built of red granite,
fluted & carved most superbly. The wall at the bottom was
three times as thick as the length of my walking stick. The
view from the top is principally comprised of the most extensive
& beautiful ruins of temples & all kinds of buildings and
carvings in white marble most tastefully executed. We wandered
about them inspecting as many as our time would admit of, lost
in admiration, & like Byron, disgusted with old Father Time -
see 18th stanza of the Siege of Corinth: "There is a temple in
ruin stands, Fashioned by long forgotten hands; Two or three
columns & many a stone, Marble & granite, with grass o'ergrown!
Out upon time! it will leave us no more Of the things to come
than the things before! Out upon time! who for ever will leave
But enough of the past for the future to grieve O'er that which
hath been, & o'er that which must be; What we have seen, our
sons shall see; Remnants of things that have passed away,
Fragments of stone, rear'd by creatures of clay!"[41]

---

38. Drunk
39. Chandni Chowk
40. Q'tub Minar, built c.1200 A.D., 238 ft. high.
41. Published 1816.

Amongst these ruins is a very large well of immense depth
which the Natives for a few annas jump down with their legs &
arms extended, closing the former just before they reach the
water. They then swim under an archway into a tank & ascend
again by an immense flight of steps. They seem to think nothing
of it, rushing out of their houses directly they know of the
arrival of visitors & jumping down one after the other till
you stop them, or all the village would be down in less than no
time.

On my return from the ruins I visited Hindoo Rao's[42] house
(the great tiger sportsman) & was shown through the rooms, well
furnished in the English style, with a great many beautiful
tiger skins spread over the floor. The garden is well laid out
& contains a tower commanding a most magnificent view. There
is also a large wooden cage containing a tame tiger called
"Motee" (the pearl) which the servants pat & caress. I then
visited the Cantonments, which are the prettiest & most comfortable I have ever seen in this country. I then rode to the
Mall, where the Bands play of an evening, excellently situated,
& saw a carriage full of the prettiest English ladies I have
seen in the East. Not a bad day's work, after a thirteen mile
march, but I was in the ancient capital of India & I determined
to make the most of my time, so I gave two horses a pretty hard
day's work.

Now for my second day at Delhi. I rode to the Jumna Musjeed,
a splendid mosque in the heart of the city with three domes &
two lofty minarets, the interior of white marble beautifully
inlaid with black. From the top of the minarets we had a very
fine view of the city, the flat white roofs of the houses, where
the Natives pray, not being obscured by smoky chimneys, had a
very pretty effect. The inhabitants keep immense flights of
pigeons which they drive up & with a flag at the end of a stick
make them fly in any direction they like. The streets are wide
& the shops well stocked & many of the houses well built, but
the goods heaped together - everything presenting the appearance
of dirt, wretchedness, & cheap & gaudy splendour peculiar to
this country. I then visited the King's palace surrounded by
an immense wall of red granite. The interior contains some of
the most beautiful workmanship I ever saw - white marble carved
into the most extraordinary & tasty designs & inlaid with
coloured stones representing in their natural colours birds &
flowers, & from the beauty & extent of the carving & inlaying
I should imagine must have taken one of the richest men in the
world a long life to get completed. Yet it appears to be
unappreciated by the present generation, who build up mud huts
against, & cover with filth, & allow to fall into ruins the most

---

42. Hindu Rao, a Maratha chief, d.1855.

durable & beautiful carvings in the world.[43]   The King of Delhi[44]
is under the protection of the Company & has got about the
palace an immense number of little boys, dressed in a dirty
uniform, half-european, their muskets, which they can scarcely
carry, twice the size of themselves. In one courtyard of the
palace about a hundred birds called "Bulbuls" are kept, being
braced by twos on an upright stick, with a crosspiece, & about
fifty servants to look after them. They are kept to amuse young
royalty. In the evening I again rode to the Mall, about two
miles & a half off, where *our band* played & astonished the
Natives. This concluded my second day at Delhi & by daylight
next morning we had drummed ourselves out.

From Delhi to Kurnaul the roads are sandy, country flat &
sometimes jungly, villages dirty & disgusting, old ruins,
especially of temples, abound - one of our baggage elephants
fell down dead in the road - large parties out daily shooting
& coursing, both of which amusements I take my part in, but
prefer the latter much - the Camp overflowing with game
including bucks, partridges, hares, snipe, ducks, quail, &
peafowl - passed a good sized canal & encamped at Kurnaul,
formerly containing two Queen's & several of the Company's
Regiments, but discontinued as a Station for troops in 1843 in
consequence of its unhealthiness - the extensive lines, Church
& fine Bungalows in all directions in a state of more complete
ruin than would take place in any other country in ten times
the number of years. Most of the Bungalows are roofless, the
roads overgrown with bushes & *trees*, & this apparently fine
Station presents in every direction the most desolate appearance.
Quitted it the next morning & passed two or three days as usual
shooting &c. & arrived at Thanesir, a large Hindoo town
celebrated for the virtue of its tank where the Natives bathe,
& containing a very elegant temple & one European Bungalow.
Two days after marched into Cantonment & took a Bungalow with
Poker & Tammy & dined with the 3rd Dr[agoon]s.

On the following Sunday went to Church in the morning. The
building where the service is performed is about a mile from
our lines & is little better than a large barn supported by
pillars of timber in their rough & crooked state, & full of
sparrows, chirping, fighting, & flying about the pulpit &
rafters all church time. The clergyman that preached is a
great sportsman & had just returned from a tiger expedition
having shot nine during a month absence. This Station is very
similar to Meerut, a large common, the Men's Bungalows (one
per Company) built along one side, a sufficient distance to
accomodate all the Reg[imen]ts, then the Off[ice]rs Bungalows

---

43. The Red Fort, built by the Emperor Shah Jehan in the
    17th century.
44. Bahadur Shah, last Mogul emperor, a pensioner of the British.

with large Compounds (gardens) in rows intersected with roads, then the native town of mud huts interspersed with large houses occupied - (by enterprising Natives or Europeans, generally old pensioners or Serjeants that have purchased their discharge) - as warehouses for the sale of all kinds of European articles of comfort, from a toothpick to a carriage. We have licked the Art[illery] here at cricket in one innings, & the 3rd Dr[agoon]s gave us a ball on the 10th, an unusually good one for India. Bungalows are unusually dear here & the roads sandy & bad - in fact it is not near such a pretty & civilized looking station as Meerut, but all our amusements are amongst ourselves, so we don't care a damn where we are stationed, in fact we are gainers by the change, for there is a capital pack of hounds here & we are already invited to the meets, so I anticipate a splendid addition to our sports.

Here the letter was laid aside for a few days, as I found I was not obliged to close it so soon as I expected, during which time we have had two or three dust storms with strong winds, the former put a stop to by some heavy showers of rain accompanied with thunder & lightning - Ther[mometer] 78 in the Bungalow every day. I have already been out once with the hounds (7 couple of Very good dogs) but our day's sport was rather below par, for altho' it ended in the death of a fox it was a very indifferent run over too clear a country for any [letter torn] excitement, but we are looking forward to better sport after the showers.

The Maj[or] Gen[eral] here, Sir *Walter Raleigh* Gilbert, has sent us an invitation to a ball at his house, but I don't think I shall go, for a ballroom loses its charms when you find all the ladies there linked in the bonds of matrimony to a lot of liverless old Soldiers. I must say there is no disposition wanting on the part of the married people at *this* Station to be social, & if you chose to call & put yourself in the way of it, you get plenty of invitations to dinner, but the 32nd are not old enough Indians yet to enjoy such wretched substitutes for English gaiety, & as they cannot go out in the sun much with impunity, prefer "reclining all day, on an ottoman gay" in the society of European literature & Indian cheroots, varied by the parades or rides in the mornings & evenings. Off[ice]rs are not nearly as bored with duty in this country - three days a week we have a parade which lasts from *six* till about *7 in* the morning. The *remainder* of the day we *are free* two days a week, on which we have nothing at all to do - on the sixth day at 11 o'c[lock] we have to inspect the Men's kits of our Comp[any] (about a quarter of an hour's job), & on the seventh we go once to Church. I like this indolent life very well, as it enables me to indulge my taste for reading, which I find no trouble in gratifying to any extent, as we possess amongst ourselves, or in our library which is supplied with the new works from England, *all* the standard works of past & present Authors, including the

Waverley novels I so often longed to finish, Bulwer's &c. &c. &c.
&c. &c.

Having nothing to do & the temperature being delightful I have
spun this letter out unconsciously to a second sheet, which
prevents my sending you with it a picture of the Jumna Musjid,
but you may expect it in my next. I have not rec[eive]d a letter
lately from Tom, altho' I wrote one to him not long ago.

I suppose you are all disgusted at the extraordinary runs of
promotion *by purchase*, which by this time I suppose in England
must have gazetted some of my juniors to Lieutenancies. Ens[ign]
Steuart is promoted in general orders in this Country. But I am
not justified in considering myself unlucky yet, so I take it
cooly, especially as Steuart intends to exchange to get to
England, so I consider I have yet a very good chance of resuming
my original position.

I was very sorry to hear of the failure of Barclay & Co. I
hope there is yet a chance of their resuming business & of John
& Arthur being all right again. How is Annie & the *batchas*?
Tell her it was Walter told me the youngest *chockree*[45] squinted,
not Ellen. Remember me to all at home, for I must heave to,
hold hard, halt, or stop this letter, or else you will never be
able to read it, for I wrote it small & close that I might not
have to cross. I hope the ensuing English summer will restore
Mother to her wonted health – (she was poorly when I last heard
from home – "Aside", about six months ago). I wish I could send
her in the middle of winter some of the balmy & perpetual
sunshine I enjoy. Well, may I be rammed, jambed, & crammed if
I cross a second page for any one so

Believe me *hona*
Tumhara pyara bhai[46]
Alfred

28. *From Ambala to Ferozepore, "a disorderly rabble" – conditions
at Ferozepore*

Alfred Bassano to F.M. Bassano   Ferozpore
(No. 20)   3 June 1848

My dear Father
    Off again you see. I had scarcely got settled in my Bungalow
at Umballa comfortably, & arranged my plans of amusement – out
with the hounds three times a week, getting some very good runs
– tamed a wolf which ran about the compound – buried a General –

---

45. Little girl.
46. Believe me, I am your dear brother, Alfred.

106

drank the promotion wine of the last batch of lucky fellows –
enjoyed the blaze of some Artillery stables being burnt down &
had an offer of a room at Simla if I went on leave – than we
were cooly told on evening parade that we were to march that same
night at 12 o'clock, afterwards finding out to our extreme
disgust that the Col[onel] (*Pattoun*) had had the order at 9 in
the morning & never let any body know. The greatest confusion
pravailed. The Servants & baggage of those who had been suddenly
ordered to rejoin from leave at Simla not having yet arrived, we
were obliged to cram our things into our trunks & drawers & did
not obtain our hackeries & camels till about ten at night, &
marched off before one o'clock, leaving our tents, baggage &
Servants in the greatest confusion, to follow just when those
lazy pipe-smoking brutes chose. We arrived at Canour, a
distance of 17 or 18 Miles, at 7 o'clock – not a single tent
pitched on our arrival & no Mess to obtain anything to eat or
drink, both Off[ice]rs & Men laying down in the shade of trees
& bushes, overcome with fatigue & disgust, not at the privations
of the march at such an inclement season of the year, but at the
selfishness & want of consideration shown by Col. Pattoun to the
feelings & comforts of those under his command, both Off[ice]rs
& Men, without an exception, ardently wishing for Col. M[arkham],
who has not yet had time to rejoin from leave to reassume the
command.

Our sudden Route to Ferozpore is to protect the frontier,
from whence, in Oct[ober] or Nov[ember], we are to march with an
Army to Mooltan to lick Moolraj, the Rajah, who keeps a force of
sixty thousand Men & has had the audacity to murder two British
Officers.[47] So you see all the rot in the papers about Lord
Hardinge having established eternal peace in India is all my
eye,[48] & if you heard the accounts of eyewitnesses of all ranks,
including Private Soldiers, you would not have much opinion of
the merits or Generalship displayed in the late actions.

Well, we scrambled through the march almost roasted in our
tents during the day (Ther[mometer] 114), snatching an hour's
or two's repose in the open air at night, having to get up at
11 or 12 to march off again, the Men straggling all over the
country. In fact, the Lilies, from being a splendid & highly
disciplined Corps under Col. M[arkham] are a disorderly rabble
under Col. P[attoun]. The country flat & sandy, interspersed
with jungle & cultivation, including some beautiful gardens full
of pomegranates, orange, lime & mango trees. Our worst march
was from Wadnee to Bhaga Poorana, a distance of twelve miles &
a half, a hot wind blowing all the way, & in consequence of this

---

47. Vans Agnew and Lt. Anderson.
48. Governor-General, 1844-8. Hardinge left India in 1848
    convinced that "it would not be necessary to fire another
    shot in India for seven years".

[the] left wing, not having heard the advance after a halt, they
lost their way during a violent dust storm, the guide being with
the right wing – the Reg[imen]t being with great difficulty
reunited by the exertions of the Off[ice]rs in riding in all
directions to find the right wing. *Capt. Gardiner* fell off his
horse & died in a few minutes. One of the Serjeants carrying
the colours & several Men fell down in the road with fits of
apoplexy, two dying shortly after. One Man of long Service went
a little distance from the road on the march & committed suicide
by shooting himself. *Immense* numbers fell out sick. Our few
doolies[49] were soon filled & the remainder were left laying in
the road to be picked up by hackeries or camels, like dogs, one
man being brought into Camp dangling to a Camel quite dead, &
by the evening the total number of deaths were seven. A coffin
was made for the late Capt. Gardiner of two tables, & the Men
were all sewed up in their bedding & buried side by side in a
separate hole before their bodies were cold, one Service doing
for all, large drops of rain falling, & forked & sheet lightning
in rapid succession flashing on the drawn swords & fixed
bayonets of Off[ice]rs & Men during the performance of this
impressive ceremony, after which we marched back to Camp, the
Band playing "Love not ye hopeless sons of clay". For the
remainder of the march we got on very well.

I visited the scene of the actions at Moodkee & Ferozeshah,
both of which places we passed, as to save time the Reg[imen]t
marched across country. A great number of bones, a few mounds
of earth, & the trace of an intrenchment, nearly choked up with
sand, is all that now marks the battle fields – the mud villages
& surrounding country, especially of Moodkee, looking unusually
thriving & well cultivated.

On our arrival here we found only two empty Bungalows –
already boned for the bigwigs. The Married Officers are crammed
into the church & left to divide it into compartments as they
like, getting out of canvass during this season of this year,
being thought of more consequence than religious instruction.
The *Sub*[altern]*s*, alas, are clapped into a large building used
as the Hospital of a Native Reg[imen]t, which they have politely
given up to us, & a pretty Bedlam we have turned it into. Boxes
& chests of drawers form the only divisions & whilst some are
smoking & singing, others are sending melons & eggs from their
breakfast tables at the heads of those more intellectually
employed. Others are trying to cut down the sparrows with their
hunting whips as they fly past, the building being full of them.
In the midst of which a dust storm comes on, fills all the
houses, so that you can scarcely see a yard, nearly chokes the
inmates & smothers your bed & tables to a frightful extent, our
heads looking as if they were covered with hoar frost & our

---

49. Litters.

faces like sweeps in ten minutes. But we are all very merry on
the thoughts of an approaching campaign. Many more Reg[imen]ts
are on their way up to the frontier & we are already belonging
to a moveable Brigade, which *designation* confers upon us the
distinction of keeping Coolies, Coolassies, & Camels in perpetual
pay, & ourselves ready to march at an hour's notice, without any
addition to our income. So you see affairs appear to be as
critical here as in Europe, which from the papers, I expect to
hear soon is in a blaze.[50] In fact, the Army is the only place
to enjoy peace in now-a-days, for being paid to fight, we don't
care what turns up, whereas you peaceful members of Society must
be in great danger of being disturbed by the riots & revolutions
which appear to be increasing in your quarter of the globe.

About the time you receive this I expect you will see my name
in the Gazette as a L[ieutenan]t, dated *24 May 48*, in which case
I don't think I can well complain of my luck, especially as I
have hopes of resuming my original position still by the
exchanges of those above me, & anticipate many changes to carry
me up the list of L[ieutenan]ts. I was sorry to see in the paper
the death of Mr. Hughes, as Walter got his promotion by it.

Give my love to Mother, Ellen & Lin, Annie & young ones, & tell
them I would write more but the Weather is so hot that I am
obliged to be wrung out & hung up to dry after every ten lines.
In addition to which a deputation from a noisy party of
Sub[altern]s close by this moment came to me to know if I would
have any mug as they were about to make a brew. These dis-
advantages will account for the blots & mistakes in the spelling,
if there are any in this letter from

Your affectionate Son
Alfred

Remember me to all my Relations & enquiring friends & tell
them we are beginning to sharpen our swords & expect the
Col[onel] to join tomorrow.

Authentic information for the Horse Guards, if not already
known - Capt. Gardiner, 32nd Regt. *died 23 May 1848* on the march
from Umballa to Ferozpore.

---

50. 1848 the year of revolutions.

29. *Dust storms at Ferozpore – amusements*

Alfred Bassano to Walter Bassano	Ferozpore
(No. 21)	3 July 1848

My dear Special Constable[51]
  I perceive by your letter of 2nd May (rec[eive]d 17 June)
that the world is wagging at home as it was wont to do in days
of yore, except that the department of wit must be rather
deficient, but I suppose you have learnt by this time to be able
to laugh at bad jokes without distressing yourselves.

This would have been the place for Mark Tapley to have tried
to be jolly in, for our opinions formed a few days after our
arrival, during which time the weather was clear & cool, that
it was not such a bad Station, have undergone an entire change.
The Ther[mometer] ever since has ranged in our Bungalow,
artificially cooled, from 96 to 102 day & night, and *dust storms*
almost every other day. One of a most violent description
accompanied by thunder, vivid lightning, & a little rain, caught
us at dinner in the Mess tent in the middle of the first course,
obliging us to jump up & even assisted by all our Khitmutgars &
Mess Servants having the greatest difficulty in preventing the
tent from being blown clean away, by clinging on it in all
directions, the dust in a few minutes covering the tables, half
filling the plates, encrusting the Meats, & reducing us to a
filthy state. It was fortunately, however, of short duration,
& the second course, thanks to the cooks, having escaped dust
free, we had the tables cleaned, resumed our places more like
dustmen than Off[ice]rs, passed the rosy, & laughed at our
misfortunes. Sometimes we wake in the morning, if so fortunate
as to have slept through the storm, with our eyes & nose filled
with dust, our hair quite white, & the bed clothes & every thing
in our rooms smothered. They say here that it will penetrate
through glass. Be that as it may, brick walls & wooden doors
let it in to a disgusting extent, a fact I am made painfully
aware of rather oftener than is pleasant.

Another dust storm came on so suddenly a few evenings ago
during the time devoted to riding up & down the Mall & hearing
the Band play, that before any one could escape all was utter
darkness & confusion. Some managed to grope their way home,
leading their horses or buggies, but by far the greater number
lost their way & wandered about, or stood still, until the storm
began to abate three or four hours after, when some of our
fellows found themselves on the other side of the Station, &
King, who was driving a buggy & made great efforts to find his
way home, was at last stopped by a wall where he pulled up &

---

51. 170,000 special constables were sworn in during Chartist
    agitation of 1848.

110

gave over the attempt, sitting patiently in his buggy till it
cleared up some hours after, when he made the pleasing discovery
that he had run his horse's nose against *his own* Bungalow wall &
been there for hours. I had fortunately overridden my cattle in
the morning & was sitting outside the Bungalow puffing a manilla
when I looked up & saw an immense black cloud of dust coming up
at a tremendous pace. I just had time to get into the Bungalow
& have all the doors shut before it came upon us & it was 11 at
night, instead of 8 o'C[lock] before dinner could be placed upon
the table for the dust, altho' we now mess in a Bungalow. But
I must change the subject, for dust storms are so numerous here
& nearly always attended with some ludicrous adventures of some
unhappy victim (generally the orderly Officer) that this letter
will be full of nothing else.

However we console ourselves with reflecting upon the
impossibility of finding a more infernal hole for a Station for
civilized beings on the face of the earth, but as we are certain
of quitting, either to take the field, if necessary, or changing
quarters, some time in Sept[ember] next, we have not found it
necessary to cut our throats or take laudanum at present. The
only redeeming quality about this place is that we get lots of
foxes & have already hunted seventeen, embracing a few slashing
runs. We have also worried two polecats, killed with hunting
whips about thirty brace of sparrows, inside the Bungalow where
they build, for chirping (16 brace in one morning), had several
races amongst ourselves, one Station Ball, a supper, several
feast nights at Mess, celebrating *promotion*, the *victim of it*
giving iced champagne (the custom of the Reg[imen]t from time
immemorial). I have not given mine yet, altho' I have appeared
in General Orders as a pucka *Lieut*[enant] & expect several steps
on the improved grades shortly – not such bad luck either, I
calculate.

By the by, there was very nearly a duel the other day between
two pugnacious L[ieutenan]ts in the Reg[imen]t (both Irishmen) –
times fixed, seconds found, &c., when one, a great blusterer,
after swearing he would not compromise the matter, funked &
apologised, which was a great pity, for we looked forward to
this playful little interlude as a means of driving away the
ennui of this dull place for one day at least.

I send you a picture of a Native Woman sitting working a
handmill,[52] which will give you an excellent idea of the costume
of many of the lower orders, altho' of course it varies much,
some wearing loose flowing robes &c. &c. &c. As they are a
very saving people they carry their wealth made up into silver
ornaments which they wear on their ancles, arms, fingers, &c. –
see picture. You must not imagine the clothes clean, but a

---

52. See plate, p. 112.

vile effluvia to issue from that gaudy Kopra,[53] which obliges
you to hold your nose as you pass. But they are by no means all
so profuse of clothing as the enclosed specimen – numbers of Men,
& some few women that have fallen under my own observation,
having about as much clothes as would make a child's pocket
handkerchief each. If any one of you want any more pictures
illustrative of the costumes of the country write & in the
answer I will enclose one, or a precious stone (already cut),
in every future reply (Davies having sent several of the latter
in letters which have safely arrived) & I have a supply of
bloodstones, cornelians, agates, &c. by me. A facetious
Sub[altern] has just brought down an Adjutant with his rifle &
dragged it into the Bungalow. It is eight feet from wing to
wing, & I enclose a feather I have just extracted from under his
tail, having a suspicion that they are what the *gals* in England
call Marabout feathers. Remember me to all at home & tell them
if they want a Native's picture or precious stone to drop a line.
Tell Annie to Khubradar ho of the butchas,[54] & don't you teach
them to take a sight at

Your affectionate brother
Alfred Bassano
Lieutenant
H.M. Lilies

"A Native Woman sitting working a handmill"

---

53. Clothing.
54. Be careful of the children.

CHAPTER THREE

"No longer a feather bed soldier but a <u>veteran</u>"
(The Second Sikh War 1848-9)

While stationed at Ferozpore the 32nd Regiment
received orders to join the Multan Field Force.
They marched out of Ferozpore on 10 August and on
the 25th joined the force under General Whish,
forming part of the left column. They then went
down the Sutlej to join the right column which had
moved from Lahore, and four marches more brought
them to the city of Multan. The regiment suffered
terribly from the heat on the march and lost many
men. Lieutenant Alfred Bassano, however, now aged
22, had gone ahead with the siege train - by river
to Bhawalpur and then across country to Multan,
where they arrived on 4th September to join the
rest of the army. General Whish had under his
command 8000 troops, with some regular & irregular
levies under Van Courtlandt, Edwardes and Lake,
and a body of 5000 Sikhs under Sher Singh - a
grand total of 14,327 infantry and 8417 cavalry,
with 45 guns and 4 mortars, as against Mulraj's
force of about 10,000 men.

On the 12th September the enemy's advanced
positions were attacked and captured, but on the
14th September Sher Singh and his Sikhs defected
and joined Mulraj, and the first siege was raised,
the army withdrawing a few miles to await fresh
troops from Bombay. The reinforcements arrived
at the end of December and the siege was resumed,
with 32,000 men and 150 guns. The city was
captured on 2nd January, and on the 22nd Mulraj
surrendered. General Whish's troops then marched
to join Lord Gough, capturing the fort of Cheniote
en route, and taking part on 21st February 1849 in
the battle of Gujarat which ended the war.

THE SIEGE OF MULTAN

30. *March to Multan - the first siege*

Alfred Bassano to F.M. Bassano   Camp before Mooltan
(No. 22)   September 1848

My dear Father
I have been so unsettled & engaged lately that I have not
been able to write a letter since the 3rd July (to Walter), but
now take up the pen with lots to say & the proud satisfaction of
being no longer a feather bed soldier, but a *veteran*, who has
outlived a sharp little affair - a short, *decisive, brilliant* &
meritorious action on a small scale - & many hairbreadth escapes,
& hope & have every reason to believe I'm in for some hard
fighting & severe Campaigns before this part of India is quieted.

After contradictory orders & rot enough to have tried the
patience of Job, & severe duty, & exposure to the sun enough to
have killed a horse, I had the luck to get out of Ferozpore with
the *first Detachment*, consisting of a Company and a half, &
embarked on board the Steam boats Comet & Meanee on the 31st
July, & proceeded down the river as a protection to the Siege
train, which was conveyed in boats - had a very jolly time of it.
I & another *Sub*[altern] had the Meanee all to ourselves, ran
aground several times - occasionally sticking for a day - bathed
in the river, saw aligators, took some pleasant walks in the
ennemy's country when the steamer was fastened to the banks, saw
Natives swimming down the river on bundles of sticks - the
facetious way they have of travelling an immense distance in a
day - & disembarked opposite Bhawulpoor on the 17 Aug[ust],
pitched our tents, established a little Mess & waited patiently
for the guns to be got out of the boats, bathed every day in the
river, gave a dinner to the Steamer *Nauticals*, got ourselves &
horses ferried across the river & rode to Bhawulpore, a very
pretty Indian town from the outside, embedded in palm trees &
surrounded by a canal, but dirty & wretched as usual in -
contains some very fine gardens however, from out of which I
plucked some of the most delicious pomegranates I have ever eaten

On the 29 Aug[ust] all the arrangements being completed, we
commenced perhaps one of the most confused marches I shall ever
see - a very few Europeans (2 or 300) & some Native Cavalry &
Infantry marching through an ennemy's country in charge of a
large siege train & sixteen thousand head of baggage cattle
(elephants, camels & bullocks), stretching for miles in the most
glorious confusion. We marched best part of every night - the
country was flat, sandy & uninteresting, interspersed with clumps
of jungle & watered by canals & channels cut from the rivers,

instead of wells as on the other side of the Sutledge – & arrived without any very serious accident than losing our way occasionally, & joined the remainder of the Reg[imen]t encamped before Mooltan [4th September]. A parade for all the Brigade ordered next day in front of Mooltan & a salute of 19 guns fired – answered by a ball from the Fort, which fell close in front of the Brigade. The town and fort are very strong & surrounded by gardens, topes of trees, & brick buildings & temples capable of being defended with great disadvantage to the besiegers. The town is very large & has a very pretty appearance from the outside. The white domes of the numerous temples & one bright blue one peeping from the palm trees & glittering in the sun has a very pretty effect.

6th Sept. A parade in the morning & report that the town is to be attacked tonight. A little excitement in consequence – mem[oranda] made, accounts squared, early dinners taken to prevent the possibility of being marched suddenly off on an empty stomach, swords sharpened (including my own), pistols loaded, & an immense deal of joking & facetiousness, which Off[ice]rs & Men must indulge in under any circumstances. The reported assault all moonshine. Guns as usual blazing away from the fort & town, night & day, principally at Lieut. Edwards'[1] rabble force in our pay, which has a skirmish or two every day with the ennemy in the most farcical manner, resembling stage fights, & always ending in the same way without any killed or wounded on either side.

7 Sept. Moved our camp nearer the town (now about two miles off), the Sappers & Miners & some Nat[ive] Inf[antry] sent out to commence operations, making trenches &c. Moved out with my Comp[any] & others (the right wing) to their relief at 6 p.m. & worked in the trenches, until relieved at 12 p.m. We were exposed during our work to the fire of two or three large guns, but the balls all whistled over our heads, or fell short, some-times unpleasantly near. I made myself as comfortable as possible under the circumstances, superintending my own Men's work, smoking or *reclining* on the *graves* of departed Natives, most conveniently situated for the purpose of watching or resting, being on a slight eminence, commanding a good view of the side from whence danger was to be anticipated, the ground being particularly adapted for a surprise, from the quantity of low jungle, topes &c. surrounding the town. N.B. The first time I was ever under fire.

8th Sept. Native Troops at work at the trenches during the day & wings of H.M. 10th & 32nd by night. Two or three Natives killed.

9th Sept. Fresh batteries constructed by Moolraj outside the

---

1. Later Sir Herbert Edwardes (1819-1868).

town to play upon us with more effect. The *Gun*[ners] & left
wing of the 32nd, with part of the 10th & the 49 N[ative]
I[nfantry] marched out to the trenches at 6 o'C[lock] p.m. & an
attempt made by *part* of *H.M. 10th* & *49 N.I.* to dislodge the
ennemy from a small building in a tope of trees near our first
parallel, which was loop-holed & defended with the courage of
desperation, & our troops were repulsed with the loss of about
60 or 70 killed & wounded, including two Off[ice]rs of the 49
N.I. desperately wounded. Great anxiety in Camp to know the
results of so much firing. Several round shot were thrown at
the same time right into the Camp, but fortunately pitched
between the tents. Col. Pattoun (of Ours) had his pony shot
under him & a ball through his cap.

10th Sept. Marched out at 12 o'C[lock] at night with the
right wing to relieve the Left, & worked under a brisk but
ill-directed fire until nearly daylight, when we were smartly
attacked from the tope, but soon drove them in again. The
round shot rattled about us like the devil. A *Native Artillery*-
man took to his heels like a frightened hare, followed by several
other *Natives*. Then a poor horse walked by with his bowels
hanging almost down to the ground. Then a European Artilleryman
limped by with his leg smashed. Then two of the Art[illery]
horses were killed with one shot & the rider's leg broken. Then
a poor fellow of our 3rd Comp[any] was borne down the trench by
four Men with a contusion on his head, succeeded by doolies
coming to carry away the killed & wounded, the bearers dropping
them with fright the moment a ball whistled by, & just before
their fire was silenced our Col[onel] Markham was shot in the
leg whilst exposing himself with rash gallantry. - Extracts
from my journal from actual observation.

11th Sept. Marched out with the right wing to occupy the
trenches for the night & enjoyed a splendid night's rest wrapped
in my cloak on the ground, as we were not required to work tonight, & are so accustomed to the perpetual fire kept up night
& day that it does not disturb us in the least.

12th Sept. Advanced in extended order with some Co[mpanie]s
of the 10th Foot, & Sepoys,[2] about 8 o'c[lock] a.m. Got into a
sharp fire from the trees & buildings in the topes - the Men
lost all order & regularity. 10th & 32nd men all mixed up
together ran up to the charge with a war whoop which must have
astonished the Seiks. Surrounded the buildings in the topes
which caused so much trouble previously & speedily carried them,
shooting & bayonetting every Man in the place. So suddenly was
the attack made & building carried that heaps of slain were

---

2. 6 Companies of 32nd Regiment; 6 Companies of 10th Regiment;
   3 Regiments of Native Infantry; 3 squadrons of Irregular
   Horse; and a troop of Horse Artillery were engaged.

piled up in every room. The remainder ran away in great
numbers pursued by the Men, & had not the bugle sounded the halt,
their trenches & batteries right up to the walls of the town
would have been speedily captured, but obedient to orders we
were obliged to content ourselves with occupying what we had
carried. The Lilies had five Co[mpanie]s engaged & lost four
men killed & thirty-five wounded, Col. Pattoun & Capt. Balfour
in entering the building at the front. The former was cut to
pieces & the latter dreadfully wounded, but now doing well.
Q[uarte]r M[aste]r Taylor was also killed & Capt. King,
Birtwhistle & Swinburne slightly wounded - rather sharp work,
for there were only 14 32nd Off[ice]rs engaged, out of which two
were killed & four wounded.

The Sepoys followed us very closely & bayonetted & shot the
wounded & despoiled the dead to a disgusting extent. Some of
the Men took prisoners, but they behaved so treacherously,
springing on their captors & trying to wrest their firelocks
from them & the Soldiers being quite infuriated & ungovernable,
shot them all. I saved one four or five times, but believe he
was shot immediately after I left him. A spent ball struck me
on the calf, but left no mark, & a Serjeant was mortally
wounded close at my side. The balls flew *singing* about as thick
as hail, occasionally varied by the rough *whistle* of a twelve
pounder close over your head, one of which came clean through my
Comp[any] whilst we were formed in close order, smack on the
chest & shoulder of one of my front rank men & breaking the leg
of the rear one, the former was killed on the spot & the latter
has had his leg taken off at the thigh. The *1st* Comp[any]
suffered more than any other - we had 2 killed & eight wounded.

Col. P[attoun] was a very plucky fellow, but sadly wanted
coolness. From the moment the firing commenced he forgot that
he commanded the force & rushed about like a madman & ultimately
fell foolishing [*sic*] attempting to enter the building with
ladders at its strongest point, when there was an entrance in
the rear, not barricaded & perfectly undefended, which any body
might have known, who was not in such a ridiculously excited
state as to be unable to use his eyes, the case, I am sorry to
say, with an immense number of the Men who, altho' as brave as
lions, are the damndest fools in Christendom, firing away their
powder & shot without any aim.

But I suppose the most interesting khubur[3] to you is relating
to myself. Well, whilst we were advancing I saw several men
all run out in rear of the building & escape to the town, &
instantly made the inference that wherever they got out was the
easiest place for us to get in, so I ran round the rear of the
building & the next moment found myself in the courtyard of the

___

3. News.

117

building, there being a doorway in the brickwork without a door, & I was not long kept in suspense as to the entrance to the building itself, for a hugh Seikh, armed to the teeth, jumped out at one of the windows about four feet from the ground, with the intention of also escaping to the town, but seeing me there before him he prepared for the attack & we might have had a very pretty little fight in the courtyard all to ourselves & we neither of us had any fire arms, but our amiable intentions were destined to be speedily & tragically frustrated, for several of my own Men, seeing me enter the building, came rushing up & one of them shot him between the eyes in a moment & down he fell, a corpse. We then entered the window & the work of destruction commenced. Every room was so full of Men that they impeded one another's motions. The consequence was, our Men stood at the doors & windows, nearly all of which were forced in by this time, & fired volleys into the rooms, where they fell over & over one another in heaps. They seemed to have an idea that the place could not be taken, for the rooms – at least some – were carpetted & furnished. Evidently some big-wig was killed in the place. There were also an old woman & child there. The latter was shot by some ruffian, but the former escaped the general massacre. In fact, it was just like a slaughter house, for altho' the Seikhs fight like devils, they have no chance against Britons. They get knocked over with the greatest contempt & confidence. The idea of a black man fighting a *gora loge*[4] is fortunately considered by the uncultivated & coarse Soldiers as too absurd to be admitted for one moment.

After the action the 1st Comp[any] were sent to hold a little mud cottage to the right, where we remained all night & day, exposed to the fire of their shot & shell, which was so badly directed that it only caused amusement. It was a calm moonlight night & the pariah dogs & jackals enjoyed themselves during the night, making a meal off one of our dead foes not four yards from one of my sentries, but it is astonishing how cool & indifferent we have become on such subjects. Our Khitmutgar brought us out plenty to eat & drink during the day, & my cooly – who stands fire uncommonly well – brought me out my cloak, a fresh supply of cheroots & a little of the cratur comfort for the night. Relieved next morning & marched back to Camp, thus ending the Campaign for the present, for on the night of the 14th the troops, stores, &c. were withdrawn & the trenches evacuated. Sher Sing, one of our Allies, having gone over to the ennemy with 5000 Men & some guns, it being found impossible to continue the works with only two European Reg[imen]ts & no British Cavalry, the climate & severe exposure to the broiling sun by day (110 in the shade) & colds & dews by night knocking up the Men & Off[ice]rs much faster than the ennemy could do with ten times the force. & we are now quietly encamped five or

---

4. White man.

118

six miles from the town with one weather eye open & lots of
support duty - our lodging being unpleasantly often on the cold
ground - waiting for reinforcements, when we shall resume our
works & lick them into fits, unless Moolraj takes it into his
head to attack our Camp, which he often facetiously threatens to
do, but I'm afraid he is too wide awake to put himself in the
way of getting such a licking as would be the result of attacking us on the open ground, in spite of our great disparity of
numbers.

I am quite well & jolly & intend soon to correspond with the
Military papers, signing myself an *old campaigner, one of the
undecorated*, &c. &c. I have not heard from home for a long long
time, but trust dear Mother & the family in its numerous
branches are all well & believe me to be your affectionate son,

A. Bassano.

28 Sept[ember] [18]48
Camp

One principal annoyance now is caused by the Native Cavalry
advanced Picquets & Sepoys, whose fears convert every cock
sparrow that settles on a bush into a Detachment of the ennemy,
& every sporting grass-cutter who goes a little farther out
than usual to get better grass for his Master's horse, is
converted into a Brigade, & in they come, running & galloping
into Camp with their wretched information, our unfortunate
selves being instantly turned out in the broiling sun, or sent
to spend the evening & night with our friends the jackals in
the jungle, the invariable result being another *sell* or a
Mare's nest. In fact, I would much rather be without them
altogether, for a more cowardly set of brutes don't exist. They
only show a bold front occasionally when acting with Europeans
who they know won't be licked at any price, so stick to them for
safety, but not on any duty by themselves - they are not worth
a damn. It was proved a day or two ago that they tried all the
morning to pot one of *our own Serdars*, but as their aim is
generally directed at the sun or stars, such a contingency is
not very likely to occur. Another time half the Reg[imen]t was
kept under arms all day in consequence of a strong report that
Moolraj was encamped on our old ground & intended to attack us.
It was even believed by a great many of our own fellows & very
strong arguments & different opinions were being furiously
advocated until the evening, when I mounted my horse, & without
saying a word to anyone (as it is contrary to orders) rode out
to the other Camp & found not a soul either there or near the
place. I then returned & proved my own opinion, got laughingly
reproved by Col. Markham, who was evidently delighted with my
breach of military discipline, & we have not had any additional
duties imposed on us since, a little trouble to ascertain the
correctness of the reports before turning us out being all that

119

is necessary & saving us from hours worked off our legs. I went
perfectly unarmed, but knowing that a good pair of spurs were
worth fifty brace of pistols, intended when I twigged the ennemy,
which I should have done a considerable distance before I got to
them, to turn my horse's head, apply the cold steel to his flanks
& there is not a man in Moolraj's wretchedly mounted cavalry that
could have come near me in a race to the Camp, with such a start.

It is currently reported here that when we have taken Mooltan
we are to march up to the Huzerah country to settle the differences of some sporting Natives, who are not sufficiently
acquainted with the British bayonet in those parts, so I hope to
become acquainted with the vale of Cashmere in time, & return to
England a great Eastern traveller. But in the mean time our
dinners here in the jungle consume best part of our pay &
drinking anything stronger than water is like refreshing yourself with liquid rupees.

31. *Skirmishes - building a battery - the attack of 7 November
- H.B. Edwardes*

Alfred Bassano to Melinda Bassano   Camp before Mooltan
(No. 23)   14 November 1848

My dear Lin
    I rec[eive]d your letter of 2nd Sept[ember] & am glad to hear
of Chris's success & long to see him in the Gazette. 5

    I suppose my letter 28 Sept[ember] to Father with the account
of the Action of the 12th Sept[ember] rather astonished you all.
But by the time this reaches you - at least it is to be hoped
so - you will be as much accustomed to hear of fights in which
I am engaged & read them as cooly as I take part in them, for I
assure you we have all become so used to being fired at that we
think nothing of it.

    From the date of my last letter to 29 of Oct[ober] nothing
particular occurred beyond the annoyances caused by false
alarms, generally partaking of the ludicrous, a loose horse one
night being magnified by a Sepoy Sentry into an attack by the
ennemy's Cavalry, wild goose chaces to catch Shere Sing with
ten thousand of the ennemy, ridiculous reconnoitring parties,
sleeping in the jungle all night when on outlying Picket, &
being almost blown up by our own rockets, which in the hands of
the Muffs who superintend them in this Brigade are much more
dangerous to friends than foes.

    On the morning of the 30th Oct[ober] I was taking my

_____

5. See Chapter Four.

accustomed ride, accompanied by Lowe & Stewart, when the former, thinking we were going too far from the Camp in an Ennemy's country & being only mounted on a small pony, returned. Stewart & I rode on until surprised, on being about to cross a large *nullah* (dry canal with banks on each side), by hearing shouts to our right, & turning round saw a number of villagers running & making signs for us to return, & on coming up told us there were twenty of Moolraj's Cavalry close by, & the next moment pointed to them defiling out of the Nullah to our left, & galloping to cut us off from the Camp. We instantly wheeled round & made for the angle of a village on the way back to Camp. It was a fair start & a beautiful race, but we soon found out the superiority of our steeds, & as they did not appear to have the fuses of their matchlocks lit, we began to chaff them, by reining in, letting them get very close, then putting in the spurs & shooting ahead again, until we got them in sight of our Cavalry Picket when it became their turn to bolt, pursued for a short distance by our Dragoons (fortunately for them *black ones*) or they would have repented their facetiousness. Two Squadrons of Cavalry & some guns were sent out about an hour afterwards & found three hundred men & several small guns on the other side of the nullah, which concealed them, & forced them to make a precipitate retreat. I had often ridden out much farther in the same direction & consequently knew the ground well, which favoured our escape, but had it not been for the devotion of the villagers in warning us of our danger, we should have crossed the Nullah & been made prisoners or mincemeat of.

From this date the Ennemy (forgetting the licking we gave them on the 12 Sept[ember]) became very impertinent, constructed a battery in a tope a considerable distance from the town, & set to blazing away night & day, the shot pitching very near our Camp & right into *that* of the humbug Edwards. Their Cavalry also began to hover about & several very exciting chases & skirmishes took place with our L[igh]t Cav[alry], & Irregulars, who killed & wounded a great many & brought in some grim looking *heads* & hung them up on the trees in front of the Camp.

The encamping grounds soon became too hot to hold Edwards & his rabble, & he requested the General would order the *Regulars* to construct a battery in front of *his* Camp, to protect him & silence their fire, in consequence of which six of our Companies were ordered out in the night (I was one of the victims *in Command of the 1st*) to comply with his request. It was pitch dark, & after blundering about in the jungle & being fired at for about two hours, we commenced sapping to form the Battery, the Engineers as usual giving very little information & contradicting one another every five minutes. However, by our own exertions we managed to make ourselves a little cover before morning when we returned to Camp having only had one man killed & a few wounded during the night. This sort of work continued by reliefs until the 5 Nov[ember] last, round shot &

small arm fire blazing away at us all the time, a good many, including Natives, being killed & wounded. I was out there three successive nights & slept as soundly as possible, wrapped up in my cloak, in spite of the noise & round shot pitching close to me. Well, we got the Battery finished at last & peppered away at theirs, but with very little effect, as was foretold by everyone with a spark of common sense from the first.

On the 6th Nov[ember] they attacked our Battery to try & capture the guns at a time when we only had 2 Comp[anie]s there, & the 72 N.I., but our fellows, well backed by the Sepoys, cheered, left the Battery, & charged them with the bayonet, which as usual soon started them, altho' there were some thousands opposed to us, but I am sorry to say with the loss of six & twenty killed & wounded of the two Companies of the Lilies engaged.

The next day Brigadier Markham took out a good force from the two Brigades & making a detour, attacked the Ennemy's position in the rear, which was defended by about ten thousand Men, & speedily captured it, capturing five brass guns, horses, bullocks, powder, shot &c. &c. Many of the ennemy were bayonetted at their guns, & a considerable number sabred by our Native Cavalry, who, as well as the Sepoys & Artillery, behaved remarkably well. Our loss was very trifling on account of the inequality of the ground, interspersed with clumps of jungle, which protected us from their fire when advancing, & the rapidity & decision with which we walked into them. I *commanded* the 1st Company, which formed part of the Reserve, & consequently thought I should be out of the best part of the fun, but Major Finnis, who commanded the *whole* of the *Reserve*, when the *British cheer*, or *Irish yell*, commenced, could stand it no longer, but waving his cap, lead us on amidst the cheers of the Men, slap into their Battery, in spite of the Rules & customs of War, to our great delight, which we very soon cleared, very few waiting for a dose of cold steel. We kept the Men very steady in this Action, & I did not allow *my* Men to fire a single round of ammunition, as there was not the slightest occasion for it. We killed a devil of a lot of them including their best Artillery-man, formerly in our Service & instrumental in the death of Anderson & Van[s] Agnew.

Since this second licking the Seiks have not shown their noses near the Camp, or caused us the slightest annoyance, & we are now quietly waiting for the reinforcements to prosecute the siege with, which are delayed so long in consequence of the general rising throughout the Punjab & the almost impossibility of sparing troops from one part of the Upper Provinces to assist the others, & the want of a sufficient number of European troops to protect so vast an extent of country.

The victories of *Edwards (the Wellington of the East)* are

all my eye & only existed in his shallow imagination. John Bull
has been most effectively gulled, & without waiting a sufficient
time to get at the facts of the case, has rewarded with a
B[reve]t Majority the greatest humbug in the Service. While he
is being lauded up to the skies in the public prints it is his
gross misrepresentations & exaggerations that has caused one
half of the mischief in the Punjaub, & instead of saving the
country millions has cost them tens of millions. The ennemy
have the greatest contempt for him & his Men. Four of our
Co[mpanie]s could drive his 7 or 8 thousand to Jericho, & Col.
Franks of the 10th swears he bought the guns which he says he
took in Action & that he has never fought a battle at all,
certainly not with any killed or wounded on either side. There
are a great many of the same opinion.

Remember me to all at home & tell them if I am extinguished
in the Mélée to look after my batta, which they say here is
almost certain to be forthcoming after the Campaign &

                    Believe me
                         Your affectionate brother
                         Alfred

A P.S.

Translation of the Inscription in Persian on one of the guns
taken by the force under the Command of Brigadier Markham on
the 7 Nov[ember] 1848. "This gun was made by Futteh Mahomed of
Lahore, pupil of Ahmud Yar, Son of the great Instructor. By
order of the Kalsagee (Runjeet Sing) high in power in the
Province of Mooltan, with a thousand contrivances, I who am
named Nursingbau, the Cloud Tearer, and aim at the heads of my
ennemies arrows like flashes of lightning, by the assistance of
the superior skill of Ahmud Yar came forth like burning fire, &
in the Hindoo Year 1878 I was ready for the destruction of my
ennemies." Note - the above mentioned year corresponds with
1821 of our Era, 3 years after Mooltan was taken by Runjeet Sing.

I have also got a translated copy of a letter picked up in
their Battery, a very *quaint document* which I may *probably* send
you home at some future time, if the climate, & my liver will
admit of the exertion.

Another P.S.

I have heard nothing of Tom since the letter I sent home.
Reed retires from the Service, which will give me another step.
We are very dull here in our tents, with nothing to do from
morning til' night, occasional races or a cock fight being our
only amusements. But I have just arrived at the rather late
conclusion that this sanguinary letter had better have been
addressed to one of the other sex, but never mind, you wrote me

123

the last, so remember me to Uncle Walter, Annie & babes, my
Aunts, Coz[en]s & friends, & let any of them read it that you
think it will amuse, not forgetting my worthy friends Hamblin &
Tipping, that sang the last song.

The *latest* P.S.

I like your joke about having ascertained that I am in no
danger here & no chance of a Campaign. After being made a
target of for about a fortnight, & nearly boned by the ennemy's
Cavalry, it is remarkably rich, like telling anyone you are glad
he only got his head knocked off by that nasty cannon ball.
Never mind, Lin. You must not think I mean all I say, so don't
be frightened, for I really cannot be serious if I try, altho'
I have had to act as parson three times the last fortnight.

32. *Christmas day - resumption of siege - capture of the*
    suburbs - looting - the fall of the city

Alfred Bassano to Philip Bassano   Camp before Mooltan
(No. 24)   15 January 1849

My dear Phil

My last letter to Melinda contained (which I hope she has
safely received) the account of our proceedings up to the 14th
Nov[ember] last, & I will now give you a brief outline of the
stirring events which have since occurred, up to the above date.

Primus - several days capital racing got up, which was of
course duly appreciated after being months waiting for
reinforcements & having nothing but drills, & a dreary waste of
canvass & jungle to gaze on. Secondly - we were well buttered
in orders for our previous exploits, & on the 30 Nov[ember] a
thousand Men, including 60 of ours, arrived from Ferozepore
with Ens[ign] Lawrance with them, who brought me out two letters,
an Army List, & 2 almanacks, almost a year old, but for which I
am much obliged nevertheless. Three drummer boys of the 72
N[ative] I[nfantry] bagged by Moolraj's Men, having strolled
incautiously too far from Camp. Three reconnoitring parties
started on the morning of the 6 Dec[ember], one, consisting of
the *Right Wing* of the Lilies & some Cavalry & Sepoys, went
round towards the N.E. side of the town, which we got an
excellent view of, but met with no adventures, one of the other
parties being more fortunate, for having met a Detachment of
the ennemy with *forty camels*, they scragged them & brought the
camels into Camp. Athletic sports got up for the Men & prizes
given. The sick & wounded sent off to Ferozepore. *19
Dec*[ember] - water *frozen* in the tents during the night.
21st Dec[ember] - the remainder of the long expected reinforce-

ments arrived. Lt. M., 60 Rifles, dined with us, & a frost at
night.

Now for *my* merry Christmas. On the 24th I was in the
Inlying Picquet & on Christmas Day the Bengal Brigades changed
Camp to our old ground on the East of the town, which took us
about two-thirds of the day, & on my arrival, tired, scorched &
dusty, I had just time to get a wash & a snack before going in
Command of *my Company* on the Outlying Picquet, where I was left
for the night to amuse myself, by sleeping with one eye open on
the softest stones I could find, & whenever I felt unusually
jolly, in honor of the season, my only vent was to visit my
chain of Sentries & see that they kept a sharp look out, instead
of sitting over a roaring fire, listening to merry songs, & the
sweet sounds of the piano, when touched by some fairy-like
fingers &c. &c. as of old. Whenever my knees knocked together
with the cold & awoke me I was greeted by the hoarse voice of
some Serjeant calling out for the Relief & damning the eyes of
some sound sleeper who did not immediately answer to his
number. On the following day (the 26th) I was Orderly Officer,
so you see I spent a *remarkably merry Christmas* especially when
you consider that *this did not* complete the joke, as you will
see by the subsequent dates. But strange to relate, I am
perpetually catching myself chuckling over my miseries like Mark
Tapley, the peculiarity & rapid changes we undergo in finding
ourselves suddenly precipitated from the lap of luxury into a
bed of flints & hardship, cannot fail to tickle the fancy of
any one with a taste for the ludicrous.

On the 27th a large force of all arms, including three of our
Companies under Maj. Case, marched off soon after 11 o'C[lock]
a.m. to recommence the Siege & drove the Ennemy, with very
little resistance & trifling loss on our side, right up to the
city walls, taking possession of the suburbs, which are of
great extent & immense strength, batteries being immediately
erected on the mounds commanding the city & Fort. The
Gren[adiers] *1st* & 2nd Co[mpanie]s were sent out soon after,
but had very little to do, altho' exposed to a sharp fire from
the city walls & Fort, which killed & wounded four or five Men.
A good many of the ennemy were killed & taken Prisoner, the
Men amusing themselves during the night, which was very cold,
breaking open the houses & ransacking them, setting fire to one
which blazed all night. Major Case & Lt. Straubenzie were both
severely wounded, but doing well. I took up my quarters for
the night in a room of the burning house which the fire did not
reach & passed a much more comfortable night than those who
remained outside in the cold.

28th Dec. A sharp fire kept up all day upon either party
that exposed part of their bodies for an instant. Our shot &
shell pitched into them very smartly, & must have done great
execution, one of the guns on a bastion of the town being

dismounted by our round shot. The day spent with great glee by
our Soldiers, especially the Sepoys, rummaging about the houses,
perpetually discovering some fresh hole containing something
worth luting - bullocks, cows, fowls, goats & large quantities
of clothes forming the principal objects boned, some of the Men
finding gold & silver coins, pice, a pistol &c. &c. which were
appropriated with great glee. Granaries of wheat, boosa, &
large store of tobacco were also found & the camels bringing out
the Men's meals &c. fared sumptuously, some of it also being
sent into Camp. My Servant made some small captures on his own
account, & William's Coolassie was shot dead by our own Men,
being taken for one of the ennemy whilst bringing out some
comforts for his master & not answering when challenged by the
sentry. I boned a fat lamb out of a fold & walked off with it
to my Company, where a loud laugh greeted my arrival, & turning
round I perceived the whole flock of sheep & goats had followed
me, to the delight of the Soldiers, who rushed in amongst them
& soon bore them all off captives. Many ludicrous scenes took
place & the droll remarks which are being perpetually made by
the Men effectually precludes the possibility of regarding your
position in a facetious light. From my experience of British
Soldiers during actual Service, they are a noble set of fellows
& the greater the danger, the more they show it. In numberless
trifling instances perpetually recurring they manifest their
good feeling for their Off[ice]rs & one another. If an
Officer's Servant has not arrived with his breakfast or dinner,
they bring you abundance from their scanty meals & insist on
your eating plentifully, declaring that they have had enough &
can't eat it, & their anxiety to prevent your exposing yourself
unnecessarily & the way they come forward if you are going on
any little service of danger & declare they are the proper
persons to go & that it is no place for an Officer, is beyond
all praise. Relieved about 4 o'C[lock] p.m. & returned to Camp.

29 Dec. Sent out again at ½ p[ast] 2 with my Company &
stationed in front of the Delhi Gate, which has been partly
battered down but repaired again with timber & earth. Found
two large depots of straw & made myself & Men comfortable for
the night.

30th Dec. A tremendous explosion took place in the Fort
about 9 o'C[lock] a.m., said to be Moolraj's principal
magazine ignited by one of our shells. It shook all the
buildings & walls we were stationed behind to their foundation
covering many of us with bits of brick & dirt & accompanied by
showers of shot blown out by the powder & succeeded by the most
magnificent view of colum[n]s & [of] dust curling in the air in
the most fantastic forms & appearing to touch the clouds,
followed by a roar of laughter & cheers from our Men. The Men
in great spirits luting the houses & foraging about in the
suburbs, one of my Company discovering a large chahti[6] full of

6. Pot.

almonds, which they amused themselves cracking whilst cracking
their jokes, having first given me a plentiful supply. I have
found nothing worth luting in my marauding excursions. Relieved
about 4 p.m. & returned to Camp. There are two or three
beautiful little temples & buildings in the suburbs, one with a
blue porcelain dome & the other with carved ceilings & birds &
flowers in various colours painted on the walls on a white
ground.

1 Jan. 1849. Capt. Brine joined & took Command of the
Company from me. Marched off again at ½ p[ast] 2 & the 1st
Comp[any] stationed almost on the extreme right close to the
Fort, which we had a splendid view of, advancing under cover
of the gardens in the vicinity.

2 Jan. Received orders to move towards the Delhi Gate &
join the other two Companies, which are to form the storming
party. After innumerable delays caused by nonsensical orders
& searching after Engineer Off[ice]rs who were never to be
found when required, we at length received the order for
assaulting the place. The storming party commanded by Capt.
Smyth immediately cheered & rushed forward & on my arrival at
the foot of the ascent with the Company, the centre one of the
party, Capt. Smyth, who had mounted the supposed breach in the
most cool & gallant manner, called out to me & said the breach
was impracticable "order your Men to retire". Both the advance
& retirement were fortunately executed with very trifling loss,
but considerable confusion in consequence of the advance
pressing on too close. The incessant fire kept up upon us was
almost perfectly harmless on account of the ennemy being unable
to depress their firelocks without exposing themselves to the
fire of the Rifles, who were stationed in the suburbs covering
our advance. But a tremendous shower of brickbats too small
to do much injury added considerably to the confusion &
ludicrous nature of the scene. Three struck me & Capt. Smyth
received one with considerable force on the head. After we
were again formed up in the suburbs with feelings of the
greatest disgust, we learnt to our gratification that the town
was carried by the Bombay Column who experienced little
difficulty, having a breach like a carriage road, & we were
immediately marched in to assist in clearing & occupying the
city, & having been detached in Co[mpanie]s the work of
destruction commenced. The houses were broken into, Men shot
& made prisoners of to a great extent, & immense quantities of
spoil collected by the Men amidst scenes of facetiousness &
barbarity beyond description. Our Comp[any] occupied a temple,
& having turned out the dead & dying, lit a fire & made themselves comfortable, continually sallying out in twos & threes
& returning laden with booty of every description, which was
examined amidst the jokes of the Men. A lot of meal was
brought in, a Native Servant speedily converting it into cakes,
which were eaten by the Men with great gusto, & the night

passed in boisterous mirth at every fresh supply of curious articles brought in for examination.

3 Jan. Still in the temple - a sacred bull, very fat, brought in, slaughtered, cut into beefsteaks & cooked in an incredible short space of time - pet pigeons, partridges, & fowls brought in, killed & eaten on the shrines of their Divinities without the slightest remorse. Camp followers & Sepoys continually returning to Camp laden with spoils of every description, bearing off the lion's share as usual. Prize Agents employed in collecting elephants, camels, horses, bullocks & all the valuable property they could lay their hands upon, but their arrangements were very incomplete & the great bulk of the property found in the place was carried away by Camp followers, who threw it over the walls to one another to escape the Sentries. Altogether the Men exercised greater moderation & forbearance than could possibly be expected. Very little money has been found, as the Natives generally bury it. The city is surrounded by a single wall, very thin but strengthened by a thick mud one, which makes it very difficult to breach. The streets are very narrow & beastly dirty as usual in all Indian towns, & contains nothing of interest. No Engineer led the storming Parties as usual in the Royal Service, but examined the breaches afterwards & reported *ours completely impracticable*, affording another instance of the lamentable ignorance & inefficiency they have manifested throughout this Siege.

From the 3 Jan[uary] to the present date nothing particular has occurred. The Fort is being vigorously besieged, but is of immense strength, surrounded by a ditch & three walls. Shot & shell are being pitched in night & day, but there appears to be no chance of effecting a breach with heavy guns & the approaches to the place are being rapidly constructed for the purpose of mining the walls. We are out on duty for 24 hours either digging the trenches or occupying them, about two days in five & the cover is so good that very few casualties occur, & those principally by imprudence & unnecessary exposure to see the effects of the shot. Moolraj has sent in a Messenger to treat with us several times & promised on two or three occasions to surrender unconditionally, the only terms we will listen to, but he never fulfills his engagements & like all Easterns only wants to prevaricate & gain time, but the General is too sharp for him & never ceases his operations against the place for a moment.

Tell Chris I rec[eive]d his letter of 18 Nov[ember] with unlimited pleasure & will answer it as soon as his address is settled. Remember me to dear Father & Mother & tell them, Lin, Ellen & Annie not to fret & say they know I shall be killed, because they know no such thing & I have considerable doubts on the subject myself, the odds being, I should say, more than a

hundred to one against it at the present moment, & as I am a
Soldier I must take my chance, & consider myself a remarkably
lucky fellow in seeing Service so early in my career. I am
unable to give you an idea of when the Fort will fall, altho'
of course the result is certain, but will write a detailed
account of it, if I escape again, immediately the event occurs.
Remember me to all my relations & friends & believe me to be
your affectionate brother

A. Bassano

It has been raining for the last two days, which has of course
delayed the operations. Shew this letter to all the family, so
that it don't matter who I write to. I have not heard from Tom
since I enclosed you his letters.

33. *Surrender of Mulraj - orders to join Lord Gough - the march*

Alfred Bassano to Walter Bassano   Sirdarpore, left bank of
(No. 25)   the Ravee
                                        30 January 1849

Dear Walter

I sent a long letter to Phil on the 15 Jan[uary] containing
the account of the fall of the city of Mooltan & have again to
announce the success of *British* arms by the capture of the Fort.
You will perceive by this letter I am still alive & kicking &
convinced of the truth of the lines which say "A man may drink
& not get drunk" "A man may fight & not be slain" "A man may
kiss a pretty girl & yet be welcome back again", but keep it
dark, I'm a coming. Well, I shall never get to the end if I
don't begin at the beginning, so here goes.

On the 16 Jan[uary] our Company were returning from duty at
the advance trenches. Capt. Brine, Chippendale, Inglis & I
were conversing as we walked along in rear of the Company, when
the ennemy twigged us from the Fort & sent such a volley of
grape & one round shot amongst us that I only wonder how any of
us escaped. The round shot struck a wall within a foot of my
body & rebounded, just missing my head, & the grape whistled all
round us, one ball unfortunately placing Capt. Brine hors de
combat, who when he fell on the ground with a very severe wound
in the spine burst into a fit of laughter & said "Well, it's
not so very unpleasant being shot after all" & continued
laughing & making jokes about the absurdity of being hit in the
rear till he drove us nearly all into fits with laughter, &
when he got into Camp & the D[octo]r was examining the wound &
asking him questions, he replied so coolly & facetiously that
the Doctor was positively forced out of the tent in convulsions.

The ball is still in & the wound anything but a joke. Brine is
sent back to Ferozepore & I am again Com[mandin]g the Company.

About the 20th the breaches began to look promising & the
ennemy to get very quiet & funky, large bodies of them coming
over to us daily. On the 21st Moolraj sent in to say he would
surrender unconditionally next morning, but as he had sold us so
many similar bargains, we continued to pitch in shot & shell like
blazes, one of the latter bursting amongst us & flooring Lt.
Maunsell, but he is still with us & rapidly recovering. On the
22nd the Co[mpanie]s were told off for the assault & every
precaution taken to cook their goose in the most approved style,
when, lo & behold, out came our worthy friend Moolraj with about
a dozen of his chief Sirdars & was quietly escorted into Camp.
Into the Fort went the 1st, 4th, & 5th Co[mpanie]s of ours, when
we found the breaches were so good that had he not given in they
would all have been scragged with very little loss. Three
sections of the 1st Comp[any] were sent to occupy Moolraj's
house, where we kicked up the Devil's delight. Port, sherry &
beer was found in abundance, the best part of which was obliged
to be spilt on the ground to prevent the Men getting drunk.
Well, we rummaged about & turned up 87 Sardine boxes full of
gold in bars & coins. Then came another Man to report he had
found a tumbril about the size of a 6 gallon cask, full of gold
coins the joke continuing all night & best part of the next day,
strings of beautiful pearls & bars of gold worth fifty pounds
each being continually found buried & in vaults, until Maj.
Wheeler, one of the Prize Agents, calculated that we had found
at least *fifty thousand* pounds worth of *gold* about that spot
alone. My Company boned something considerable amongst them, in
spite of the precautions taken, & report says some of the
Off[ice]rs in the Fort fingered a little, *including* Brigadier
Harvey, who was reported officially in consequence. None of
our Officers cribbed anything except a few valueless curiosities
& a few curious old gold coins, which we made no secret of, but
told the prize agents we meant to appropriate, having too great
a regard for our characters & Commissions to be tempted into
roguery.

On inspecting the Fort we found it immensely strong &
surrounded by a ditch 25 feet deep & 30 wide, & lots of large
guns & a few mortars, the latter not much use. Many of them
were knocked over & rendered useless by our shot & shell, &
almost every building in the place was knocked to pieces, the
stench of the half buried Men, dead cattle & filth being enough
to breed a pestilence. The sufferings of the garrison must
have been dreadful, & many were reduced to the alternative of
eating the entrails of camels to avoid starvation. Moolraj is
an intelligent looking Man, about thirty years of age, but
having facetiously tried to put himself into communication with
the townspeople & escape, they have clapped the darbies on him
to prevent any more of his jokes.

An order having come out for us to march with 2 Reg[imen]ts
of N[ative] I[nfantry], a few Cavalry & light field pieces on the
27th Jan[uary] to join Lord Gough & extricate him from his
difficulties, for altho' he is perpetually writing despatches
announcing victories, the loss on our side is so great & the
advantages gained little or nothing, that it appears to all here
that he is rather in a pickle. A battle[7] he fought about a week
ago, the 24th Foot were almost cut to pieces, having lost 13
Off[ice]rs killed & 10 wounded, besides half the Men being killed
& wounded. We held our ground & took some guns, but we also
lost some, the exchange being anything but satisfactory. The
9th Lancers & *14 Dr*[agoon]*s* ran clean away & rode over our own
Artillery, which of course played the devil with the arrangements, for you can't blame Sepoys when Englishmen run away like
a pack of cowards from about three hundred of the ennemy. They
are now entrenched & building batteries & stockades in the
presence of Lord Gough & bullying his Pickets daily, which don't
look much as if they had been licked. However their arrangements are all the better for us, for we shall catch them all
huddled together, & there is another large force only a march
or two in our rear, coming up with some heavy guns, howitzers &
mortars, escorted by H.M. *10th & 60th Rifles* & a large force of
capital Sepoys & Irregular Cavalry, also some English
Artillerymen & the 2nd Bombay *European Fusiliers*, so as the
Americans say, if they don't get a tarnation good licking when
we arrive they never will. A few shells amongst them as they
have boxed themselves nicely up for the purpose will astonish
their weak intellects. I am very sanguine as to the result &
hope to have two medals at least on my breast when I return to
England. The Governor-General has also decided that Mooltan is
to be luted for the benefit of the troops, so I look forward to
prize money. The Prize Agents are left with the Garrison of
Mooltan to dig & search for concealed treasure & also to levy a
contribution on the town, so if they are successful we shall
come in for something considerable. Altogether I think things
look promising & am in excellent health & spirits. The nights
are getting pleasantly mild, which makes our roving gipsy life
much more jolly. Another circumstance has also contributed
largely to our comfort & chance of getting safely through the
Campaign, vizt. the departure of *Col. Brooke*[8] for Bombay, who
was all bully when out of danger & in action a frightful funk &
perfectly foolish, causing the greatest confusion & making the
Men so unsteady that the consequences might be disgraceful in
any hard fought field. But we are now, thank God, the merry
32nd again, with cool, courageous & pleasant Field Officers who

---

7. The battle of Chillianwala, 13 January 1849.
8. Private Waterfield wrote at the same time, "There's not a
   man in the Regiment would not sooner be led into action by
   the youngest subaltern than by Colonel Brooke ...", *Memoirs*
   (1968), p. 87 [22 January 1849].

will do their best to keep up the credit of the Lilies in a pleasing way to all parties, at the Mess table, or in the *battle field* (rather poetical).

I rode all about the place before leaving Mooltan, but saw nothing of much interest, & in fact was very glad to get away. We have now had three very pleasant marches & are encamped on the banks of the river "Ravee", which I believe we cross tomorrow. The country passed through is the same as usual, flat with clumps of jungle, but rather more verdant. The villages are all surrounded by mud walls & bastions of the same material loopholed, showing the warlike propensities of the Natives in these parts, but a red jacket, white face, & pair of pistols ensures the greatest civility from the villagers. The beggars at this side of the Sutlege are remarkably flattering. They ask for a pice & keep repeating we shall conquer wherever we go, but we are not so green as to be taken in by that sort of blarney. What we all hope for, as the season is advancing rapidly, is to get one good mill & then march into quarters, for altho' we are becoming great veterans we are not such fire eaters as to wish to be fighting for ever, especially in the hot season. However, we must take our chance. We are only doing what we are paid for, & after all, there is a great pleasure in travelling over such an extent of country, altho' we seldom come upon anything worth going five miles to see. Yet the perpetual change induces you to hope to be rewarded every time you move by coming upon some wonder of Nature or Art that will repay all the inconvenience or annoyance we have suffered.

Well, I have nothing more to say in the shape of news. Write a little oftener if you are not too lazy, & if I am killed, remember that it gives you an excellent claim for a Commission for one of your increasing family, if you get any boys, & mind & pack them off to India & don't put off having the most promising youth noted on the List in good time. Also tell Father to look after my batta or Prize money which, if we are to believe all reports, will at all events be well worth having, & the produce of my effects would, I hope, bring something considerable. I have no debts of any description in this country & I therefore go into Action with an easy conscience from the knowledge that, altho' long delayed, whether I am spared or not, all the expenses that I have put Father & Phil to will be amply & abundantly repaid. The unavoidable delay, I can assure them, [h]as been as annoying to me as inconvenient to them. But enquire of anyone conversant on the subject, letting them know of my perpetual change of Stations & knocking about, which is fearfully expensive, & I will venture to say that their only surprise will be how I have managed to keep out of debt in this country at all & at the same time keep up the necessary appearances of an Officer.

Give my love to Annie & the babies, & tell her never to let

them plait their hair, for if I suddenly return some day & don't find an abundant crop of ringlets I will cut them off with a shilling. Also to keep them clear of gooseberry bushes & not let them grow up too fastidious about smoking. I forget my other English peculiarities & tastes about what is necessary to bring an European female to perfection, so I will leave the remainder to Annie's good taste. Another thing I have just recollected - don't let them learn "The Battle of Prague"[9] for goodness sake. Give my love to all the family in its numerous branches & details. Also remember me to all my friends, & tell any of my female friends & acquaintances, not forgetting little Clara King, *Annie Speller, Kate* &c. &c. not to poison themselves or pine away on account of my long absence, for I have not yet married a darky & they may still have a chance of catching *the Captain* (when I get my promotion), altho' he's getting very wide awake.

Well, now for a poetical wind-up. The Sun is sinking in the distant horizon & reflecting its long shadows from the beautiful jungle surrounding my tent & stretching down to the glass-like surface of the winding Ravee, which is reflecting the clear blue of an Eastern sky on its calm surface. Ma, bah, bar, goes a flock of sheep just driven past my tent, entirely destroying the gush of beautiful language I was about to pour out to ease the overflowing of my overwrought feelings & desires, principally caused, I believe, by the want of a cheroot, which this letter has kept me out of for the last hour. The loss caused by the flock of sheep must be very annoying to you, but I am much obliged to the sporting young lambs, who run frisking about by the side of their dams, as they have enabled me to gratify my desire for a weed at last. So adieu, & don't forget the *puffs* of

Your affectionate brother
Warlike Alf of the Lilies
about to settle the affairs of
the Punjaub & extricate Lord
Gough from his difficulties

---

9. A favourite piano piece.

THE BATTLE OF GUJARAT

34. *The capture of Cheniote - battle of Gujarat*

Alfred Bassano to F.M. Bassano   In camp at Goojrat
(No. 26)   1 March 1849

N.B. Goojrat is a small town on the opposite side of the Chenab
not far from Ramnuggur.

My dear Father
    My last letter to Walter left me at Sirdarpore on the banks
of the Ravee on Route to join the Grand Army, nothing particular
occurring except the usual inconvenience of a march & Col.
Brooke rejoining again, to our great disgust, until we arrived
at Cheniote, an insignificant fortification at the foot of a
rocky hill which completely commanded it. Here we found Sheik
Emam-oodeen, one of our Allies besieging it & Narain Sing with
a small force defending it, having only three or four guns
between them, the Sheik's judiciously planted on the hill. But
partly from want of powder & the usual indolence of Natives,
very little damage was being done on either side. One attempt
which the Sheik had made to carry the place by assault failed
with a trifling loss on both sides. On our arrival we sent in
a chit demanding unconditional surrender the next morning, or
the place would be blown about their ears, & in the mean time I
took a walk, reconnoitred the Fort, ascended the hill & found
the Sheik's Artillerymen lounging about smoking & scarcely ever
thinking of blazing into the place. I pointed their gun & sent
a ball flying into the middle of one of their largest houses,
crumbling one of the walls about their ears, & then ascended
the loftiest summit of the rocks & obtained a very fine view of
the surrounding country, town, fort & river Chenab which could
be seen winding about for miles & having some rocky islands at
the broadest parts. The next day the Brigade paraded at
6 o'C[lock] a.m., marched to the Fort & received Narain Singh
as a Prisoner of War. His followers, amounting to 1200 fighting
Men, were then marched out, disarmed, & everything of value
taken from them & given to the Sheik. The Prisoners were also
made over to him, with the exception of Narain Singh, whom we
handed over to the Political Agent at Ramnuggur. He is a
remarkably handsome looking cut-throat & a regular Mark Tapley
under difficulties, drinking his two bottles of raw rum a day,
& eating a bottle of Chilli pickle with great glee.

    Ramnuggur contains nothing of interest except filth to an
astounding extent & a bridge of boats. We remained there three
days & then marched 11 miles further up the left bank of the
River where we again stopped three days, moving off about 2

o'C[lock] p.m. on the 19 Feb[ruary] to the River side, which the
Brigade forded, & bivouaced on the opposite bank without their
tents, marching off at daylight next morning & joining Lord
Gough – leaving my Company behind to unload Camels & send the
baggage across in boats, which we completed & crossed over ourselves about 3 o'C[lock] next morning, slept about a couple of
hours on the ground & commenced reloading the camels at daybreak,
which we completed by 11 o'C[lock] a.m. & hurried off to join
the Reg[imen]t at Lord Gough's Camp, a report being prevalent
that an Action was to be fought today, & on arriving at the
ground, we found that the Army had moved on towards Goojrat.
Off we went again, under a broiling sun, never stopping once to
halt, making the best of our way through the enormous quantity
of baggage belonging to the Grand Army, which we at last overtook
& joined our Reg[imen]t on the march, the Brigade halting &
pitching their Camp about 5 miles south of Goojrat, the report
of the Action being only a sell.

The next day, the *21st Feb*[ruary], we moved off about
8 o'C[lock] a.m. with the Army formed in order of battle towards
Goojrat, which was occupied by the Ennemy, their Line extending
on both sides of it. The Artillery opened upon their position
between 9 & 10 o'C[lock] & a cannonade commenced which lasted
some hours, our columns steadily advancing nearer towards them,
their fire doing very little execution. On nearing their
Encampment we perceived the Ennemy, to our great surprise &
delight, without any defences of any description, drawn up
partly in line on an open plain, waiting to receive us, their
Off[ice]rs some distance in front waving their tulwars,[10] & even
having the audacity to try & get their Men to charge us. They
then opened an ill-directed matchlock fire & treated us to two
or three showers of grape, but it did not check our steady
advance for one moment, and immediately after we returned the
compliment with such a shower of grape, canister & musket balls,
that they all took to their heels at such a devil of a pace that
it was useless for any but Cavalry to pursue them. We then
halted & piled arms, sending two or three Companies into the
town to clear it & take the Fort, which was soon done as the
Garrison laid down their arms, & the guns taken in our vicinity
having been collected, we anxiously awaited news from the other
Brigades, being soon relieved by intelligence from all parts of
the Field of the total defeat & flight of the Ennemy, hotly
pursued by our Cavalry & Light field pieces, which followed them
for fifteen miles, cutting to pieces immense numbers, including
one entire Reg[imen]t which attempted in vain to make a stand.
All their baggage & guns were captured, altho' a few of the
latter have not yet been found, as they abandoned them all over
the country. About an hour after dark we marched to Camp, which
was pitched about two or three miles beyond Goojrat. The next

---

10. Swords.

morning Gen. Gilbert with a large force marched off to follow the remnant of Shere Singh's Army & to settle our differences with Attok & Peshawur, leaving two or three Brigades here in daily expectation of receiving orders to march back to Cantonment & *repoze* on our laurels.

The Battle from the first commencement was a beautifully managed affair, more like a parade than an Action, yet nothing could be more decisive. Their dead are lying about the country in all directions, wherever they made a stand being marked by rows of them & a little stronger perfume. At the beginning of the Action they made an attempt to outflank our right, which was frustrated in the coolest possible way by Col. Franks with the 10th Reg[imen]t, which he moved off to prevent it. Until this occurred we were in Reserve in Rear of the 10th, this fortunate accident bringing us up to the front to fill up the gap. But I must refer you to the papers for a regular account of the Action, for no individual can tell what is going on much beyond his own Regiment. The small list of killed & wounded on our side & the decisive results confirm the opinions of all the old veterans at present with us that it was the ablest display of Generalship they have ever seen.

War has made fearful ruffians of us all. Our chief amusement is to ride about & look at the dead bodies & see what they were killed with, the conversation consisting of jokes & such observations as "By George, that was a smasher in the ribs", "That fellow was lanced", "This chap got a slashing cavalry cut", "Come this way, here's where the grape knocked them over", "There's a fellow with his jead knocked clean off by a round shot", &c. &c. &c. The jackals, pariah dogs, kites, & vultures appear to be the great gainers by war in this country, for no one ever thinks of burying the bodies & there they remain just as they fell, until all the tender ones are eaten up & the tough ones decayed, the bones remaining as a memento of the fight for years.

But I suppose you are getting sick of the horrible, altho' as I have told you in former letters the ludicrous is always largely mixed up with it. We are quite as ignorant here as you are in England as to whether this victory will finish the War or not, & to tell you the truth I don't know anybody that cares, altho' we often get papers informing us of our critical situation & hinting at the probability of our being cut to pieces. Ignorance is bliss, & we never dream of such a contingency ourselves.

I expect to get two medals, one for Mooltan & the other for this last splendid victory, & if the Prize money turns out well I don't think I shall have done so badly by coming into the Army. There is a report that Lord Gough claims to share with his Forces the Mooltan booty, but the injustice of the claim is so glaring that I don't think there is any fear on that account.

I was delighted to see in the Gazette Chris's appointment to
the 70th & that he intended to try his liver in this Presidency.
Before this letter reaches England, I suppose he will be on his
passage out, so it is of no use my prosing on the subject of
Bengal & young Men who will leave their anxious Mothers to come
out to be scorched in a barren land, teeming with pugnacious
Seiks & rampant boa constrictors. By the bye, talking of boa
constrictors, who should walk into my tent the other day but
Bridgeman Wigst[r]*om*, or some such name, of the 14th Dr[agoon]s
& shake hands furiously with me. I didn't know him from Adam &
wondered what was coming next, when he began to enquire if I had
heard from Walter lately. Mutual explanations ensued & I soon
found out he was a very nice fellow, well known to the family,
sent home something a short time ago for the late Mr. Hughes &
Walter - asked him to dinner - head shaved couldn't come - been
very seedy - couldn't go with the 14 Dr[agoon]s to Peshawur -
Walter very bad correspondent - see me again soon, Lahore or
some such place - recovered from illness - able to dine with
me - Adieu.

I forgot to tell you I commanded my Company in the last
decisive Action & had great difficulty in preventing them from
breaking their line & charging the Ennemy against orders.

Have you got my Commission as Ens[ign] yet? If so, keep it
in a dry safe place & on obtaining my L[ieu]t[enanc]y in the
regular course put it in with the Ensigncy. Do you ever hear
from Tom now, as I have not the slightest idea of his whereabouts?

I hope you & dear Mother are happier & more comfortable in
your new residence, especially as you have got rid of the last
of the family in so advantageous a way for his own prospects.
Everything appears to turn out so auspiciously for the welfare
of the family that I begin to look forward at no very distant
day to a return on leave to Merry England to cheer you & Mother
up with my nonsense & wonderful stories of the stirring scenes
of a Campaign, & beat you some more games at cribbage, & tell
Mother I won't insist on doubling her again at vingt'un. I am
writing great rot, but if it makes you laugh it is labour well
bestowed, for from the tenor of the letters I get from England
I am afraid that my departure banished mirth from the old house
at home. If so, I will restore it to an improved tone some of
these fine days. Nil desperandum is a motto you don't appear
to act up to at home with any energy. Why, if you saw me laying
on the ground (on outpost duty) with a bit of carpet over me, on
a tempestuous night, raining every half hour, or pushing off &
loading boats up to my knees in water more than half the night
& marching under a broiling sun all next day, having had nothing
to eat but a crust of bread & a drink of muddy river water for
forty hours, & this sort of unpleasant duty is not long coming
round. A Subaltern for the last seven months has seldom had 24

hours of anything like rest or comfort. I have not been
reposing on a bed of feathers, but as long as I enjoy good health
I don't care a pice & take everything very coolly & am always
jolly under the most miserable circumstances.

Give my love to dear Mother, Annie, Ellen, Lin, & the rest of
the family & tell them they don't give me much trouble acknowledging the rec[e]p[tio]n of letters, which I invariably do under
any circumstances. But I suppose my long absence is causing a
rapid evaporation of the interest taken in me. Well, if so, it
is perhaps all the better, for then if I go to swell the game
bag of some enterprising Sikh, with a taste for intelligent
Feringhees,[11] it won't be of any consequence. Gammon! I am
sorry to hear that John & Arthur have not got fresh berths yet.
Remember me to them & Aunt Ryle, & tell Hamblin if he writes me
the threatened letter, I will give him a long one on foolscap
in return, written in the blood of England's Ennemies drawn for
the purpose if he likes, & believe me to be

Your affectionate Son
Alfred (at present a Centurion)

III

THE END OF THE WAR

35. *March to Lahore - at Lahore - March to Jullundur*

Alfred Bassano to Philip Bassano   In camp at Lahore
(No. 27)   5 April 1849

My dear Phil
    Still knocking about in all directions and improving my
acquaintance with the country. On the 13th Ultimo we marched
from Goojrat to Kuttata, & on the 20th to Wuzirabad, a good-
sized & bustling town, with several fine houses & beautiful
gardens in the vicinity, containing terraces, fountains, marble
baths & painted ceilings &c. &c. in Eastern profusion. We made
two or three picnics to the finest gardens, but our principal
amusement there was going to see the vanquished Seiks coming in
daily to deliver up their Arms & trust to the clemency of the
Britons for their lives. Forty thousand are said to have given
up their weapons already.

    On the 28th we were again drummed out on the road to Lahore
which we reached on the 2nd of the present Month & are now

---

11. Europeans.

encamped under the walls with the Thermometer 104 in the shade
of our tents wondering what is to become of us next, for we have
got a Route for Jullundur & did not expect to be detained on the
road any more, but for some political reasons here we are,
without any knowledge of when we are to make another start of it,
& from the numerous reports current, very doubtful whether our
destination will not be again changed. In the meantime the
weather is getting fearfully hot to be in canvass & the Men are
doing their best to assist the climate by getting drunk every
day by hundreds, & as by dint of robbing houses, cutting throats,
& plundering the dead bodies for the last six months, there is
no lack of tin amongst them this delay before a large town is
giving us endless trouble & filling the Hospital. One Man was
found drowned in the River this morning, having evidently fallen
in last night, probably dead drunk, as he had stiffened with a
smile of peculiar satisfaction on his face. In fact, the more
life is endangered by natural causes, the more reckless &
indifferent men become, & the zeal with which they hasten their
own end by drink & exposure to the sun without even their hats
on, is worthy of a better cause. I read the funeral service
over a Serj[ean]t two days ago, who died really very much
regretted by Men & Officers. The former were cracking their
jokes over the sale of his effects the next day, & the latter
continued merrily off from the funeral to the Mall & afterwards
to dinner with the 98th. But a truce to these horrors, which
must be anything but interesting to you, & only show what a set
of callous unreflecting ruffians war & a bad climate make of
Men. By the bye, the annexation of the Punjaub has considerably
improved our prospects as far as climate goes, for the nights
are almost invariably cool & the heat of the day is of a dryer
& less enervating description, & though of course it will take
a few years before the new Stations are complete & comfortable,
yet the prospect of completing the best part of an Indian
Service in the Punjaub is decidedly refreshing.

But you want me to tell you something about Lahore, so here
goes. From the outside it is a remarkably pretty place, in fact
I think I am justified in using the word "Grand" - fortified
you know, which means moat, counterscarp, glacis, rowny, walls,
embrasures, bastions, Fort, drawbridges, & Soldiers, all mixed
well up together with trees, fine houses overlooking the walls,
lofty minarets, mosques with gilt domes &c. &c., altogether
forming a very imposing sight from the exterior. Now for the
interior - magnificent gateways, fine palace, pretty gardens,
beautiful temples, elegant mosques, imposing minarets, narrow
streets, painted ceilings, wretched hovels, coloured stones &
marbles beautifully inlaid, filth, ferocious Men, pretty women,
pariah dogs, half-starved ponies, miserable cripples, Rajahs,
elephants, &c. &c. all mixed well up together, so that you
cannot get at any of the interesting without going through a
great deal of the disgusting, & add every description of
unpleasant smells with a small proportion of rose water & eau

de cologne, & you will be able to form some idea of the prettiest
& most interesting town in India I have yet seen (barring Delhi).

Now for the vicinity - cantonments passable, topes of trees
some, very fine temples & tombs, especially one of the latter
which contains the remains of the Emperor Juhangeer, & numerous
very fine gardens & quaint mosques, one of the former, between
three & four Miles from Lahore, is beautifully laid out with
tanks, terraces, fountains by hundreds in rows intersecting the
gardens in all directions, water-falls, marble baths, temples,
&c., arches with inlaid & painted walls & ceilings, shady walks
amongst orange, lemon, pomegranate & mulberry trees, the latter
now covered with luscious fruit, & all clothed in perpetual
verdure. But with the fall of the Rajahs we may date the
decline of Eastern luxury & the charms of a residence in India,
& these magnificent gardens & works of art are falling into ruin
& decay now the country has fallen into the hands of the
civilized, but in many things lamentably niggardly, Britons. I
obtained a sight of the crown jewels through the politeness of
Sir H. Lawrance, the Resident. The pearls, diamonds, rubies &c.
are of a surprising size & beauty, & the Koh-i-noor - literally
"Mountain of Light" - is a magnificent diamond *larger* than a
pigeon's egg, & is said to be worth a million & a half of money,
& if reports can be relied upon, is going to be presented to Her
Majesty by the Hon[orable] Company, who consider they have got
an excellent pretext at last for bagging the magnificent
precious stones formerly belonging to the Rajahs of the Punjaub.

I see by the papers that Chris has been blown into Milford
Haven,[12] but I suppose soon got off again. I have nothing more
to say, but wish I could hear something of Tom. Remember me to
all at home & Believe me to be

                    Your affectionate brother
                    Alfred

P.S. I wrote this letter at Lahore, which was too late for
the Mail, & on the 10th April started again for Jullundur which
we reached on the 18th instant & are again stationary. The
country passed through was uninteresting as usual & Umritsar
the only place worth seeing. It is surrounded by a wall &
contains one of the most splendid Seikh temples in India; the
floor being beautifully inlaid with coloured marbles & precious
stones, & the doors, walls, ceilings & domes plated with silver
& gold, embossed & inlaid with looking-glass, the whole being
almost surrounded by water contained in a magnificent tank, the
Natives, to our great disgust, making us take off our boots &
leave them outside before permitting us to inspect its beauties.
The Fort of Govinghur (now occupied by our troops) is a most

---

12. See Chapter Four, Letters 44-50.

well built & very strong fortification close to the town.

Our present Station is a very nice place, but wofully
deficient in Bungalows, all there are being for sale, & none for
hire, most of them being not one bit better than an English
stable or barn. Most of our fellows have already purchased
however, at exorbitant prices, but I have great hopes of getting
six months' leave to Simla, as my application has I believe been
forwarded this morning, so I have every prospect of recruiting
my health in an English climate & avoiding the inconvenience &
annoyance of a bad purchase, having very little doubt that when
I come down from the hills again there will be plenty of
Bungalows for a moderate rent.

I got a letter yesterday from Chris in the Cove of Cork & see
by the papers that he has since been blown into Milford Haven
& started again. Direct all your future letters to Jullunder,
Punjaub (*via Bombay*) until you hear from me to the contrary.
Remember me to all at home. In haste,

Your affectionate brother
Alfred. All right, 19th April 1849.

CHAPTER FOUR

"Your beloved Sawbones"

While Alfred Bassano was encamped outside Multan,
and Tom Bassano was working hard in South India at
his first efforts at coffee planting, their brother
Christopher Bakewell was waiting for the regimental
appointment as Assistant Surgeon which would make
him the third Bassano in India. Christopher was
24 years old, two-and-half years younger than Tom,
and a little over two years older than Alfred, and
the brother on whose education most money had been
spent. In the early part of 1844 he had entered
the Medical Department of King's College, London.
He was a diligent student as well as a light-hearted
young man, a favourite with the young ladies with
his luxuriant whiskers, his fine singing voice and
his playful ways[1] - as well as an expert skater on
the Round Pond in Kensington Gardens. During his
four years at King's College he attended lectures
on botany, chemistry, physiology, descriptive and
surgical anatomy, the practice of medicine, materia
medica and therapeutics, forensic medicine, surgery,
and midwifery - as well as attending medical practice and clinical lectures, surgical practice and
clinical lectures, and midwifery practice and
lectures on the diseases of women and children, all
at King's College Hospital. During his third year
he acted as the professor's prosector, during the
surgical anatomy lectures of Professor Richard
Partridge.[2] From the 1st May to the 1st November
1848 he was the Physicians' Clinical Clerk for the
in-patients at the hospital, after having passed an
examination for the post, and on the 18th August
1848 was admitted a Member of the Royal College of
Surgeons, one of fourteen successful candidates at
that time. He had studied medicine with the intention of joining the Queen's service and going out
with his regiment to India, and the letters received
from his brothers in India confirmed him in his

---

1. See Chapter Five, Letter 75.
2. His certificates are all in the Bassano papers.

142

intention. Not long after arriving in India in 1846
with his Regiment, the 32nd, Alfred had written a
long letter encouraging Christopher to go to India
as an army surgeon, in the 32nd if possible, and
advising him on the outfit which he should take
with him.

I

36. *Advice for an Assistant Surgeon going to India*

Alfred Bassano to Christopher Bassano   Chinsurah
(No. 5)   10 November 1846

Dear Sawbones
  A *subject* to discuss & afterwards to *operate* upon.

  I intend cramming this chit with convincing arguments showing
the peculiar advantages accruing to an Army Sawbones by proceeding immediately (if not sooner) to the beautiful East & the
circumstances under which they are most manifest. In the first
place - if possible get appointed to a Reg[imen]t on its
augmentation for India (Bengal preferable of course). If
successful in this you will go out in Medical charge of one of
the ships conveying part of the Reg[imen]t & on arriving at your
destination you will receive 15/- a head for every Man or Woman
of the Reg[imen]t who may be disembarked *alive* - (doubtful if
any under *your* care) - Officers included, & children half price,
amounting to no inconsiderable sum. The following is the amount
received by our Assistant Surgeons - Dr. M. £180, Dr. C. £130,
Dr. D. £146 - putting you completely on your own hands at once,
as the necessary expenses on your arrival in the country will be
under £40, leaving you at least ninety to remit at once, which
with your advance pay, about fifty, will enable you to pay for
a liberal outfit without the slightest inconvenience, & before
you have been six Months in the service, leaving you with money
in your pocket and an income of about £400 a year and an
expenditure of about half that sum. This is not a golden dream
but a pleasant reality, which being interested I have ascertained
without the shadow of a doubt & saw the bills on the Hooghly
Bank for the above sums sent to our D[octo]rs on their arrival
here. And as Reg[imen]ts are always sent up the country on their
first arrival you can easily get removed to the *Lilies* when a
vacancy occurs, the expense of changing the buttons & facings
being very trifling. But I would not have you miss an opportunity of getting into *my Reg*[imen]*t* on any account, but only
tell you in case there should be no vacancy when you are ready,
& to stop you from going to any other Station. And even in the
event of your being lucky enough to get appointed to the 32nd at

once, they always send out a D[octo]r in charge of a Detachment
of his own or other Reg[imen]ts & I think there can be no doubt
the [East India] Company issue the same allowance of head money,
& if so, which you can ascertain, you are sure to come in for
something handsome under any circumstances.

2ndly. Our Ass[istant] Surgeons have been fetched away in
buggies several times to the bungalows of sick residents,
returning in about a quarter of an hour with twenty Rupees in
their pockets, which is not to be sneezed at.

3rdly. You can have a splendid *spider preserve* of a *very
large* and *superior* breed, and there is *no climate* like this for
the *growth* of WHISKERS. Now - *don't* get excited. I know what
you would say. Ye gods & little fishes, an extensive pair of
whiskers & a spider preserve! If this don't bring you to India
I'll swallow the first Bengal tiger I catch without salt.

4thly. There is very little to do, as the Company's
Apothecaries do all the duty work & you only have to go to the
Hospital occasionally to superintend. In fact, your prospects
are *excessively* brilliant, as the necessary expenses of a *Bones*
are much less & their income considerably larger than a
Sub[altern]'s.

Well now, as you've made up your mind to come to this land of
cholera & enlarged livers I'll proceed to give you some advantageous hints which, in connection with the enclosed list of
necessary articles, must regulate your outfit, & this timely
notice, by removing all doubts of what will be serviceable
hereafter, will enable you to arrange your purchases in such a
manner as to get up your private stock to the requisite articles
by the time of your appointment. & you must bear in mind that
as soon as you are stationary for a short time, your room must
be made to look as furnished & comfortable as possible, for as
luggage is easily & safely transported about, under the care of
a Sub[altern] & baggage guard, the weight allowed to be carried
at the expense of government being also very liberal, don't
leave anything that is the least likely to prove useful or
ornamental. Chairs, tables, bedsteads and *chests* of *drawers*
may be *hired* or purchased here for a mere trifle, the *latter* a
very necessary & convenient article of comfort. And decorations
should be *purchased* on arrival here, either at Calcutta or the
H[ea]d Q[uarte]r of your Reg[imen]t, where you can get rid of
the old boxes mentioned in the list, if of no further Service.
& don't fall into the error I did of supposing the boots good in
this country, as they go to pieces in a few days, English ones
being quite at a premium. Keep your six p[ai]rs of white
trowsers clean to land in & wear ashore, using your canvass &
checks for the passage, which you can get washed on board. In
fact, the Soldiers' wives will wash & iron many things, such as
your white jackets &c., but as it depends a great deal on the

144

Captain & Com[manding] Off[icer] you must not reckon on it.

The first time you go on shore at Calcutta take a good fitting *White* jacket, trowsers (loose straps) & waistcoat (holes for Reg[imen]t buttons) & give them to a native tailor to make twelve suits, as they have not much idea of measuring, for which you will pay thirty or forty rupees, *the lot*. & any purchases you have to make, go to the China bazar, asking the price, and however cheap it may appear, offering about one third or less, as they are the greatest rogues in Christendom, nobody ever giving a native what he asks.

I'll tell you about your Servants, horse, and travelling, with our mode of living &c. when I'm a little more conversant on the subject, and also give you an insight into the language – in fact make an oracle of you. But there is one thing I have almost forgotten to mention, which is, that every Assistant Surgeon is forced to purchase a Medicine Chest for board ship use, for which he gives twenty pounds – but it is your own & fetches ten or twelve with ease at the end of the voyage. As Medicine is very dear here, and you could obtain the necessary things for very little, you will in all probability make money by that apparent loss.

Acknowledge the receipt of this Chit & take care of it, paying no attention to any hints you may receive from Buffers who have already sufficiently fried their tripes in India, or read in Books on this country, as the Authors must in most cases be people of no observation, impaired upper stories, or never been here at all – as I read an immense deal of the manners & customs of the Natives &c. in Modern works on my passage out, thinking to derive a great deal of information from them, but in reality they are only calculated to mislead, & you will have plenty of time to write & ask me anything about which I have not been sufficiently explicit.

We are supposed to be now in the enjoyment of what they facetiously call here the cool season, the Ther[mometer] having been caught in the fact of stopping for a short time as low as 85 in the shade. This occurred a few days ago, but it appears to have been so ashamed of itself that to the present time it has kept itself day & night two or three degrees above that. But I don't feel it unpleasantly hot & consider anything under ninety comfortable enough.

Now if you are beginning to entertain the idea that you'll come to some news presently you are very much mistaken, for having confined myself to professional subjects so long I don't intend to let you get any thing else out of me, but for your private information refer you to the letters for other members of our distinguished family which will accompany this. My object in giving you all such a dose at once is that there will

145

be but one more English Mail previous to commencing our march &
I don't expect to be able to write much till I am again
stationary at *Agra*. But if you don't cross your letters in
future & tell me more of the news and fun that's going forward
in your quarter of the globe, positively & actually I'll strike.
I don't refer to you in particular but all the entire family,
Father & Mother excepted, but as I expect soon to see you out
here you are more under my control, & if you don't attend to my
suggestions the first thing you get on joining the Gallant 32nd
will be - A Smack on the Head from

Your affectionate brother
Alfred

P.S. If you don't like it, lump it.

[Enclosed List]

N.B. A medico is nearly always in plain clothes.

1 Regimental Coatee (with buff belt & breast plate) (if 32nd).
  Loose bullion epaulettes.
Frock Coat and scales.
1 Shell Jacket (Cloth) - materials for another of Cashmerette
  (if 32nd) only a plait of 2 gold shoulder cords *not 3*.
1 Pair of Cloth trowsers (plenty for a D[octo]r)
Cocked Hat in tin case.
Forage cap - d[itt]o - (if 32nd, small badge as sent to Cork).
Sash.
Sword with rings for *sling* belt (if 32nd, hilt lined with white
  glazed leather).
Sword knot (if 32nd, of white leather like the one sent to Cork)
  (gold sword knot *no use* in *32nd*)
Black sling Belt (if 32nd, a morocco *sling* belt, the *sling* of
  leather cords not straps)
1 Military stock.
2 pr. gloves & glove trees.
1 Set of Reg[imenta]l buttons with rings for white waistcoats
  (same size &c. as on shell jacket)
6 pr. White trowsers (drill) - (2 pr. canvass for voyage).
3 White Jackets.
3 White Waistcoats (2 with holes for Regl. buttons).
1 Doz. shirts (linen fronts), 4 Doz. (Muslin) all white - with
  what you have.
3 Doz. Socks (2 - or all - white)
12 Flannel waistcoats.
2 Doz. towels.
4 pr. sheets.
1 Counterpane.
3 Blankets.
Hair Mattress & pillow with leather case like I bought at Cork -

6 pillow Covers.
pr. white cotton gloves.
Doz. white handkerchiefs, those of mine plenty good enough.
Brown Holland short cutaway Coats.
Brown Holland cap with peak.
large dirty-clothes bag.
Dress Coat.
Frock Coat.
Shooting Coat, with buttons of a kind of stuff, & very short -
dark mother of pearl, *or same*.
Black Venetian or zephyr coat, single breasted, & buttons not
seen.
Great Coat.
pr. black dress trousers.
pr. of summer trowsers (1 Darkish).
or 4 waistcoats.
scarfs.
several light neckerchiefs of silk, cotton & gauze.
White chokers.
Black hat in *leather case*.
Cap with peak of same stuff, black & white, check the kick [?].
good pr. of braces.
pr. kid gloves & 1 pr. of dogskin.
Brush case & bit of pipeclay.
pr. patent leather boots - 3 pr. of Common leather - 2 pr. of
Oxonians - 1 pr. pumps, Slippers & *boot trees*.
Writing Desk & any small ornamental boxes of mahogany &c. you
may have in the house.
Table cover.
pair of large hair brushes & comb & the one you have.
tooth brushes.
pr. nail brushes.
r. of boot hooks.
corkscrew.
tumbler.
Button hook.
Razors, oil, soap, tooth powder &c.
white covers for dressing table & any china ornaments or scent
bottles to decorate a dressing table you may have.
looking glass.
Work bag well stocked.
Seidleitz powders - soda & tartaric acid & particularly essence
of ginger, capital things.
Metal wash hand basin & can, thus [drawing].
Prints, pictures, books, amusing & instructive, as many as you
have got.
Bullock trunks.
portmanteau & any number of old boxes with your name legibly
painted thereon that you may require.
shabby clothes, useful & often worn.
Also provide yourself with a good sized oval tub to wash in,
with a lid, so that when travelling it will contain your jug,

basin, &c.

Very useful additions to Gents wishing to lay out a little more
money on their outfit - vizt. double-barrelled gun in case;
pr of small pistols; Rifle; Saddlery including bridles, brushes
&c; powder flasks, shot pouches, caps, powder, bullets, shot,
wads. &c.

The above list, I think, includes everything, & is worth £10
to any one appointed to a Reg[imen]t in India, or at least in
Bengal, making some slight alterations in the things which only
apply to D[octo]rs. You can make a decent & intelligible list &
destroy the original, giving a copy to any friend who may
require it.

II

"THE GREATEST EXCITEMENT PREVAILS HERE ABOUT
THESE APPOINTMENTS"

Early in November 1848 Christopher Bassano went
to Chatham to await his posting.

37. *First days in Chatham*

Christopher Bassano to Melinda Bassano   7 Trout Row
                                                  Chatham
                                                  12 November 1848

My dear Melinda
    I recieved the tin box yesterday morning and in it your note
enclosing the watch guard which my friend Martelli opened
without any difficulty. I am very pleased with its neat and
elegant appearance and return many thanks.

    I am sorry to hear that Mother is not yet convalescent, and
also to say that my cold does not get any better. Tell Walter,
if you see him before I next write to him, that the P[rincipal]
M[edical] O[fficer] appears not to have been informed that Adams
and Fife are Acting Surgeons, as they have received no intimation, though Hyde, the next man, has had an official letter
appointing him.[3]

    Remember me to all my friends and tell Hamblin not [to] talk
so much at cards nor throw them on the table before the game is
lost, also to become steady in his old age and get his skates

---

3. Walter was a clerk in the Army Medical Department office.

148

ready for the winter. I have been wandering all over the country in search of a sheet of water without any success, the largest pond I have discovered being about the size of your parlor. I shall write to Father when I have paid my bills and I shall then be able to calculate my expenses. I trust he has got rid of that troublesome cough and that he does not meander about in the cold before getting up. I spent a very pleasant evening at Mr. Lewis' last Wednesday and I was much pleased with Mrs. L. who is not much above five & twenty. In writing to me address to my lodgings as there is a delivery at half past 8 in the morning. Tell Walter this, and believe me Dear Melinda,

Your affectionate Bro[ther]

C.B. Bassano

P.S. If this be in time to stop my instruments from coming here tell Walter I don't want them, as I intended getting them repaired at Evans'.

38. *Expenses - recreations - medical stores*

Christopher Bassano to F.M. Bassano   7 Trout Row
                                        Chatham
                                        15 November 1848
                                        $9\frac{1}{2}$ p.m.

My dear Father
    You may probably think I ought to have written to you ere this, but the fact is I seem to have been doing nothing else in my leisure time but writing letters from the time I came here, and knowing I must write to you respecting pecuniary matter I put it off until I could form some idea of my future expenditure. I have just paid my bill here which amounts to £1 - 0 - 1 for the week ending on Sunday, and I believe the mess bill is about the same, but as it is not necessary to settle that more than once a month I shall not trouble my head about it at present. I have had numerous other expences as the cost of travelling, boxes, washing, &c., which have dipped pretty deeply into another Pound, and I can therefore see pretty clearly two pounds a week is non[e] too much. You however know me pretty well by this time, and I am sure you will not imagine for a moment I could, or would, spend more than I found necessary.

    I hope your cough has disappeared and that you are still as comfortable in your new house as you were. When does Dr. Clerk leave the Board? Remember me kindly to him and I hope his move is accompanied with promotion - also to the other gentlemen in the Board. Give my love to Mother, Ellen, and Melinda. I hope

to hear something satisfactory about Ellen.[4] I have not had
time to write to her yet, I regret to say, and I might say the
same of many others, but I really seem to have done nothing else
but write letters since I came here. Send me your portfolio by
the first opportunity, for I have nothing to write upon.

I spent a delightful evening at old Lewis' last Wednesday - I
think I mentioned it to Melinda. I saw him in the store house
yesterday and he entered into a long story about the great
difficulty he had in keeping up the supply of certain medicines.
I told him there was not any Iodide of Potash in the Surgery,
one of the most useful medicines in the Pharmacopea, indeed I
might say the most useful. I am in the Surgical division and I
can only get about a quarter of a yard of common plaister at a
time, not enough to strap one man's leg. Economy in such
thing[s] is certainly being penny wise and pound foolish, as it
keeps the men much longer in Hospital.

I intend writing to Tom and Al if I can get time before the
mail starts.

I hope to see some of you here shortly. The trains from
Gravesend run nearly every hour throughout the day. Remember
me to Hamblin and any enquiring friends, and believe me, my
dear Father

Your affectionate son
Christopher

39. *Expenses - news of the next Gazette*

Christopher Bassano to F.M. Bassano   7 Trout Row
                                             Chatham
                                             21 November 1848

Dear Father
    I recieved the Post Office order for £3.0.0. this morning.
I shall endeavour to make it go as far as possible. I have been
trying this week to do with as little as possible, but I find
the items in the bill exactly the same, except an increase of
1/6 for firing & Candles. I shall not however again have a
common sitting room with a man for it leaves no time for study
or anything else. I am very sorry to hear that you and Mother
are still on the sick list. If Mother requires a Doctor I
wonder you don't get Dr. Davies, for from what I have seen these
Army Doctors are not of much use.

---

4. See Chapter Five (IV).

If this arrives before you send the parcel will you put in it
Thompson's Dis[pensar]y, also Quincy's Lexicon.

Tell Walter, Linney came down here this morning to bring me
news of the next Gazette. It is quite a joke here about the
tailors always bring[ing] the news, and the chaps are always
pumping me to know how they get it. Mopsticks was wrong about
the thimble, but I don't object to recieve the promised seal.
On the contrary, T have wanted one a long time and indeed
intended buying one the day I came here.

I will write a few lines to my long friend the first opportunity, meantime, believe [me] to remain

> Your affectionate Son
> Christopher

40. *Awaiting a posting*

Christopher Bassano to F.M. Bassano   7 High Street
                                             Ordnance Place
                                             Chatham
                                             Wednesday 12 a.m.
                                             [December 1848]

My dear Father
    I recieved your laconic letter, following Walter's of a
similar description, the other day, and I regret exceedingly not
having heard from either of you since, especially at this, to
me, anxious time. I have thought it very unkind of Walter,
inasmuch as although I let the cat out of the bag accidentally
about the information he so promptly gave me respecting the
W[est] I[ndies] appointment, and which had he intimated the
annoyance it might cause to the parties concerned, which I was
quite innocent of, I should have kept it strictly private.

I called on Lewis tonight and spent another jolly evening,
licking him two games out of three at cribbage for sixpence a
game. I am going to his house again on Saturday next to dinner.
He dines at six o'Clock and he pressed me in the *strongest*
manner possible to request you would come down on that day to
dinner, saying at the same time he should be most delighted to
give you a bed which he has *always ready*. Mrs. Lewis, who is a
very comfortable lady, joined in her intreaties. I have therefore only stated what they have said, and if you will avail
yourself of their offer, do. But on the other hand (and I don't
see any reason why you should not accept the invitation), if
you prefer sleeping at an Hotel, as Mathews' friend did last
Saturday just opposite this house at the cost of 2/6, you may
do so, or sleep in my room - nothing would give me greater

pleasure. Mathews' father did the same thing, but slept at a
friend of his in the Dockyard, and he enjoyed the trip, he told
me, amazingly. He is a jolly old fellow, and he gave me an
invitation to his house when I came to London. His residence
is in Church Street, just by Paddington Green. He also told me
that, contrary to what was expected, only one Reg[imen]t of the
three was going to the Bengal presidency, and I think he believed
that to be the 83rd. He does not appear at all anxious about
what appointment his son may get, and he thinks there can be
little doubt that I shall get an Indian Reg[imen]t. He behaved
very well to me and expressed his obligations to me for having
been so friendly to his son (who is still living with me).
Williamson has returned from London tonight and brings news of
Adams having exchanged from the 82nd to an Indian Reg[imen]t.
(I suppose the sneek has been trying to get one himself). Is
this true? I also recieved a Lr̃e [letter] from Crisp this day,
in which he informs that the man he exchanged with is, or has,
returned and that they will want two Ass[istant] Surgeons
besides. The greatest excitement prevails here about these
appointments. Who is to have the 12th Lancers? Of course it is
too expensive for me, although it would be jolly to serve under
my esteemed Friend Anderson.

Poor Hardy lost his wife this morning and he, in addition to
[h]is weak state of mind, has now half a dozen children to
provide for.

I expect to be blown up by old Pink tomorrow for not having
obtained leave of absence for tonight, but when I explain to
the old fool where I was, he will with his usual civility (to
me) shut up.

I this morning had a bathe in a cold bath as salt as the sea
just beyond Brompton Barracks, and although the water was cold
I have recieved great benefit notwithstanding. My health has
been during the last week first rate.

I hope Mother and you are quite well, together with Melinda
& Ellen. Tell Melinda to remember me to Mr., Mrs. & Miss King
(alias Clara). If you see John or Arthur also pay my respects.
Tell Hamblin that he is a great humbug not to drop me a line,
or beat up to my quarters. Write to me by Friday, and in the
meantime, believe me your affectionate son

Christopher.

I leave the next page to acknowledge the receipt of any Lr̃e
which may arrive by tomorrow's post.

I recieved Walter's letter by this morning's Post, and tell
him that I should be glad if he would ascertain what terms
Linney will make my uniform, but at the same time I have no idea

152

of getting epauletts &c. from him, as the cheaper way would be
to get them at the regular houses as Al did. I wish you would
look out all Alfred's bills you can, so that I shall have some
guide. I am waiting to get my appointment before I apply for
leave in order that no difficulty may arise, so you need not
expect me yet. Tell Walter, Matthews' Father expected to have
had the names in for India at the beginning of this week. I
believe he is humbuging me about them.

Yours affectionately,
Christopher.

III

VOYAGE TO INDIA

On the 22nd December 1848 Christopher Bassano
was appointed Assistant Surgeon in the 70th
Regiment, under orders for India. He got his
uniform from Messrs. J. & G. Linney, Army Outfitters
of Regent Street, and early in January 1849 sailed
for Cork to embark with his regiment for India.

41. *Military outfit*

Bill from George Linney, 23 Regent Street.[5]   6 February 1849

	£	s.	d.
A dress scarlet cloth full dress Coatee richly [*illeg.*], lined with silk, & including silk linings.	8	0	0
A pair rich gold work [*illeg.*] Epauletts	5	12	0
Patent Springs.		7	6
A Sup. Scarlet cloth Shell Jacket, including silk linings	3	3	0
A Sup. Scarlet cashmere [torn]	–	–	–
Two pairs Gold Shoulder [torn]	–	–	–
A pair Unifm ----- trousers, Scarlet stripes [torn]	–	–	–
A Grey Milld Beaver --- Coat, lined through	3	5	5
A rich Gilt Regulation sword	3	0	0
A rich Gold Sword Knot		13	0
A Black Morocco Sling Belt		18	0
A full dress Cocked Hat	3	0	0
Two forage caps	2	2	0

5. The bill is torn.

2 pairs Buck. Gloves	4/-		8	0
1 Military Stock			3	0
6 White Jean Jackets	10/-	3	0	0
6 White Jean Vests	9/-	2	14	0
1 dozen Unifm Vest Butts.			5	0
A Brown Twill Angola Sporting Coat, lined through				
A do do Vest		3	3	0
Two pairs summer --- trousers		2	10	0
A Pr. Glove Hands			7	0
An Airtight Japan Coatee Epaulette Case		1	5	0
A Cocked Hat Case			6	0
A Sword Bag			4	0
A pair Best Bullock Trunks Iron Bound		3	10	0
A pair Grey Milld Buckn Trousers		1	10	0

£57 3 6

10 per cent discount   5 14 6

£51 9 0[6]

42. *Waiting to sail*

Christopher Bassano to Charlotte Bassano   Cork
                                                    13 January 1849

My dear Mother
     I find by Walter's L̃re of the 10th (received on Friday
morning) that you have not recovered from the fatigue caused by
my departure. I hope however you have ceased to mourn after
your beloved sawbones. I regret leaving you all, but from what
I have seen, I have every reason to believe that I shall spend
a very pleasant life in the fighting 70th. The Surgeon [Harvey],
although a rough looking fellow, is a gentleman at heart, and
has behaved very kindly to me. And in the Assistant Surgeon
Johnston I already have found a most sincere friend.

     I have made several purchases at Cork, and from what I have
seen I believe every thing may be obtained as cheap or cheaper
here as in London. I bought a first-rate hair mattress for 30/-,
the hair at 1/2 per lb. and of the best quality, at a shop like
Shoulbred's, and also about 3 yards of Kid[d]erminster carpet
for 3/-, 3 yards of chintz for curtains at 8[d], all the best
quality. At one shop, nearly as large as Rippon & Burton, I
laid out £3 in tin bath, jug, bason, hammer, chisel, nails,
filter, gimblet, Lamp - Goblet, Candles, Soap - Blacking, Lunch

---

6. £40 was paid on 15 September 1849, the remainder not until
    14 June 1854, by draft dated Ferozpore, 14 April 1854.

Tray, Matches, Hat & Coat hook, Oil, &c. I think I have every
thing but the trousers Walter speaks of, and I admire his coolness about our stop[p]ing here 2 weeks when we are positively
to start on Monday. I think the chances are that I shall not
get my trousers if he has sent them by Liverpool. However it
will not grieve me much, and if it will afford him any pleasure
I'll be beautifully sick in the Bay of Biscay and bottle the
pieces for an emetic and send them him.

I called today & paid my respects to the ladies in the
Regiment, as I thought it would be the only time they might see
me as I used to was, and they seemed to think it a mark of great
attention and were delighted to see me. Col[one]l Galloway's
wife is [a] scrumptious woman and so is Johnston's.

I shall most likely be able to send you a few £5 notes before
I start, but don't be disappointed if I don't, for I have not
bought either pistols, gun, or paid my Hotel & Mess a/cs. I
intended writing to Melinda, but it has just struck two o'clock
and I want to get a good night's rest. But tell her I hope
before this the cigar cases are on their way, for nothing will
disappoint me more than not recieving them. Give my love to
her, as well as Ellen, Father & the rest, and if I have time to
write again before I start of course I will. Tell Walter that
if I had known about Miss Wigstrom earlier I might have called,
since I went twice to Passage which is 8 or 9 miles from Cork.
I may however have an opportunity tomorrow or Sunday. I am
daily expecting to hear from you, but I suppose you are too busy,
so believe me to remain, my dear Mother,

Your ever affectionate Son
Christopher.

Mrs. Hamblin gave me a most beautiful purse which when I pull
out of my pocket the fascinating Cork ladies in the shops
invariably begin to admire and even, to my great dismay, insist
upon having it in their hand, although it is full of gold.

P.S. Enclosed a P.O. order for £5 out of my pay which I
rec[eive]d this morning.

43. *Delayed by gales*

Christopher Bassano to Melinda Bassano   Cove Harbour
                                                18 January 1849

Dear Melinda
    I recieved you[r] paper box crushed to atoms yesterday, also
a Letter this Morning. Fortunately the cigar *cases* were not
injured and I may think myself lucky at getting them at all.

They are both very beautiful and I scarcely know which to like
best. I hope to be able to give Al his in the course of a few
months, if I am not turned into the sea to feed the fishes.
That parcel from Linney has not yet come, so I shall be in a fix
for trousers. There is no Chance of our leaving this harbour so
long as the present south-west winds prevail. It has been
blowing a fearful gale all night, and is at the present time
causing the ship to rock about dreadfully. Some of them already
feel queer. My small cabin is not yet to rights, and is not
likely to be, for I have had so much to do that I have not had
any time. I have written a short Lre to Al today, but in consequence of the movement of the vessel and the darkness in my
cabin I cannot tell what I am writing, so with love to all,
believe me, Dear Lin,

Your affec[tionate] bro[ther]
Christopher

I am the most responsible person on board, and every body
come[s] to me about every thing. The officers are very pleasant
and so are the crew.

44. *Blown into Milford Haven*

Christopher Bassano's diary   February 1849

The ship Diana, having on board a portion of the 70th
Reg[imen]t, sail[e]d from the Cove of Cork on the 20th Jan[uar]y
1849, and after beating about the Channel for a week put into
Milford Haven. The Troops were ordered to disembark, and
billets in the Town of Milford and the adjoining villages were
obtained for them. The cargo having been partly removed, about
70 Cwt. of biscuits were found damaged, and a large portion of
the water was found to have leaked out of the casks. The
Officers were billeted at the Nelson Hotel where they remained
a fortnight, and on the 12th Feb[ruar]y re-embarked with the
Troops. One soldier deserted, but was brought back, having been
taken into custody at Haverford West. A few days after this the
men refused to work, and six of them were taken before the
magistrate & sentenced to two months imprisonment. The Captain
however got some fresh hands and on the Morning of the 25th
sailed from Milford with a fair Wind.

Christopher Bassano to F.M. Bassano

[1] Ship Diana
     Milford Haven
     27 January 1849

[2] Nelson Hotel
     Milford
     Pembrokeshire
     30 January 1849

My dear Father
    I am now safely anchored opposite the Town of Milford where
I think there is every probability of remaining a fortnight or
three weeks since the Captain informs us that he will have to
write to the Owners in London to know what he shall do. I have
written to the D[irector] G[eneral], but I do not intend writing
to the Staff Office in Bristol, which I believe is the nearest
station to this where a Staff Surgeon is stationed. What is to
be done with the Troops I do not at present know. The Captain
tells us we were in great danger, but I am glad to say I was not
aware of it, and I have to thank God for our safety. I wrote
to Walter today giving a hurried account of the knocking about
in the Channel.

    Since writing the above three days have elapsed and I have
now (Tuesday morning) just disembarked together with the whole
of the Troops & Officers for the purpose of remaining at Milford
& Hakin(qy) (two small villages separated by a narrow river)
until the cargo has been taken out and a hundred or two tons of
ballast shipped. I am living at the Nelson Hotel with my
brother officer[s], who are right good fellows, and if I do not
spend as jolly a time as I ever did in my life it is a wonder
to me. I began to appreciate dry land after having been tossed
about in a gale for a whole week. The Captain has not heard
from Messrs. Phillips, the owner[s] who reside in London, so he
does not know exactly what will be done, but he is of opinion
most decidedly that the cargo must all be taken out. When we
embarked, the ship was noticed to hang over to the Port side a
little and since we have been at sea it has increased, and now
she appears as if she had had a shift of cargo, and I understand
today that she has a cargo of salt which is believed to have
dissolved on one side. I only heard this today.

    The opinion here is that we will be three or four weeks
before we can again embark. We have - at least our Capt.
Durnford has - written to Cox's to supply some money for this
unlooked for event, but I should think the East India Company
or the owners should falk [*sic*] out since we have all recieved
our pay until May next & the greater part has been spent.

    I hope you an[d] Mother are well. Rem[em]ber me to all my

friends and believe me
My dear Father
Your affectionate Son
Christopher

P.S. Send some London papers please. We want particularly to know about the other ships.[7]

46. *At Milford Haven*

Christopher Bassano to Charlotte Bassano   Ship Diana
                                               Milford Haven
                                               28 January 1849

My dear Mother
You, I have no doubt, have been extremely anxious about your beloved Sawbones, but thank God we have managed to come again to an anchor without having suffered any very serious inconvenience.

I am at this moment writing at the Nelson Hotel in Milford Haven having this morning come on shore with three of our Officers for the purpose of attending divine service and offering up prayers for our safety. I know not yet whether we shall remain on board the Diana while they unload her or have to put up at the Hotel, but under any circumstances I dare say I shall run short of tin if we remain here many weeks, and I almost regret have[ing] sent home my £10. I understand that all the other Troop ships put back to Cork and I am not at all sorry we came to this side of the water since it seems so much more like home, though I should have preferred a more convenient place for getting to London, and were there a Railroad to this town I do think I should get away for a week.

I posted a Letter about 5 o'Clock last night for Walter and another which I gave to the Captain about 8 o'Clock to the Director General, though I am not certain if I should have done so, but I dare say there is no harm in so doing. I have a letter partly written to Father on board the vessel, which I had not time to finish last night. I should like to know what the Hall[8] have done about my medicines. I find my bill amounts to about £19 and that it is customary to have the money deducted from our pay at Calcutta. So unless they have made some arrange-ment with the E[ast] I[ndia] Com[pan]y I shall have to pay in the same ratio as the rest.

---

7. Carrying the rest of the regiment. On the cover of this letter is a pencil note giving Tom Bassano's new address c/o John Wells, Calicut, Malabar.
8. Apothecaries' Hall.

Tell Walter to inform me if there has been one cold day since
I left London, since it has been with us a continuance of
warmish winds. It is rather cooler today & I am anxiously looking forward for some skating. Send me some London papers, and
anythink else likely to be interesting to me. I believe I wrote
to Melinda ackn[ow]l[e]dg[i]ng the receipt of the cigar cases.
I hope she & the whole of you are well and in excellent spirits
as I am. Remember me to my Aunts and Cousins, also to Uncle
Walter, Hamblin, & in fact any one, requesting them all to write
to me. I would willingly write to them had I sufficient time on
my hands.

Well, dear Mother, for the present believe me your affectionate Son
Christopher

I am now just going for a walk about Milford and then intend
returning to the ship. The post leaves here at 5 o'clock daily,
& as this will be in time this afternoon, I expect you will
have it on Tuesday morning. Excuse this scrawl - I had to mend
my pen with the carving knife.

47. *The ship Diana*

Christopher Bassano to Walter Bassano   Nelson Hotel
                                                        Milford
                                                        1 February 1849

Dear Mopsticks
    My poor *breeches*, which I am so annoyed about, are not
American drill, but *two pairs of thin doe skin* which Linney
promised to make me and about which I swear you have not said
a word. I might well be in a fix since I have only one pair of
them, and those very thick. As to getting drill at Cork, I only
had your L̃re a day or two before leaving, so that I only had
time to get one pair. This is the fifth time I have been at
great pains to explain it to you. If you don't blow up Linney
and cease your cheek, I'll pull your ear.

    What the devil do you want to know? I have told you in
every Letter I have written that Capt[ai]n Durnford & Lieuts.
Willis, Buc[h]anan, Chute & Crawley, together with myself are
all batchelors, so who are the Ladies you would have me dilate
upon? It is just possible the last Gent[leman] alluded to may
take unto himself a wife, & the most graphic description of
her shall be given, but I am doubtful if I can possibly do it
in so short a time, and certain objections may arise in the fair
lady, as well as in St. James'[s] Street.[9] What cock and bull

---
9. Army Medical Board Office, at 13 St. James's Place,
   St. James's Street.

159

story were you sticking into me about Philip having £800 a year?

I am glad to hear about Tom. I shall write to him addressed
to Mr. Wells at Calicut, Madras.

The number in my ship are as follows: 1 Captain, 4 Subalterns,
1 Staff, 7 Serjeant[s], 7 Corporals, 1 Drummer, 145 Privates,
19 Women, & 25 Children, being together 210, and this number I
shall to the best of my power endeavour, while here, to increase.
I went into the Kitchen on Sunday last to wash my hand, but for
the express purpose of seeing five or six amiable kitchen maids
and strongly recommending their immediate union with certain
privates who I should make it my business to recommend to them,
so that I expect before we again embark to add twenty or thirty
Welsh women to our number.

After writing that letter to Father last night I went on
board the ship an[d] to my great surprise found about 70 Cwt.
of biscuits just brought on deck fron the hold so hot you could
scarcely bear to touch them, and my friend Crawley declares he
saw a man's coat burnt off while carrying a sack. Persons
acquainted with this sort of bread as well as the officers
belonging to the ship are of opinion that the ship would soon
have been on fire, and this idea is also strengthened by the
above named gentleman having noticed the coating of tar inside
the ship having been melted and combining chemically with the
bread - and his veracity none can deny. But say what they may
it was a most providential escape. The owner has arrived
today - or a chief clerk named Webb - and he thinks it may
possibly be put to rights in a week or ten days, but others
consider a much longer time is required. They have not yet
taken out the salt, but I hope they will remove it all. I spoke
to Mr. Webb this morning about my cabin & the Captain suggested
making it larger. I was thinking this morning of writing to the
East India House, or the owner, demanding one the size specified.
Should I write to the D[irector] G[eneral] giving a monthly a/c
of the sick? I thought of writing to Appleton to know if the
East India Comp[an]y would pay our debts here. We expect to
hear from Cox's tomorrow about our month's pay. How is Ann &
the babies? It['s] post time, so I cannot say more, so for the
present
                    Believe me Dear Walter
                    Your affec[tionate] Bro[ther]
                              Christopher.

P.S. Dam the trousers - send a newspaper or two.

48. *The hotel - and countryside*

Christopher Bassano to Melinda Bassano

Nelson Hotel
Milford
Pembrokeshire
4 February 1849

My dear Melinda

I am sorry to find by your Lre that the Cholera has made its appearance in Kensington[10] & I hope none of you are making yourselves uneasy about it. I am much obliged to you for the Illustrated London News which you would have sent. I hope it will arrive tomorrow.

At this Hotel there are three young Ladies, daughters of the Hostess, one of whom afforded us no little amusement last night by playing on the piano & singing. Her voice is excellent, and it was great fun. We sent in word we should like to hear them perform, and after a considerable lot of rum te tum &c. we got them into the room, but for some time we could not prevail upon them to sing, because from what they had heard I was considered a first rate vocalist and musician,[11] and Mr. Crawley a very facecious individual (and in his manner like Al) commenced cracking his joke & setting us all laughing, so that the fair damsels thought we were poking our fun at them. As we became more grave they assumed more courage & then we had no end of glees &c. to our hearts' content. We all went to church this morning and had a very appropriate sermon delivered.

The country about here is very like that around Cork, consisting of hills & dales. The rock is red stone and the inhabitants make their fires with a mixture of mud from the river & small coal. This they make up in heaps like mortar and then form it into pieces about the size of your fist, which pieces they place in a very judicious manner in the grate, leaving a hole in the centre for the air to pass up. It does not blaze but burns very like coke though longer.

I wish to write to Tom this afternoon, so dear Lin, believe me your
                    Affectionate Bro[ther]
                    Christopher.

---

10. The first cholera epidemic reached Britain in 1832; this (1849) was the second great epidemic in Europe. The family was living at 7 Wiple Place, Church Lane, Kensington.
11. The Bassanos were descended from a family of Venetian musicians.

161

9. Ready to sail again

Christopher Bassano to Charlotte Bassano   Milford Haven
                                                  15 February 1849

My dear Mother
    I have not sufficient time to pen a long epistle, but I
thought you would like to have a line from me in reply to yours
which I received yesterday morning. I am happy to hear your
health is so good and I hope now that we are all away you will
live happy and comfortable with our old Dad. I went on shore
yesterday to bid adieu to the fair ladies in Milford. I did not
succeed in my endeavours to walk into their affections, but
exceeded my expectations in making away with the money. I found
after paying all that I was £11 poorer than when I landed, but
it's astonishing how fond men in the army are of making the
money fly and it seems so catching that I can scarcely refrain
from joining them. My first act however when I arrive in India
will be to send home sufficient to pay all expenses incurred,
and then I shall be happy.

    The ship is now at the mouth of the Harbour and the wind just
sufficiently to the north to enable us to sail, so with love to
all, believe me to remain
                        My dear Mother
                        Your Affection[a]te Son
                            Christopher.

50. More delays

Christopher Bassano to Walter Bassano   Milford
                                               21 February 1849

Dear Mopsticks
    I slept at the Hotel last night after spending a pleasant
evening with Dr. Byers' daughters, and this morning went on
board with Captain Pugh and an officer to take the men prisoners
to Haverfordwest, the nearest town where a magistrate resides.
What will be the result I know not, but I fancy after being
reprimanded they will return to their duty. If not, I imagine
the Captain will be some time remanning his ship.

    In a country paper in a paragraph dilating on the qualities
of some very early lamb it was stated that the Officers of the
70th expressed theirselves highly delighted with the repast.
I regret it was not mutton.

    How is Annie & the babies?   Tell Frank[12] I must have her in

---

12. Annie Francis, aged about four years.

162

India. She can come out with Ellen & Melinda. I think after
Tom wrote such a long letter it is a disgrace to each of you
not to have replied and to make out Melinda the cause is making
much worse of it. I begin to think I shall require a fresh
outfit before I start. I have not heard from you for some time.
I dare say you will have time after receiving this & believe me
Your &c.
Christopher.

51. *The voyage*

Christopher Bassano's diary.   February–June 1849

25 February 1849.
    Sailed about 12 o'Clock with a North-East Wind from Milford
Haven after having remained in that Harbour a Month.

Sunday, 26 February 1849.
    Ther[mometer] 50°, wind N–W very light. Divine Service
performed by Capt. Pugh. A whale made her appearance near the
ship this morning.

8 March 1849.
    In the Latitude of Madera today, that Island being about 30
miles on our larboard bow. At 10 p.m. saw a partial eclipse of
the moon. Dance on the deck with the officers and soldiers'
wives, Mr. Chute Dancing with Mrs. Hazleton and displaying great
taste in the Irish jig.

9 March 1849.
    Tied a bottle to the rigging and fired with pistols.
Buc[h]anan broke it and I cut the rope nearly through with the
ball. We afterwards had some gymnastics.

Saturday, 10 March 1849.
    Amused ourselves in the afternoon by jumping with crutches,
&c.

Sunday, 11 March 1849.
    Splendid day, wind N–E by E. Capt. Pugh read prayers.

12 March 1849.
    Flying fishes and porpoises seen today.

14 March 1849.
    Saw St. Nicholas[13] this morning at 12 o'Clock. We sailed
along the shore for some time without seeing anything but goats.

---

13. Cape Verde Is.

Dined at 3 o'Clock. Bore in for the shore after dinner. The
captain then lowered the boat and manned it with some of his crew
taking on shore Capt. D[urnford], Willis, Buc[hanan], Chute, &
myself, leaving Crawley in charge. We landed at a most beautiful
creek called Freshwater Bay and were soon surrounded by natives
who seemed glad to see Capt. Pugh & his boy. Saw near the shore
a number of cocoa nut trees.[14] Buc[h]anan climbed up one and
threw down a few, by the milk of which we refreshed ourselves.
Saw a vin[e]yard, grapes not formed. Returned to the boat, but
found the boy Frank's mother had not arrived - waited until
about 8 o'Clock, when she arrived & the place was lighted up with
Cocoa nut leaves. Women pretty - bought some eggs, goats, fowls,
nuts, Bananas, &c. for a few shirts, some calico, and a raysur
[razor]. I had a bathe in the sea, and on leaving them about
9 o'Clock we had a most affectionate parting. The natives
offered up a prayer on the beach after we had left, for our
safety, which was quite necessary since we were not sure until
we had pulled nearly three hours if we should ever get to the
ship that night, and I believe we should not, had it not been
for me and Willis taking an oar each and pulling so manfully.
The captain was of opinion that the ship was fifteen miles from
the shore and was drifting from us at the rate of three miles an
hour.

Thursday, 15 March 1849.
    Saw St. Jago and Togo.[15] The peak of Togo, a volcanic
mountain, is 9670 feet high, and presented a most beautiful
appearance.

Monday, 19 March 1849.
    Mr. Fitzpatrick caught a small shark.

Wednesday, 21 March 1849.
    Commenced making a set of chessmen. Played a game at
Backgammon with Buchanan, *and although he had taken off several
men and I had three or four men on his table, yet I beat him,
and lost a dice overboard.[16] At 9 p.m. Buchanan went on the
poop and the third mate having informed us that there was a shark
about I threw over the line and soon after the shark took it and
he was soon hauled up and proved to be a blue one. I dissected
the next morning his jaw.

Thursday, 22 March 1849.
    At 7 a.m. a ship was seen and soon after a boat was lowered
and the 1st Mate took some L̃res on board for us. She turned
out to be the John Bartlett from Port Adelaide to London.
Finished our chess men. At 12 p.m. we had a heavy shower of

---

14. Here is a rough sketch.
15. Cape Verde Is.
16. This sentence from the asterisk is crossed out.

rain which we all went out into perfectly naked.

Friday, 23 March 1849.
    Capt. Pugh nearly harpooned a shark, the [*illeg.*] having only hit him on the tail he soon extricated himself.

Saturday, 24 March 1849.
    At 7 o'Clock a.m. saw a ship 5 miles off which sent a boat to us to know the longitude. While the boat was alongside I had a bathe. The ship was the Adelaide from the Coast of Africa bound to Madeira. Several women complaining of an eruption resembling itch, but which appears to be Eczema Solare.

Sunday, 25 March 1849.
    A calm this morning, so I lowered myself from the bow by a rope & had a bathe in the sea. Divine Service read by Capt. Pugh. Caught a shark about 1 o'Clock and tried to Catch some dolphins.

Thursday, 29 March 1849.
    Exchanged names with the Robina, but they did not seem to understand what we said in answer to some queries they put, so the conversation fell on the deck.

31 March 1849.
    Crossed the line, and endeavoured during the night to create a false alarm by crying out "Shark", but in consequence of the over excitability of Buchanan the plan did not succeed, so we were made April fools ourselves. Had some good songs from the sailors, some of whom were shaved.

Sunday, 4 April 1849.
    Caught a Tiger shark.

Monday, 2 April 1849.
    Perfectly calm. Twelve ships in sight. Caught a large Tiger shark.

Tuesday, 3 April 1849.
    I hooked a shark this morning, but he got off and was again hooked by Willis, who allowed him to break the line and escape.

4 April 1849.
    Sixteen ships in sight. No wind.

Friday, 6 April 1849.
    Strong breeze, supposed to be the commencement of the South-East Trades.

10 April 1849.
    Sustained a reverse at Chess from Durnford. Played with Buchanan giving him a castle, and saved a licking by getting a

stalemate.

11 April 1849.
   Strong breeze from S.E. - rather cool.

Sunday, 15 April 1849.
   Wind blowing hard and a heavy swell running.

Monday, 16 April 1849.
   Wind fair - air cool.

Thursday, 19 April 1849.
   Latitude 30° 26 South, longitude 22° 46 West. Fair Wind.

20 April 1849.
   My birthday.[17] Wind N.E. While at dinner we saw the first
Albertros.

21 April 1849.
   A calm. Caught an albertros. I and the second mate skinned
him.

Sunday, 22 April 1849.
   Saw a cape hen and a stinkpot, the latter a black bird with a
yellow beak, and so named on account of its unpleasant smell.

24 April 1849.
   Saw several albatross & Peons. Also large numbers of whale
birds and Stormy petrels.

25 April 1849.
   Carried away our port main brace bumkin, and our port main
topsail stensail Boom.

26 April 1849.
   Large numbers of birds about the ship today. We amused
ourselves with firing at the Peons. I killed four out of six
I fired at.

Tuesday, 1 May 1849.
   A dead calm today until three o'Clock when it commenced
blowing and at four the wind increased to a strong gale, and in
about a quarter of an hour every sail was taken in, and we
sail[ed] during that night under close reef topsail. Our main
Royal sail was blown to pieces before it could be got in. The
sea soon broke over the deck and the hatches were fastened down.
I, Captain Pugh, Durnford, & Buchanan played a rubber at whist
though the ship was tossing about so much that we were obliged
to hold our cards while they were being dealt.

_____

17. His 25th.

166

Wednesday, 2 May 1849.
    Wind blowing a gale, sea breaking over the ship every minute.
At four o'Clock I was called to attend Mrs. Mahoney, and about
half past 5 o'Clock I brought into the world a female child.

3 May 1849.
    Sea very high, and the ship rolling about fearfully. Had a
good night.

Friday, 4 May 1849.
    We found we had made about 200 miles since the gale
commenced and we are now just to the east of the Cape.

Saturday, 5 May 1849.
    A fine day. Saw a ship about 10 miles ahead this morning –
came up with her about one o'Clock and spoke with her for about
five minutes. She was one of Green's ships, the Windsor, 1000
tons, bound to Calcutta, having lost her fore & main mast a few
nights ago. Several passengers were on board. She was out of
sight from the deck by sunset. Calm in the evening.

Sunday, 6 May 1849.
    Weather fine and nearly a calm in the morning.

7 May 1849.
    A squall came on about one o'Clock, and the wind continued
to blow hard during the rest of the day.

8 May 1849.
    Caught an albatross. Saw a ship about 10 miles to the north
of us.

9 May 1849.
    Carried away a boom this morning during a squall. Heavy rain
in the evening accompanied by lightning.

18 May 1849.
    Main topsail Hallyards gave way – no one hurt.

Saturday, 19 May 1849.
    Fancied we saw the Island of St. Paul about 12 o'clock a.m.
About one o'Clock p.m. we saw the Island of Amsterdam, which at
first look[ed] like a whale. Buchanan, Willis and myself let
out a reef in the main topsail and I came down a rope from the
topsail yard to the mizen mast.

Sunday, 20 May 1849.
    I was called up at two o'Clock this morning to attend Mrs.
Madden, who at about half past three was delivered of an
apparently dead child, which however I managed by various means
to resuscitate.

Tuesday, 22 May 1849.
A soldier who had been labouring under consumption for some months died almost reduced to a skeleton, and was cast into the sea at 11 o'Clock, Capt. Pugh having read the burial Service over him. A shoal of porpoises surrounded the ship at 3 o'clock p.m. I fired at some of them, but no doubt missed. Won 5/- of Buchanan, and 7/6 last night, at Whist.

Sunday, 27 May 1849.
Mrs. Beldham confined. The child was only a six month foetus and did not live above two or three hours.

28 May 1849.
A court martial held by Willis, Chute & Crawley - I and Capt. Pugh were witnesses. He was sentenced to 40 d[a]ys hard labour. Saw a booby in the afternoon.

29 May 1849.
O'Reeff's Court Martial confirmed. Buchanan read it on parade.

Saturday, 2 June 1849.
Two or three men and women presented themselves with Scurvy.

Monday, 4 June 1849.
Durnford's birthday. Almost perfectly calm in the morning and quite so in the evening when Willis, Buch[anan] & Mr. Fitz. jumped overboard, and had it not been for me Buchanan would have met a watery grave.

Tuesday, 5 June 1849.
A light breeze sprung up and increased towards the evening - which seems to be the S.W. monsoon.

Thursday, 7 June 1849.
At noon we were in lat. 1.15 North, and about 85 E. Longitude.

[19 June 1849 landed at Calcutta]

CHAPTER FIVE

Three Bassanos in India
(1849-52)

With the arrival of Christopher at Calcutta in June 1849 the three youngest Bassano brothers were now all living and working in India, although for the three and a half years when they were all there together they never met. Tom was working hard in the South at coffee planting, Alfred was serving with his regiment in the far North-West frontier area, while Christopher spent his first 18 months in or near Calcutta, before moving up the country to Meerut and Cawnpore. He too was leading a busy life. Neither Tom nor Alfred wrote many letters home, but Christopher wrote twenty[1] during his first two years, before he too lapsed into silence once the novelty of new scenes and a new way of life had worn off. He also wrote twenty-three to his brothers and sister Ellen during this time, but none of these have survived.

I

"DEAR TOM ... HE HAS HAD A HARD LIFE OF IT"

Tom Bassano found his life as a coffee planter rather different from what he had envisaged when he left the sea at the end of 1847. He worked for his first employer for a year and then left him for another master, with whom he also stayed for about a year. Nothing was heard from him for a year after he had left the sea,[2] but during 1849 while he was working for John Wells of Calicut he sent home several letters, but again during the whole of 1850 there was silence and his family became very worried about him, especially his mother,[3] but having once

---

1. Christopher kept a note of letters sent, and to a lesser extent of those received. 14 of the 20 survive.
2. The first letter was sent 27 December 1848. See Letter 52.
3. See Letter 80.

more found a new master in late 1850 or early 1851 he wrote home once more. He was to manage the estates of this family (Morris) for about five years.

52. *Fall of Multan - plans to open estates - the ginger business*

Tom Bassano to Walter Bassano   Choroor
                                                 31 January 1849

Dear Walter

Glorious News! Mooltan has fallen - Alfred's name not amongst the killed or wounded. The Gallant 32nd figured conspicuously in the breaches, being part of the storming party. Alfred will be at the top of the Lutenant's list as almost all, or one half, of the Officers above him are killed. Every paper I take hold of - Colonels, Capt[ain], Qua[r]termaster &c., one after [an]other killed. In fact I think he is now to get a C.B., as my master says. In fact it has been taken with comparative little looss on our side. He will get any quantity of prize money, as it is said the fort is half full of rupees.

As regards myself, I am getting on swimmingly ginger scraping. They have made a fine thing of the Pinu Estate at Wynaud, having plucked 1200 cwt. off it, a ma[i]den crop of 300 acres. Tell that to any West India or Ceylon Coffee planter and they will not believe you. I wrote to you about the coffee pl[antation]s in [my] last letter. If you and Philop - I will write to him about it - can manage to put 20£ a month together, or a third party - Ellen - another 10£ a month, and remit it to me, I will open an estate for you which shall be a fortune for you, wives and children. With this 300 rupees a month I will keep myself, work like a horse of course, get a lease of land by paying something about 3 rupees a month, and go on quitetly [*sic*] clearing 100 acres a year - and an estate of 300 acres is something considerable in 3 years. It was Mr. Wells, my master, said this was the best plan, as it is what he is doing at this present moment for a brother. He is with me for 2 or 3 days ever[y] 20 day and [then] up in his mountain home cutting away. Ther[e] are 3 new estates now opening, but the people see so clearly what it is that they are keeping it dark as much as possible. Of course, opening your estate we would dispence with all permanant buildings untill the estate had payed itself, and then begin upon permanent works. Mud huts can be made like little pallases, as far as comfort goes, and what more dose a man want? Of course, I don't want you to think I offer to do this without some motive. I should expect to becom[e] a share holder in time, and that you can settle yourselves. But I assure you, it is not a thing to be laughed at or thrown away, if it is in your power. But I think time flys so fast that ere this you must be getting a good salary, for if I remember righ[t], yours was an increasing salary, and if your famamily [*sic*] has not encreased

170

of late so fast as at first, you perhaps will be able to manage
it. At all events Philop might of himself, if his salary is as
I was given to understand in a letter I got from you once,
telling me he was on the War Office Est[ablishment] and that he
would get £800 a year in a short time. Consider about it both
of you, but don't laugh at the skeem, as I have been on shore
more than a twelve month and not at all anxious to go to sea
again. If I did, ther[e] is a command open for me at Calicut
this present moment. But I think the situation I am now in bids
fair to be a good one, and a perminant one, only it is very hot.
In the hills it is cool and healthy. Mr. Grant wants me to join
him on the [? Pinu] estate as a manager to one of the branches,
a salary of 100 a month, but between the good situation I am now
in, the command in the estate, in perspective of yours, I want
some one to advise me which to take, or which to keep. This
ginger business is a curious sly business, as I find by the
ginger being quoted in the Newspaper that this ginger realises
a 100 percent. The money is gliding throw my hands like wild
fire, 60 miles from my master, and when he comes he never looks
into my account book, but only talks away, and ask[s] if I want
more money. It is not his mone[y], but the Mr. Remington, a
large house in Bombay, he being agent at Calicut for them.

For goodness sake, write an answer to this sharp, as I am
anxious[ly] looking for home news in answer to my first letter
of Dec[ember] 27th, since my arrival here. Another letter I
sent this month, and then as per promise a letter every month.
I hope you, Annie, and little children are well. The last from
you Annie was not so well. Give my love to her and all the
Famaly my Mother included, and to conclude, believe me to remain
your affectionate Brother Tom.

Excuse hast[e] and scrawl; as my work is having the accounts
of 5 Station[s] to look to and Cast a/c to all in my hand [it]
is no sinecure birth, my pen never being out of my hand when at
home, and obliged to visit three station[s] a day, while the
ginger purchase is going on. T.B.

Tell Philop about it. I will write him next month as there
is plenty of time to talk about it, as you can't commence till
Oct[ober].

Tell Cris I will write to him next month.

53. *Expectations*

Tom Bassano to Charlotte Bassano
Lakadee
22 April 1849

My dear Mother
I received Father's letter in which he begs of me to send a
letter to you every mail. It shall be done for the future. I
am glad to say hitherto, since writing my first letter, I have
sent one by every mail except one, as I was waiting to here from
you all first. I am very much grieved to hear you are so unwell,
but am glad to hear that you have left the large house, and are
now in a nice quiet place, and trust ere the spring is over you
will be perfectly restored in health. You must not make yourself uneasy on my account, as I am living well and comfortable,
with every comfort a man can wish for, and quite my own master
as Mr. Wells lets me do just as I like. And [you] know I have
half a dozen trades at my finger ends, so should one fail I
always have another to clap on to. But there is not much chance
of my shifting now that I am opening a coffee estate on my own
a/c, and when it pays I shall send for Melinda to see this
beautifull country, and then by that time Alfred and Cristopher
will be high up in the service, and let that be the signal for
us all to come home togather. And then, please God, we shall
see our dear mother carve the large joint of rost Beef so often
enjoyed by her sons, and the china Bowl of punch made by your
own hand. Happy days in store, my dear Mother yet. Don't fret.
All though far apart, picture to yourself the joyous meeting it
will [be], Alfred in the red coat, Cris in the Blue, and Tom in
the broad-Brimmed planter's hat. Don't fret, Mother, or you
cannot improve in health if you do, but look forward to the
happy meeting it will be, and believe me to remain your ever
affectionate son Tom.

54. *Coffee planting and ginger scraping*

Tom Bassano to Ellen Bassano[4]
Choroor
29 December 1849

My dear Sister
Your long and interesting letter of the 31st of October duly
arrived. You talk of coming to me. I only wish it lay in my
power to receive you in a proper manner. I should be too happy,
but as I am always living in mud houses, 15 feet square, tents,
and sometimes no house over me at all, it would be rather a
difficult matter to receive a sister under such circumstances.

---

4. Copy in Ellen Bassano's hand, with improved spelling and
   punctuation added, not always happily.

You may see by the place this is dated from that I have again
shifted my quarters, and in two or three months more I shall
again make another shift. I will tell you how all this happens.

I left the Sea to turn Coffee Planter, and of course to begin
a Coffee Estate in the Wynaud Jungles you select your spot, then
build a little Shed to keep you from the dews of a night and
commence cutting jungle, and when the ground is burnt build a
better description of mud house - mud floor, rather nice things,
and very damp for a lady. That finished, get into it and you
are pretty snug for the monsoon, that is, rain for six months.
This monsoon, we had at the estate I was on 245 inches in 5½
months, so you can imagine a mud house is not a very comfortable
thing.

Well, after building Mr. Smith's bungalow and planting
160,000 coffee plants - which cannot be planted without being
superintended with one's own eyes - you may naturally conclude
it is not over pleasant or dry work, but as I was a sailor and
used to all weathers I thought nothing of it, to boot, scrambling
over slippery steeps, and high hills. Well, after doing all this
I left Mr. Smith and joined a Mr. Wells. His work lay on the
Malabar Coast amongst a turbulent and most savage race in all
India, and will some day give more trouble than the Seiks. This
business was to scrape ginger, of which I prepared and sent to
England, 2000 cwt., costing twelve rupees a cwt. and selling in
England 108s/- per cwt. upon the average, the cheapest and best
ginger he ever had. This work was over in April, having been
living in tents since November. He had then just commenced a
Coffee Estate, was very kind to me and asked me to go and carry
it on, which I was too glad to do, not liking the low country.
The Wynaud Jungle being 3000 feet above the sea, all very pretty
and romantic whilst health lasts, thither I went - no house, a
little place about 10 feet square to get into until I could build
a house. And as I had got some experience in building matters
during the time I was with Mr. Smith, and as he told me a young
man was coming out from England to do the ginger business and I
was to look after the Coffee Estate, it made me very zealous to
do everything very well and cheap. I built a Splendid mud
bungalow of 60 feet long, 3 rooms 20 feet, a six feet veranda
all round, 2 bath rooms, and a nice chimney, country farm house
fashion, taking the plan from the farms when at Scarborough, and
to boot, boarded the floors, all for £25 (250 rupees), planted
280,000 coffee plants almost with my own hands, as their future
growth depends upon their being well planted, he at the same time
holding out hopes that he would commence a place for myself and
cut and plant ten acres a year for me, all of which being said
in such a sincere manner I took for granted all true. But as
soon as the fine weather commenced he tumbled me out, sent me to
coast to attend Oil business, and went up there in the nice cool
country with his wife and family. The young man arrived and he
went to Coffee Estate - I remained to be gulled on coast, all of

173

which I took very quietly. This was in August, so you may guess I was not idle to build a bungalow and plant so many plants in so short a time.

November came and my twelve months was finished. I then told him that as I had been with him twelve months, and during that time had disbursed about 30,000 Co. Rs. and he had always taken my books and never acknowledged the a/c, although he was always very particular to get receipts of any sum of money placed in my hands, and so I declined to serve him longer, and as the promises he had made of opening an estate for me were not yet begun, and I seeing no prospect of his beginning it, although Mr. Remington had said in my presence he was to do so. He said if I left him I should be using him very badly, as it was now the eleventh hour, and he could get no one to commence the ginger business for him. Well, I stuck out for 200 a month and a clean receipt for the twelve months' books, and say no more about the coffee estates in perspective. So he sat him down and wrote me a letter acknowledging the whole of the a/c, and that if he did not open the estate for me in less than a month he would give me 500 Co. Rs. in lieu thereof, and at the end of the ginger business, that is in March. So here I am again in canvas tents, scraping ginger.

I wish you had such a School as I have a pandale, that is a place shaded with leaves, with 1000 women scraping ginger, and as Cris says some of them truly "are very interesting" in their almost naked state. Another pandale full of boys, 600 preparing the ginger for the women; another with ginger being weighed ready for the boys. From the women it is laid out to dry, and the beautiful romantic smell from four acres of ginger laid out in the sun is delicious. Three stations I have like this, all clearing 120 cwt. a day.

After the ginger is over, if I should not get a comfortable berth in the opening of a nice little estate that I can take a share in, I will embark for either England or Calcutta first, see Cris, and then come home and come home to eat the next Xmas dinner. Do not think I am almost mad to be writing such down in the mouth letters and then such high spirited ones. Hitherto I have, in the fulness of my heart, listened and trusted to what people promise verbally, and then built castles in the air, but I have gained more experience of the manners of the world amongst shore people in the last 12 months than the whole of my life before. Not that I have any fault to find in my master more than he is a man of straw. If the people he draws upon in Bombay were to dishonor his bills he would be a beggar tomorrow. In fact, merchants in India are worth nothing, the second sort commission agents in particular cannot call their lives their own, so you see I cannot be well situated when I find all this out. I thought all the money he spent was his own at first when I joined him.

I had a letter from Chris to day. He mentions having heard
from home and all well. Tell Melinda I hope Caroline is well.
I will write to Uncle Walter next opportunity. Glad you
mentioned it as I thought not a soul took any notice of the
affair, after all the late hours I sat at it after having been
planting all day. I will let you know shortly whether I shall
be at home at Christmas dinner next year, please God.

Believe me
                    My dear Sister
                        Your affec[tiona]te Brother
                            Tom.

I am sorry to hear so bad an account of so many old Bayswater
friends. Does not Phil ever write to any one? I think I never
had a letter from him since coming to India.

Although I work hard I generally get good pay, 100 per month
(£10) and spend 50 out of it per month, so I must not find fault
especially to get £50 as a present. I am anxious to try coffee
a little longer, as I am sure it will pay, and when it is well
found out, there will be a rush of capitalists here, and of
course the parties on hand will walk into good berths.

Love to Aunt and Arthur. Kindly remember me to all the
Thompsons, Uncle &c.

55. *Managing the Morris estates*

Tom Bassano to Walter Bassano   Tellicherry
                                                  6 March 1851

My dear Walter
    I take this opportunity to fulfill my promis[e] of a letter,
being a little more settled in my affairs than I have been since
the death of my kind superior, things being now in proper trim
untill we here from the partner concerned in England, the
Supreme Court here having placed me in charge of all the
property to continue the working of the Estate &c. I am on the
Coast as you will see by address, and garbling and packing the
coffee for shipment. The ship will be here in a few days.
After having shipt it I shall again mount the Ghauts to the
Coffee Estates. I find I have very kind friends here who have
written home to the Morrises, knowing them, and tell me they
have mentioned my name in a favourable point of view, the Civil
Judge having behaved like a brick, also the Collector & Doctor.
I am still in excellent health and passing a very pleasant time,
the whole of the residents being very good fellows, and being a
feed every night at one of their houses they do not leave me out,
so being very Jolley. In my last to Father - which I hope he

175

received, also the letter of the 6th Febr[uar]y containing my
letters of recom[men]dation - I mad[e] a sad mess I think, but I
was so worried and out of spirits, the event being so sudding
and unlooked for. But I suppose he has called on the Morrises
and arranged matters to all of your satisfaction.[5]

I wrote to Alfred a few days since and shall write to
Cristopher tomorrow or so. I hope you and Annie are quite well
and the little family. As I write this I almost wish the affairs
of M. will come to a smash, if only for the sake of se[e]ing you
all again, for I think I should make a bolt home in that case.
Remember me kindly to Annie, and love to Dear Mother, and tell
her we are sure to meet again. Melinda wrote me to send a size
of my foot as she wished to make me a pair of slippers. I
should like to see the colour of them very much. She must have
received my letter with the size enclosed. See to this, as I
have the receipt of the letter, and since Phillop's description
of never having received a letter from me since I had been in
India is quite a stagger, and I don't believe you receive the
half of the letters I write, as I never get an answer to half I
send to you. I hope Ellen has not left for Sidney[6] as I shall
be able to invite her out here should I get charge of poor
Morris's affairs. Mind and make her wait and see how things
turn up. Write me on receipt of this, and don't forget to
bulley Melinda about the slippers and let me know her defence.

Your ever affectionate
Brother
Tom.

II

"I HAVE NOT A BETTER YOUNG OFFICER IN THE REGIMENT"

While Tom Bassano was working hard coffee
planting and ginger scraping in the south his
brother Alfred was with his regiment at Jullundur
and Peshawur, except for an interval during the
winter of 1850/1 when he was on escort duty with
the Governor-General, Lord Dalhousie.

---

5. See Letter 79.
6. Ellen had sailed for Australia the previous November.

56. Col. Frederick Markham to Lord Fitzroy Somerset

19 August 1850

[Extract]

... You may remember a protegée of Mr. Coleman's and Mr. Fergusson's, a Mr. Bassano, whom you gave me on our being ordered for India, he has turned out remarkably well - I have not a better young officer in the Regiment...

57. *Amusements*

Alfred Bassano to Melinda Bassano

Jullundur
23 September 1850

My dear Lin

I have become so lazy in letter writing latterly from want of practice that I can scarcely muster sufficient resolution to commence the task. However as I have received one from you & promised an answer here goes, altho' I don't know what to write about. The old topic of scenery &c. will not answer as I have been so long stationary, but my next letters will, I hope, be more interesting, as it is almost settled that I am to go with two of our Companies as a Guard of Honor with the Governor General this cold season, perhaps up to Peshawur & into Cashmere, but this is very uncertain.

The Regiment does not move this year I am sorry to say as I love variety & have imbibed a great taste for knocking about foreign countries. There has been very little amusement of any description for the last six Months, as is always the case in the hot season, but the weather becoming rapidly pleasant again, a change is coming o'er the spirit of our dreams. The Gun. Company gave a ball about a week ago, which I enjoyed very much & remained until a late hour or rather an early one. Another ball & supper is to be given on the 1st of next Month by a sporting Serj[ean]t in E.I.C.S. to celebrate his marriage with a fair widow formerly belonging to my Company. All the Officers are invited and a great deal of fun is anticipated, & my Company have announced their intention of giving another on the 10th Oct[ober] next, previous to going on Escort duty, so you see we have some little gaiety to look forward to, even in this out of the way place.

I have not heard from Tom lately, so imagine he must be on his way to England again, as he hinted at having some intention of revisiting the white cliffs of Britain in one of his former letters. Chris seems to like the country very much. His Reg[imen]t is ordered up to Meerut & will commence their march

177

some time in October or November next.[7] It is one of the
pleasantest Stations in Bengal, so he is very lucky in being
ordered there. Give my love to Annie & the piccaninies. How
are they all getting on, for I am quite ignorant of both the
quantity & quality of Walter's family, as I never hear from him
by any chance.

I nearly put a premature stop to my letter writing a few days
ago taking my horse "Sultan" over a ring fence. He caught the
bamboos & pitched heavily over on the other side. The ground was
fortunately soft, or I should have broken my neck, as I alighted
right on my head. However, I had the satisfaction of seeing the
Ensign who was following me share precisely the same fate, & as
neither of us sustained any damage it was rather ludicrous than
otherwise.

Give my love to Mother & all at home, and make my salaam to
enquiring friends & tell Father, if possible, to get Chris
transferred to the next Cavalry Reg[imen]t ordered to India
(12th Lancers, I imagine) on the augmentation, as the pay is
120Rs. a Month more & the expenses exactly the same. In fact,
if he could manage it, which I think there is no doubt about, he
will have the satisfaction of knowing he has wonderfully
improved his prospects. Well, I am getting tired of writing, so
enough for the present from

                        Your affectionate brother
                        Alfred Bassano

58. *On escort duty with Lord Dalhousie*

Alfred Bassano to Philip Bassano   Jullundur
                                              6 February 1851

My dear Phil
    I have been knocking about the country so much for the last
four Months on Escort duty with the Gov[ernor] Gen[eral] that
I have been unable to answer your letter of 4th Oct[ober] last
sooner, also one from Father of the 19th of the same Month, &
even now as I am in the Sick Report & unable to sit up for long
I shall not be able to write you a very long one. My sickness
is not of a very serious description, altho' it may be a Month
before I am able to knock about again.

    I had a very pleasant trip with the Gov[ernor] Gen[eral].
The two Co[mpanie]s, mine & the 3rd, joined his Camp at the foot
of the hills on the 29 Oct[ober] at a place called Roopur, &

_____

7. See Letters 77 and 78.

having waited a week for his Lordship, started with him on a tour of inspection through the Punjaub. Some parts of the country we passed through was rather pretty, but there was nothing worthy of an elaborate description during our progress. The sacred & beautiful tank at Umritsar, which I described in a former letter, was illuminated at night in honor of the Great Man, also the town itself. I went down to see it on an elephant with gorgeous trappings, & amused myself, with two or three more lively sub[altern]s, by introducing our sticks into first floor windows, knocking the turbans off dignified looking natives, & smashing the lamps of oil, causing it to fall on the crowd below, & many other eccentric proceedings, to the great horror & disgust of a sober minded Captain, who had the misfortune to trust himself on the same elephant with us. However, we arrived safely at the tank, ascended to the top of a house prepared for our reception, when the most magnificent illumination I ever have or ever shall see burst on my view. From the steps of the tank to the loftiest minarets was one blaze of light, & even the water itself was covered with floating illuminations, in the midst of which, high above you, fireworks were being showered down from the minarets & house tops, fire balloons descending in all directions ./* .. ? - / - & - : . - In fact, it beggars description, so I have imitated Sterne & put a lot of marks which your imagination must interpret. Well, it was a case of to your tents O Israel, so we mounted our elephantiasis & having gone through a similar series of eccentricities, with a few dangerous improvements, we arrived safe in Camp, nothing further of any importance occurring until our arrival at Lahore, where we all received three invitations to balls during the ten days we stayed there - one given by the 14 Dr[agoon]s, one by Sir H. Lawrence, & one by the Gov[ernor] Gen[eral], all of them very good ones. Invitations to dinner also poured in & a grand fete was given by Sir H. Lawrence in the Soldiers gardens. So you can guess we led a pretty merry time of it until our departure for Wuzeerabad, where we also stayed ten days, having invitations to dine out every day during our stay, also one ball. But the great scene was the meeting of the Gov[ernor] Gen[eral] & Gholab Sing, first in the former's tent, & then the return visit, magnificent present[s] being exchanged on both occasions. Being on the Guard of honor I had a splendid view of the whole proceeding & was in the centre of the tent during the conference, Sir H. Eliot being interpreter. I afterwards went down to Gholab Sing's Camp with Dr. Dunlop, who had been requested by the G[overnor] Gen[eral] to make a sketch of him, & had a private interview of about a couple of hours during the time Dr. D. was making his portrait. After this we were relieved by two Co[mpanie]s of the 10th & returned to Jullundur after an absence of three Months just in time for a ball the night of our arrival, & two days races during the next week, which brings up the time very nearly to the present moment.

I have not heard from or anything about Tom for upwards of a

year. Chris is flourishing & on the march to Meerut, if not now
there. I suppose from the last letter I received from Father
that he has now retired & gone to live in some snug little
retreat in the country with Lin to look after & take care of dear
Mother. I hope Ellen has changed her mind about leaving England,
for in spite of the strange tales told by travellers (myself
among the number) there is no place like it. Give my love to all
at home, not forgetting Annie & the babies, & all my Official
friends. There is lots of promotion & announced promotion going
on in the Regiment, so I shall have plenty of steps shortly, if
everything goes on as expected.

Having arrived at the end of my paper with nothing more to
say

>   Believe me
>   Your affectionate brother
>   Alfred.

59. *March from Jullunder to Peshawur - life at Peshawur*

Alfred Bassano to Melinda Bassano   Peshawur
                                                     15 March 1852

My dear Lin
    I have at length made a slight effort to return to England,
with what success remains to be proved, but the Colonel has
forwarded an application from me for the Invalids. I am not
an Invalid myself, but to proceed to England in charge of sick
Men in October next. He has strongly recommended it, but you
must not be too sanguine, as it will all depend on the number of
applicants, & whether they are senior to me or not.[8]

    The march here from Jullundur was a very pleasant one through
quite a different style of country. Instead of miles of plain,
without a spot of ground higher than a molehill, the last march
has been through low ranges of hills, ravines, rocky dells,
ripling streams, &c. &c., but do not imagine it was very
beautiful, for with few exceptions it was about the ugliest
country ever created, looking exactly as if it had once been a
fine & well cultivated tract of land but was now worn out.

    I rode over the Battle field of Chillianwallah, & of course
thought all sorts of heroic things, as people always do under
such circumstances, or get credit for doing, which amounts to
the same. I also brought away some bones, but on my return to
Camp the Doctors declared one was the jawbone of an ass and the

---

8. Alfred went to England on leave in early 1853.

rest had once belonged to some respectable old cow. At
Manikyala I visited the tomb of Bucephalus,[9] a very ancient
looking ruin, built of pumice & sand stone. At a place called
Hussein Abdal there are some warm springs and a beautifully clear
stream running through several small tanks full of very large
fish. They are not allowed to be caught and are very tame in
consequence of being constantly fed with chupattis & grain from
the various visitors, native & European, who go there. The place
is sacred, the native story being that the stream was dried up
when a fakir struck his hand on the stone leaving an impression
and causing the water to flow again.

    The Fort of Attock seen from the opposite side of the River is
very picturesque,[10] but like everything in India, distance lends
enchantment to the view, for no sooner do you go inside to make
a closer inspection than you find it is a filthy place, scarcely
worth looking at.

    Well, I have now taken you rapidly over the Hyphasis,
Hydraotes, Acisines, Hydaspes & Indus,[11] shown you the tomb of
Alexander the Great's horse, and landed you safely in Peshawur,
a Cantonment surrounded by hills, full of such turbulent tribes
of barbarians that we sleep with loaded pistols under our pillows,
& occasionally get fired at coming home from Mess on dark nights.
Altho' the station is begirt with sentries with orders to fire
on any one approaching their posts, & overrun with Cavalry
patroles, yet some how they get in & out during the night and
actually got safe off with three Stand of arms from our L[igh]t
Comp[an]y and 5 from the 53rd Reg[imen]t, taken out of the
Barrack rooms full of men during the night, & as for your horses,
any morning you may get up and find your Stables empty.

    Tell Father & Walter that Col. Markham will arrive in England
about the same time as this letter, & intends to call on Father
at the A[rmy] Medical Board Office & explain to him what an
acquisition to the Service I am & how grateful the country ought
to be to him for having conferred upon them the benefit of my
Services. There is no doubt I have done the State some service
in my time, but am too modest to let them know it.

    By the bye, in your last letter you talk of pretty female
cousins of mine that I never knew coming to stay with you, as if
they had grown up like so many mushrooms in my absence, to say
nothing of little nephews that I never heard of before. However,
you may drown'd the latter, but don't tell Annie I said so, but
have a grand collection of the former, viz. the pretty cousins of

---

 9. Favourite horse of Alexander the Great.
10. Sketch enclosed.
11. The five rivers of the Punjab - now Sutlej, Ravi, Chenab,
    Jhelum and Indus.

the fair sex, all ready to receive me on my return with open
arms, when for the first week I shall *allow* them to kiss me as
often as they like, but after that must positively put them upon
an allowance for fear they should get too fond & kiss me to
pieces, as I am very delicate with so long a residence in the
East, in fact I may say interestingly so.

Now having succeeded in getting you & dear Mother into a fit
of laughter, and being very fond of teasing, I intend to make
you both cry just by way of variety, by telling you that a force
of 3000 Men under Sir Colin Campbell have just left the Station
with the supposed intention of Chastising some of the hill tribes
& altho' only 600 of the Reg[imen]t & H[ea]d Q[uarte]rs have
gone at present, & I have been doomed to remain ingloriously
here as Acting Adjutant & Q[uarte]r M[aste]r to the Companies &
Depot left, yet if there is anything serious to be done he must
have a large reinforcement out, when I shall do my best to join
in the expedition, which will I hope take place very soon. In
fact, there must be much more fighting before this part of the
country is settled. Now, set your fears to work & imagine all
sorts of impossible accidents occurring to me & when you have
finished the catalogue of casualties, perhaps you will find
leisure to laugh again when I tell you that my present app[oint-
men]t of Adj[utant] & Q[uartermaste]r not only entails upon me
the management of upwards of 300 Men, but, *miserabile dictu*,
100 Women, each one of the latter thinking that I have nothing
earthly to do but redress her particular grievances, and as they
always tell them to you in dozens, all speaking at the same time
and invariably wandering into an account of their life &
prospects from birth to the present time, interspersed with
abuse of one another, you can imagine what a pleasant time of it
I am enjoying.

I have rec[eive]d a very satisfactory letter from Ellen, but
as she mentions having written home I need not mention its
contents. Chris is all right & has heard from Tom, who is also
salubrious. Give my love to all at home, not forgetting my
pretty cousin Jane, and believe me

Your affectionate brother
Alfred.

III

"MY SHEET ANCHOR ... IN THIS COUNTRY IS LIME JUICE OR FRUIT"

Christopher Bassano landed at Calcutta on the
19th June 1849 and was stationed at Dum Dum for the
first four months of his service in India. He then

moved to Calcutta until December 1850, when the
Regiment embarked for Cawnpore, arriving on the 6th
February 1851. From there Christopher went to Meerut
to do duty with the 29th Regiment - he was recalled
to his own Regiment, the 70th, at Cawnpore in
September 1851. He was at Cawnpore from then and
throughout 1852, but apparently wrote no letters
home from June 1851 until February 1853.

60. *First day in India*

Christopher Bassano's diary   June 1849

On the 19th June 1849 I landed at Calcutta at one of the
Ghauts near Fort William where there were a sufficient number of
carriages to convey the whole Detachment, consisting of about
200 Men, women and children, to Dum Dum. I had but one or two
sick so did not accompany them, but remained in Calcutta that
day, by which means I was able to leave my cases of instruments
at the Medical Board. This was, however, what I should not in
future do, inasmuch as any accident occurring to the men on their
way attended with fatal results might have very justly caused me
to be severely reprimanded.

I arrived at Dum Dum in the evening of the same day, and to
my great delight found myself located in a Bungalo[w] occupied
by an old college friend of mine, Mr. Miles of the Company's
Service, and his friend Dr. Parker - of whom I had also some
recollection of at college. I cannot help remarking the great
difference between the number of London Medical men in the
Company's Service as contrasted with those in the Queen's.
During the four years I was at King's College no less than ten
students obtained appointments as Ass[istan]t Surgeons in the
Company and only one besides myself during the same period in
the Queen's S[ervi]ce. Numbers of the students, & these the
flower of the flock cheifly, will not accept appointments in
the Queen's Service, but with scarcely an exception all are
anxious to obtain appointments in the Company's service. That
there is some reason for this there is no doubt, and an explanation of it is no difficulty. The difference in the pay &
retiring allowance is not by any means the sole reason, for were
such the case you would have men enter the Queen's Service to
whom money is no great object (and of whom there are a large
portion) but how rarely is this the case. A medical man in the
H[onorable] C[ompany]'s Service is treated as he should be - he
has that assistance which converts his office into what as a
Surgeon or M.D. he has only a right to be troubled with. But
these remarks are misplaced here and I shall comment upon them in
my memo book.[12]

---

12. Not found.

Christopher Bassano to Philip Bassano   Dum Dum
                                                         2 July 1849

Dear Phil
    I sent a letter off to Father this morning by your friend
Miles and Parker who are gone to Calcutta, and it being a very
cool day I had a regular overhaul at my things, and just as I
finished I found the letters I spoke about to Father, viz. one
from you and Father of the 23rd Feb[ruar]y, one from Melinda
22 d[itt]o, and another from Tom, dated 22nd May. Tell Father,
if I did not mention it in my letter - which I believe I did -
that I found my volumes of Creevey's Anatomy, and also that I
shall like very much to go on with the Lancet from the 27th
Jan[uar]y, as I intend to have them all nicely bound. Your
Letter contains suggestions from Mr. Croomes and yourself - I
think those from the latter much the best, since 5/- a day
would go very little way towards paying £10 or £12, but I fear
it is too late to write to E[ast] I[ndia] C[ompany] as you
recommend, and if it were not, I don't much like doing it by
myself.

    Tom's letter is from Lackadie, and he talks of being on the
point of starting to his mountain retreat, and also of starting
a small plantation on his own a/c, but he is still open to an
offer to commence as manager on a large scale, and has written
a long yarn to Al, which I hope to receive in Alfred's next
letter. He is going to plant this monsoon 300 acres, but not
for himself, and so he says I am not to expect to hear from him
for some time. He received a Ľre from home about the same time
as he did the one I wrote. He seems in excellent spirits an[d]
signs himself the *Jangle Wallah*.

    July 11th. I found I was too late for the mail & so I have
been obliged to wait for the Bombay mail. I bought the other
day a poney of Miles, with an old saddle and bridle, for
Co.Rs.110. She is as handsome a mare as any in the place, but
I find her rather small for riding, and as Alfred told me I
certainly should prefer a large country horse, and I almost
wish I had bought one instead. I am thinking of getting a buggy
& cabriolet in order that I may go to Hospital without getting
regularly soaked to the skin as I have been on one or two
occasions. There is some talk of our going to Calcutta when the
90th Reg[imen]t go up the Country. I hope it will not be for
some time, for I am not yet tired of Dum Dum. The Artillery
Officers here are going to give a Dinner and Ball to General
Whish this month, which is to be a grand affair. I suppose the
70th will join them either as guests or inviters - it is not yet
settled. Remember me to Mr. Matthews, young Stewart, and any
friend who may inquire after me, and try and get me into the
Cavalry. I can quite understand that Alfred has but just been

able to live on his pay here - even with great economy the
expenses are frightful. I saw Cumming of the 32nd at Mess, and
he says Alfred is by no means extravagant.

> I remain
> Dear Phil
> Your affectionate Bro[ther]
> Christopher.

62. *"Things here [are] so monotonous"*

Christopher Bassano to Walter Bassano
Dum Dum
4 August 1849

My dear Walter
    Since I wrote to Phil and Melinda I have not heard from home
and I find things here so monotonous that really I have but
little news for you. I expect the Ball which is to be given to
Gen[era]l Wisch on the 6th by the Officers of the Artillery and
to which the 70th Officers are invited will be something very
grand, though as a ball rather slow in consequence of the
scarcity of ladies and the difficulty of getting them to dance.
I was rather surprised by the Paymaster informing me the other
day that he had received a letter from Calcutta saying that I
owed upwards of two hundred rupees for my medicines and they
would charge it in the Regimental a/c, so no doubt it was an
omission on their part in not deducting it in the first instance
and I may think myself lucky at having just enough money to
carry me through this month. There is good foundation for
believing that this Regiment will be sent to Calcutta for a few
months and it is said that Col[one]l Bigg intends returning to
England. I shall be sorry to lose him, as he is a sensible man
and I know he is much liked by all the Officer[s]. Capt[ai]n
Durnford, who is living with me, I believe will not purchase, so
he will have the mortification of being again passed over.

    I find quite enough to do here and am likely to have more if
the Reg[imen]t goes to Calcutta. There are now about fifty men
in Hospital with Dysentery, and many of them are now being
admitted with fever. Cholera seems to have declined altogether.
I leave my bungalo[w] between five and six, and seldom return
from Hospital before nine o'Clock to breakfast. Then come the
junior officers' chits saying that they have got a severe pain
and would I give them a call. I think from one Officer I must
have had since I came here, on an average, three Notes a day,
all about nothing - so the other day I blew him up and told him
I would no longer attend him, and Harvey having mentioned it to
the Col[one]l the youth got reprimanded. I find what the other
Medical Officers told me when I first came here that I should be
troubled to death with the Subalterns quite true, for they seem

185

to think our only pleasure is in prescribing.

Capt[ai]n Pugh invited us to Tiffin on board the Diana and
gave a most sumptuous meal, everything having been sent from
some house in Calcutta.

Yesterday our servant came to tell us that a large snake was
in the Compound, so Durnford got his gun and as the heart was
passing from one branch of a tree to another he shot him as dead
as mutton, to the great delight of the natives. I was very
quietly riding my poney the other night without looking about me
when she suddenly stopped short before a large dirty puddle, the
result of which was that I went head first into it, and was
suddenly changed from a white to a black man. I mearly
scra[t]ched my face a little, so I did not care. It is astonishing how soon one gets over the prejudices against the blacks.
They are a much handsomer class of people than I have yet seen,
and really the women are exceedingly interesting. - But this
greasy paper is enough to make one swear!

How about the Cavalry, for I begin to think the sooner one
can make some money here the better. Eaton[13] tells me he is
trying to get a Horse Reg[imen]t. He is a great swell, but a
very good fellow.

I am in a melancholy mood just now having been suffering
from indigestion during the last two or three days, and in this
country anything of the sort causes great depression. I have
no doubt the Ball will set me up again.

Give me a long yarn about the Regatta and anything else
amusing, and excuse this short chit of mine. I hope Annie and
the two pets are well. Remember me to our mutual friends in
the Board office and all other friends. How does Uncle Fred
get on with the fair sex? I have no doubt the end of it will be
that he takes unto himself some ugly old dowager with lots of
tin and gives her so much soft soap that she slips down the first
week never to rise again. If the letter I sent by the last mail
should not arrive I have another bill ready to send Father for
£100, fifty of which he will give to Linney. It is merely a
duplicate of the other. I must post this letter today at Dum
Dum & so must reserve an a/c of the Ball for the next mail.

> I remain your affectionate Bro[ther]
> Christopher

---

13. Assistant Surgeon, 70th Regiment.

Christopher Bassano's diary   September & October
                                           1849

1 September 1849
    Right wing of 70th marched to Calcutta, Johnston[14] & myself
being left in Med[ical] Charge of the sick at Dum Dum. Dum Dum
about 10 miles from Calcutta and a very pleasant St[atio]n. The
Artillery Mess house is a handsome building and its internal
economy very judiciously arranged.

1 October 1849
    The left wing of the Reg[imen]t came into Fort William today.
I took charge of the sick leaving Johnston at Dum Dum. Rained
heavily all day - my luggage all saturated with water. I somewhat regretted the change, having spent a pleasant time in Dum
Dum with the Art[iller]y. The only thing worthy of comment as
regards the men is that 84 died from the date of arrival in this
country to the 1st Sept[embe]r when the right wing were ordered
to Calcutta. There can be no doubt that the crouded state of
the barracks was the chief cause of so many deaths, since not
only were the daily admissions at the latter end of August 40
times greater than in the first three or four days in
Sept[embe]r, but the deaths, of which there were five or six
daily, immediately stop[p]ed on the other half of the Reg[imen]t
obtaining sufficient room in the barracks. The chief mortality
was from Dysentery and cholera. The Dysentery was of a very
severe form, in some cases running its course in a few hours,
and these cases the men died from loss of blood. I had an
opportunity of making a P[ost] M[ortem] examination in one case
where a man had passed an enormous quantity of blood, but to my
surprise there was no abrasion of the [*illeg.*] coat of the
intestine. There existed however, from one end of the large
intestine to the other, patches of raised mucous membrane
varying in size from that of a fourpenny piece to half-a-crown
and resembling venous nevi - in fact they consisted of enlarged
capillary vessels, which in the course of a short time would
have been converted into sloughs, but as the man had died so
soon this had not taken place. This stage writers do not
mention. For Treatise on Dysentery see notes by C.B. Bassano in
Med[ica]l Register. Lime juice is the sheet anchor in Dysentery
- fruit an excellent remedy for vomiting in cases of Cholera.

---

14. Assistant Surgeon, 70th Regiment.

64. *Balls in Calcutta*

Christopher Bassano to Melinda Bassano   Fort William
                                                       8 December 1849

My dear Melinda
    I believe I have not replied to you[r] two last chits and I
have not time to refer to them. I recollect however that you
were much offended at my throwing some of the numerous chits I
recieved on my arrival on the floor. I really do not recollect
having made such an assertion and if I did I must have been
inebriated. I think I said that I lost or mislaid them, but
never mind, dear, it does not magnify.

    I am in what they term here the vortex of society, although I
have made but few calls since I have been in Calcutta. I dined
with Sir Laurence Peel[15] a week or two back, and I have been to
several grand Balls. Last night a lady gave a fancy dress ball
on a most magnificent scale. You can form no idea of a ballroom
in India – one room here is equal to half a dozen in England
and instead of, as you might suppose, being warm, they are much
cooler than those in England, even in the warm weather. Last
night however, in consequence of the cool season a good fire was
kept in one room, and really the amusements of the evening were
excellent, and the various costumes, as you may imagine amongst
people who have been in every quarter of the globe, could not
be surpassed. One gentleman was dressed as a South Sea whaler,
having a tight dress made of a sort of [*illeg.*] rope all netted.
Another came dressed as an adjutant, having a large beak
projecting from the back of his head, and a body and tail from
the front of him, so that he walked backwards to make the joints
of his legs look more natural. A third would consist of a
Postman who came in with a bundle of letter[s] and a bell.
These letters were distributed by calling out the names of the
respective ladies and gentlemen to whom they were addressed. Of
course the contents were full of nonsense, but displayed great
taste, one spooney officer of ours had a drawing in his letter
of three spoons &c. and I have no doubt they were all amusing
to the parties to whom addressed. I was not selected, so I
suppose I had no particular weakness. The tallest man in the
room was dressed as a Welsh peasant with a short red dress,
another as a beggar with a [*illeg.*] child in a shawl behind his
back. The ladies' dresses were very beautiful. I went in
Regimentals as I could not afford to buy a dress, having just
purchased a buggy which has left me about 200 Rupees in debt.
I go to a ball at the town hall every fortnight with the
officer[s], the people of Calcutta having invited the whole
Reg[imen]t, and on consideration the 70th Band was allowed to
play there, so that there are two bands and but little or no

---

15. Chief Justice of Bengal.

188

waiting between the dances. The room is about the size of Old
Smalley's Chapel and comfortably full, so you may give a guess
at the stile in which ye Indians live. This is very pleasant
while it last[s], but six or seven months broilings soon make
you meek I have no doubt.

I fear they are working you too much at home and I hope your
exertions will not interfere with your health, which is of
primary importance. Remember me to my numerous Lady friends,
and give my love to dear Mother and Ellen. I have no time to
write to them as the mail is off tomorrow, and I nearly forgot
to mention that should you have any companion[s] who sit on seats
in Kensington Gardens by themselves reading, you must immediately
drop their acquaintance. Take this advice from your ever loving
an[d] affectionate Brother

                    Christopher.

65. *Medical and family gossip*

Christopher Bassano to Walter Bassano   Fort William
                                                 9 December 1849

My dear Mopsticks
    The receipt of your Letter of the 19th Oct[obe]r & the
favourable state of the weather here and a variety of pleasant-
ries has enabled me to forget what has for some time annoy[e]d
me, and now I feel as jolly as ever I did in my life. Yesterday
& today were the t[w]o first since I have been in India that the
sun has ceased to shine when it has not been raining, and you
cannot conceive the great relief to the eyes. I have been during
the last fortnight much affected on one side of my head in consequence of having ridden slowly from Calcutta to the Fort about
eight o'Clock one cool morning with a forage cap on. The sun
seemed to have had some influence on the side of the head
exposed, and I get a slight headache now every time I go into it.

I called on your friend [?Mowatt] soon after I came to
Calcutta, and he is the only person who has not returned my call
or noticed me in the least. Everybody else either invited me to
dine or made themselves very polite. He suggested that he did
not think they were very favourable to his brother in the 9th
at the Medical Board. I am not sorry, for every invitation is
an expense of about three or four rupees, and by giving your
friends an invitation to the mess in return you are let in for
at least eleven or twelve rupees for wine thro' bad management,
and what with the mess guests, which are officers invited by
the regiment & which consist of the officers in the Troop ship
on their arrival here, together with dinner given to heads of
departments and to native Regiments when they come into the Fort

to relieve each other every month, they manage to run up most formidable wine a/cs. The mess expenses alone during the first month equaled the pay of a subaltern, and in many cases exceeded it - and drove most of them into the Agra Bank.

I bought a buggy and horse a few days ago for 470 Rupees, and if it will last me twelve months without being injured I shall be satisfied, as I can then sell it without much loss to buy an English one for going up the country.

There [is] some chance of a row here with the inhabitants of the Sikim territory, the Governor having seized upon two Doctors for searching for plants in his country and passing the boundary. Several detachments have been ordered to Jardeeling [sic] and it is reported that the Doctors have been put to death and that the Government intend taking the territory.

I am a member of the medical board at present sitting at Calcutta, and should Alfred wish to go home I can send him for a couple of years with ease. I sent home Grey of our reg[imen]t the other day, and on his arrival in London I suppose he will have to appear at your office. He is on Board the Seringapatam.

Tom sent me a long letter a few days back and is still anxious to get up the Estate. If it pays so well he will soon be able to increase what he has already commenced on his own a/c. He seems in good spirits and seems determined to remain and do his best. Alfred says that he soon brought him to his senses by sending him a Chaffing letter with a little abuse.

I am sorry to hear Hamblin is dead, but I suppose Uncle Fred is married to Mrs. Yates and is now doing the paternal to his sisters. Remember me kindly to them all. I hope Annie has tamed you a little, and if you send any more of your half sheets with nothing in them I shall write only once a year. Tell Francis I will come and see her when there is a railroad all the way home. I hope she is [a] very good girl. I suppose the little godchild begins to talk a little.

I dare say it would be advisable for me to remain in this regiment a year or two, because then if I do not wish to come home I shall have made up my mind to stop here until promotion, but at present I am inclined to think I shall prefer at the end of that time going home and returning to India as full surgeon.

I must however conclude or I shall be too late for the Post. I have enclosed a letter written to Father some time ago as also another to [letter torn] and one to Linny, and in hopes you will be a little more liberal with your News next time believe me dear Walter

Your affec[tionate] Bro[ther]
Christopher

The only pun I have heard since I have been in India is small
stud at the E.I.C. because they have only two Galloways and a
little Hay.

66. *Duty at Calcutta*

Christopher Bassano's diary   Calcutta
                                                   1 January 1850

On my arrival in Calcutta I was ordered to live in the
General Hospital, a large b[ui]lding consisting of three
separate portions & Officers' quarters forming a distinct
Building. I am now in the Fort doing Eaton's duty and like the
change uncommonly. Had a row with Dr. Hare who took possession
of my quarters during my temporary absence. I complained to
the authorities, and the Dep[ut]y Governor ordered him to hand
them over again to me. I did not return to them as by Johnston
coming in from Dum Dum at the time, I was ordered on permanent
duty in the Fort. I am in great force just now, parties
innumerable, the Calcutta people very polite. Weather most
delightful. Bought a buggy & horse of Dr. Boyd for Rs.470.

67. *Life in Calcutta*

Christopher Bassano's diary   Calcutta
                                                    1 March 1850

The last few months have been most delightfully spent, not
only from the magnificent weather in Calcutta during the last
four months, but also from the extreme politeness & kind feeling
of the inhabitants to the 70th Regiment. Parties have been
innumerable, and at many of them our Band have sent forth their
soft strains. I have made too many acquaintances & friends to
treat them all with the attention they deserve. My buggy has
been of great use to me and I do not think I should have enjoyed
such good health had I not possessed it.

68. *Expenses in India - gossip*

Christopher Bassano to Philip Bassano   Fort William
                                                    7 April 1850

My dear Phil
    I fear I have not written to you since I left England
although I recieved a long epistle from you on my arrival in
India. But really it has been only the last few Months I have

been at all comfortably settled, and the time has but just come
that enables me to sit down quietly in a comfortable room and
reflect upon what I have done, what I have not done, and what I
might have done. I find that I have the credit of receiving
Rs.225 per Mensem, but in reality, since I came to this country,
I find by turning to the Paymaster's account, that although for
nearly four months at Dum Dum my pay was 255 Rs. per month,
being 30 R. for House rent extra, I have actually only had paid
over to me during a period of eleven Months Rs.2053, or little
more than Co.R.186 per month. Had I been paid in full the sum
total would be Co.R.2502. Now the deduction is due to the
expense of keeping up the band, bringing out a billiard table,
and paying mess subscriptions, the latter not including the
expense of paying my share of every mess guest, and of whom there
are not a few, as we are obliged to invite every Officer to mess
who leaves his card. This latter expense however causes our
wine a/c [to] be very large, and even at the present time I
cannot get mine below Rs.50 per month, although I generally take
beer. These expenses, which an individual officer cannot avoid,
are disgraceful to the service, and I think the actual amount of
pay a man recieved ought to be sent to the Comm[and]er in ch[ie]f
in order that there might be some check upon such extravagance.
I have told you as near as possible, and I assure you it is
correct, what I get a month, and now I will just give you a list
of what I am *obliged* to spend - which I enclose. You will thus
percieve that although a subaltern has credit for recieving an
allowance which without investigation appears liberal, it is in
fact but just enough to maintain him in *India*.

I wrote a long letter to Walter on the 8th ultimo, and the
enclosed, which I hope you will deliver to their respective
owners, will have most of the news worth relating in Calcutta
that I can recollect, and I must defer replying to Mopsticks'
Lr̃e of the 19th Feb[ruar]y with its excellent puns (and which
only came to hand yesterday) until a mail or two hence.

You have heard of Wemyss of Alfred's Reg[imen]t. He is a man
with (from all a/cs) much interest in the C[ommander] in
C[hief]'s Office. I was to have been on the medical board the
other day to decide whether he was ill or not, but I got
Johnston to take my place as from what I have seen and heard
about him I should have ordered him to join his regiment. He
has been living a most dissolute life in Calcutta for some time,
and although he has been four years in the Reg[imen]t he has
never done a day's duty, and so fully aware of his scheming and
idleness is Col[one]l Markham that he has written to the Horse
Guards to say that although he is the Senior Lieut[enant] for
purchase he will not allow him to do so unless he joins his
Regiment. I did not like to have anything to do with it because
it might have been said that I was interested in the matter.
The result of the board was that he got leave to Simla until
October next, at which he was much disgusted.

You will shortly see in London the Nepal Princes who have been in Calcutta some time, and who honored our Ball with their presence. They are dressed in the most extravagant and beautiful costume, and they are to pay Rs.50,000 for their passage to England. They have no end of tin to spend, so I calculate they could not go to [a] better place than London to spend it.

Wa[l]ter says nothing about the Cavalry in his letter. I should like to get a Reg[imen]t that will remain out here five or six years if possible, so that I can then go home for a short time and return to India as a full Surgeon. If I could not get one out here the next coming out would do very well, say 12th Lancers. I have become a first rate horseman, and my Cavalry seat is considered excellent. I shall send an official application to Sir James by the next mail, which I expect I should have done long ago. I intended writing to Uncle by this mail, but find there is not time. Remember me to him, also to Messrs. Matthew, Fergusson, and some others whose names I forget at this moment. I am glad the Commander-in-Chief has drawn attention to the number of officers who get leave from this country. I think it is the greatest humbug that ever was perpetrated and should be stopped. Send me a long letter by return & believe me

Your affectionate Bro[ther]
C.B. Bassano

P.S. Can you find out the composition of that sticky stuff they put on paper to catch flies? If you can let me know – it would clear our rooms of musqetoes capitally. If you have an army list send it out. I will pay the postage.

69. [Enclosure in the above]

Expenses absolutely necessary

	Rs.	
Wine a/c at mess	50	per month, not including what you drink in your quarters if you take luncheon.
Breakfast & dinner at mess	50	per month
Kitmutgar	8	" Up country extra
Bearer	7	" servants are
Dobie	5	required for
Beastie	5	your tents.
Water	2	

Rs.127

	Rs.	
Horse-syce or groom	5	per month
grasscutter	4	do
stabling & food	12	
Punka pullers (2)	8	
	29	

Total   Co.Rs.156

Leaving *me* only 30R. a month to buy furniture, pay palenkins and in fact anything connected with domestic arrangements, and save up money to buy tents and horses.

I certainly have lived under my pay since I came here only because I have from being on duty at the Hospital escaped going to mess. But where is the extravagance in Alfred which Walter persists in, but in which I am glad to hear you differ? He comes into this country with sixty or 70 Rupees a month less than I do, and no doubt had just as much deducted from his pay, together with the expense of an early march and the purchase of a Tent. It is [a] surprising thing to me how he has managed to keep afloat as he has. He has had a splendid charger given to him by the Col[one]l he tells me, which looks well. He complains about none of you writing to him and seems rather surprised.

Tom is at work with the ginger. I have not heard from him for some time.

This is a most beautiful cloudy morning, the first for some months. You can have no idea how much relief it is to the eye. The mail starts at 4 o'Clock today for England. A salute of guns have just fired, and I must go and get my breakfast, so fare the[e] well.

70. *Death of an uncle*[16] *– reply to complaints*

F.M. Bassano to Christopher Bassano   [2 June 1850]
[mutilated]

... therefore taken out Letters of Administration in order to realize and divide his Property (above £4000) according to Law: viz. one third to myself, one third equally between Bro[the]r Philip's children, and the other third equally between Bro[the]r Henry's children. Melinda is writing to Alfred, but as you probably know Tom's address better than we do, I must request

---

16. Walter Bassano, senior, tea dealer.

you will inform him of his Uncle's lamented death, especially as he said in his last letter that he thought of being at home at Xmas. Ellen is writing to you by this Mail.

My Clerk, Mr. Millar, was taken ill with pulmonary disease 6 months ago and has only just returned to the Office, which together with private affairs has thrown more labor upon me than I am able to compete with.

I think your last letter to me is dated 10th December, but I cannot condescend to answer the graceless and ill-judged complaints contained in it, and surely I had a right to expect better things from one in whose behalf I have done more than for any two of my children. If however it turn out for your advantage I shall be well repaid for the outlay.[17]

Philip and Walter went with me to sign Papers requisite for my realizing and distributing your lamented Uncle's property, which is chiefly in East India Stock - 3 of your cousins being Minors I shall be obliged to keep their shares in the Funds till they are of Age. I remain your affect[ionat]e Father, F.M. Bassano

I suppose one Guinea a year to the Widows's Fund will be enough for you to pay till you can afford and think proper to give more. If you marry in the Service the previous Subscription of one or two Gui[nea]s p[e]r ann[um] will give you the option of joining the Society for the benefit of your Widow. But I am not a sufficient Calculator to say whether [the] money could be better employed.

71. *Concerning exchanging into the Cavalry - sickness in the Regiment*

Christopher Bassano to Walter Bassano   10 Rampart Barracks
                                             Fort William
                                             3 July 1850

My dear Walter
    My last to you was dated March 8th, and I have now time to acknowledge your abuse of the 19th Feb[ruar]y, which I alluded to in the last letters I sent home dated April 8th to Philip, with notes to Ellen & Aunt Ryle. Snip Snap Snorum[18] seems to be your evening amusement. I don't wonder at Uncle Fred indulging in childish games, but how the rest of you can find amusement in such is past my conception. How am I to send Mr. Clark my £4-4?

---

17. This paragraph has been scribbled out.
18. A children's card game.

It is to[o] small a sum to send & I am not any to the good at
present, so I shall not send until I can at the same time pay
off other small scores. Rem[em]ber me to him & Theophalus, and
next mail I must write about the museum to Sir James.

I wrote to your friend Wigstrom a short time back, asking him
to give me an idea of the expense attending an exchange into the
Cavalry, and he wrote back immediately saying that he was trying
to go home with the invalids this year, and that he would, if
successful, effect an exchange with me, previous to so doing,
and that he would moreover, because I was your brother, exchange
with me for £200 less than he could get from any one else. He
said that I should not be at any more expense in a Cavalry
Corp[s] than my own, and he said he had written three times to
you but had not heard from you in reply. I wrote saying that I
had no money to exchange, that I had no idea of borrowing any
for that purpose, and that if I had any I should not consider it
worthwhile to risk it as I was at present placed, thanking him
at the same time for his offer, which however amounted to
nothing, as he did not say what he could get for an exchange.

I suppose you have not heard from Tom. It is now six
month[s] since he has written either to Alfred or myself and I
am inclined to think he is on some other tack, which is Alfred's
idea also. In Alfred's Reg[imen]t I perceive Capt[ai]n Brine
has been brought to court martial & if not found to be insane is
to be reprimanded.

I am in very good health indeed and I wish I could say the
same of the Officers in the Regiment who are nearly all so
disgusted with the country that they are continually fancying
and making themselves ill. Two of them died of Cholera, as you
know before this, and Major Edwards died of Fever a short time
after, and what was very odd, all three of them had but just
before returned from a Buffalo expedition on foot, exposing
themselves to the sun all day and walking about 30 miles a day.
The rest of the party were also more or less affected. I think
another year here will be the death of half of them, and yet
there is nothing to complain of. The reason is that they cannot
sit down and amuse themselves by reading, so they wander about
an[d] grumble at everything, or go to sleep all day. The rains
have now commenced and the thermometer in the room with the
windows open is about 85° and indeed before the rains set in it
was only on two or three occasions as high as 90°. I am
thinking of publishing a book for the advice of medical officers,
entitled "One year in India", but I cannot find time to set
about it, so my good intentions will I dare say end in smoke.

Calcutta is perfectly quiet, no fun of any description, and
India generally is tranquil, and as long as the 70th remain
here, no doubt it will continue so. A lady living in the Fort,
who has been a particular friend of mine (and who is the wife

of the Garrison Assistant Surgeon, Dr. Bedford - a very nice
fellow) is going home with her children, three in number, very
young, and as she has two young children at the Grammar School
at Kensington, she wishes to get a house with about 8 rooms in
that neighbourhood, and in consideration of our intimate
acquaintance, and from the fact of my having received great
kindness at her hands, I have no doubt Ellen or Father or some
of you would put her in the way of comfortably settling herself
down. She is to take over some nicely worked cambric handkerchiefs &c., if she can get them made in time. I gave her the
order a few weeks ago having been so much pleased with some she
had had worked for herself. She will therefore do herself the
honor of calling on Mother, and I have no doubt every kindness
will be shown her. She does not start for some months however,
but I should like to be able to tell her that my friends will be
glad to see her and assist her in any way.

    I only began this an hour or two before post time, so excuse
its brevity, & with kind love to Ann Frank, and the chota bihe,[19]
Mother, Melinda, &c. &c.

                    Believe me Your affectionate Bro[ther]
                            Christopher.

72. *Summary of life in Calcutta*

Christopher Bassano's diary   Calcutta
                                                31 August 1850

    The heat has not been by any means oppressive during the last
few months. I have lived in the Rampart Barrack, Fort William,
and the temperature of my room has seldom exceeded 86°. I am
as comfortable as I should wish to be. It is however difficult
to get on without spending more than one's pay, and I find most
of the Sub[altern]s have had to go into the Banks. Had I not
had four or five hundred rupees to start with I must have
followed in their track. The 70th Reg[imen]t is much liked by
the inhabitants. The expense of giving large public dinners,
which are very frequent, are a source of great expense to the
junior officers, most of whom however have not been called upon
to pay their wine accounts and there is consequently a large
amount owing the wine fund.

---

19. Little brother.

Christopher Bassano to Walter Bassano

Fort William
6 October 1850

My dear Walter
    If you have any regard for me don't send any more of your humbuging Letters, like that of the 30th April 1850, No. 13863/5.[20] I, Harvey & Johnston had the benefit of reporting on the fusty old papers, and if you are not satisfied you may go hang yourselves. The four presses full of dirty dry drafts and Returns, in a godown which had not been open for years, soon produced in our hearts that peculiar depression of spirits, accompanied with languor and lassitude, which at my suggestion and Harvey's expense, was only removed by a few bottles of Bass Pale Ale and a mild Manilla cheroot. After three days fatigue we succeeded in wading through them and our report has elicited great applause from Dr. St. John,[21] who wrote a letter to Harvey expressing his deep regret that he should have had so much trouble, and his sincere thanks for the efficient and satisfactory manner in which the report was made, and begging him to communicate his sentiments to Johnston & my own dear self, and I have no doubt in consideration for my services he will put me into the first good appointment he has vacant. And should he not do so, I see no reason why you should not have written to me since last February, when I wrote to you on the 8th March & 3rd July, and another thing, I see no reason why either of us should send letters via Southampton *prepaid*, let me have no more of your bully about foolcap, for I bought a Cashmere smoking cap the other day to send home for you, but the cap seems to fit me so well that I do not know how to part with it, nor how to get it home, together with other things I have been buying, as I understand they will be detained at Custom house unless the duty be paid. I bought a Bombay cribbage board for Father, a d[itt]o-card case for Melinda, some d[itt]o paper knives for ye brothers, and a box of agricultural implements for knitting to be given to little Frank. As to the rags for the dear creatures, there will be no difficulty.

    The shabby 70th (for such we shall be called if we do not give a return Ball before leaving Calcutta, which from heavy expenses I fear must be the case) are to proceed to Meerut. The first wing are to embark about the end of this month in steamers, or rather to be taken in by flats, so we must be muffs, and according to the present arrangement I and Harvey will proceed with the second division, and as the steamer will take nearly two months to carry the first wing to Allahabad and

---

20. An official letter from the Army Med. Dept.
21. Inspector-General, Army Med. Dept.

return with the 18th Reg[imen]t to Calcutta for the left wing,
I shall not leave here till the middle of Dec[embe]r. The
Count,[22] however, may be arrested for debt, or he may if he feels
inclined to go up with the last wing, be sick, or his Lady may
be dangerously ill at the last minute, both the latter very
common circumstances to obtain an object, and in that case I
shall be obliged to take his place. I am going to sell my buggy
and horse to the highest bidder, and I dare say I shall get
nearly as much as I gave, although its appearance was not
improved by the capsize the other day. I have ordered a new one
to be built, and I intend sending it up to Allahabad by the
steamer, and if you or Philip will kindly send me a copy of our
crest and coat of arms I shall esteem it a favour. My last
bread seal I broke making an impression for the coachmaker. I
have no doubt you think me a most extravagant fellow, but I find
from experience that the money I was obliged to spend daily in
Polkies[23] and Garries[24] amounted at the end of the month to
twice nearly the expence attendant on my buggy and horse.

Do you know any member of the Skating Club? because I want to
know whether they elected me a member. I paid my subscription
to young Stavely and Mr. Antrobus promised to propose me at the
first meeting in 1849. By a clause in the rules I cannot be
called upon for subscription when abroad, so I shall be an old
member if I by a fluke return to England, as I hope to do in a
year or two.

I wrote to Father and Mother this day month in two letters
which I suppose arrived together, and I enclosed a Lře to
Phillips, Shaw & Lowther, and if you can get anything out of
them by appealing to their honor it will be very satisfactory.
Perhaps a note from Father would have some weight. But if
they have any bowels they cannot refuse payment. I sold my
medicine chest last month for 30 Rupees, much to my disgust.
I was much gratified to find my friend Dr. Thompson a K.C.B.
He and I are great cronies. I have dined & tiffined with him
two or three times lately, which is quite a treat on account of
his English butter, combined with his agreeable society.

I have not heard a word about poor Tom, nor has Al. I
suppose he is on his way home by this time, an old muff.

If you can spare time, perhaps you will send me a copy of
"Old King Cole" (Tipping version), and any other song you think
would suit my sweet voice, and while I think of it, make my
kind regards to Tipping next time you see him, and also Uncle
Fred. Is he still spooning after Mrs. Yule? And does she still

---

22. Assistant Surgeon Eaton, 70th Regiment.
23. Palanquins.
24. Carriages.

open the door and watch him out of sight? Tell him, if everything else fails to come to Calcutta. He is just the man to get
on in business here. And also request him to make my salaam to
his sisters & nieces &c. I would have stolen a number of
sketches from an artist here for Mrs. Pidgeon, the other day,
only the gentleman watched me so carefully, and seemed so choice
of them that I did not dare, & not only from laziness, but also
from ignorance I have made no attempts at drawing myself.

How long are they going to be at the Horse Guard[s] filling
up the vacancies (don't say "you made", because I didn't) in
this Reg[imen]t? I wish you could give me some news in that way
before it is generally known. I hope there are to be no more
such vacancies, and judging from present appearances I think
there will be but little mortality in future. The thermometer
is in this room 86° and I am quite cool & comfortable. Last
week it was just below 80° and to show you how soon one becomes
climatised I wore cloth clothes as I should in England with
comfort. I have not had time to complete my Report on the
diseases of India and my original views, but I hope to do so
shortly.

What is the game at knock 'em down, which you were anxious
to play me at, at the time Ellen concluded her letter to me?
What a mess you are making of the Thames Regatta this year, and
how you're spoiling those Parks with your exhibitions, &
occupying the only eligible ground for the accommodation of all
the poor pickpockets who have no other place to take their daily
rest.[25]

I was told the other day that your friend Wigstrom had
obtained two years' leave on med[ical] certificate, but I have
not seen it mentioned in the papers here.

Much to the amusement of the congregation this morning and
the annoyance of the clergyman, a jackdaw or Rook made his
appearance in church and perched himself just over the
preacher's head on one of the punkah irons, and flew down on
the sacrament table for the ostensible purpose of receiving it,
but perhaps to [?gobble] up the bread and wine - this was
ill-bred indeed. Let me have some more news & believe me my
dear Mopsticks

Your affectionate Bro[ther]
Sawbones.

Oct[obe]r 8. I have written expressing my intention of
subscribing to the Museum B[ui]lding Fund. I hope you will be

---

25. A reference to preparations for the Great Exhibition, in
    Hyde Park.

able to read this letter & just answer its queries by return of
post, via Bombay to Meerut, or abide by the consequences.

C.B.B.

74. *About to leave Calcutta*

Christopher Bassano's diary   Calcutta
                                                     19 October 1850

    The first, or left, wing of H.M. 70th Reg[imen]t started for
Meerut in two Flats for the men and an accommodation boat for
the officers, each of the three being tugged by a steamer.
They are to go as far as Allahabad by steam and there remain
until the right wing arrives. Everything in Calcutta slow at
present. Col[one]l Warren gave us a ball[26] and the inhabitants
are very sorry to lose us. Another year however would send half
of us to Chowringhee (No. 1).

    I have ordered a new Buggy, having sold my old one and horse
for R.400, so that I have only lost R.70 by it. My finances
are not in a flourishing state. On leaving Calcutta I fear I
shall be about six or 700 rupees in debt at least. We are
however fortunately to be paid a month in advance.

    I have succeeded in curing all the oppthalmic cases and we
shall leave Calcutta with scarcely more than two or three cases.

75. *News from friends at home*

Harriet Hamblin to Christopher Bassano   Twickenham
                                                2 November 1850

                                    [received Jan. '51, ansd.
                                    July '54]

    I am quite ashamed, Dear Chris, that I have allowed so long
a time to pass without answering your letter, especially as you
are so unconscionable as to expect us to write six times to
you[r] once ... We are very dull here just now ... I am the
old lady and obliged to keep them all in order ... for I assure
you they are very unruly. Ellen says she thinks they would be
much more if you were here ... [Uncle Fred] made enquiries
respecting the skating and desired me to tell you that you were

---

26. On Tuesday, 31 December at 9½ o'clock, Treasury Gate, Fort
    William, a "bal costumé".

duly elected a full member of the skating club. Uncle Fred had
some very "spiff" skating at Hampton Court last winter ... Of
course you have plenty of dancing, as you say Calcutta abounds
in young ladies. I suppose it is hardly fair to ask how many
you have had the impudence to kiss since you have been there.
I expect they are not to be innumerated ... Grandmamma and
Aunt Louisa have returned and the latter says I am to give her
love to you and say she thinks of you very much and more
especially when she sees any mistletoe. How do you progress
with the black Lady and her thousands? I hope, if you succeed
in gaining the Lady's affections, you will not bring her to
England. It would be so horrid to see you with a black Wife,
but I give you credit for better taste ... Your Brother Phillip
dined with us a few Sundays back. We had a lot of fun with him,
but we are more afraid of him than we were of you. I suppose it
is because you are so much more impudent ... Sarahanne (or
Sarah-ranne) has been very anxious to write to you. You are
still an especial favourite of hers - the enclosed is quite her
own ... How does India agree with you? Has your hair become
any greyer? Tell us about it when you write ... Grandmamma
and Aunt Louisa unite with my sisters & self in best remembrances (or love), whichever you please ...

[enclosed - written in a childish hand]

Dear Chris, I have been wishing to write to you a long time, but
I have been waiting for Harriet to write to you again. I
should like to see you very much, and I hope you are quite well.
I hope you will soon come back, as I am sure they all would like
to see you. I hope by the time you come back you will have left
off playing your tricks. We are all quite well. Have you left
off climbing down the tiles as you did? I suppose you have no
time for it now. As my Cousins are writing all the news to you
I will only add my love and pray believe me, Dear Chris, that I
am still you[r] affec[tiona]te

                    Sarahanne Thackthwaite.

76. *Family, regimental and general news*

Christopher Bassano to Walter Bassano   Fort William
                                               7 December 1850

My dear Walter
    Yours of the 19th Oct[obe]r arrived here yesterday and my
letter to which you allude no doubt was that of July 3rd, and I
have since written twice, my Sept[embe]r 8th to Father & Mother
with a L̃re enclosed to the ship owners, and Oct[obe]r 7 to you
and about the Museum to your office.

I have entrusted to the care of Lieut[enan]t Rae of our
Reg[imen]t, who has just exchanged into the 27th, a parcel containing a cribbage board for Father, a card case for Melinda,
2 knives for you and Phil, one for your son and heir, and a
knitting box for my dear little Annie Francis, the latter
scarcely either useful or ornamental. They are all Bombay style
of architecture, and if seized upon by the custom house, a large
duty will be levied upon them. I addressed them in large letters
to the Army Medical Board office, and I am not certain whether
Rae will not deliver them personally since he has promised to
call on Father and Philip to give you any information about me &
I hope he will. You will find him as nice a youn[g] fellow as
ever breathed, and as he is going home overland by this mail, he
and this L$\tilde{r}$e will arrive about the same time. I did not like to
trust the H[an]dk[erchie]fs with him because I thought he might
lose them.

The son and heir seems to have caused a great sensation in
your family. Melinda thinks he has too large a nose, and the
nurse thinks he is on that a/c sure to live. I hope he may.
Ellen has trusted herself to the wide world, and poor Aunt Ryle,
Melinda informs me, died in July last, and very sorry I am to
hear it. Melinda thought I had heard it before, but she was
mistaken, and if important events are communicated to me casually
three months after they occur in future I shall inflict summary
punishment on all of you. Sir James has retired, you say, and
Philip is living at Brompton. But where do you think I am going
to? Why, instead of the Reg[imen]t being stationed at Meerut,
orders have just arrived ordering us to Cawnpore, the former
being the best, the latter the worst, station in India. I am
now sorry I ordered a new buggy. I sold my old one and horse
for R.400 to Dr. Trousdell of the 29th Reg[imen]t last month,
and I dare say I shall sell my new one when I get to Cawnpore,
where I intend coming the economical dodge, as I understand it
is a cheap place, and no opportunity must be lost now-a-days.
They have been cutting the head money, or allowance for bringing
out troops to this country, in those cases where a Medico comes
out with his own Regiment. I hope there will be a reform in
our service with respect to the Med[ica]l Department, now Sir
James has retired. The first thing they should do is to raise
the pay of Ass[istan]t Surgeons to 13/- a day, and then they
would get a few more decent fellows into the service, but I have
no space to say what I should like to say here. I must wait a
little longer for the good time coming.

I had a miniature taken of myself yesterday and it has just
come home. It is almost in full length, with my regimental
cotee. I shall go on board the steamer tomorrow and see if Rae
will take it also for me. The position is as you see here
depicted.[27] The hole in the face is shown and only just. It

---

27. Drawing - this photograph still exists.

is a daguerrian type, so is quite correct. I must present it to my dear Mother, who I hope has acted up to my instructions about her teeth. The weather here is now most delightful. I am glad of my warm trousers and a shooting coat. In my room thermometer is however only 75°.

The left wing of our Reg[imen]t started from Calcutta in the Steamer on the 19th Oct[obe]r and were safely taken to Al[l]ahabad, where they are remaining for the head Quarters, but now that we are to go only to Cawnpore, it is thought they will be ordered to march there at once. The three steamers are expected here in 3 or 4 days, bringing down a wing of the 18th to Garrison Fort William, and we shall embark for Al[l]ahabad in them, but some doubts arose yesterday as to these boats being required to take up the Commander-in-Chief, who landed here yesterday, and in that case it is possible we may march all the way.

Do you get copies of Medical Committee[s] held in India to determine the sanity or not of men? Because I sat on one by order of the C[ommander] in C[hief] the other day, and I brought the man in sane, in opposition to the two senior surgeons who were on the board with me. P[riva]te Jno. Murphy of our Reg[imen]t was the man. I had just obtained a week's leave, when in the middle, just as I was enjoying myself at Hoogly with Lt. De Quincy, with whom I was knocking about the River in a Bateau or boat, I was ordered back for the confounded Board. We started again and amused ourselves by calling at all the Town[s] on the Hoogly as far up as Chinsura. I had some shooting, but not of a description to brag about.

Alfred wrote to me a few days back saying that two com[pan]ys of the 32nd were to accompany the Gov[ernor) Gen[era]l through the Punjaub and that he happened to be in command of one of them and was anticipating a very jolly journey.[28]

Let me know what they intend doing with your office as soon as you hear. Don't forget what I mentioned in my last. I want "Old King Cole" & a few other songs if you can get them. I gave out the riddle last night about White Arsenic at mess, and it was properly felt. This week I suppose will see the 70th out of Calcutta, so you must address your letters to me at Cawnpore. I am not certain whether they should come across country from Bombay, but if you do not specify that outside I dare say they will come thro' Calcutta.

Your affectionate Bro[ther]
Christopher

---

28. See Letter 58.

77. *Calcutta to Cawnpore to Meerut*

Christopher Bassano's diary   Calcutta
                                               20 December 1850

The head Quarter of H.M. 70th Reg[imen]t embarked today on
board the vessels which took up the left wing to Allahabad and
brought down the 18th Reg[imen]t to take our place in the Fort.
I have been for some days busy in calling on my friends and I
leave Calcutta by no means tired of it. Our destination is now
changed from Meerut to Cawnpore and the left wing are still
waiting for us at Allahabad where we shall proceed by steam. I
am in the Nerbudda steamer in tow of a troop boat.

                                               22 December [1850]

We are now in the Sunderbunds, a space enclosed by the mouths
of the Ganges, and a very peculiar appearance presents itself.
The rivers through which we pass are for the most part not wider
than broad Canals with trees hanging over the banks so that you
seem to pass through an immense forest, which it is, although
the trees are for the most part small. Tigers abound here, but
none presented themselves. On getting into the Ganges we had
plenty of sport in the shape of shooting Crocodiles or
Alligators. I shot several, but none were killed. When they
are not hit they remain quiet, but when struck jump about most
vigorously.

I spent my Xmas Day 1850 on board the Accommodation boat with
Col[one]l & Mrs. Galloway, Majors Timms & Durnford, Capt[ai]ns
Mulock, Reynolds, Evatts, L[ieutenan]ts Buchanan, Blady,
Rutherford, Scheberres, DeQuincey, Crawley, &c. & a very jolly
night we had.

The most remarkable part of the journey is the peculiar state
of the bed of the Ganges, which is continually shifting and even
altering its course for miles. The bed is composed entirely of
fine white sand and a bank formed of this extending seven or
eight miles has a peculiar appearance from its being so flat.
With the exception of Benares all the places we stopped at were
very stupid & uninteresting, but this City from the river has a
most splendid appearance, & emerging from the Centre of the
crescent on the bank of the Ganges on which it stands are two
minarets or lofty towers, about 200 f[ee]t high, from the summit
of which the country may be seen an immense distance. The town
itself is peculiar in having such lofty houses and narrow
streets without from one end to the other there being a single
open space of any description. I wandered about for two or
three hours with Saltmarsh in search of the minarets, but could
not either find them or our way out of the Town until we chanced
to meet a man to whom we could make our desire known.

On the 19th Jan[uar]y we arrived at Allahabad. I had no tent
so borrowed one of the Hospital tents of which we had one or two
to spare. We succeeded in getting excellent beef for the men on
the river. The married men and women had one portion of the
deck of the flat consigned to them, but there was no partition
between them and the single ones and I had some few complaints
made to me about it. Capt[ai]n Digney fed us tolerably well,
but in the Accommodation boat the[y] faired sumptuously.

19 January 1851

Disembarked and encamped at Allope Baghe, Allahabad, where we
remained encamped 3 days previous to commencing our march for
Cawnpore.

6 Feb[ruar]y [1851]
[to March 1851]

Arrived at Cawnpore and I must confess I was not particularly
gratified by the march. The encamping grounds and surrounding
country had daily the same appearance. Our marching distance
avaraged about 13 miles, and the men stood it well. The weather
being cold most of the officers walked best part of the way,
some all, but the Col[one]l not knowing much about the country
insisted on all the officers remaining with the men. Some few
robberies were committed. A Camel to carry one's tent is a
great comfort. Cawnpore seems a pretty good station, but it
extends over too much ground, it being six or seven miles at its
extreme points. An order that an assistant should proceed to
Meerut to do duty with H.M. 29th Reg[imen]t has just arrived &
I intend to try to get it if possible. Eaton has been put in
orders, but does not wish to go so I am to take his place.

Started for Meerut about the 12th Feb[ruar]y 1851 for the
purpose of doing duty with H.M. 29th Regiment. It is 27 days
march from Cawnpore to Meerut, but as I wanted to see Agra on
my way I took an extra day or two. Had my new buggy drawn by
coolies. I enjoyed the march amazingly, and was much pleased
with the Taj and the other buildings at Agra. Two marches from
Agra shot a most beautiful peacock. My march into Agra
commenced at 5 o'C[lock] a.m. and I did not arrive there until
6 p.m. The distance I went over that day must have been 40
miles. Fortunately on my arrival there however, I found an old
friend (Hansbrow) with whom I remain three days.

*8. *The Sunderbunds – the Ganges*

Christopher Bassano to Charlotte Bassano

> Hon[ora]ble John Com[pan]y
> steamer Nerbudda
> [22 Dec. 1850-3 Jan. 1851]

My dear Mother

My last letters dated Dec[embe]r 8th to Melinda and Walter were probably too late for the mail, although they made me shell out a Rupee fine. I am at present in a very comfortable Steamer enjoying myself to the utmost. The head Quarters left Calcutta on the 20th Dec[embe]r and we dropped down the river Hoogly that afternoon en route to Cawnpore, our destination. The Hoogly at this time of year is not navigable except for country boats, so we had to go down almost to the mouth of the sea. We then intersected a number of small rivers called the Sunderbunds, many of them containing salt water which opportunity I embraced and had a series of salt water baths, much to the benefit of my health. The rivers we are passing through vary in breadth from that of the Thames at Gravesend to about twice the breadth of the canal, and nothing is to be seen on either side but low trees extending close to the water edge, in fact the whole country for miles around seems like a garden of weeds, abounding in deer, wild boar, & Tigers, but no human beings.

Dec[embe]r 31st. We are now in the Ganges, a most remarkable river, in some places three or four miles wide, in other[s] narrow. At this time of year the water is low, and immense flat sands are left which look in some places like a table cloth a mile or two in length. The banks fall down on one side and are deposited at another part of the river, so that its bed is continually changing. Along the flat sand great numbers of alligators lie basking in the sun, much to the relief of the monotonous character of the river, and afford us opportunities of displaying our skill with the rifle. I hit five out of the first six I fired at, turned one over on his back, & shot another down the throat as he was basking with his jaw open so wide that a child might readily of walked into his jaw.

At Rampore Bauleah, the third station we coaled at, my friend Dr. Bedford met me, he having just been appointed Civil Surgeon there, and then came the Judge, Mr. Cheap, with whom a number of us dined, he and Bedford having agreed to amalgamate their dinners in order to give us a good feed. I made no bones at paying my respects to a splendid haunch of venison & a variety of other dainties with which the table abounded. In the morning he kindly sent on board a quantity of fresh butter, fruits, vegetables, &c. all of which are in great request as nothing of the sort can be obtained at the small villages through which we pass.

I sent my likeness home, as I told you, by Lieut[enan]t Rae, by the last overland steamer which left Calcutta on the 8th Dec[embe]r, together with the Bombay things, and I have given Mrs. Capt[ai]n Braddell the Handkerchiefs (six in number) to put into the L.P.D.Cy. when she arrives. She is the wife of Capt[ai]n Braddell of the 70th who has just sold out, and she will in all probability arrive in England about the middle or end of March by the ship Wellesley (I think one of Green's). It is a first class ship and left Calcutta about the 12th Dec[embe]r. One marked for Annie, 1 for Mother, 1 for poor Aunt Ryle which Melinda may have, one for Melinda marked, and one which she may have without a mark. If you can send Ellen hers do so, if not Mother may do what she likes with it.

I should like to know whether my College certificates are being taken care of for me as they may be useful.[29] Tell Walter not to bully me any more about foolscap; since I am now a Mofussilite he will no longer see this kind of paper[30] - the reason is easily explained. A sheet of foolscap weighs half an ounce, and that is equal to four letters in India, about a quarter of that weight being the standard for one letter. And as letters sent to or recieved from the upper provinces are charged with postage, viz. about 10 An[nas] or upwards of a shilling, for every fourth of half an ounce, the Indian correspondent finds he must make light of his postage or it becomes very heavy. From what I know however I am not like to find any inconvenience from your Lres. I merely explained it because we used to wonder why all Alfred's letter[s] were marked "paid" and yet bore the postage from India.

I did not mention I think that I had a merry C[h]ristmas, and I wish you have had the same. Col[one]l Galloway stood Simpkin in commemoration of its being the second Anniversary since he & I joined the Reg[imen]t. About twenty of us sat down, Mrs. Galloway & Mrs. Buchanan being the only ladies on board that [?flat - letter torn]. The Band played some melodious strains as is their custom every evening after the three steamers have anchored.

Jan[uar]y 2nd. On New Year's Eve my slumbers were disturbed by some soft music just before 12 o'C[lock], and you cannot concieve how be[a]utiful several of our native airs sounded on the water, played in the most soft and imposing style. Yesterday, New Year's Day, the steamer stopped to take in Coal at Rajmahall, close to a range of hill[s], so I took the opportunity of having a long walk. I saw some splendid old Ruins of an old palace built on an eminence, and below this the bones of a Cow which had been half eaten the night before by a tiger.

---

29. These still survive.
30. See Letter 80, n. 34. This letter is written on ordinary
    foolscap -- succeding letters on very flimsy paper.

Today we have been passing at the foot of the hills, the sight of which, combined with a cloudy day, has in no small degree elevated my spirits. I took a sketch or two for Mrs. Pidgeon, as they appear so extraordinary after being at the lower part of Bengal for nearly two years where the country is as flat as a pancake.

I have not heard from Alfred since I last wrote you. I suppose he is busy with the Gov[erno]r-Gen[era]l. I got Culloway to apply for the appointment of medico to the C[ommander] in C[hief] for me, but although he promised after a little jaw to do all he could after wondering what the Reg[imen]t would do if they lost me, yet he would not let me write about it. I attended his levy and had a nice conversation with him a few days after it had been given to Dr. Franklin, but he is only to have the appointment for a short time, so perhaps it is as well I did not get it. I must endeavour to become unpopular in the Reg[imen]t as then I shall have no difficulty in getting plenty of leave and permission to apply for a better appointment.

In a few minutes we shall be at Bhaglepore, so I must post this letter. Nothing particular today, except more hills and one or two b[ea]utiful Rocks in the middle of the river. Major Timins' rifle went off by accident and shot a man between the arm and chest. Let me know where Ellen is to be written to when you hear from her as I may not get a letter for a year or more, the steam communication is so indifferent. Send Melinda to Paris for about 6 months, but to a first rate school, or not at all. Rem[em]ber me to any friends, and don't forget the advice I gave you about eating plenty of fruit in the summer *daily*, get a new set of teeth and I will remain your affec[tionate] Son Christopher.

Bhaglepore, Jan[uar]y 3rd, '51.

9. *Thanks for presents – news about Tom – family news*

Charlotte Bassano to Christopher Bassano
(letter finished by Melinda)

7 Church Row, Kensington
19 March 1851

My dear Christopher
    It is impossible for me to express the delight I felt on the receipt of your kind present – you could not have sent me one more valuable. I think it very like you, but wish it had been done on ivory.[31] I could then have hung it up and had it constantly before me. Melinda is as much pleased with it as I

---

1. See Letter 76.

am - indeed so we are all. Poor Lieut[enant] Ray was seized with
paralysis as soon as he arrived in London and confined to his bed
at the Colonnade hotel. His Mother wrote to say we could have
the things. Your Father called first, and I went a week after.
His Mother took me to his bedside and I was much pleased with
him - he seems a very nice young man. Phil called about three
weeks after, but he had been removed that day into the country,
and we have heard nothing since.

You will be glad to hear that my health is very much better
than it was. Dr. George, a medical gentleman in the neighbourhood, who was called in when I had the cholera, attended me
again last summer for about two months, and has quite set me to
rights although I am so thin I have scarcely a bit of flesh on
my bones.[32] Still, I feel very well, and am more comfortable
than I have been for many years in every respect, for when your
Father got the Derby money about a year and a half since he
paid Slipper and Child, which was a great relief to my mind.
But we had many words over it, you may be sure, for he is just
as stingy as ever. You say get a set of teeth. You may be sure
I will as soon as I can, for I have only two left and they are
quite loose, but I shall not go to your friend for then he would
be too expensive for me.

I have been quite miserable for a long time about D[ea]r Tom
as we had none of us heard from him since he left his last
employer, and I felt fully persuaded he was dead. But I am
happy to say Phil has just had a letter from him. He writes in
good spirits haveing got a new master, and a coffee estate of
his own just by. I hope God will bless his honest endeavors,
for he has had a hard life of it.

Your Aunt Thompson has had another fit of sickness, but has
got over it again, much to our astonishment, but her son Joseph
Dean is no more. Your Father is going to his funeral next
Thursday. He has been ill about two months with a disorder of
the lungs. He has left his property - about 8 or 9 hundred
pounds - to his Mother, which will be very acceptable to them I
am sure, as they are very much put to it to make a liveing.
Arthur is left executor. He is still with Mr. Gurney Barkley,
who is going on again. John has got an excellent situation in
the Royal British Bank.

I cannot write any more for I have got the rheumatism so bad
in my hands I can scarcely hold my pen, which is a very bad one,
so you must excuse it. We have just rec[eive]d a letter from
Christopher Bassano of Derby informing us of the death of his
Mother, your Uncle Henry's wife. Aunt Thompson sends her kind

---

32. She was in her 66th year.

ove & best wishes for your welfare & I remain, My dear
Christopher
                    Your most affectionate Mother
                         Charlotte Bassano

Dear Chris
    Mamma wants me to finish this letter as her rheumatism is so
bad it is rather troublesome to her to write, but you must
excuse me writing much because we have to go into mourning for
Joseph Dean tomorrow, and I have a good many little things in
the way of dress to get ready. We are all delighted with the
beautiful presents you sent us, particularly your portrait. I
did not think it so much like you the first moment I looked at
it, but I think it very much like you now, & the more I look at
it the greater resemblance I see. Someone told them at the
office - Lieutenant Willis, I think - that you have had a fever
& had your head shaved. Why did you not tell us? It accounts
I suppose for the absence of your luxuriant curls, which we
missed in your Daguerreotype. I think my card-case is most
beautiful. You could not have selected a nicer present for I
had some cards printed about a year ago & could not afford to
buy a handsome card-case & so I did not have one at all. Mamma
has told you, I see, that we have heard from dear Tom again -
not that I was quite so despairing about him as Mamma was, but
younger hearts are always more hopeful. His employer, Mr.
Morris, died a few days after Tom wrote, & his brother called
on Phil & frightened him in such a manner, for Mr. Morris
expressed himself in such a way as to make Phil think at the
moment that it was our poor Tom that was dead. He seemed very
anxious to retain Tom's services, & Phil thinks that he, or
Father, could make a more advantageous arrangement than Tom has.
Mr. Morris said he did not think they should quarrel about terms.
But you will hear all about [it] from Tom & I have not room to
tell you any more.[33] We have not heard from Alfred for ever so
long - he is quite losing his good character as a correspondent.
Give my love to him when you write. I must write in turns to
each of you I suppose now. That will be once in four months to
each of you. Will that do? This paper is villainous to write
on, my dear Chris, so pray excuse the writing & Believe me to
remain
                    Yours affectionately
                         Melinda

    I was obliged to finish the last few lines for Mamma,
because I am in a hurry to take the letter, so don't puzzle
your head about the difference in the writing dear Chris. M.B.

---

33. See Letter 55.

Christopher Bassano to F.M. Bassano[34]   Meerut
                                                        9 April 1851

I arrived here on the 10th March to do duty with the 29th
Reg[imen]t after an [?amusing] journey from Cawnpore spent most
agreeably, and I was not a little improved in my health by it,
since I never recollect being so [?strong] and healthy in my
life. I found Walter's letter of the 10th Dec[embe]r waiting
for me with the Armorial bearing, and I a few days after
recieved yours of the 18th Jan[uar]y expressing your anxiety
about your hide & seek son Tom. I wrote accordingly to him,
and enclosed it in a letter for the postmaster at Calicut, who
will open & return Tom's letter to me, should he know nothing
about him. I shall hear therefore in a few days, and if nothing
satisfactory results, I will make further inquiries. Why poor
Mother should mar her happiness about him I cannot understand.
He cannot be dead, or we should have heard about it. I hope
Mother received my letter from the Banks of the Ganges
"Boghlepore", and Walter a subsequent one written a few days
after I left Agra (dated March 4th),[35] both of them containing
a history of my journey from Calcutta, and although addressed
to individuals were written as family letters. The remainder
of my journey was not so amusing. Wild fowl &c. became scarce
& the weather rather warm for walking twenty miles a day.

I have very little at present to say about Meerut. It
appears a much better station than Cawnpore, and is considerably
cooler. My Thermometer until three days ago was, in the house,
as low as 75°. It is no 80° and the air outside about 100°.
This, people seem to think warm, but I don't find it so myself.
The C[ommander]-in-Chief was here the other day, and a grand
fancy dress ball was given to Lady Gomm, but I did not honor
them with my company, as I knew nobody in the station and had
made up my mind to be quiet. Some wag here in the Civil
Service, (a son of S[i]r Joseph Hume), wrote a critic on the
ladies at the Ball and scandalized them so severely that a
meeting was held to know what they should do to the culprit.
And it was settled that he should not be admitted into society,
and a written apology was sent to him to sign, but he wrote
back to them saying he could not put his name to an apology
containing a grammatical error, so he wrote a mild one himself.
The verses were very well written, and only gave the ladies
what they deserved, I have no doubt. If they appear in the
newspapers I will send one to Walter, as he seems rather

---

34. This letter is written on very thin greasy paper, some
    lines so faint as to be illegible, some written over by
    CBB. See comment in Letter 81.
35. Not found.

disgusted that I don't give him some scandal about the ladies.
Just like the married men!!! Why, if I were to write about the
scandal against the ladies of one Reg[imen]t in India, it would
fill a volume. Nobody who has never been in India can form any
idea what a rum lot of females are married to Officers in India,
and how freely all their faults are conversed and canvassed at
the mess table. No matter whether good or bad, mention
anybody's name at the table and I defy you hear a word in favour
of him or her from the moment they were born. For my part, I –
like Uncle Fred – take no part in such conversation, and never
retail what I hear against ladies.

I am living in a nice little Bungalo[w] with my friend
Ass[istan]t S[urgeo]n Miles of the 1st Bengal Fusiliers, who you
and Walter I think have seen. Perhaps a slight outline of my
house would be interesting, so I have enclosed it.[36] I regret
there are but few fruit trees in the garden, for I am still as
great an advocate for fruit as ever, and make it a portion of
my daily meal.

Do you know Dane, the surgeon of the 29th? He is a queer
fellow and not much liked, I fancy, by the officers. I have as
yet got on very well with him, and on my joining, he handed
over to me all his ophthalmic patients – about eight and twenty
– having heard of my success in that department. He appears to
have had great disputes with the Col[one]l about these men
being invalided for ophthalmia, and I quite agree with him that
no man ought to be invalided for that disease while inflammation
exists, and from what I have now seen and from my own experience
I have no hesitation in saying that ophthalmia in Reg[imen]ts
in India would form the most inconsiderable disease in a
Reg[imen]t if the men knew how to live and the Doctors knew how
to cure them. When I took charge of the ophthalmic cases in
Calcutta – which I did at two distinct and distant periods – the
number was about the same as in this Reg[imen]t, and I in the
first instance reduced the number during one month to about half,
and subsequently, just before I left Calcutta after having had
them about two months under my charge, reduced them from 25 to
4, and on leaving Calcutta there was not a case of a week's
standing. The same result is now manifest in the men under me,
and although several of them are nearly or quite blind [I]
have no doubt that in another month or two these will be the
only cases in the books. My sheet anchor in this disease, as
well as nearly all others in this country, is lime juice or
fruit; without administering this in nearly every case of
Ophthalmia & Dysentery in this country, other judicious treatment becomes perfectly useless, and in many cases absolutely
injurious. I have been preaching this ever since I was in the
country, and I am now glad to find others are of the same

---

36. See Letter 82.

opinion. But until soldiers in hot climates are recommended to
eat fruit by Medical men, or until that article is served out to
them as a portion of their rations, they will continue to die of
Dysentery and become the victims of cholera; and ophthalmia will
still be at the top of the list. I am however becoming prosy on
the subject, perhaps of little interest to you.

I percieve that Dr. Smith is to take Sir James['s] Place,[37]
and I am very glad of it for several reasons. I think, from
what I have seen & heard of him, he is well calculated for the
office, and I now begin to look forward for some changes in the
medical department better adapted for the times we live in and
the advancements lately made in science. Perhaps the day is not
far distant when a med[ica]l officer can obtain a decent pair
of forceps to pull at a tooth, or an urinometer & its appendages,
or a few new and valuable medicines, all of which he has been
accustomed to, but which are at present beyond his reach, and
when indented for produce the utmost surprise. Perhaps also a
few newly discovered diseases and medicines will be added to the
list, and the vast number of old & useless ones be erased - but
not by medical officers in the army, but by professors at the
Colleges who are the only men up to all the new dodges. The
chief thing which I hope will take place however is that some
inducement should be held out for officers to practise their
profession in the army and not by great assiduity and activity
place themselves in a worse position than if they did only what
they were obliged to do. Such is the case out here, and thus
the more value attached to a Medical Officer the less chance he
has of the slightest recreation. I assure you I have been
obliged - independantly of my wish to see India - to leave the
70th on the 1st opportunity, just to get a little relaxation
from the continual daily walk through the Hospital, knowing that
the only answer I could get when I required change was "that I
could not be spared". As long as Medical Officers are considered as unfit to be recommended for leave of absence on the
same ground as other officers how are they to recruit their
strength except by having recourse to malingering, which no
doubt many of them are forced unwillingly to have recourse to.
It surely requires no great amount of brains to see that
Med[ica]l officers, who are never for a moment at rest or free
from calls, are the men who require the most indulgence.
Perhaps now that the Secretary-at-War will have the patronage,
he will find from experience that appointments are only coveted
in the Queen's service from their necessity, and that he will
see the propriety of recommending their pay and position being
exalted.

The 14th Dragoons are here, and our friend Wigstrom in great
force. He complains about not having heard from Walter in reply

37. As Director-General, Army Medical Department.

214

to three letters. He is [a] fast fellow & something in Eaton's style. I was on a Board with him and Dr. Stewart a few days ago for the purpose of condemning Hospital clothing, and I never saw such a particular and slow old coach as Stewart. I wish I had thought of applying to go home with the invalids as Walter mentioned in his letter, but I doubt if I should have been recommended by the Col[one]l. I rec[eive]d a letter from Alfred the other day, and he goes on much as usual. There was some talk of the 32nd being ordered to Peshawur, but they now say not. Wa[l]ter may well call the Museum movement a swindle and say I appear very flush of money. I was some time before I could make up my mind to acquiesce with the notion. There are much better museums in London than ours, and at Chatham it is of some use to medicos, whereas in London nobody would think anything of it.

Strawberries are in great force at Meerut just now, but the fruit suffered considerably a few days ago from a hail storm such as I had never before seen. The pieces of ice were as large as [a] pigeon's egg and in such large quantities that the ground remained white for nearly an hour. I collected a large box full by dint of great exertion amongst the niggers whose hands & feet were quite frozen by the fun, and I have heard that in some parts there were regular flakes of ice as large as hens eggs. The Hills are said to be visible from Meerut, but I am sorry to say I have failed to get a sight of them.

I shall make an effort to get six months leave after this summer is over and pay Alfred and Simla a visit if I succeed. I heard from Alfred on my arrival here, but he does not seem so jolly as he used to be, and still complains of the paucity of European letters which come to his hands.

Tell Wa[l]ter to give me a long account of the Great Exhibition, and little less of his cheek. And if you can write a letter to any of the bigwigs who can do me a good turn out here do so. St. John for instance might be put up to favour my application to come home in charge of invalids and then I might volunteer for Africa, and get my promotion. I often think I should like to do that, for I have come to the conclusion that climate is the greatest rot in the world as to your injuring your health, and I would just as soon go there in that respect as any other place. I was glad to hear of the birth of Wa[l]ter's son and heir & that his good points are so well developed. Melinda thinks his nose to[o] big, but it's a good thing, and I have no doubt he will be very intellectual, for all people with large noses do great things in the world.

I have enclosed a letter - or rather, I intend doing so - to Messrs. Phillips, Tiplady & Co., if I get a reply from the Paymaster at Cawnpore in time to send with it, but if not, I will write to them next mail.

215

(P.S.   It has not come so I will write by the next.)

[Copy of a letter from Phillipps Shaw & Lowther,
23 November 1850, addressed to C.B. Bassano, Esq. M.R.C.S.L.,
Assistant Surgeon, H.M. 70th Regiment, 10 Rampart Barracks,
Fort William.

Sir, We are in receipt of your letter of the 6th
Sept[embe]r and in the absence of Capt[ai]n Pugh from
England regret that we cannot give you a satisfactory
reply.
    All we can say is that in all the very great number
of ships we have for many years past dispatched to India
with Troops we have never yet had such a claim made upon
us, and we conclude you must have made it under a mis-
apprehension.   More especially as regards the medicines,
seeing that we had under the superintendance of the
Hon[oura]ble E[ast] I[ndia] Com[pan]y to supply the ship
with a medicine chest for the Troops & also one for the
Crew.
    On the return of Capt[ain] Pugh we will question him
on the subject & if necessary again write you.]

The above is a copy of their letter and I have written for a
memo showing that I had to pay for the medicines, and thus will
be able to shew they have almost told a crammer in writing the
above.   Capt[ai]n Pugh went to Bombay I think, in somebody
else's employ, after I fancy having a row with them, so if they
should ask him he will support me, especially as I wrote him a
certificate of having treated us all well & been of much service
to me.

Address your letters to me via Bombay and give my love to
the dear creatures in our circle, and believe me

                    My dear Father
                        Your affectionate Bro [sic]
                            Christopher.

81. *Miscellaneous gossip*

Christopher Bassano to Walter Bassano[38]   Meerut
                                                       9 April 1851

My dear Mopsticks
    I may as well give you a little abuse in reply to yours of
the 19th Dec[embe]r, and for fear you should not be able to

---

38. Enclosed in Letter 80.

216

read the commencement of Father's letter, which seems to get fainter & fainter every day, I may as well mention again that I wrote to you on the 4th March & to Mother on the 3rd Jan[uar]y. Ink is so bad here, and this dry weather if you put your pen down for a few minutes the nibs twist back like a puppy dog's tail. Talk about dogs - I have just had two pups given me as something very fine, and Miles has promised me one of a breed which are likely to be very valuable. I have driven my new buggy with a large horse of Miles', and it certainly looks, as you say, stunning. I don't see much use for a buggy here & if I can't sell it for a hundred rupees more than I gave I shall be rather sold. Tell me all about the Med[ica]l Board, what they are going after. I hear that they propose abolishing some of the distinction made between the medicos. I don't care about that for I see no reason why a Surgeon in a Corps should not, if he choses to remain in it, be just as well off in a pecuniary point of view as if he were made a Staff surgeon. I am however very ignorant of the real state of my brethren, so am perhaps wrong. Old Dane here seems to get information in a very mysterious manner, and he gives it out to you in a peculiar manner. Dr. Thompson of the 24th has just arrived and wishes to be attached to the 29th, and I fear they will be sending me back.

[The next eight lines are scribbled out.]

If you or any of you take in *Punch* I don't mind having recent numbers occasionally. The Atlas for India or Home News would be acceptable. These 29th chaps are not so flush of newspapers as the 70th and the mail has been in a week without my being able to get hold of the news. Did you find Indian news interesting? Did you speak to my red-nosed fool of a friend in the scating club, because for God's sake don't. Did you drink my health on Xmas day? Did you get the smoking cap I didn't send you, poor old beast. If you give me so much cheek I'm blest if I don't tell The[ophilus] to lick you. I hear that The had proposed to a gal & she objected for some good reason. Is it true? I cut Sir W[illia]m Gomm for not taking me on his staff, and Alfred has cut the Gov[erno]r Gen[era]l because he didn't take a fancy to him. How is the young hopes, Harry Phil? I should like to have his likeness taken. Perhaps Melinda might make a happy hit in that line as well as in Singing.

Give my love to Annie and the kids on my birthday[39] & [I] will drink all your healths & if you think of it just tell me the year I was born in, for I have not the least idea of my age. I expect I am damned old. I am however not so grey as I used to be, which is remarkable and very gratifying. Did you tell me Liz was married? What a screamer she must be by this time!

---

39. 20th April. He was born in 1824 and this was his 27th birthday.

If she is not married you may give her a kiss for me - I dare
say she will be able to put up with the delusion, and I have no
doubt would much sooner have that operation performed by your
affectionate

Brother Chris

Why don't they make a staff surgeon of Father? Now would be
the time to agitate the question. He will be a great muff to
retire without making a push for it.

82. *Family gossip*

Christopher Bassano to Melinda Bassano[40]   Meerut
                                                 9 April 1851

My dear Linney
     On the other side is a mild plan of my bungalo[w] which may
afford you some little amusement. I hope you have given up
your tuition duties and have taken to a domestic life. Why, the
next thing will be another dear sister running off to colonize
instead of remaining at home to look after poor Mother in her
old age. I might excuse your going to France for a few months,
but nothing more. Has no one fallen in love with you? I am
afraid you do not encourage the bashful young gentlemen who are
so fond of you. There are but few officers good enough for you.
They are a poor set of muffs generally speaking, but if you
particularly admire the red coats I might pick out one very
readily who would do. When I come home I will look after this
little affair for you. I strongly suspect you have nobody to
trot you about but Philip, and he is not fond of amusements.
Tell him he has not favored me with a letter since I have been
in India, and Arthur also beg to write me a line. I am anxious
to know what he and John are doing. Give my love to Mrs. John
Ryle and young Boneparte her son, Aunt Thompson and nieces Eliz
& Anne. My bonny Kate also must not be forgotten, and the dear
creatures at Twickenham, Sarah Nan &c. Mrs King & Clara kindly
wrote me a note and I am ashamed to say I have not been able to
answer it. Remember me to them, and tell them that my
correspondence is really so very extensive that they must not
be offended at my delay in replying. I have now been here a
month and have been doing nothing else but write letters, to say
nothing of the expense. Everybody who I come across in India
seems to keep up an occasional correspondence, I suppose because
I am such an agreeable fellow. You will say I am more conceited
than ever, but just look at my daguerratype, if you have

---

40. Enclosed in Letter 80. The first page consists of a
     drawing of his bungalow, with a description. Pinned to it
     is a "feather out of the peacock's topnot I shot".

recieved it all safe, and mark what a disagreeable fellow I look, but how profoundedly intellectual. I long to hear Walter's abuse about it.

I suppose you have by this time received the Handkerchiefs I sent home by Mrs. Braddell in the "Wellesley", and the cribbage board for Father &c., by my friend Rae. Take care of yourself in that monster "Cristial Palace" and don't let those omnibus fellows put Mother into the wrong bus. When do you stare a small bucket out of countenance? When you look a little pale in the face. Has Mother got a new set of teeth yet? I wrote to her on the subject of her jaw, but received nothing but Wa[l]ter's instead. This is contrary to cocker, so you must insist upon Mother writing to me. I want a new watch guard, for everybody bullies me for putting my shoe ribbon round my neck. My watch goes as well as it did the day I bought it, so I have had my four guineas worth out of it nobody can deny. Alfred's thoughts and his paper always come to an end together, and mine seem to have terminated simultaneously today, so for the present

> My dear little Lin
> Believe me your aff[ectionate]
> Christopher

Description of bungalow

No. 1 My consulting Room, where I may be supposed writing this letter at (1a) the table
(b) a couch I intend getting

2. My bedroom (a) bed (b) baggy cushions (c) chest of drawers (d) boots (e) case for drawers (f) carpet (g) matting

3. Bath Room, with a cask of beer made in the hills and which I bought to bottle off

4. Dining-Room with table & chairs (a) china chest

5. Common Sitting room (a & b) two small tables (c) a large table with Miles' books and writing apparal (d) large table with dimity cover (e) sundry chairs beautifully striped with gold at 1/8 per chair (f) the chest Savory gave me standing on a bullock trunk with the table cover in it Mother bought, and wine glasses &c. in front (g) my Chinese rocking chair

6. Waiting room.

7. Miles' bath room & writing room

8. Miles' bedroom

9. Pantry

83. *Ellen in Australia - Tom's affairs - life in Meerut - Alfred - attempts to get home - gossip*

Christopher Bassano to Philip Bassano   Meerut
                                                         27 June 1851

[Note on letters sent]

Walter dated Dec[embe]r 8th,[41] with   )
enclosure to Melinda   )
)   receipt not
Mother Jan[uar]ly 3rd,[42] posted at Bohglpore)   acknowledged
)
Walter March 4th,[43] posted at Allyghur   )

April 9th[44] I wrote to Father enclosing a note to Walter and
Melinda with a copy of Philips Tiplady's letter.

My dear Philip
    Yours of the 19th April arrived only on the 17th inst.   The
latest English news here is the 7th May containing the account
of the Exhibition, and the next mail is due tomorrow, which
should bring news up to the 20th May.   Had Walter received a
Letter which I wrote him from Allyghur on 4th March last, containing the account of my journey from *Bohglepore* (from which
place I wrote to Mother on the 3rd Jan[uar]ly) - not answered -
and of my joining the 29th?   I should have heard from some of
you by the last mail across country from Bombay.   I am therefore
afraid it did not arrive.   Tell Mother I recieved hers and
Melinda's of the 19th March on the 11th May[45] and I will answer
them next month.   I am glad they are so pleased with my image.
I wrote to Wa[l]ter on the 8th May enclosing him a letter to
Phillip Tiplady in reply to theirs of Nov[embe]r last.[46]   I also
had the gratification of hearing of Ellen's safe arrival at
Melbourn[e].   Her letter is dated April the 9th and she had been
there a week.   She enclosed me one to Tom, not being certain of
his address.   If you have not recieved a letter from her you
will like to hear how she is &c.   She does not say much about
the voyage, only that it was rather tedious, and that she was

---

41. Letter 76.
42. Letter 78.
43. Not found.
44. Letters 80-82.
45. Letter 79.
46. Not found.

so ill for a month that she could not keep the least thing on
her stomach and they expected she would have died. A calm however for a week came just in time to save her and she is now
very well. She did not like Adelaide, but seems to speak well
of Melbourne where the people appear much more respectable and
wealthy. She was kindly recieved by those to whom she had
letters of introduction. Dr. & Mrs. Black she mentions, and
Capt[ai]n Conran introduced her to a lady who knows Dr. Peleau's
brother and has written to them on her behalf. She was living
at the Hotel where she was eaten up by mosckettos, bugs &c. She
was however just about to take private lodging. House rent she
says is very high, but all thing[s] taken together it is not
much more expensive than England. She does not seem in good
spirits, and I don't wonder at it, poor girl, in the unsettled
state in which she is in. She was disappointed in not having
recieved a letter from home and attributes it to the Post Office
where they are extremely irregular; in fact she begs me not to
write to her until I hear from some of the family where she is
settled, so let me know if you hear of her whereabouts first.[47]

I am glad you told me all about Tom, although I had just
before recieved a letter from him; I dare say you wrote to him
by the same mail you did to me. I however told him how difficult
it was under the circumstances of the two brothers quarrelling
to adjust matters, and I quite think with you that he should not
be taken in as a partner unless he could be protected from any
future delinquencies likely to involve him in their affairs.
Let me know as soon as anything is settled, as he is such a lazy
chap at writing I may not get another letter from him for some
months.

Excuse me for having made such a preamble about my own chits,
but I seldom get the dates of them mentioned, so unless I allude
to them over and over again I fear they have miscarried. The
weather until about a week ago was most intolerably hot so that
it was impossible to sleep at night, the Ther[mometer] standing
at 96° all night. A few heavy rains have now cooled the air
again and I hope we may get more shortly. You are mistaken in
supposing I like this place better than Calcutta. Fancy what
there can be to like in a place where you cannot stir out during
the whole of the day, and when you take a drive in the evening
nothing on earth to see or do but a few people on the course
puffing and blowing and trying to look happy when they do themselves the honor of bowing to you, and giving you the trouble in
return to lift your hand up and bring every muscle in the body
into action by bowing again to them. The most lively thing that
has taken place was a Masonic Ball at which nearly all the
crannies (half casts &c.) in the station were invited, together
with the wives of the Serg[ean]ts of all the regiments and other

---

47. See Section IV, below.

decent women. It was given in Wigstrom's house, and a supper was laid out for 300 people. The women danced capitally and came out with the Lancers & Caledonians in great force. Nearly all the officers in the station were at it and they made themselves as amiable as possible to the ladies and fraternized with the Soldiers to a great extent. You can scarcely concieve how elegantly some of the women were dressed. In fact a soldier's wife in India is not the same person as at home. Little tea parties occasionally amongst the regimental ladies keep up ones esteem for the fair sex, otherwise I don't know what we should come too.

I wrote a private letter to Dr. St. John begging him to let me take home the recruits this year, not that I much expect to get them, but I might manage to take them down to Calcutta by the assistance of Dane's influence with St. John. I and Dane get on capitally and he declares he will speak very highly of me to the Inspector General, so I am in hopes something may turn up. Dane knows how to appreciate *talent* and feels under a great obligation to me for my zeal in the Ophthalmic ward and has mentioned me in his annual return. There is nothing like keeping up the steam, so I shall before I leave the 29th get as much out of them as I can for my services. If I can get Col[one]l Congrieve to write me a good letter to Mountain it would be a great service to me. I should think if Father knew St. John he might give him a hint that anything worth having would be acceptable to me. If I could only get home with invalids next year it would be very jolly, perhaps £100 in my pocket for head money and if not I should be in pocket by the trip.

So Willis told them I had had my head shaved in Calcutta which accounted for my hair being so short at the time I had my likeness taken. It is all a cram. I only had it cut short because it was all dropping out after I had the attack of acute Rheumatism. I have been very seedy with Rheumatism during the last week, and indeed thought one day I should have been laid up with Rheumatic fever again, but it has gone off and I have only had some pain in my elbows & wrists. They will probably be gratified to know that my hair is now very thick and curly and that a large stack of whiskers are making their appearance. My horse was very frisky the other day and began jumping about, and while I was licking the brute he threw his head up and gave me such a blow on the jaw that it nearly stunned me. My lip was cut clean threw and is not quite well yet, and what annoyed me most was that I could not eat or laugh for the pain until yesterday.

I was just as disappointed as you about Alfred losing the adjutancy. He did not assign any reason or even allude to it in his letters. He expects to get a month's leave to Kangra in Sept[embe]r, but he is not so communicative as he used to be. I fancy he does not enjoy such good health as he used to do.

So poor Joseph kicked the enemy, but it's not to be wondered at if he continued the old game. I am glad John Ryle has got such a good situation. Remember me to him & Mrs. John Ryle to whom I hope they sent the handkerchief I had made for Aunt Ryle. I want to hear how they like them, which you did not say. I would have sent you & Walter home something more worth your accepting, but I could not spare any more cash when I left Calcutta. Walter doesn't tell me what they are about to do with the Medical Board. I suppose all my friends in the War Office are well. You must make my respects to Fergusson & rem[em]ber me kindly to Matthew Gurney & Melinda's friend & some others whose names I forget, also to my friends at Twickenham and Uncle Fred, who you say has gone back to spoon about Mrs. Yule. Why doesn't the old "monument" write to me? I am not much in the humour for writing this morning for it's so damned hot, so I am afraid this is rather [a] dull, stupid letter, but you must make the most of it and believe me to remain, my dear Phil

    Your affec[tionate] bro[ther]
        Chris

This Letter will have to go through Calcutta in consequence of the steamer not touching at Bombay. But you must still address my Letter per Bombay steamer, as they still come across country if so addressed. What is our friend Tipping after? I understand he is married. Make him my salaam and try and find some lady with a *few thousands* who will put up with my ugly mug, for if I can get home I shall either try something in that line, or volunteer to Africa to get my promotion. I hope Mother is all right again. She ought to have a month or two at the sea side. You put that about for hers & Father's sake. Father's favorite place, Broadstairs, would brace them up beautifully. I suppose you meditate a continental trip, though this summer would not be favourable for such an excursion on account of the Exhibition. I am anxious to hear from some of you about it and how long it is likely to remain open. Why are the men of Sir John Franklin's expedition like the inhabitants of Ferozepore? Because they are Ferozepore fellows. Perhaps this is an importation, but never mind. Mopsticks' babies all right? I should like to see the last born. Walter should have a daguerratype of the family taken. How spiff Annie would look.
CBB

84. *Summary of life in Meerut*

Christopher Bassano's diary   Meerut
                                               September 1851

    I arrived at Meerut in March and have been doing duty ever since with H.M. 29th Reg[imen]t, and since the time I was in

Calcutta I have not enjoyed myself more – Meerut is a most
excellent station. The road[s] are plentiful and good. Fruit
better than in any other part of India I have visited. The Hills
are seen clearly from this station. I lived most of the Summer
with Miles who was doing duty with the 1st Bengal Fusiliers.
Pamperdoo and Pamperdee, the two famous dogs, were born in April,
Miles' spaniel being the mother and Pretty, Johns (14 Drag[oo]ns)
the father. Sent Alfred the brother and sister of these up to
Jullundur. Tried hard to get leave to see Alfred at Jullundur,
but failed in consequence of a few cases of cholera having
occurred in the 70th Reg[imen]t at Cawnpore and my services being
urgently req[uire]d with my Regiment.

85. *Application for leave*

Christopher Bassano to Col. Galloway[48]   [September 1851]

My dear Colonel
    I wrote to Dr. Harvey a few days ago beg[g]ing he would write
me a line stating he had no objection to my obtaining leave for
three or four months from the beginning of October, but I have
not yet heard from him on the subject.

    May I beg the favor of your forwarding my application for
the above time for the purpose of seeing my brother in the 32nd
before he marches to Peshaur. I am aware that you and Dr.
H[arvey] have complained about the distribution of the medical
officers, but as before the time that I can now possibly join
the reg[imen]t the cold weather will have set in, Johnston will
have resumed his duties, and [*illeg*.], it cannot appear incon-
sistent on your part to grant me the indulgence which I solicit.

    The surgeon of the 29th is in the Hills for this month on
sick leave, and as there are now 400 men on the sick list they
cannot let me go until his arrival, or that of the other
Ass[istan]t Surgeon who is now about passing through Cawnpore
and who I suggested [to] Dr. Harvey should get attached to the
70th for a few weeks, as by that means all difficulties would
be overcome.

---

48. Draft.

86. *Leave refused*

Col. T.J. Galloway to Christopher Bassano   Cawnpore
                                              14 September 1851

My dear Bassano
    I have this moment received your letter and regret that I
cannot comply with your wish. On the 29th of last month I
applied officially for you to be ordered to rejoin the Regiment,
and I have done so subsequently unofficially. In fact you are
much required here. Johnston is very ill with Dysentery and
unable to do any duty. Eaton has been some time in the Sick
Report and is likely to continue so, leaving all the work on
Harvey who has not got his Sanatory Report prepared. We lost a
man last night by cholera, another three nights ago, and last
Month 4 by cholera, besides Major L'Estrange's daughter and some
of the soldiers' children. We have had many other deaths besides
those from Cholera, so that you must really see that you are
required with your Regiment.

    I think you might see your Brother who is at Jullundur
without much trouble. I suppose it is not more than two days
dawk from Meerut.

    It is now finally settled that we remain at Cawnpore till the
next cold season when we go to Lahore.

    Mrs. Galloway desires her very kind remembrance and believe
me

                            very truly yours
                            T.J. Galloway.

87. *Regimental movements*

Christopher Bassano to Capt. Durnford[49]   Meerut
                                              19 September 1851

My dear Durnford
    I recieved a Letter from Schriber last night in which it
would appear that you still expect to be sent to Lahore which is
quite at variance with a demi-official Letter the 29th had, and
a similar one it was understood had been sent to the 70th (now
ten days ago). He tells me that I may expect to be ordered to
Cawnpore, but nothing is yet decided here on that point, tho'
I suppose from what the Col[one]l wrote I may expect something
of the sort - for what purpose however remains a problem.

---

49. Copy.

88. *Summary of life during 1852*

Christopher Bassano's diary   Cawnpore
                                               December 1852

Have been living on the bank of the River Ganges during the
year. Went to Lucknow for a month's leave.

IV

"ELLEN HAS TRUSTED HERSELF TO THE WIDE WORLD"

The eldest of the Bassano children, Charlotte
Ellen, born in 1812, almost became another of the
Bassanos in India. She taught in a girls' boarding
school at Hillingdon, and then for some years ran
her own school without much success.[50] For several
years from early 1846 she contemplated going out to
India, but receiving no encouragement from her
brothers already there,[51] she at last decided to
strike out on her own and in November 1850 set sail
for Australia from Gravesend on board the *Anglia*,
landing at Adelaide and moving on from there to
Melbourne, where she obtained a post of governess
at Geelong until the end of 1851. The next year
she went as governess on the Hepburn sheep station,
at Smeaton, twenty miles from Ballarat. During her
first two or three years in Australia she remained
very unsettled and there was still talk of her going
out to India to become housekeeper for her brother
Tom.[52]

89. *Voyage to Australia*

Ellen Bassano to Philip Bassano   Anglia
                                               9 December 1850

My dear Philip
    We entered the torrid zone the day before yesterday and are
now in the trade winds and are proceeding at the rate of $7\frac{1}{2}$
miles per hour in the right direction, which has put us in
Spirits, for hitherto the weather has been very much against us.
On Saturday we were in a perfect calm, the Ship's only motion

---

50. See Letters 5, 10.
51. See Letters 15, 54, 58.
52. See Letters 55, 94.

being that it sometimes pointed north, at another time turned to
the South. On Sunday half a mile an hour was our Speed, and thus
it has been on other occasions. We had a very rough sea for 12
or 14 days after we left Plymouth. The greater part of the time
the wind was directly against us and I have been exceedingly ill
for 15 or 16 days, which has made me so weak that I cannot walk
without clinging on to everything in my way. One day I was sick
11 times, on other days nearly as frequently. The doctor's
medicine had no effect on me. He said he could not tell what to
do with me and the passengers made up their minds that I should
make the third body committed to the deep. Our gallant captain
said he must take me in hand: "He had cured Mrs. Gardner (his
wife) with Salt fish when everything else had failed". However,
he could not make it take effect on me. One of the passengers
then gave me a dose of castor oil and that, with the succeeding
calm weather, effected a change in me, but I suffered much more
after the sickness ceased from extreme weakness. I was advised
to sit up on deck as much as I could, but the pain it gave me to
sit tottering there without anything to rest my back against no
one can have any conception. I have been stronger these last
three days.

Dec[embe]r 29th. Latitude yesterday, 16 S. Longitude, about
34 W. There is a Ship in sight which will be up with us in
about half an hour, so I have not time to add much. I have been
very well in health since I began this letter and find the
voyage very pleasant. It is very warm at night and has ·been
for this last fortnight, but beautifully pleasant all day on
deck. We have had two days of pouring rain and caught an
enormous quantity of rainwater. We have had a little baby ill
ever since it was put on board and it died on the 24th. This
makes 3 deaths.

Yours &c.
Ellen Bassano

90. *Geelong — the gold rush*

Ellen Bassano to her mother Charlotte   Geelong
                        and sister Melinda   6 December 1851
(No. 4)

My dear Mother
    I received a letter about three months since from Philip
dated Feb[ruar]y 18th (which I shall soon answer), also one
from Father, Melinda and Walter by the same post. These are all
that I have received since I have been in the Colonies. Philip
sent me word you were very well but even thinner than when I
left home. This climate seems to agree with me; I have gained
much flesh especially in the legs: my stockings will not pull up

to their full extent. I do not know how I shall like the heat
which is to ensue, but at present it is not too much for me.
On a few occasions it has been more overpowering at home. The
rays of the sun have more power than in England, but there is a
coolness in the air not met with there, so when you keep quiet
it is very pleasant. The thermometer stands at 78 today in the
Shade. We have had hail on several occasions during the winter
but neither ice nor snow – they are of rare occurrence except in
the interior, and then by no means severe. We have had a great
quantity of rain during the winter, and the weather is at all
times uncertain and changeable: the variableness of England is
nothing to it. You remember Honey Lane in bad weather thirty
years ago? Few of the roads and Streets of Geelong are better
than that, and some considerably worse, drays sinking into the
mud as low as the axle-tree, and then in dry weather the dust
is tremendous, and occasionally when there is a high wind it
quite obscures every object. I have not received any letters
from Christopher or Tom. I begin to fear our wily Captain did
not put my letters to them into the Indian post as he promised
after he had arrived in India.[53]

Great excitement exists in consequence of the recent discovery
of Gold. Bathurst near Sydney was the first field and since that
time they have found it in larger or smaller quantities in many
other localities. Ballarat (put the accent on the Second
Syllable giving the second "a" the same sound as that heard in
"far", the "r" following it rough) – (it is a native name) –
near the township of Bunningyong about 60 miles from Geelong
has yielded an enormous quantity, and nearly all the men in
Geelong have been there digging. Hundreds have made immense
fortunes; hundreds have also met with disappointment and been
ruined. Mr. Strachan[54] went to the spot to make his own remarks.
He describes it as a sight which you must see to form any conception. There were about four thousand on a very small space
of ground all at work with picks or cradles as fast as they
could go at it, and the utmost order prevailing amongst them.
He has bought very largely to send to the London market. It is
being shipped in the Hero, which has on board, from various
merchants here and at Melbourne, £110,000 worth. There is now
a rush to Mount Alexander, about 110 miles from Geelong, and
they say the yield exceeds the first named place, and with less
fatigue. The number there is supposed to be about 12 thousand.
They pay £3 per month for the privilege of digging: it was
thirty shillings. It goes to government. There is scarcely
any labour to be obtained, which in many instances causes a
total cessation of trade. But perhaps you know all this from
the London papers. I have seen all the "Illustrated News" for
the last eight months. What a stir the Crystal Palace seems to

---

53. See Letter 83.
54. Her employer.

have caused! Father asked me if I should like a newspaper sometimes. I should a weekly one, when it contains anything
important. The postage is one 1^{d} and they had better be directed
to the Post Office, Melbourne, for I do not think I shall be here
much longer. With best love to you, Father, Philip, Walter,
Wife and family

> I remain
> Yours affectionately
> C.E. Bassano

Dear Melinda
    The last letter I wrote home was to Walter, No. 3, and with
it one to Mrs. King. If any number fail coming, I should like
to know... The first Legislative Council is now sitting. Mr.
Strachan is returned as the representative of Geelong. The
Gardens are now at their greatest height of beauty. Soon everything will be scorched up with the heat. When we are visited
with a hot wind the edges and outside leaves of many of the
flowers are shrunk and withered as if they had been held over
boiling steam. I hope you all appreciate the woods that were
exhibited belonging to these colonies, for if you had any as
beautiful as Mr. Strachan's light wood card tables sent, I am
sure they were worthy [of] attention. The tables alluded to are
formed of three species of lightwood - the fronts and sides of
a kind of dotted, feathered and speckled wood which is the root
of the tree, the slab of the trunk which is light brown grained,
and the legs of another sort. The [*illeg.*] Pine is also a very
beautiful sort of deal, nearly as soft looking as satinwood.
I hope you will be able to make this out - my ink is so thick
and my table about half a foot too high.

> I remain
> your affectionate Sister
> C.E. Bassano

91. *Description of Smeaton - the gold rush - journey to
    Smeaton - adventures*

Ellen Bassano to Philip Bassano   Smeaton
(Letter 5)   15 March 1852

My dear Philip
    Thank you for your very long letter which gave me a little
of everybody and everything... I am glad to hear Mother is so
well, but poor Tom! the silence is very alarming. I have not
had one letter from any of them in India nor any from London
since my letter to Mother, No. 4. I have seen all the accounts
of the great exhibition, but I should like very much to hear

from you what London was like during the time, with a little
account of all the grotesque characters it must have drawn
together. I should like to know the beginning of Papal
aggression: the papers which I have seen follow up what has
before been treated of, but as I did not see the first papers
I do not understand at all. Both the Miss Saunders are very
near sighted: they never know anybody in the street, and have
offended many in consequence. The letters cannot be put into
the Melbourne Office without a pre-postage: they would lie in
the dead letter office if so sent. But send them unpaid from
London, if they would be surer, for I cannot think that two
letters are all that have been written in one year and four
months.

I left Mr. Strachan on the 24th of December and remained a
visitor with my best friends Mr. & Mrs. Nicholson until the
24th of Jan[uar]y when I left Melbourne for Smeaton, 110 miles
up the bush, 20 miles from Ballarat and 30 from Mount Alexander.
I again have been fortunate to obtain a salary of £50 per annum.
I shall be here for a year. The Squatters always make engagements binding for that time, because it is so great an expense
to get people up the country. Captain Hepburn has been in the
Colony about 16 years and has 60,000 sheep beside cattle on his
run. There is a family of nine children, the eldest twenty,
the youngest four years old. My pupils consist of one boy and
four girls out of the number. The house consists of eighteen
rooms and [is] situated on an elevation in a park-like country
with hills in every direction that you turn your eye, some less
than half a mile's walk from us. The view from the tops of
course is very extensive, but not varied like English scenery.
The rivers are too small to be seen at any great distance: the
want of water is the great drawback of this country. Captain
Hepburn has a tank which holds a six months supply of water,
being filled in the rainy season off the roofage, which now that
it has been standing some time has a filthy smell and is the
colour of dirty ditch water. This they call beautiful water: it
is certainly very philosophical to be contented with such things
as you can get. Luckily I never wish to drink, so I can laugh
at those whose thirst obliges them to relish it. There have
been many wells sunk in various parts of the country, but the
water is generally brackish.

Of course you read the colonial papers and know as much as
I can tell you concerning the gold mines. It is the opinion of
Captain Hepburn, Mr. Strachan and many other intelligent men
that the whole country is one vast gold field, of course more
productive in some localities than others. The sole engrossing
topic is gold, and the diggings. The excitement is immense.
All men of capital are buyers of the precious metal. The state
of society and trade in general is very much altered through
the sudden discovery. The Publicans and Linen drapers are
reaping a famous harvest. I wish poor Mrs. Ramsey had come

over when she thought of so doing, but now the good will of a
business would be a most enormous sum. There is scarcely a
servant to be had, they are all married up. The first thing a
successful digger does on his return to Melbourne, is to obtain
a wife. The length of the banns is quite tedious to listen to
Sunday after Sunday. Sometimes a whole party of newly married
people will parade the streets of Melbourne for two or three
hours after the ceremony to show their gay dresses, and turning
into sundry public houses in their route. Others will hire a
vehicle of some kind, and drive furiously about, and when they
see any of their friends, a loud hurrah is set up, and hats and
handkerchiefs waved as a passing salute. Cheese and bacon are
two and sixpence per pound; milk one shilling per quart. House
rent is preposterously high and the population is so much
increased that there is not sufficient accommodation for them
and they are obliged to pitch their tents in the suburbs. All
buildings &c. are at a stand. Working men have all turned
diggers and generally speaking it is this class who have been
the great gainers in the gold fields. The work is too laborious
and the discomfort too great for respectable people to endure,
notwithstanding I know many gentlemen who have turned diggers
and who look exceedingly well, and who do not dislike it very
much. It was calculated that about fifteen thousand men were on
Mount Alexander a short time since, out of which number rather
more than half could not obtain gold, but some few realizing
immense fortunes, the rest getting rather more than they would
at their respective occupations.

In driving from Melbourne to Smeaton the boy let the wheel go
over a stump, shooting me and all the parcels into a waterhole.
Captain and Mrs. Hepburn were in another chaise just before, and
on looking round all that was to be seen of me was my bonnet
just emerging above the water. There were about thirty diggers
on the spot who were proceeding to the gold fields and who were
particularly polite and useful on the occasion. Among other
civilities, one offered me his handkerchief to wipe the mud from
my face, observing that "it was rather fishy" "but I must not
mind that". I had to walk a mile with the water dripping out of
me before we came to a house. I dare say three pounds would not
replace all the clothes I spoiled on the occasion, but I did not
take cold. I have not had a cold since I left England. I was
again upset - at least I jumped out to avoid it - about a
fortnight after I arrived at Smeaton. A visitor of the Captain's
took me for a drive, and the horse took alarm and began leaping
and kicking with all his might. The chaise was very much
injured and that was all. We have had several bush fires since
I have been here, and about three weeks since I mounted a small
hill near the house to take a view of one about ten miles distant
which was raging in terrific grandeur, and in coming home again
missed my way, and got into a forest, where after walking about
for hours in the hope of reaching the house I was obliged to
take a night's lodging in a hollow tree, which had an opening

on both sides or I might have got a nap, but the draught
obliged me to get out and dance the polka occasionally to keep
myself warm. At dawn of day I decided on making to one of the
hills thinking I might see the house from the top, but in my way
came to a road, so thought I had better keep it until some one
passed of whom I might enquire. After having walked some miles
the wrong way some diggers gave me the proper direction. But
although nothing alarmed me during my ramble, at home they were
in the greatest consternation, for the bush in some parts is so
thickly timbered and so trackless that if any one gets into it
he rarely finds his way out, but perishes of hunger, and Mrs.
Hepburn pictured the worst and sat up all night in great anxiety.
The Captain's brother and son, with two other men, were galloping
about all night in search of me. Guns were fired off, the house
illuminated, and bonfires lighted, but I was too far off to see
any of them.

I think your letters had better be directed to Mr. Germain
Nicholson, tea-dealer, Collins Street, Melbourne, for you see
there is no certainty in my own address and there is no post up
the country, and rarely any communication between Melbourne and
the country during the winter in consequence of the rain standing
in marshes and valleys and preventing travellers from riding
backwards and forwards. Any letters that may arrive in Melbourne
after June I most probably [will] not receive till November up
the country.

I think I shall be very happy here. They are just such an
amiable family as the Woosters. I came solely because Mr.
Nicholson advised it. Otherwise I was resolved to open a school,
and had got the promise of several pupils. But he said that I
was the most fortunate woman in the world, that Mr. Strachan's
was the first of the Merchants, and Capt[ai]n Hepburn's the
first of the Settlers, that two to match them in liberality and
standing could not be found in the colony, and just at this time,
when all was so unsettled, I should have less anxiety in a
situation. So, of course, I was obliged to act by his counsel.
I should think the gold will induce some of our friends to leave
England for the Colony. I shall then see them, I hope, and hear
all about you. I wish I knew whether Rose [*illeg.*] obtained my
£20, for I would have it sent out in dresses &c., they are so
very high just now. The Captain sets off for Melbourne tomorro
early, so I have not time to tell you anything else at present.
Give my love to all my relations and my best respects to all my
friends if you please, and when you next write treat of everybody and everything as you did in the last, and if any of your
acquaintance come to the Colony they will meet with hospitality
and good cheer if they will give me a call in their way to the
gold fields. With best love
                 Believe me
               Dear Phillip
             Your affec[tiona]te sister
               C.E. Bassano

P.S. Captain John Hepburn, who is one of the parties gone in
search of Sir John Franklin, is cousin to the Captain. Plenty
of warm clothing is required in this country tell people who are
coming. Sore eyes are very prevalent in the country: thick
matter collects in the corners of the eye in great quantities
is one disease, and another called the blight which swells the
eyelid to the size of a walnut and quite closing it; this last
is not attended with pain or discolourness. I have escaped all
at present.

I am so accustomed to write Port Phillip with two lls – that
is the reason I have made the mistake in your name.

92. *General news*

Ellen Bassano to Philip Bassano   Smeaton
(Letter 6)   27 October 1852

Dear Philip
    I trust you received the letter I wrote to you soon after my
arrival at Smeaton which was in Jan[uar]y last, giving you an
account of Capt[ain] Hepburn, his family, my own good luck, &c.
I now proceed to answer yours dated Feb[ruar]y 52. I was indeed
glad of the news it contained respecting poor Tom. How unfortunate he has been! I wrote to him directly to the address you
sent me. I received a letter from Christopher about 3 weeks
since (the first I have had from India since I came to the
colony) but he gave me the reasons of his silence. I suppose I
shall hear from the others in time. Poor Alfred is better,
Chris tells me. Perhaps he has been too much shaken to write to
any one. Your account of Janey was very interesting to me ...
What numbers of people have died since I left to be sure! ...
tell her [Mrs. W. Tipping] to stick to her text of not coming
out to Australia. It is fit for no one who cannot work like a
horse, endure as much as the houseless beasts of the field, and
be ready to take advantage of everybody at every turn and in
every transaction. Now I perceive why the Americans are so
different in character from the Mother Country. I have other
letters arrived which I will answer in due time, but if you
received my last letters you will understand why I have been
silent for so long.

    I think I shall send about £80 worth of Australian gold home
for you to turn into money for me, but I dare say the gentleman
who brings it will not leave the Colony until Jan[uar]y or
Feb[ruar]y so I shall send another letter purporting how I wish
it laid out for me, and how you are to receive it &c., for I
do not know myself at present. Captain Langden is the gentleman
who will have charge of it. He has just sold his station and
stock to Captain Hepburn for £7000, which he intends to bring

233

home in the form of Australian gold, and he will dispose of mine
in London with his own and hand you over the money, if you like
that better than disposing of the gold yourself. But I thought
you might all like to have a look at it perhaps, which you cannot
do if he sells it for me. Captain Hepburn originally sold the
station to Captain Langden for £1400 or £1700, about nine years
ago (it adjoins Captain Hepburn's). If you have an interview,
do not retail a word that Captain Langden says respecting the
Colony or its affairs, for his name is another word for false-
hood, no one believes one syllable he says, he has such a
particular talent for invention. I think you find in the London
papers every copy of the colonial affairs that are worth extract-
ing from the Melbourne ones, for all the London papers in which
I have observed any notice of the great finds and other matters
connected with the Colonies have been perfectly correct. So,
with best love to all

Believe me
Your aff[ectiona]te Sister
C.E. Bassano

P.S. [written inside envelope] Read Arthur's letter before
you send it. I always intend the open letters to be perused for
your general information before they are forwarded. Address my
letters to Mr. Germain Nicholson, Collins Street, Melbourne.
There is no post up the country.

CHAPTER SIX

Two Bassanos in India
(1853-5)

Early in 1853 Alfred Bassano went home on leave and did not return to India until February 1855. The two remaining brothers both found life hard, Tom still working for a master and not on his own account, and Christopher faced with a bad cholera epidemic in the regiment which carried off his superiors and left him in charge. They were both very unsettled and thought of joining their sister in Australia, but Ellen herself was not happy and proposed joining Tom in the Wynaad as his house-keeper. Her eldest brother, Philip, offered to pay her return passage home, and Christopher sent her money for the same purpose, but all "too late" as by the time she had received these offers she had married her employer's brother. Christopher made several attempts to get home to England in charge of the invalids, and finally succeeded.

93. *Family gossip – Alfred's return home – complaints of overwork*

Christopher Bassano to Melinda Bassano   Cawnpore
                                                          22 May 1853

My dear Linney
    When next you favour me with a letter just by way of variety take the opportunity of writing when you are *not* in a hurry. One would suppose that you were Secretary to the Female Slavery Abolition Society, or that you were at the head of the Society for the conversion of the inhabitants of Katmando. What say you to sit down and write a few lines tomorrow morning giving me a sketch of the new house and finishing your letter in the course of next week without "making an effort". Never mind when

the post leaves for India, but when your letter is finished quietly walk over to the nearest post office and put it in the box, addressed [*illeg.*] office, or merely put Via Southampton and underneath per Bombay.[1] Take care also that you do not pay the overland postage, but just go over to a Stationers and buy a quire of paper or two, that does not weigh more than this sheet that I am writing on, and having written as much as you think proper, put it in the post, mind *unpaid* and no envelope, by that means you will save yourself a shilling and me another. I shall also get your letter a fortnight sooner, and I hope an additional supply. Do you understand me, you little imp?[2]

I wrote to dear Mother on the 17th April last & I think I told her to make no end of apologies to you for not having answered yours of the 19th Feb[ruar]y 1853. I also told her that you were to have the three handkerchiefs which you had already got, viz. the one I sent to poor Aunt Ryle, the one without any mark, and the t'other [*illeg.*]. I am sorry I did not write to you last mail, as you do not seem to know much about Alfred, but by the time you get this he will have arrived, or if not the chances will be that the ship has gone to the bottom. The odds are much in favour of its performing the latter fête [*sic*], for I recollect there having been a long argument about the ship when I was going over to Cork and it seemed to be the general opinion that she was an old crazy bark and totally unseaworthy. (Of course I hope she will be all right). Her name is the "Earl of Balcarres" and by a letter I recieved from Alf at Kurrachee, dated the 4th Feb[ruar]y, he mentioned that he would be off in about five or six days. He said he had had a very disagreeable march, and had been done out of a lot of money by his Pay Serg[ean]t. I wish I had been going home with him, or was likely to follow him this year, for I have been suffering from a bad cough lately the symptoms of which I don't at all like, and I have no doubt a sea voyage would set me to rights. I have however no chance, for I wrote to the Inspector Gen[era]l when I was at Meerut and he kindly gave me a slight snub. Nobody cares a bit about the health of Doctors, and they care d[e]uced little for one another so that any poor devil is kept at work until he is nearly dead. If I should die, which of course I don't intend doing if I can avoid it, I will leave you all my property, except a hundred and fifty pounds which I will make over to Father if he wants it, but if not you must have it all. Now don't laugh, because it's no laughing matter. I should much prefer going home and taking myself a wife however, so if I should by any chance do so you had better have one ready for me to pounce upon. She must have some property, or I shan't close. I will then bring you out to India and get you married to that young fellow you used to be

---

1. He gives here an example of his address.
2. For Melinda's reply see Letter 97.

so spoony upon in Pick[er]ing Terrace. He is out here in Civil
Service and has grown such a fine fellow. I think Alfred might
come the same dodge, for by the time he returns to India he will
be able to get some Staff appointment up in the Hills. If I am
able to get the Staff at Landour where Dr. Johnston of our
Corp[s] is now for two years, I shall be able to save about two
thousand pounds. I am not certain yet whether we shall move
this year further up the country: it will depend upon the result
of the war in Burmah.

June [*sic*. Should be May] 30th. Tell Phil I have his last
letter before me, dated April 19th [18]51, and ask him what he
means by saying he wrote to me last when I gave him a stave in
reply dated 27th June [18]51 from Meerut.[3] Also ask him to send
me a red or blue book, with all the Gov[ernmen]t offices in, if
he can spare one. I think by the new postal arrangements they
can come overland tolerably cheap. The mail of the 24th ultimo
came in yesterday, and I see they are about to reduce the number
of Queen's Reg[imen]ts in India and give the Com[pan]y three
additional ones. I had a great dream last night about Mopsticks
and his house and I thought I saw Annie Frances and all the
others. Does Frances recollect me now? I suppose but little.
Is she as pretty as she used to be, for I thought in my dream
she had grow[n] so ugly & had a dreadful squint. Why don't you
tell me something about them, for that fellow Walter is in a
rage with me for something and never writes. I had a jolly
account of Tom the other day and a long letter from Ellen. Tell
Alfred to write me a letter on his arrival in England, and with
love to all believe me my dear Linney

Your affectionate Brother
Christopher

94. *Life as a planter – Tom begs Chris to visit him*

Tom Bassano to Christopher Bassano[4]   Manantoddy
                                                         1 June 1853

My dear Cris
    So your Birthday has just past and gone. Well, old boy, many,
many happy returns to you. So Alfred has gone home. I wish I
was on the road and [could] be at the meeting. What a happy
one, dear brother! The ship he has gone home in is the finest
and quickest in the merchant service, so he will have a quick
voyage.

---

3. Letter 83.
4. Replying to one from Christopher dated on his 29th birthday.

Ellen asks to come to me here. I have told her not, as I
shall come their perhaps shortly, and one of my proprietors is
just dead. The chances are that the properties will be sold;
besides the place in a jungle like this is no place for her. I
suffer from jungle fever much. Don't let the Family know this
for the world, as Mother will be alarmed, but I fear before long
I must cut it. I enclose you the advertisement you asked for.
Send it to Ellen when you have done with it: perhaps [it] will
amuse her. She tells me she has lef[t] her situation and that
her address now is care of Mr. Germain Nicholson's, Collin[s]
Street, Melbourne, Australia Felix.

Why don't you exchange into a regiment in this part of the
world, Cannanore, Mangalore, or Bangalore? At each of the
former, European regiments are stationed. It would be so jolly.
You could get a month's leave and come and be with me here at
my Splendid Bungalow, the dining hall being 35 foot by 24, one
sitting room, & 3 Bedrooms, quite in Europe stile, Beautifully
furnished &c. And as for the Expence in coming, what is that
to you? You are provided for life, sick or well. Try and
exchange like a good fellow, and cure me of jungle fever. You
and your princess! Come and see the stunning fair girls of this
coast, the Niars and Lentias. I keep a splendid little girl of
15 year old - took her M ———————— and been keeping her ever
since. We purchase them here for 25 Rs., never been toutched,
no fussing about it, considered a great honour amongst them to
be broken by a saib, and to be kept is their greatest vanity.
Rather astonish your week nerves this part of the Country, I
guess, so don't talk to me about princesses. I am sorry you
had a split with Father, for he is brick of the first water, and
no flies. Make it up sharp like a good Cris. We will all meet
at home yet, and have one of those jolly Pudding[s] of Mother's,
please God, and the stunning Punch out of that China bowl.

Regarding my affairs, I have 20,000 coffee trees planted and
100 acres of land and may plant 10 thousand more this monsoon,
24 head of cattle, and 1500 Rupees in the Oriental Bank. I
wish you would exchange. I would kill the fatted Calf for you,
if I could only get a look at you. Or get 3 Months and come
and see me.

                    Your affectionate Brother
                              Tom

I heard from Philip by last mail. They are all well and
Walter has another boy. TBB

P.S. Write sharp about exchange or leave as this solitude in
the jungle will kill me. TBB

95. *Cholera epidemic in the 70th Regiment*

Christopher Bassano's diary

Cawnpore
June 1853

Came in for Charge of the 70th Reg[imen]t in consequence of
the death of Surg[eo]n Harvey. Had an immense deal of trouble
in consequence of the severity of the Cholera, but managed to
get through everything to the satisfaction of the Authorities.[5]

96. *Proposal by Christopher to settle in Australia*

Ellen Bassano to her mother, Charlotte
[Incomplete]

[postmarked
Melbourne
13 August 1853]

... in which he surprises me with the intelligence that
Alfred has left for England. Please to be very particular in
your next letter with respect to how much he has changed, and
what he found different in England after so long an absence, and
if he has come to England for good, &c. &c.

Christopher seems inclined to come here and form a practice,
and asks me my opinion as to the scheme. I put him in possession
of all the facts bearing on the subject and left him to make his
own calculations and conclusions. My own opinion is that it is
a fine field for a clever medical man, but that opinion I did
not express to him, because I thought if he should not happen to
succeed, I should never forgive myself for advising him to throw
up a certainty for an uncertainty.

I wrote Mrs. King a letter by the Eagle and please to tell
her that I have had the letters of the dead letter office looked
over as far back as September 1852 - any letters previous to that
time would be returned to her ... As this Colony draws thousands
weekly how strange it is I have never met with any person who
knew me at home. My kind regards to all who know me and with
best love believe me

Dear Mother
Yours affectionately
Ellen Bassano

5. See Letters 98-100, 103-4, 112-13, 115.

[Here follows a list of articles to be sent out[6] - incomplete]

1 Dark green French merina dress sufficient to make two bodies, and if the fashion of working the front in a pattern is not going out I should like one cut out from the piece and sent to the dressmaker to be worked. I suppose Melinda's pattern will fit me, but I have sent a piece of cotton the width of my chest, from armhole to armhole, measured over my dress. And please send me a sleeve pattern.

1 light silk sufficient for two bodies.

1 summer bonnet ribbon and 1 winter d[itt]o with linings &c.

1 Winter shawl.

1 Summer d[itt]o.

2 very nice collars and 2 ribbons or neck ties.

2 thin dresses.

1 light and one dark pair of gloves.

4 Prs. white stockings.

6 yds. flannel.

1 sheet red Morocco paper.

2 prs. scissors - 1 pr. Tweezers.

1 neat and good dress waistcoat (gentleman's).

1 pr. Fur cuffs.

1 nail brush - 1 Dressing comb.

1 Black lace veil with plain middle.

1 Green net veil. 1 Blue d[itt]o d[itt]o.

Materials of whatever is worn for half day bonnet caps.

4 yds. black satin ribbon, width of this line.

2 doz. hairpins, let the largest size measure the length of this line and decrease in size down to those very fine little pins in this shape [drawing].

---

6. The box was received in November 1854. See Letters 118-20.

oz. black silk. 8 oz. short whites.

ome white, brown, and black thread.

doz. bootlaces.

dozen of lace for night caps.

d[itt]o for nightgowns.

Swiss cambric dresses.

Domestic Medicine book.

Here the page is mutilated]

cookery book.

inings and trimmings for the dresses.

   Please to air them before packing, and kindly look at the
ists sent home last December for farther particulars respecting
uch articles as I now again name, and if the twenty pounds
bout to be forwarded will afford anything in addition to what
s here set down, select me anything you like from the December
ists. I should like a few seeds of vegetables, herbs and
ruits, if you can get any without much trouble. This has been
 very severe winter. On two occasions ice the thickness of
alf a crown. I have had chilblains on my hands and feet.

..

   P.S. [On the inside of the envelope] I should like a steel
usk, if you can get one, just three times the length of this
nvelope, and narrow in width, and a few back bones. I make my
wn stays.

7. *Reply to Christopher – Alfred in England – description of
   the new house*

elinda Bassano to Christopher Bassano[7]   6 Elysium Row
                                                        Fulham
                                                        18 August 1853

ly dear Chris
   I am going to write to you this morning, *"not in a hurry"* as
ou so strongly object to it, & although having rather an

_____

. Reply to Letter 93.

aversion to favoring my friends with unpaid letters, I will comply with that request too, as you so particularly wish it. Your account of your health makes me very uneasy. Pray, dear Chris, apply for leave of absence again. Alfred says there is no difficulty about getting it, if you come home at your *own* expense, and as you have money you can do so. I dare say the voyage home would reinstate your health, and if a winter in England would be bad for a cough complaint, sorry as we should be to part from you, we must only have you for the summer. Have you had medical advice? I have a great opinion of your skill as regards other people, but I don't think physicians understand healing themselves and I wish you would get someone to prescribe for you, if you have not already done so. Mamma sends her love to you & says she will write to you soon, & begs you will be more liberal with your letters.

Alf has got home safely about the 12th June, and I dare say you can picture to yourself how pleased we were to have *one* of our wanderers home, & how we wished we could add the rest to the family circle. He is altered & yet he is *not* altered, if you can understand that. When I rushed to meet him at the door it struck me he looked so like Tom, & I think he has grown like what Tom was when he left home, tho' not much like the portrait of himself that Tom sent home. I think he looks more like a seafaring, than a military man. He brought home a quantity of things, too numerous to describe, all very beautiful. He gave me a splendid inlaid envelope case, the same pattern as that beautiful card case you sent me, & a lovely silver filigree brooch set with turquoise. The rest of the things were very handsome: a beautiful card case for Mamma, a pen box for Annie (besides other small things), a case of Indian butterflies, which makes a very pretty ornament for our oak room, & a group of Sikh & Afghan arms which the boys have arranged in the hall. But I must stop this, for I have such a great deal to tell you & I shall never get it all in if I don't.

Papa has bought me a piano. Phil got it from Collards & put £10 that I might have a rosewood one which I otherwise should not have had. It cost £42 to us, but I think the regular selling price would be between £50 and £60, but Phil got it through his friend Ollivier.[8] It is a very nice instrument.

Phil & Alfred have had a trip up the Thames. They took a boat at Richmond & rowed up to Lechlade some distance beyond Oxford, & as high up the river as they could go, nearly all the rest of it being private property. Mr. John Hamblin invited Alfred & me to go on a water excursion yesterday: there was a large party of us consisting of his daughters, Betsy Hamblin,

---

8. Robert W. Ollivier, Music Seller and Publisher, 19, Old Bond Street, Piccadilly.

I really wish you had given me an account of Cashmere, but I hope you will gratify me in your next. I should like very much to travel in India, but if there is any travelling in store for me it will be through bleak Scotland. I have had chilblains each winter in this mild Climate, so do not know how I shall come off if we ever retire to Scotland. I trust your recommendatory letters will procure your promotion, and how does Alfred stand? Near the top of the Lieutenants or not? Thank you for sending me a receipt for pomatum. You sent me plenty of news about home which I had not heard. Write me as soon as you can and tell me all news, domestic and political. Did you see Miss Catherine Hayes in Calcutta? She is the best vocalist these shores have ever been able to boast. I suppose she was quite second rate in England. Ask Philip. I never heard her at home but was much gratified on hearing her in Melbourne. What a game about the lotion producing a prolific crop of carrots! I cannot recommend you any lady possessing £100 per annum and I advise all men to keep clear of Australian ladies, if they can meet with a fair partner elsewhere. They are the most errant flirts and jilts that man ever made love to. I think they lead the men on for the sole purpose of having the pleasure of either at once refusing them or of jilting them. I suppose the reason is, because they know that there are about ten Jacks to one Jill. How vulgar I am becoming, am I not? This is a capital country for common people. Pray do not marry for money alone, you can never be happy.

Benjamin is gone out for two days to buy sheep. That is always the opportunity I take for writing. I am so lonely that I drop off to sleep in doing anything else. Remember me to all enquiring friends and believe me

> Dear Christopher
> Your very affectionate Sister
> C.E. Hepburn

32. *About Ellen's letter to Tom in 1852*

Ellen Hepburn to Philip Bassano   Glendonald
(Letter 17)   13 July 1855

My dear Philip
    I have just received a letter from Christopher [means "written to"] which I was going to send by post, but on second thoughts thought it best to enclose it to you in case he may be at the Crimea by the time it arrives in England. I have not anything to write about now I have told you every thing about Australia. There is nothing fresh ever, in the bush. We are quite well and doing well, although not as well as we were doing some months since. I am sorry to hear from Chris, that dear

Mother is almost Blind.

Tom writes in good spirits. I trust his produce sent to
England realized what he had anticipated. He seems to be more
settled now, but he has often changed his mind. I wrote to him
in '52 to say I should like to come to him because he had said
he wished he had let me come to him when I left England. On
this he made arrangements to receive me, but before he posted th
letter to tell me to come he had an illness and made up his mind
that I should not come to "such an unhealthy hole", but that he
would sell off and join me. So I sent him every information and
at the same time thought it right to communicate to him that it
was probable I should soon marry in case I should mislead him by
remaining silent on the subject. Then instead of seeing him as
I had been led to expect he writes to say "come to India
immediately. I have had my house altered and made convenient
for you. Ladies have their health in this country. There are
letters of introduction waiting for you at all the Ports. Do
not delay." This last epistle reached me a month after the knot
had been tied, to the infinite amusement of Benjamin, who had
been hoping that he would soon be here to enter into partnership
with him. [The] concern would be much better [for] two who had
an interest in [it, than for] one.

Please remember me kindly to John and his wife, thanking him
for his kind enquiries, and with best love to you all, believe
me, dear Philip,

Your affectionate Sister,
C.E. Hepburn

133. *Christopher arrives in England*

F.M. Bassano to Christopher Bassano   6 Whitehall Yard
                                          Opposite the Horse Guards
                                          (Late St. James's Place)
                                          26 July 1855

My dear Christopher
    Many thanks for yours of 24th Instant, which is truly
gratifying to us. We are not aware that you can avoid going to
Chatham, and we must regret that it is not possible for either
of us to get leave of absence to meet you at Gravesend. Our
present Office is in Whitehall Yard, and our address is No. 6
Elysium Row, Parsons Green, Fulham. Your dear Mother is very
poorly from the puncture of a skewer in the finger, but is much
better these two days.[22] I understand you will be obliged to go

---

22. She died a few days later, 30 July 1855.

o Chatham before coming to London.

Yours affectionately,

F.M. Bassano

34. *Claim for passage money*

:.B. Bassano to Secretary, Hon. E.I.C.　　　　6 Elysium Row
Fulham
1 August 1855

ir

I have the honor to bring before you the following particulars
·ith a view of obtaining the amount of my "passage money",
:o.Rs.1200, in lieu of "head money" for medical attendance on the
·nvalids just arrived from India in the ship "Marlborough" and
:o beg the favor of your submitting my claim to the Honorable
:he Court of Directors.

In General Orders by the Commander in Chief dated respectively
:he 5th October and 29th December 1854 I was appointed to the
·edical charge of the Calcutta party of Invalids from Umballa to
·alcutta and also directed to do duty with them on the voyage
:o England, and I was under the full impression that my passage
·ould have been provided for me at the public expense. On my
·rrival at the Presidency however, I found that the 135 Invalids
·ere to be divided between two Ships, and that the Government at
·alcutta would not recognize my claim to a free passage informing
·e at the same time that I might find my way home how I pleased
·nd that the Commander in Chief had no authority to order me to
·o duty with the Invalids on the voyage. I may here mention that
·n consequence of my name having been prominently brought to the
·otice of the Commander in Chief by the Superintending Surgeon
·f the Cawnpore Division I received a highly complimentary letter
·rom the Adjutant General of the Army expressing his Excellency
:he Commander in Chief's approbation [in pencil "satisfaction"]
·f [in pencil "at"] the laudable exertions made by me during a
·evere Epidemic in 1853 and it was in all probability on this
·ccount that the General Order directed me to do duty with the
·nvalids in order to ensure my passage being paid as a reward
·or my services.

I beg to enclose copy of the G.O. as also a letter from the
·ecretary to the Government of India in reply to an application
· made through the Brigade Major "Queens Troops" to obtain
·edical charge of a Detachment of the 96th & 98th Regiments
·umerically sufficient to cover the expense of my passage; from
·hich letter you will also perceive that application had
·reviously been made by the Brigade Major for my passage with
:he Invalids at the public expense.

Trusting that this application may meet with the favorable
consideration of the Honorable the Court of Directors

> I have the honor to be
> Sir
> Your most obedient
> Humble Servant
> C.B. Bassano (late Assistant Surgeon H.M.
> 70th Regiment)
> Assistant Surgeon 9th Lancers
> late in Medical Charge of Invalids
> per Ship "Marlborough"

CHAPTER SEVEN

Crimean Interlude
(1855-6)

I

TO THE CRIMEA WITH TULLOCH AND MCNEILL

Following the disastrous winter of 1854-5 when
the British army wintering on the heights above
Sebastopol was destroyed by sickness, a commission
was appointed to enquire into the question of
supplies for the British army in the Crimea. Not
only had the army been without supplies, but the
road from Balaclava had been impassable so that
there had been no means of transporting the supplies
to the army, even when they arrived. The two
commissioners were Colonel Alexander Tulloch, R.E.,
and Sir John McNeill, and with them went the eldest
of the Bassano brothers, a clerk in the War Office.
They travelled via Marseilles and Constantinople,
arriving on 12 March 1855, just before Philip
celebrated his 38th birthday (18 March), and
remained there taking evidence for about three
months.

35. *Constantinople – voyage to Balaklava – taking evidence –
the siege*

hilip Bassano to Walter Bassano   Balaklava
                                                   14 April 1855

ear Walter
   Your letter of 30th ult. I received in due course and was
ery glad of it as it was the first I have received from home

since I left. I am very much obliged to you for the trouble you have taken in packing up the things. Tell Bob I am also much obliged for the *assistance* he rendered you and am sorry you coul not find enough liquor to keep your spirits up with. With respect to the Bath, the best way is before having screwed it quite tight to twist some thin dry string into the joints and then finish the screwing up. The moisture of the water, if it oozes through the string, will swell it water-tight. Or perhaps you may find among the odds & ends in my tool chest one or two leather rings for putting into the joints, but I think a bit of thin string does it more securely. I have had one or two of my letters from the War Office enclosed in Col. Tulloch's packets. But if you have any others for me you can direct as before, leaving out the *Steam Transport Gothenburg* as we have changed our quarters to another vessel, and perhaps may change again. I am glad that Ellen is pleased with the things we sent her. Is she getting on comfortably? I wrote to Al & Tom from Marseilles on my way out enclosing to Tom the duplicate Bill of Lading for the Hoes I sent to him, and as you do not say you have heard from him I am in hopes they will arrive before he leaves for home, if such is his intention. Since my arrival here I have been so hard worked that I can scarcely find time to write private letters, which will account for so long a silence.

After writing to you I did not see much more of Constantinopl proper, but what I did see of it was if possible infinitely more disgusting, filthy & abominable than Pera & Galata. You go over to it by a rough Bridge of Boats which they open to let Vessels pass up & down the Golden Horn. There is a toll house upon it and money taken, but Englishmen always see them at the devil before they pay a farthing, and so I followed the same example. Heaps of stinking slush ankle deep, crooked lanes about 2 yards wide, skulking dogs, swarms of busy people in every variety of Costume swarming with Vermin, and dirty ramifications of Arcades called Bazaars, where you get most infernally cheated if you attempt a purchase, are the principal features of Stamboul. Notwithstanding the unprincipled character of the Shopkeepers I attempted a purchase, the only one I made there, & from having made all the necessary enquiries previously as to price, I think I was not very much taken in. I bought half an Oki ($1\frac{1}{2}$lb.) of Turkish Tobacco & $\frac{1}{2}$ doz. in Books of Cigarette Papers. The style of smoking in these parts is almost univer- sally in the shape of Cigarettes (except among the Canaille) and so I have fallen into [the] habit to a great extent and have become quite expert in making them. For the above purchase I paid 20 pence.

Well, after remaining at Constantinople for 5 days we embarked on Board the Emperor Steamship for this place on the 10th March, having as Companions in addition, Milton & [?Hugger] of our office. We started in the afternoon on a fine day and had a beautiful view of the Bosphorous up to the Black Sea,

which we reached before dark. The shores of the Bosphorus are
most charming, studded all the way almost with Palaces, Mosques,
Beautiful Suburban Villas & Villages, Minarets, lovely Bays,
High grounds, quantities of Shipping, and everything capable of
assisting in rendering the scene beautiful, but perhaps the
illusion would have vanished like Constantinople if I had had an
opportunity of stepping ashore. 11th. Steaming across the Black
Sea, weather still very fine & warm, only one or two vessels in
sight all day. 12th. On getting up soon after daylight found
ourselves skirting the shore of the Crimea, a fine bold, rocky
coast, without a bit of Beach, Cliffs perpendicular into the
Sea, of a reddish Marble, and about breakfast time arrived off
Balaklava, where we lay to outside waiting for permission to
enter: could only see the tops of the masts of the Vessels
inside. A good deal of delay in signalling with the Authorities
on shore, the particular nature of the conversation we could not
understand, rather annoying as the wind had freshened into a
good breeze right on shore, began to think that perhaps there
was too much sea to attempt the narrow entrance. In the midst
of the signalling a deal of smoke appeared amidships and a cry
of "Fire", and sure enough the ship was on fire in the Galley.
The crew rushed to the Buckets and in about a quarter of an hour
all was safe again, and a signal hoisted from on shore that a
berth had been allotted to us and we might enter, so in we went,
the place almost chock full, Upwards of Two Hundred vessels,
visited by the Admiral who had in the course of the morning
allotted the "Gothenburg" for our residence, and placed her very
comfortably along side the only berth but one where vessels can
have a landing stage to the shore, all the Saloon & Cabin out of
it having been handed over for our accommodation, very snug,
comfortable quarters. Since which time I have been almost
incessantly occupied taking down the evidence in the rough all
day, Copying it out fairly in the evening, and doing other
Official business, Writing letters &c.

When we arrived the mud had almost entirely disappeared and
there was nothing at all discouraging in the appearance of the
place or in the appearance of its Civil & Military Inhabitants.
It is a fact that those who have managed to get through the
Winter without going on the Sick List are in the most robust
state of health, but if a chap once knocked under, the want of
Comforts to get him right again was almost sure to Cook his
Goose, so to speak. We have finished taking down evidence here
and have had a Hut and a Tent erected for us up at the Camp to
transact our business in, where we have been at work for the
last two days. At first it was our intention to go and live
there, but on second thoughts we were of opinion that we should
be more comfortable on board ship, so we have given up all idea
of roughing it in our hut, and as we have managed to get ourselves well mounted it makes a pleasant ride morning & evening,
about 5½ miles each way. The hut is in the lines of the 14th
Foot in the 3rd Division, and we can sit at work and see the

Bombardment going on at the same time. The horse I have bought is a cream colored charger and I am now quite an excellent horseman.

After our work is over we generally go as far forward as it is safe to see how the siege progresses, and since they have set to work in good earnest we can go where a week or two ago we should have no more dared to show our faces than the man in the moon. But now the Russians do not waste their shot on individuals, having something better to do with it. Some parts of the ground we have been over is literally strewed thick with Cannon Balls from the Russian Guns. We have been expecting for some days past an attack on Balaklava, but I do not think it will take place now. If it does, I hope the fight will last all day because there are some Capital heights to go on to, quite out of harms way, where a good view might be had of a Battle in the Plain.

The Rail, or rather Train, road is progressing and nearly finished. It is not intended for Engines to run on, the sleepers being merely laid down without any foundation: there is [a] stationary Engine to drag the Carriages up an incline, but otherwise the work will be done by Horses.

The Vessel we were first living in, the Gothenburg, was so suddenly ordered home that I lost an opportunity of sending home a lot of Crimean relics which I might perhaps have collected. However I sent home a couple of Sticks by Mr. Lees the Purser, who lives at Eel Brook Common, and who promised to call on Mother and let her know all about how we are getting on.

Well, as it is very late I must shut up.

> Yours very Affect[ionate]ly
> P.H. Bassano

P.S. 15th April. Nothing particular has occurred since yesterday except the arrival of the 10th Hussars from India. The firing today has been rather more brisk than usual. An assault is expected every day.   P.H.B.

In a month from this time we shall most likely be returning.

136. *Continuing the investigations – the campaigns*

Philip Bassano to Walter Bassano   Balaklava
                                                           11 May 1855

Dear Walter
     I wrote you on the 15th April last acknowledging receipt of

your letter of the 20th March, which I hope you received. I entrusted it to Major Anderson of the Artillery to post it with his letters, which he told me he did the same day. We are still living on board the Paraguay d'Hilliers, and as we are all well mounted we have managed to carry on our investigations at the Camp without any inconvenience and have relinquished our intention of living up there. As we had not come prepared with the necessary things for such a life Sir John thought our Establishment would cut a very sorry figure and I think he was right. We have however got a Camp bed and a few things in our hut up there, and a man who looks after and takes care of the Establishment, which consists of 2 Huts and a tent, the principal contents of which are the aforesaid bed, a few Camp Cooking utensils, 3 deal forms and a table, and our ration of forage which we draw there. And one of us occasionally sleeps there for a change.

What a sell the late bombardment was. They certainly are managing to make a great mull of it somehow or other. A general officer, I need not say his name, but who commands one of the Divisions, took us round to a part of the French Attack one day where the best view and the closest one to the Town can be obtained, and explained to us the operations, and he gave us as his decided opinion that a successful attack might with certainty be made at that part, but for some reason or other no attempt was made. We have not yet got the London papers containing the account of the cessation of the Bombardment. I expect there must have been a jolly row at home about it. It is said by most of the officers that the French General Canrobert is the cause of it. He is not game to run the slightest risk. And Lord Raglan, easy going soul, gives in to him. Then the expedition again which left this about a week ago to attack Kertch returned in a few days having, it is said, been recalled by Canrobert. It makes me quite savage to think that 100,000 men can do nothing. If they really cannot take the place Sebastopol, they are surely strong enough to take the Field and Chevy the Cossacks from one end of the Crimea to the other, and then starve out the city. There is actually a hill within a mile of this place where a Cossack Picquet has been stationed ever since we have been here, and who can see every movement that takes place between here and the Camp, and who is allowed to hold possession of the Post. On one or two occasions they (we) have made a reconnaissance in force beyond it and driven the fellows in for the time being, but as soon as we retire they are back again. It is a very dangerous & distant outpost for them to hold, but no attempt is made to drive them permanently away from it.

We are nearly drawing our labours to a close and I shall not be sorry when it is over as I have been so precious hard worked, at it continually from Breakfast time till 11 or 12 at night, with scarcely time to take a stray $\frac{1}{4}$ of an hour for a pipe. And a week or two ago I was almost knocked up with the work: though much better now I am not nearly so well in health as when I left home. I am accosted with exclamations of "Good God! Why, what is the matter with you? Have you been laid up?" and such like. But I am not ill, mind you, but I suppose it is the work has made me look fagged in the face and careworn, and I dare say the journey home will freshen me up again. We expect to leave in about a fortnight and to be home about the middle of June. If Chris has arrived I hope he will not be packed off to the Crimea before I get home. Even then, I may stand a chance of meeting him on the way. But it is not settled yet which way we shall come home. I think most likely it will be Athens, Venice, Milan, Turin, Switzerland, the Rhine, & Paris. The alternatives would be Malta, Smyrna, Marseilles &c.

Tulloch says that Balfour has been made a member of the new Medical Board & that Dr. Smith has been driven in to retirement. What a shame if it is so. The evidence we have taken brings all the wants of the Army down to the point of insufficient means of transporting the supplies, which have been ample, from Balaklava to the Camp, and the reason why the commissariat Transport was insufficient was that the Q[uarte]r M[aste]r General did not keep the road in repair, which was the means of killing or knocking up the Mules. This is what it resolves itself into – R.O.A.D.

I hope you are all well at home, but I shall not be long after this reaches you to satisfy myself on that point. This is a Country that Father would glory in, it being covered with wild Flowers. It is, taking it altogether, the most beautiful Country imaginable, scenery and every thing. Nothing I have seen elsewhere at all comes near it.

Yours very affect[ionate]ly
P.H. Bassano

137. *Expecting to leave for home*

Philip Bassano to Melinda Bassano   Balaklava
                                                     17 May 1854[5]

Dear Lin
    I got your letter of 21st April all safe yesterday and was glad to hear that you were all well at home with the exception that Mother's eyes do not get any better. I enclose this with one I wrote for Walter a few days ago but which I have not had an opportunity of posting before.

    It will be about 10 days before we leave this on our way home, and I think we have settled upon going through Trieste, Venice & Piedmont. I am better than I was when I wrote Walter's letter not having worked quite so hard and have taken exercise more regularly. We are going to shift our quarters again into another Ship, the situation of the one we are in not being first rate, being at the head of the harbour in an abomination of Stinks. The one we are going to is the Dinapore, and she lays near the mouth of the harbour. Sir John McNeill has been laid up by the aforesaid smells, having had a slight attack of Cholera. The place has agreed with Col. Tulloch exceedingly well. He has got fatter and was never in better health in his life. There is another expedition fitting out which I hope will result more favorably than the last. What its destination is I cannot say.

The Weather here for the last 3 or 4 days has been fearfully hot: $84\frac{1}{2}$ in the shade. I thought I should like it but it is rather too much for me. I am glad to hear such good accounts from Ellen. I hope if Chris comes home he will not be packed off to the Crimea before I get back. If he goes through France, Meurices is the hotel at Paris that we stop at, but after that we shall not be travelling on the same road, and if he has got further than that before I reach there there will not be much chance of meeting him. I am quite tired of this place and shall be very glad to get out of it. It is of no use my asking you any questions as there will not be time to get a reply to them. There has been quite a commotion here with the arrival of the Piedmontese the last few days. They are the best accoutred and best looking troops out here, not excepting our own, and I have no doubt will fight well. 10,000 of them have landed.

> I remain, Dear Lin,
> Yours affectionately
> P.H. Bassano

138. *"A new bit of country to ramble over"*

Philip Bassano to Walter Bassano   Balaklava
                                                     1 June 1855

Dear Walter
    I wrote to you & Lin on the 24th Ult. which letters I hope you got all safe. We have nearly brought our labours to a close and will leave this in 3 or 4 days on our way home – or a week at latest. We shall have a few days work to do at Scutari, so it will most likely be 10 days after you get this before I shall be with you, because as we propose taking it easy via Athens, Trieste, Venice &c. this letter will travel much faster than I shall.

We have shifted our quarters to the Dinapore, which lays in a much more healthy part of the harbour, near the mouth, and I feel quite all right again, though the Colonel has not been well for a day or two past. The second expedition which sailed from this for Kertch a short time ago has had a much more favorable result than the first one having taken the place without the loss of a single man, together with the capture of about 140 guns & 100 Vessels laden with grain for the supply of the Russian Army. The Army is now in capital spirits and quite ready for an assault on Sebastopol, which will most likely be begun in a few days.

Since the arrival of the Sardinians the Allied Army has been in a position to take up more ground and have extended their lines up to the Tchernaya & the Valley of Bardar, which has been quite a godsend to us in the shape of a new bit of Country to ramble over. I went over it the first day it was in our possession and a more lovely ride I never had. The fields were a thick mass up to the horse's belly of all the most beautiful flowers you could imagine, and the Valley of Bardar is beautiful beyond description. Every one agrees in saying this is the most lovely bit of Country they were ever in. The Weather however is intensely hot, so much so that you cannot with safety go out in the middle of the day, but there is generally a nice breeze which sets in in the afternoon and the evenings are delightful. I took a ramble a day or two ago over the field of Inkerman, and had gone outside some of the Batteries where there were several people about, some much further in advance than I was, when I was stopped by a French sentry who said it was not safe to go any further, so I just turned my horse about for a few yards, and then turned round again to survey the Russian heights on the other side of the Tchernaya, and while contemplating the beauty of the scene and the recollections associated with the place I saw a puff of smoke from the other side, and was just beginning to wonder whether I was in a dangerous place when the ball from the gun ploughed up the earth and raised a cloud of dust about a hundred yards before me and almost in a straight line between me and the aforesaid gun, accompanied in the next second by the boom of the gun and the whistle of the shot, and after bounding down a hollow between me and where it first struck the earth came to a stand at an unpleasantly short distance from me. I therefore turned my horse about in a very short space of time and bolted, thinking discretion the better part of valour.

I hope we shall not be troubled at Trieste or Athens on our way home by any vexatious quarantine regulations – it is not unlikely as I believe there is a good deal of Cholera about at Constantinople as well as here – because it will be a most infernal bore.

I hope Father, Mother, Annie &c. are all well and I hope Chris will be at home when I arrive. I suppose Bob is at the present time preparing to begin his Piscatorial excursions on the Thames. This is the first day of the season, and by the time I get home he may have got a good place ready baited for me. Remind him of it.

                    I remain, Dear Walter,
                     Yours very truly
                      P.H. Bassano

139. *Medical Department gossip from the Crimea*

[*Illeg.*] to Walter Bassano   Crimea
                                                2 June 1855

My dear Bassano
     As matters are now going you might as well drop me occasion-
ally a few lines more particularly of Departmental news.   I
trust that Dr. Smith is well, or better than he was some short
time since, and that he is now installed permanently at the head
of affairs.   I don't know where they could pick up so hard a
working and talented head in spite of the abuse which I believe
has only been lavished in ignorance of facts.   I was very much
pleased in reading the evidence of Lord Hardinge to see the way
in which he spoke of our Chief.   It was well said and in good
time.   Cholera is now amongst us but chiefly attacks the New
Comers.   I hope, please God, I may be preserved from it, but I
have not and never had the slightest dread in this way.   I am
not at all funky but mean to see the end of this affair if I
possibly can, God willing.

     The weather is now tremendously hot and our P[rincipal]
M[edical] O[fficer] is often excessively nervous and irritable
upon slight matters, but I know there is great excuse for him
under all circumstances.   There is, however, *entre nous*, one
weakness in him which I certainly regret to see and that is, he
is often prejudiced for or against a person without *good reason*,
and whether he professes to be a disciple of Lavater or believes
in love at first sight I can't say, but his likes and dislikes
often appear to me to be taken at first sight.   There is a man
here by the name of Elliot, Surgeon Ord[nance] Med. Depart., who
moves about a Satellite of the Sun.   Of course, the object or
gilded ball in the distance is promotion.   Everyone can see it
and I really think it would be a very good thing were E. away
from head quarters, and I could give my reasons, but a close
tongue &c., and I have said more to you than perhaps I ought.
The P.M.O. has recommended him most strongly more than once.   On
my word it is a matter of surprise to me, for I cannot see what
he has.   I know many of his brother Officers despise him.   I
wish the Chief would promote him, if it would rid Head Quarters
of his dodgery.   He seems to be getting too great a hold on the
Doctor, and if I could see any apparent talent in him to
recommend him it would not be a matter of surprise, but I can
find nothing of the kind & his influence may become mischievous.

     The last Week has been very quiet about Sebastopol, although

                            287

the French & Russians are constantly more or less Shelling each
other. I sometimes get a run at night to visit the lines, but
very rarely, for one is Expected to be in attendance from morning
to night, and very properly, for really on such a Service there
is little or no help for it and you do not know the moment your
Services may be urgently required, as was the case the other
Even[in]g when the Expedition to Kertch was ordered. Doubtless
you have heard of the success of this Expedition. I should much
have liked to have been with this affair, as I have been in every
other and should have liked the change and excitement. I went
down near the Trenches three nights ago about 12 o'C[lock].
They were most active in bringing up powder, shot and shell, and
have now a vast quantity stored ready for the third bombardment
which is expected to open every day.

Every one is anxious, every one is weary of the dull monotony
which each day produces. Society you have none but your own,
and the time given to labour permits not a thought of seeking
either Society or recreation. Amid all this you have perhaps
reason to think your efforts may not be appreciated as you feel
they ought to be. The only hope one has when you fall back upon
yourself is that such a state of things cannot last for ever and
a change must come.

I have ample employment for the two Clerks you have sent me
out. They seem very nice young men, but as it appears they
were told by Mr. Wimbridge or some of you at the Board they
would have nothing to do out here, they are somewhat disagreeably
deceived and when awakened at 5 a.m. in the morn[in]g — I this
morn[in]g aroused them at this hour — to come to work, and kept
at it late in the Evening, I find a Sigh invariably Escapes them
at your deception.

Yours ...

140. *Journey home*

Philip Bassano to Walter Bassano   Black Sea
                                        Wednesday, 6 June 1855

Dear Walter
    We are already on our way home, having left Balaklava in the
Dinapore on Monday, in which ship we had been residing for
about a fortnight. The Dinapore sailed with us for Kamiesch to
put us on board the Mail packet, in which I now write, and which
sailed from that place at about 7 o'clock last night, the said
packet being nothing more or less than his French Imperial
Majesty's Man-of-War "Chaptal" screw. Before leaving the
Dinapore we sailed in her as near the mouth of the Harbour of
Sebastopol as the Men-of-War would let us, and had a Capital

View of the place on a new side. The people were walking &
riding about the Harbour, and none of the houses appeared to be
in the least damaged.

We shall leave Constantinople next Monday and proceed via
Trieste and shall most likely be in London by the 2nd of July.
We made I think rather a precipitate retreat from Balaklava.
The place got positively too *hot* to hold us. Sir John & the
Col[onel] got unwell, the former hav[in]g had a second attack of
Diarrhoea, the Cholera getting very bad in the harbour and the
heat something frightful, poor Old Admiral Boxer being a Victim
at last to Cholera having stood the brunt of all the other
attacks which have been aimed at him from home for some time
past. In him the public have lost a valuable servant. I have
been quite well for the last fortnight, which is more than I had
been previously. I shall post this at Constantinople to go on
with this mail. I hope they are all well at home.

I remain, Dear Walter,
Yours very truly
P.H. Bassano

II

"... DEAR CHRISTOPHER ... CUT OFF IN THE PRIME OF LIFE
AND A STRANGE LAND"

Philip Bassano arrived home from the Crimea in
July 1855 and at the end of that month Christopher,
assistant surgeon in the 70th Regiment reached
England after his six and a half years service in
India, having travelled in charge of the invalids
and with one year's leave due to him. However,
because of the better promotion prospects during a
war he determined to go out to the Crimea, and
transferred to the 9th Lancers, and after only about
one month in England sailed for the Crimea, first
to Scutari and then to Sebastopol with the troops
employed in destroying the docks. Later he served
as medical officer on the transport *Gibraltar* which
carried the sick from Balaclava to Scutari, as well
as in the General Hospital.

141. *Before leaving for the Crimea*

Christopher Bassano to Melinda Bassano   [Sandcliffe]
                                                      26 August 1855
                                                      Sunday afternoon

My dear Melinda
    I arrived here last night about 7 o'C[lock] and reported
myself to Dr. Menzies. There were two deaths from Cholera last
night, but the disease does not seem very severe and I don't
think there are more than twenty men now labouring under it. I
am living at an Inn on the sea coast and I dare say a residence
here for a few days will do me much good, but I should like to
know how long I am likely to be here. Ask Walter to write to me
and tell me if he thinks I should be justified in running over
to Paris for a day after I am discharged from duty here, for if
I cannot get overland that will be the only Chance I shall have
of seeing the Paris Exhibition. Don't mention this to anyone
else because whether I get a wigging or not I may do it. Send
me, like a duck, my great coat (blue) and that pair of trousers
(black) which you will see in my room and address them CBB at
Roberts Hotel, San[d]cliffe, nr. Folkestone, Kent. Also put into
the bundle that book I bought with German, French & Italian
sentences in it for I can't make these German chaps understand
my lingo.

                    Your affectionate Brother
                        Christopher

142. *First days in the Crimea*

Christopher Bassano to F.M. Bassano   Karabolnaia Villa
                                               Sebastopol
                                               28 October 1855

My dear Father
    I just take this opportunity of giving you a line, for a few
days ago I got something in my left eye and the inflammation is
now so severe that tomorrow I may be unable to write at all,
even today it causes me much pain. I wrote to Ellen from Kamosia,
but I only now post the letter to her. On the 23rd we came into
the harbour of Balaclava and on the 24th I rec[eive]d orders to
go to Sebastopol with a Medical Chest, three or 4 bearers
(stretchers) and my case of instruments. On the 25th I sent all
off but my case of instruments which I am sorry to say have not
yet arrived, nor have I heard from you whether you sent them off.
I wrote to you at Malta begging you to do so and again at
Constantinople. I hope they will soon arrive. Well, on the 25th
I started and called on Dr. Hall to explain my difficulty about
the instruments, but he was out and I wrote to him yesterday to

say he had better let me have an Ass[istan]t and an order on
the Stores for a [illeg.] case until mine arrives, but I
have not yet got an answer. I am as you may imagine rather
uncomfortable with my eye, and this morning when I woke the
[illeg.] was so great that the corner seem[e]d quite in a hollow
and I fear tomorrow it will be worse and there are no medicos
here. The Russian shells as you may imagine are playing all over
the town, but they fire chiefly at the French side, but quite
enough come near the house I live in to make it uncomfortable.
The night before last two rockets came and settled about a dozen
yards in front of my house and yesterday they saw the men
repairing the roof so they fired at the house and one of the
balls hit the house next to mine. Another house below me was
all knocked to shivereens. We must however all take our chance
and if I do not get injured I shall have the pleasure of saying
I was the first P.M.O. in Sebastopol. Should anything happen to
me I leave all my Effects to Melinda. I will send you a longer
yarn in the course of a few days if my eye will permit.

> Your affectionate son
> Christopher[1]

143. *A trip to Brighton – "don't go near the cannon balls"*

Melinda Bassano to Christopher Bassano   6 Elysium Row
                                            Fulham
                                            18 November 1855

My dearest Chris
    I received your letter to me along with Papa's, & am very
glad I did so, for I should have felt uneasy about your eye,
which I am fortunately prevented from doing by the favorable
account you give of it in your latest dated letter.

    Frances & Melinda send their love to you & beg me to thank
you for their trip to Brighton, for which they were indebted to
you. They were all there servant & all, for three weeks, the
last of which I spent there with them also, & very much enjoyed
it & very sorry I was when it was over, but the Doctor returned
home then, & of course we were obliged to return with Walter.
What a pretty town it is & so full of gay people. You could
fancy you were in London, only you see no poor people, & everybody looks so happy & smiling, as if they had nothing in the
world to do but to amuse themselves & a very pleasant occupation
I think it is. I came home as frisky as a kitten. We walked
about a great deal whilst I was there, for although we had a

---

1. There is a sketch map of the dockyard showing CBB's house.
   This letter was used as his will and Melinda got about £400.

great deal of rain, the town being built upon a hill, & the
footpaths nicely paved with red brick (which gives the town a
very pretty appearance) the place dries up in a few minutes, &
all Brighton turns out again. We made an excursion to the
"Devil's Dyke" one day, a distance of five miles from Brighton.
We hired a donkey for the children & a perambulator for the baby
& managed the distance very well. The road to the Dyke winds
amongst the lovely Downs, but on the ascent all the way untill
you reach the Dyke, & then a view of a totally different character bursts upon your sight. Instead of the lovely undulating
Downs, a valley of great extent & beauty lies at your feet, &
exclamations of pleasure & surprise burst from our lips. It
really was *beautiful* & coming upon it so unexpectedly increased
our admiration. The day was very fine & the air most exhilerat-
ing. We packed our dinner in the perambulator & sat down on
the hill & enjoyed it with this splendid landscape at our feet.
We stayed there an hour or two & returned home tired, but
gratified.

I have not forwarded your note to the Editor of the
Illustrated London News for I thought it would suit you as well
if we looked at the pictures & read the news before transmitting
it to you. Papa thinks it will be more sure to reach you, & you
will have the *felicity* of seeing either Papa's or my handwriting
on the paper. The latter I am sure will prove an *immense* source
of gratification to you. Papa got me your cheque cashed, but
I hope you do not anticipate being detained in the Crimea long
enough to exhaust *five pounds* in the purchase of a weekly paper.
I am daily hoping for a termination to the war followed by your
speedy return home. Write often, dear Chris, never mind if you
don't always get an answer, for we cannot find subjects of
interest so easily as you can in a country where everything you
see must be as new to us as it is to you.

Mrs. Bedford has not paid me her promised visit yet. Arthur
has been to Paris since you left home but I have not seen him
since his return. He called at Annie's & enquired very kindly
after you. Dear Mamma's gravestone is put up & looks very nice.
I shall be glad when you come home again to see it. God bless
you, dear Chris. Don't go near the cannon balls for the sake of

Your affectionate Sister
Linney

P.S. Your instruments were shipped in the steamship Sardinian,
by Hayters & Howell, the latter end of Oct[ober] or the beginning
of November, but they will have reached you I have no doubt
before this. The freightage was 5 shillings, which Evans will
charge to you. Papa wrote to you about them last Monday & the
Monday before. Adieu.

144. On duty at the General Hospital - miscellaneous news

Christopher Bassano to Walter Bassano   General Hospital
                                                  3rd Division
                                        8 December 1855

My dear Walter
    I rec[eive]d your note a few days ago and I am obliged to
you for thinking about the Cavalry. I shall send in an application for one, but do you think after being out here a while I
could not get on the Staff in London, and would it not be a good
thing for me? Mowat has been very civil to me and desired to
be kindly remembered to you. He is in General Orders tonight
for leave till the 29th Feb[ruar]y and leaves this directly.
He has been P.M.O. at the Gen[era]l Hosp[ita]l and I am sorry he
is leaving us. When that dreadfull explosion took place he got
me posted here, but I did not come in for any of the operations
and I dare say unless I am attached to a Regiment I shall remain
here all the winter. I am living in a hut with Dr. A. Smith and
am tolerably comfortable. Beatson takes charge of the Hospital
vice Mowatt. I am glad to hear my instruments are on the way
but I have not yet heard of the arrival of the "Sardinian" and
until I get them I cannot apply to Hall for any separate charge.
I should have been very jolly in Sabastopol as far as quarters
and servants went, but I found it very dull with only two or
three fellows there and I am not sorry Hall appointed me here,
for I have seen no end of practice, but the civilians have had
it chiefly to themselves. I got some Russian helmets in
Sabastopol last week and some other curiosities. The weather
has been very boisterous and some few nights frosty with a
little snow. The mud is like pea soup all over the place and
everything looks and is as wretched as it can be and the sooner
I am out of it the happier I shall feel. I bought a very nice
English horse for £20 but I have not been able to get a stable
for him and I fear he will kick the bucket if I do not look
sharp about it. I am glad you took all the babies to Brighton
with you. I hope they are all well. Melinda has not given me
a line since I left. Ask her to write to me.

    There is a sham here tonight that the Russians have cut off
a French outpost, but there is no attack expected. My belief is
that the Russians will make off before we take the field in the
Spring. If they don't I suspect not many of them will get out
of the Crimea. The men are very healthy and the food is capital.
I have been living chiefly on my rations lately, but as I have
no regular Servant or accommodation for cooking I am unable to
have things as comfortable as I should like. Most of the Troops
are huted and those who are not soon will be. I see the "Times"
continues to have occasional hits at Dr. Andrew Smith. Who is
likely to succeed him? Have you heard anything of the Civil
Surgeons being made 1st Class Staff? I hope it is not in con-
templation, for although they are very good fellows it would be

unjust to put them so high up. Some of them here were with me at college and were junior to me. I wrote home for the Illustrated L[ondon] News. Will you tell them to have it sent to me addressed General Hospital *3rd Division*, otherwise it goes to Balaclava and I have to ride in for my letters. I have seen nothing of Kirkland's last pay certificate. I suppose it is at Scutari. I forget what I made out in my bill for Shorncliff, but they only allowed me 1 -13 - 0 and said that the War Office had disallowed the detention allowance. Give my love to Annie and the babies and if you have any newspapers send them out and draw the postage from Melinda if you are obliged to prepay them. Tell Father that I think I have rec[eive]d all his letters and that I will send him an order for my cash.

Your affect[ionate] brother
Christopher

P.S. Fancy the wine I ordered at Fortnum & Mason's before I left has only just arrived. At least I hear this evening that the ship "Preston" in which it was shipped has arr[ive]d ... I shall pay 5/- a bottle for it by the time I get it if they don't charge extra for bringing it on from Scutari to which port it was shipped. Don't forget to send me a plum pudding by some private conveyance to Balaclava direct.

145. *Cigars for the Crimea*

Colvin Ainslie Cowie & Co. to Christopher Bassano

Calcutta
21 December 1855

Dear Sir

We have the pleasure to acknowledge receipt of your letter dated 2nd Nov[embe]r and beg to inform you that by the present opportunity we have dispatched a case containing 2000 Manilla Segars to the care of Messrs. Briggs & Co., Alexandria, whom we have requested to forward the case to your address by the first opportunity.

We are &c.

To Staff Surgeon C.B. Bassano, British Camp, Scutari, Per Hindostan, viâ Alexandria.

Christopher Bassano to Walter Bassano

Steam transport
Gibraltar No. 183
[postmark 21 January 1856
Rec^d 1 February 1856]

My dear Walter

Will you send the enclosed to Dr. Smith if necessary. I hope
you have had a jolly Xmas and I wish all a happy new year. Some
fellows out here have had plum puddings sent out to them, some
have none. I wrote to Father on 30th Dec[embe]r enclosing an
order for £100 and again on 6th Jan[uar]y enclosing cheques on
Kirkland for £50 & £25 which I hope he has rec[eive]d all right,
and I also have written to Kirkland for my last pay certificate
and my a/c, which I wish they would send, for I find I must draw
my pay out here. There is nothing doing in the Crimea except
that they are blowing up the Docks and have nearly completed
their operations. I had a little skating the last time I was at
Balaclava and to my surprise I was as steady on the ice as I
used to be. I hope to get a little again when I return for it
is freezing down here and we expect to go back in two or three
days. I embarked 104 men, Invalids, the last trip and we were
to have gone on again to [*illeg.*], but unluckily when we arrived
at Scutari a supply of coals was required and so they had all
the men landed at Scutari.

Will you send that cloth shell jacket I left in my trunk to
Linney and ask him to put a fresh lining to the collar and
reduce the dimensions of the jacket to my size, but tell him I
am two inches larger round the waist than I was when I left. I
don't know whether I left two cloth jackets, for I had two, one
which I had made when I went out to India and which had a piece
let in all down each arm. If this one is in my trunk it may be
thrown away, but if it is a cloth one without a piece let in
down the arm (formerly Dr. Harvey's] it is the one I wish to be
altered so that it may fit me. In the same parcel will you put
a pair of *new* summer trousers which I left in my drawers and
send them out by a friend or through the arsenal at Woolwich at
the Gov[ernmen]t expense. If they come in the usual way they
are so long on the road.

You give me no news from the M[edical] B[oard]. I am very
sorry I got Med[ica]l Staff uniform for I am quite ashamed to
be seen in it. A man may now be anybody with V.R. on his cap
and I have unluckily lost my cap cover. I see young Stewart of
the War Office is here in the Purveyor's Office. What has he
been after? He dined on board with me the other [day] and from
what I could make out he has been obliged to leave the W[ar]
O[ffice]. Kertch was reported to have been retaken by the
Russians, but it is al[l] a hoax. With love to Annie & the

babies believe me

                    Your affect[ionate] bro[ther]
                         Christopher

P.S. Do you have to pay more than 3d for my letters if I do not
write outside "Officer's Letter"?

147. *Death of Christopher at Balaclava*

Copy of letter to F.M. Bassano   Balaklava
                                                  3 February 1856

My dear Sir
    It is with a feeling of deep regret I have to communicate to
you a sorrowful intelligence. In the performing of an arduous
duty, attending to the Sick on board the Steam Ship Gibraltar
your son must have caught a low fever which apparently did not
develope itself to cause any alarm, neither did he think himself
the imminent danger of his state till he went into Hospital.

    It is sad and mournful to me to relate your son has gone to
his long Home. His death was calm and resigned. He knew full
well (as he stated to the Orderly) the inevitable result.
Everything was done for him that could be done and his suffering
was comparatively little. He entered the General Hospital on
Thursday morning Jan[uary] 31 and died on the Friday afternoon
at about 3 o'Clock, Feb[ruary] 1st. He was buried yesterday,
Saturday Feb[ruary] 2nd at the Cemetery of the Castle Hospital,
followed by a numerous party of friends and a Company of
Artillery stationed at Balaklava. His effects &c. I will see
to their proper disposal. Any thing that I find you would be
likely to reserve I will take care of and remit. Sympathizing
with you in your bereavement, Believe me, my dear Sir, ever
yours

                         F. F.
                         Apothecary to the Forces

148. *About the death of Christopher*

F.M. Bassano to Tom Bassano   16 February 1856
(Copy in F.M.B.'s hand)

My dear Tom
    I have not heard from you since your dear Mother's death.
Another visitation of Providence almost as lamentable has now
fallen heavily upon us in the death of our dear Christopher at

Balaklava on the 1st Instant. He was in excellent health during his short leave of absence in England and I think would have been able to complete his service in India if he had returned to that station, but he declined doing so on account of delaying his promotion, and he therefore decided upon accepting immediate promotion for Service in the Crimea. He proceeded to Scutari in September last and thence to Sebastopol with Troops employed in destroying the Docks. His subsequent duty was with the Invalid Soldiers from Balaklava to Scutari, on board the Gibraltar Steam Ship. His frequent letters did not lead us to apprehend that his health was declining, and the first account we had of his illness and death was published in the Morning Herald of Friday last, the 15th February, viz. "French Camp, Kamiesch Road, Crimea. 2nd Feb[ruary]. A Mr. Bassano who was a great favourite in the British Medical Staff died at Balaklava yesterday". The Official Report arrived at our Office on Saturday 16th inst. stating "that he was landed ill with fever and appeared for a few days to be progressing without any very bad Symptoms till the morning of the 1st February when he was seized with a strong convulsion fit and died almost immediately with all the symptoms of Cerebral effusion". I wrote to Ellen and Alfred yesterday and have some hope that my health will be spared to me till you and one or both of them come back to England. At the same time I know you cannot return if your own prospects would suffer by the movement.

149. *Christopher's effects*

War Department to F.M. Bassano   15 April 1856
(Copy by FMB)

Sir
    In expressing to you the regret of the Secretary of State for War at the death of your late son 2nd Class Staff Surgeon Christopher Bakewell Bassano which took place at the General Hospital Balaklava on the 2nd [*sic*] February 1856, I am directed to inform you that the sum of £223.12.5 has been paid into the Commissariat Chest to be credited to his non-effective account.

    The Military Secretary has further reported that the articles reserved for the friends of the deceased were transmitted to England in charge of Dr. Jephson, 1st Dragoons, who sailed for England in the "Andes" steamer on the 24th February last.[2]

                    I am &c.

---

2. Endorsed by FMB "W.O. 15/4/56. Death of Xtopher the proceeds of effects about £400 received by Melinda".

CHAPTER EIGHT

Brothers Meet
(Alfred & Tom Bassano, 1855-8)

Alfred Bassano returned from leave in 1855 shortly before Christopher left India, and spent two years with his regiment in the hills of the frontier area before being moved to Lucknow. He took part in the battle of Chinhut and then went through the siege in 1857, finally succeeding to the command of the regiment (though only a captain) because of the death or sickness of the more senior officers. After the relief of Lucknow he got six months leave and decided to visit his brother Tom on his coffee estate. This was the only time any of the brothers met while in India. Alfred was 32 years old and Tom not quite 37, and they had last seen each other nearly fifteen years before. After this meeting Alfred returned to England with his regiment and never again served in India. He continued to serve with his regiment, retiring on half pay in 1872.

Things had at last begun to look up for Tom. With help from his eldest brother Philip he had been able to leave his employers and set up on his own account. He paid his first visit home in 1857.

RETURN FROM LEAVE AND SIEGE OF LUCKNOW
(Alfred Bassano 1855-8)

50. *Summary of Alfred's career, 1854-8*

Alfred Bassano to Mr. Gaffney

Union Hotel
Ootacamund
24 June 1858

My dear Mr. Gaffney

Better later than never. I believe I promised to write to you from India on my last visit to your hospitable house in the delightful little village of Buntingford, and as God has spared my life in these hard times I must redeem my promise by giving you a brief outline of my second Indian career.

I had a tolerably pleasant voyage out. We jumped overboard several times, and bathed in the Sea, shaved our heads, played écarte, backgammon, & whist all day, eat dolphins & flying fish, caught sharks and talked Sentiment, arrived at Bombay, stayed at a hotel for a fortnight, visited the cave of Elephanta, took a steamer to Kurrachee, stayed about a week, eating oysters, riding, & driving about, then again by steamer to Mooltan, a pleasant journey of about a month up a river, scenery tolerably pretty at some places (a great many agreeable ladies on board, most of them married, but one spinster, an amiable and beautiful girl, who nearly upset all my philosophy again). Thence by mail cart to Lahore, 208 miles in 18 hours, drove myself, 6 hours less than the usual time to the astonishment of the Post Office officials, licked lots of the Coachmen and syces on the road, stayed one day, thence again by mail cart to Jullundur, came an awful smash into a Banyan's shop on the road through the stupidity of the Syce, picked myself up and off again to Umballa, where I arrived just in time for dinner at my own mess about a week before the Expiration of my leave. Stayed about a fortnight at Umballa when we had the luck to be ordered to the hills in March '55, & were quartered at Kussowlie and Soobathoo for nearly two years, delightful place, beautiful scenery & an English climate, snow sometimes 3 feet deep in the winter. Got a great deal of leave, went over the country shooting & admiring the scenery, & set to raising a pack of hounds, then marched to Lucknow (suffering dreadfully from Cholera on the road) where we had splendid quarters given to us gratis in a palace on the banks of the "river Goomtee". We bought two 4 oared cutters & with my pack of hounds prepared to pass a very pleasant time of it hunting, rowing, shooting, riding & driving, not to mention lots of balls, parties, private theatricals, & archery meetings, then out broke the mutiny, most of us losing nearly everything we possessed in the world. I lost 3 horses, a pack of hounds, my share of two four oared cutters, an expensive lot of saddlery, all my tents, furniture and half of my personal baggage.

Then came the unfortunate fight at Chinhut[1] where I got a grape shot through my foot & lost another very fine horse, which I had taken from the Enemy only a few days previously. Then the siege, the first half of which I passed in a state of filth & misery in a dark sort of store room in the Residency having my foot dressed, & being enlivened by the whistle & fall of bullets, round shot, and shell in every part of the house. One of our own Officers was killed in the mess room and another had his leg smashed by a round shot which took off the leg of the mess table first. Then two or three rooms fell in & buried two parties of the Men, who were playing whist in the ruins. Then fierce attacks, and rumours that the Enemy had stormed another part of the garrison. An incessant din of musketry, shot, shell, & cheers, made it remarkably agreeable for a sick man who could not move from his bed. However I soon got all right again, and then took my share when others were laid up or killed. I commanded one sortie taking nine guns and driving the Enemy into the river, shooting and bayonetting them by dozens. I afterwards succeeded to the Command of the Regiment,[2] and took it out of Lucknow.[3]

Since then I have been knocked about with the Cornish Choughs sleeping on the ground sometimes wet through or bitterly cold, & sometimes scorched & choked with dust. We were engaged with Sir Colin Campbell kicking the Gwalior Contingent out of Cawnpore,[4] taking all their Guns &c, after which I appropriated two buggies, a boat, & several round tables belonging to the Enemy, & our Reg[imen]t having been sent into quarters at Allahabad on account of their severe losses, with no immediate prospect of being Engaged again I sold off my property which I had again accumulated & numbered two horses, a galloway & a pony, and got six months leave, travelled about 17 hundred miles by Railway, steamer, carriages, horses, bullock Carts, palkies &c, &c., and after numerous ludicrous & dangerous adventures arrived at Ootacamund, where the scenery is beautiful in the extreme, Climate at present like England in March & April, showers, high winds, cold & warm alternately, sit over a wood & peat fire, & drink hot whiskey punch every night. The Station is very large, houses magnificently furnished, each standing alone, generally surrounded by beautiful gardens & shrubberies, a lake with rides & drives about 7 miles round in the centre, and the ladies are perpetually getting up picnics to Fair Lawns, Lovedale & other romantic spots a few miles off. I am living at

---

1. 30 June 1857.
2. 27 September 1857.
3. 22 November 1857.
4. 6 December 1857.

a very comfortable Hotel, but am perpetually dining out, anyone
from Bengal being quite lionized here. I am only about 80 miles
from Tom, and intend directly my health is completely restored
(it has not suffered much) to go and see him. I rode with a
party of four two or three days ago on a shooting expedition 12
miles out and home to Dinner with a few head of Deer, having
ridden 24 and walked about 15 miles over steep hills. Not a
bad day's walk for an old Indian Invalid, Eh Doctor!

Give my kindest remembrance to Mrs. Gaffney, your daughters,
Son, and Mrs. Green, who I trust are in the enjoyment of
uninterrupted health, and all the kind friends, both old & young,
I met with in merry Herts, too numerous to mention by name.
Give my love to all the young ladies. I'm an old Man, a Field
Officer now, so they must not be offended, and tell Miss Vaughan,
if she has not changed her name, that the "Woodlands" still ring
in my Ears. I hope she continues to practise it occasionally.

Well, I must hold hard, as they say on the turf, or I'll be
filling an Acre of paper with nonsense which might be pardoned
in a sentimental Lieutenant, but does not become a dried up
Major. Adieu. I hope an English Railway will before long
shoot me out of "Where"? Echo answers "Ware".

> Yours sincerely
> Alf Bassano, Major
> H.M. 32nd Light Infantry

151. *Alfred's debts — thoughts of applying for a Crimean
regiment — "I am leading a very quiet retired life"*

Alfred Bassano to Philip Bassano   Kussowlie
                                               24 September 1855

My dear Phil
    I received your letter containing the melancholy intelligence
of the death of dear Mother. I wish Tom as well as Chris could
have seen her before she died.

    I am very much obliged to you for your kind offer of
assistance, especially considering your own scanty means. I
have also received and declined a similar one from Tom. Now,
to be Candid with you, I will not deny the fact of my being in
debt, but if I stay in this country the amount will soon be
liquidated by me without assistance, and in the mean time it
does not cause me the slightest inconvenience or anxiety. The
only nuisance of owing money at this particular time is that it
prevents me from applying, or getting Father to do so, which
would do as well, perhaps better, for a *Company* in a Reg[imen]t
in the Crimea. Now if you think this War will last and can

afford to give me a chance of distinction, for I am really just in the state of mind to storm a breach or do anything desperate, try and get me *promoted*, that is to say if the E.I.C. or Gov[ernmen]t pay the passage of Officers on promotion from India to the Crimea, which I am almost certain they do. And provided also you could lodge (to say without inconvenience would be humbug) from £50 to £100 - fifty would do if I sold my horse, pony, saddlery, &c. well, but it would not do to run the risk without being sure of the larger sum to get me out of the country if actually required, especially as my horse has gone lame twice lately, which has not improved his character for efficiency.

If you get Father to send in an application you can make him mention, in addition to my services, that I will join whatever Regiment I am promoted in with the greatest possible expedition.

You now know exactly under what circumstances *only* I shall ever again require assistance, vizt. being called on suddenly to leave the country within a year or two from the present time. So unless you think it is worth while to get Father to have a shot at the Authorities for my promotion, you need never have any more anxiety about me or my fortunes, and do not be annoyed at my scarcely ever writing home, as nothing but the pleasure and excitement of being engaged in another War is likely to enable me to recover sufficient spirits to be a good correspondent again.

Make your mind quite easy. I am neither drinking to excess or committing any other eccentricity. My temper is certainly slightly soured, and I now occasionally have a row, otherwise I am leading a very quiet retired life studying Persian, Hindustanee & Arabic, and breeding foxhounds[5] [with] a view to obtaining an appointment and finishing my [service] in this country as free from thought as possible in the enjoy[ment of] my favourite sport, hunting. That is to say if I cannot [manage] to get engaged in the present War. The Regiment is [remaining] in the hills another year, so I shall not suffer much [from the] climate which is lovely. I have a fire in my house all [day] and soon we shall have snow on the ground.

Give my love to Lin, Annie, Fan Fan, [——————] and ask Lin and *Fan Fan* to drop me a line occasionally ev[en if I do] not reply, which is a trick I have got [into with no] probability of breaking myself of. I [heard] from Tom. He seems to be really getting on now. I intend to try and get a year's leave to go & see him, when the Reg[imen]t goes down the country.

When the present War is drawing to a conclusion tell Walter to keep his wits about him and put Chris into a Regiment about to be ordered to this country or already here. He can please

---

5. A piece of the letter has been cut away from here.

himself about coming out or remaining here, as he can *merely*
pocket one thousand pounds for an exchange to home, & even now
he will be better in the Crimea in a R[e]g[imen]t than on the
Staff & no chance of being put upon half pay in case of an
abrupt conclusion to the War.

Remember you must not attempt to get me promoted unless you
feel convinced I shall be in plenty of time to come in for lots
of fighting and get out of the break, for I am getting up to the
top of the L[ieutenan]ts in the 32nd and I feel more convinced
now than ever that it does not pay for a poor man to leave the
only country where he can preserve his independence and pay his
Tailor's bills, without considering very carefully what he is
about, even if he is only quitting it on leave, as I now know to
my cost.

Have they promoted you yet in the War Office, or Walter in
the Medical Board? It is high time you both of you got a lift.

If I *pass* in the *language* and get on the roads it will nearly
double my pay and decrease my expenses.

Give my love to all at home, and ask Lin to tell Fan Fan she
is quite old enough now to write to her uncle occasionally.
You can direct & post it for her.

Your affectionate brother
Alfred

152. *About promotion*

Alfred Bassano to Philip Bassano   Kussowlie
                                                24 October 1855

My dear Phil
        As I have got so many steps lately and shall probably be
senior Lieut[enant] by the time this reaches you, I think you
had better not do anything about getting me promoted in another
Regiment, if such was your intention, as the expense I should be
put to would not compensate me *now* considering my present
position and chance of promotion in my own Regiment. I hope
you have not put in an application. If you have, cancel it, as
I have come to the conclusion that I must not think of quitting
this country until I am out of debt. The anxiety is too annoying, in fact I could not do it. There is a rumour that we are
to go to Umballa, but I don't think it likely.

When you write to Chris advise him to try and get into a
Regiment. However, I suppose he knows best what will suit his
convenience without any telling.

I have no news to tell you. There has been great excitement in the Regiment lately in consequence of such a run of promotion, and I don't think it has stopped yet so I suppose I shall soon be a Captain and independent of the World.

Have you got your promotion yet, and Walter his? Tell me in your next, that is to say if you take the trouble to answer my exceedingly stupid letters. I seem to have lost all idea of writing, and get so disgusted at my own miserable productions that I expect before long I shall cease to write altogether. In fact, I have nearly done so as it is, and have heaps of unanswered epistles from my friends in all parts of the World.

Remember me to all at home and give my love to Annie, Lin and the little ones, and

Believe me your affectionate brother
Alfred B.

153. *Adventures on leave - promotion - life at Kussowlie*

Alfred Bassano to Melinda Bassano   Kussowlie
                                                     1 May 1856

My dear Lin
    I received your letter containing the melancholy intelligence of the death of Chris a day or two after I had seen it in the newspaper. It certainly appears as if misfortunes never come singly by the rapidity and number that have fallen upon me lately.

Tell me in your next if you have heard from Tom as my last letter dated some Months ago has never been answered, and we used to correspond very regularly. Also about Ellen, whether she writes in good health and spirits.

I have been travelling again over the hills to Mussoorie and back on a Month's leave - magnificent scenery and good sport, but I unfortunately fell over some rocks on the banks of the Jumna and broke my right thumb, turning it completely back, the two bones protruding from the flesh. I was twelve days march from any European habitation at the time, and no other means of conveyance, so was obliged to set it myself and dress it with the waxed cloth used for putting round bullets, the nearest approach to anything medicinal in my possession. However, on my return to the Reg[imen]t a fortnight after, the D[octo]r (Old Scott) told me I had made a splendid job of it, and it is now quite well again, only larger than the other and a little stiff in the joint.

I was just meditating another trip into Chinese Tartary and
Ladak, having been promised *six Months'* leave, when the
Paymaster died suddenly, and the Q[uarte]r Mast[er] (Giddings)
succeeded him in the appointment temporarily, and the Colonel
offered me the Acting Quartermastership, which I immediately
accepted and resigned my leave, as it gives me upwards of a
£150 a year extra, and I may possibly hold it for ten Months, or
until I get my Company, which in the present state of my finances
is not to be sneezed at. In fact I expect *soon* to get my
promotion as I have several strings to my bow, one of our
Colonels being on his way home and intends to try and get some
appointment in England, which if he succeeds in doing and gets
the step to go in the Reg[imen]t *without purchase*, the Seniors
of each rank obtaining their promotion have agreed amongst
ourselves to make up a purse of two thousand pounds. I have also
had some communications from one of our Captains relative to
giving me a step, but at present he wants more than I have any
intention of giving. The Regiment is now altogether at
Kussowlie, 7000 feet above the level of the sea with a lovely
climate, just like England only more regular in the seasons and
lots of sunshine. Ther[mometer] at this moment, the middle of
the day, 71 in my room and a very cool wind blowing outside. I
am getting up a kennel of dogs to hunt when I go down to the
plains in October or November, and received from Agra a few days
ago two couple of half bred fox hounds, a present from Col.
Carmichael who is on the Staff of the Lieut. Governor of the
North West Provinces. Ladies & pianos are very plentiful here,
even young unmarried ones, and we actually get tolerable music
and singing.

Remember me to all at home and give my Love to Annie and the
young ones and believe me

Your affectionate brother
Alfred

154. *Casualties of the 32nd Regiment at siege of Lucknow,
30 June-22 November 1857*

[The Return of Casualties, dated Cawnpore, 29 January 1858, lists:

4 officers, 111 non-commissioned officers and men, killed in
action at Chinhut, 30 June 1857

6 Officers, 174 non-commissioned officers and men, 3 women
and 6 children killed, died of wounds, or died of disease,
during the siege, 1 July-22 Nov. 1847

8 officers, 185 (of whom 55 died later) non-commissioned
officers and men wounded, 30 June-22 November 1857 (including

Capt. Alfred Bassano, 30 June, severely)

Also: 3 officers, their wives and two children; 82 non-commissioned officers and men, 43 women and 54 children supposed to have been killed at Cawnpore on or before 27 June 1857]

155. *Alfred Bassano at the battle of Chinhut, 30 June 1857*

Extracts from *A Personal Narrative of the Siege of Lucknow ...,* by L.E.R. Rees (1858), Chapter IV.

[The British force consisted of 300 men of the 32nd Regiment, and about 300 others (including 150 of the 13th Native Infantry, and 125 troopers of the Oudh Irregular Cavalry, mostly Sikhs) under the immediate orders of Brig. Gen. Sir Henry Lawrence.]

"Many of the Europeans had indulged the previous evening a little too freely in liquor ... They moved on confident of success, and without making any preparations for covering their retreat, should they meet with a reverse, a contingency of which neither Sir Henry, his counsellors, nor any European individual of the force ever contemplated the possibility.

* * * * * * * * *

"The village of Ishmaelpore was filled with the enemy's sharpshooters. Colonel Case, at the head of his 32nd men, gallantly led them up to it, but fell, struck by a bullet ... Captain Bassano, seeing the Colonel fall, went up to assist him. 'Captain Bassano', was the noble speech of the wounded hero, 'Leave me to die here. Your place is at the head of your company. I have no need of assistance.'

* * * * * * * * *

"The order for retreat was now given, but the 32nd still kept up a brisk and murderous fire, many men firing more than a hundred rounds of ammunition. Poor gallant Lieutenant-Colonel Case was still seen on the roadside, lying with eyes wide open, with his sword firmly grasped, in the midst of the corpses of his own brave companions in arms. Lieutenant Brackenbury was shot next, and Thompson, the adjutant, was mortally wounded. Captain Bassano was likewise wounded in the leg, but succeeded in arriving safe in the Residency, through the intrepidity of a sepoy of the 13th Native Infantry, who carried him for a considerable distance on his back. The men were now panic-struck, and retreated towards Lucknow as fast as they could go ..

* * * * * * * * *

"When approaching the iron bridge, men, women, and children,
rich and poor, crowded around the weary and thirsty men, and
offered water, which was greedily swallowed. Nothing could
exceed their kindness, - a proof that we yet had friends in the
city, and found many sympathisers among the natives."

* * * * * * * *

156. *Alfred Bassano's wound*

Proceedings of a Committee of Medical Officers   Allahabad
                                                  19 April 1858

    The Committee find that Captain A. Bassano, H.M.'s 32nd
Regiment, was wounded by a Musket Ball on the 30 June 1857,
which passed through his left foot fracturing two of the bones.
The wound did not heal favorably, assumed a sloughing action,
and several pieces of bone had to be removed. He is still lame
and the wound does not seem permanently healed.

    The Committee is of opinion that Captain Bassano received a
severe and dangerous gunshot wound of the foot, but in its
permanent effects not equal to the loss of a limb.

157. *Siege of Lucknow*

Alfred Bassano to Tom Bassano   Cawnpore
                                              6 February 1858

My dear Tom
    I received your welcome letter only today altho' it is dated
more than [a] Month back. Make your mind easy. I am all serene,
having perfectly recovered from the effects of the wound altho'
it was rather a bad smash, a grape shot slap through the foot,
in on one side & out on the other, cutting my boot right off my
foot. However I managed to walk about 4 Miles & ride two, and
do a little fighting besides on the way home from that disastrous
business at Chinhut, after which we were besieged for nearly 5
Months, during which time I flatter myself the 32nd left their
mark pretty well defined in the blood of some thousands of the
brutes. Our loss however was fearful as you can imagine, one
weak Regiment against about 50 thousand, holding a lot of
indefensible houses for upwards of four Months. We lost 13
Officers killed or died of wounds, the remaining eight all
wounded badly once or twice with *one* exception, vizt. Capt.
Lawrence, the only Combatant of the 32nd who went right through
the Siege without being touched.

I commanded the Regiment for nearly two Months during the
latter part of the Siege, every Capt[ain] but myself being
killed & Major Lowe wounded.

I have since been in a fight under Sir Colin Campbell, when
we licked the Gwalior Contingent out of Cawnpore, taking all
their guns and Camp equipage - & the Chief is now preparing for
another advance on Lucknow, but I don't think we shall be taken,
being so weak.

I shall write to Lin by the next Mail, but have been nearly
driven mad with work during the last year, in addition to fighting, being President of 14 Courts of Adjustment, Mess Pres[iden]t
Sec[retar]y to Library, Boat Club &c. &c., so you can fancy I
have not been idle.

Give my love to Father & Lin and all at home next time you
write & if by chance I should be knocked over there is about
200£ of mine at Cox & Co., part of which I have just sent home.
This and the money due to me here will I think clear all my
debts & reimburse Father & Phil most of the expenses I have put
them to.

If I can get leave I will certainly pay you a visit this hot
season, as I hear we are to go to Darjeeling in the hills near
Calcutta. If so we shall soon be on the march down. What are
you doing? Coffee planting again? I thought you had sold your
Estate, but I suppose have bought another. I met Pemberton of
the 60th Rifles who came out with you & has now gone home again
without the fingers of his right hand, blown off by a shell in
the late fights here.

Cheer up, old fellow, I'm not scragged yet. I hear you are
getting *beastly* fat. Drop me a line addressed to care of Messrs.
Gordon, Stuart & Co., Calcutta, as we shall probably soon be on
the move again.

Your affectionate brother
Alf Bassano

158. *More about the siege - the settlement of Alfred's debts*

Alfred Bassano to Melinda Bassano   Cawnpore
                                                     14 February 1858

My dear Lin
     I received your welcome letter after being shut up without
news from home for five Months, seeing the Reg[imen]t gradually
wasting away by shot, shell & sickness to a perfect skeleton.
However, we held the place & would have done for some time

longer & I flatter myself for every one we lost two or three
hundred of the ennemy bit the dust. I was shot through the foot
the first day of the Siege but got tolerably well about 3 Months
before it was over, hobbling about in the trenches but too lame
to go out in the Sorties until the last Month of the blockade
when I began to be active again & headed one Sortie when we took
7 guns and drove no end of the ennemy into the River, shooting
& bayonetting them like dogs.

When the Siege commenced we had 23 Officers present with the
Reg[imen]t, not including the Doctors, Paymaster, & Q[uarte]r
M[aste]r who are non-combatants, out of which number we *buried
thirteen* (including Cawnpore), eight of the other ten being
wounded once or twice, many very seriously, and another laid up
with Cholera nearly all the time so he ran very little chance of
being shot. In fact, only one went positively through the Siege
without being touched, viz. Capt. Lawrence.

I commanded the Reg[imen]t for nearly two Months, drawing £43
a Month Command & Horse allowance in addition to my pay. I was
giving *£3-4* a lb. for bad moist sugar & could have sold a few
bottles of wine I had for 5£ a bottle, but preferred making it
into hot punch & entertaining a few friends in the trenches of a
night. I lost almost all my property, three Horses, four or
five saddles & 10 bridles, a pack of hounds and several shares
in two four oared cutters, one of which had been built in
England and cost £50. However, I believe we shall get compensa-
tion, but not sufficient to cover our losses. All my tents &
other property were burnt by the ennemy.

What rot appears in the papers about the operations in India!
Most of the accounts that lead John Bull must be written by
people who have never been in the country, much less in the
places they describe. What a God Almighty they make of the late
Gen. Havelock. You should hear the opinions of those who
served under him. A few unpleasant truths could be told by
first rate Officers that would rather astonish John Bull. The
Times correspondent will arrive here today. I wish he had been
in Lucknow. Since my arrival here we have had one more fight
turning out the Gwalior Contingent who had again got possession
of the town after licking Gen. Wyndham. However, we had a
rattling force to do it with & Sir Colin to Command.

I am living in a Bungalow on the banks of the River close to
where all the ladies & women of the Regiment & Station were
murdered, commanding a splendid view of the two boat bridges
leading to Lucknow, which is 48 miles from here. The road now
day and night is a mass of hackeries, Camels, guns, horse & foot
soldiers, all going to Lucknow. It is to be hoped to take it
this time. We are so weak and short of Officers that I don't
think we are likely to go back, but will be left to Garrison
this place.

Don't go & let this letter or extracts get into print as seems to be the fashion now, to the great disgust of the senders.

There is a rumour that we go to Darjeeling in the hills this year, and another that we go home, but I don't know what truth there is in it. I'm afraid they can't spare Troops from India yet as the fighting is by no means all over.

Tell Phil I have sent a couple of hundred pounds home to Cox & Co. and will be able to return the money himself & Father kindly supplied me with directly I am settled. Also ask him to tell Linney the Tailor that I will send him an order for the Amount of his bill directly I get my batta (£102) which will, I believe, be paid next Month. If I should by chance get slain my credit at Cox's and at the Reg[imen]t, with the sale of my property (for I have again got two horses, a pony, a cart & buggy) and have just got clear of my Indian debts, will be no inconsiderable amount.

Give my love to Annie, Fan Fan, little Lin, Harry & the *chota Butcha* "Alfred" whose existence I was not aware of until the receipt of your letter, and tell me in your next if there are any more, as I may have missed the intelligence of a brace of twins or two previously, by the loss of your letters.

I received a letter from Tom a few days ago and answered it by the same post. I will write again this Month, but have so much to do having been during the last year, on acc[oun]t of the paucity of Officers, Mess & Canteen President, Sec[retary] to library, and President of 14 Courts of Adjustment on Deceased Officers' Estates, no sinecure I can tell you.

Tell Fan Fan if she don't write to me soon I will send two Sepoys to kill her and bring out little Alfred to rear.

Your affectionate brother
Alfred

Love to all at home.

THOUGHTS OF AUSTRALIA AND VISIT HOME
(Tom Bassano 1856-7)

159. *Advice on going to Australia*

Ellen Hepburn to Tom Bassano   Glendonald
                                                31 December 1855

My dear Brother
    I have received a visit from your friend Mr. Farrer. He seems
to be very much pleased with this country, and was going to
persuade you to throw up what you have in India and come out. I
sincerely trust if you make up your mind to do so it will be for
the best and that you may be prosperous. At any rate I will do
what I can to make you happy as long as you remain with us. I
think it was in Sept[embe]r or Oct[obe]r that Mr. Farrer was with
us and I said I would write immediately, but I have missed the
posts in the following manner. It is some days after the paper
is printed before it reaches us up the country, and then if
business takes Mr. H[epburn] another way, they lay at the
Creswick Post Office some days longer, and then my letter has to
be written, taken to the post four miles off, and then down to
Melbourne – so that unless the Ship happens to be advertised a
considerable time before leaving the Port you see I am too late.
I now am going to adopt a different course, viz. send my letters
to a friend in Melbourne to be posted by the first mail.

    I suppose Christopher is in England by this time. I have not
had a letter from any of them at home since last Nov[embe]r
twelvemonth. If there were fewer of them I should think they
were dead, but they are very busy in other ways, I suppose.
Send me word any news you may have from that quarter, and
remember any thing concerning Alfred will be quite fresh to me,
as we have never corresponded.

    I trust you will be able to sell your plantations to
advantage. Do not be headstrong and throw them up for nothing,
because a little capital to work on is so highly advantageous
in this country, for without it you may drag on for years
without being able to do any good for yourself. Salaries were
very low before the Gold was discovered, and they are now
falling again, for the gold fields do not yield a quarter of
what they did, and everything is coming down. Vegetation is
beginning to be extended and plentiful – and it is the opinion
of many that there will soon be an overplus in that line. It
is my opinion that there will soon be a standard price all over
the world by means of the easy transit that is now effected
everywhere. Mr. Farrer said he would call on Benjamin's Agent,
viz. Mess[rs] Heape Brothers, and show him your coffee, also

leave some there for me to taste. I have not heard from Mr. Heape that he did so, but he may for all that.

When you come into the country you had better direct your boxes to Mr. Benjamin Hepburn, Glendonald, care of Messrs. Heape Brothers, Merchants, Lonsdale Street. See that they are properly given into their hands and then they will be safe until Benjamin has a dray up, when they can come up the country with our goods. Then you had better buy a horse and saddle and come up to us as fast as you can. You can get horses cheaper in Melbourne than here, and it will save travelling expences, and you will feel independant when you can mount your own nag and do as you please.

We are mowing at the present time and we have had nothing but heavy storms ever since we began, so we begin to feel apprehensive that it will not be worth much. He has not made a very good year - his sale of sheep and cattle is over at Creswick. He has been able to dispose of a few at a diggings sixteen miles off these last few weeks, and that is all that is doing. If things do not mend again, we have not much to look forward to.

Our new house, on property which Benjamin purchased last year, is finished, but we shall not go into it until February twelvemonth, that is the time our term of this Station expires. So if you come before that time you will have the pleasure of another move. I hope you do not dislike dogs and cats and Turkeys and fowls and Duck, because we have swarms, and do not bring me a monkey or a parrot, for sometimes I am almost mad with those I have. Benjamin too is going to add to the collection by introducing pigeons and rabbits. But be sure you bring a few seeds of flowers, fruits and vegetables &c.

Prepare yourself for seeing a very shriveled up old thing in the person of your Sister, not a bit like she was when you saw her last in Bayswater.[6] Neither shall I know you, for your likeness which was sent home was not recognized by any of them. I have got Father's sent out to me. It is capital, just the same as he was when I left. A happy new year to you and a safe voyage out and with best love believe me

Your very affectionate sister
C.E. Hepburn

Please write immediately on receipt of this. My address is:

Mrs. Benj. Hepburn, Glendonald, Post Office,
Creswick, Victoria, Australia Felix.

---

6. Ellen was in her 44th year, Tom in his 35th year. They had not met for 12 years.

Ellen Hepburn to F.M. Bassano   Glendonald
                                             27 February 1856

My dear Father
   It was with extreme sorrow that I received intelligence of my
poor Mother's death. Christopher wrote me the mournful news
from Scutari and does not enter into many particulars, supposing
that I had heard it before, but if any of you wrote I never
received the letter. I should be very glad to hear all the
particulars of her illness and last moments, whether she was
conscious that her end was approaching, and whether she was
happy at the thought of leaving this world of trouble. It will
be a cause of great comfort to Chris and Al that they visited
England once more before her death, but poor Tom! how he will
grieve that he is too late.

   I suppose that there is something wrong as I do not receive
any letters from England. I saw a notice in the Argus newspaper
that there were thousands of letters to persons in these colonies
which were lying in the dead letter office in London in consequence of the proper Stamp not being affixed. You had better
make the necessary enquiries. The last letter I have received
from home was from you telling me that you had sent my box, dated
July '54, which I received in the Nov[embe]r following. The
letters I have written home since that time have been as follows:
to you Nov. 9th/54; to you and Philip Nov. 23rd/54; to Philip,
poor Mother, Melinda and Walter's two eldest girls Jan. 1st/55;
to Christopher, who I knew was on his way to England, July 12th/
55; and to Philip (Number 17) July 13th/55. So please write by
return of post and tell me everything that has taken place in
England for the last two years, and do not forget ole Uncle Mark
among the catalogue - he is a wonderful old man, if still alive.

   I am waiting for Benjamin to come in, and then we shall drive
down to Melbourne to procure furniture for our new house,
situated about three miles from this Station, on property which
he bought about a year and a half since, which I think I told
you all about. The cottage consists of two parlors, 3 bedrooms,
a storeroom, and a kitchen, all on the ground floor, and a
Verandah nearly all round the house, with outhouses consisting
of Stable, Coach house, and Servant's room. Please address
henceforward, Mrs. Benj. Hepburn, Forest Hill, Post Office,
Creswick, Victoria.

   This summer has been a very cool, pleasant summer, with much
rain, but the hay crops have suffered much in consequence. It
has been nothing but build up stack and then pull it down again
to dry, all through the harvest, and although there was the
most luxuriant crops ever witnessed, what remains unspoiled will
only pay expences. Benjamin has not been able to make money so

rapidly this year as he did last, the sheep and cattle Markets
being also dull, and much competition, but still we have not any
cause of complaint.

[Letter unsigned]

P.S. I am now in Melbourne purchasing furniture for our new
house. March 8th.

161. *Instructions on how to reach the Hepburn station*

Ellen Hepburn to Tom Bassano   Glendonald
                                                                20 March 1856

My dear Brother
     The Viscount Canning is advertised via Madras, 25th March.
If it should be true to its time this may reach you before you
leave India for this country, if it still be your determination
to come and join us, and when you arrive you must come to
Ballarat by coach, and then by the branch coach to Creswick.
Benjamin will very likely be on the township of Creswick. If
you make enquiries at Shearer and Hassels Store or at the
American Hotel, and if he should not be there, any of them will
direct you to Mr. B. Hepburn's new house at the foot of Forest
Hill. It is about three miles from Creswick, and you can walk
it. Leave your carpet bag in Mr. Benj. Hepburn's name, care of
Anthony and Vines, and it will be quite safe till we send for it.
The bulk of your luggage must be left in the care of Messrs.
Heape Brothers, Merchants, Lonsdale Street, Melbourne, until
some of our drays are loading for us, when the luggage will be
conveyed up to our house for you. The coach will not bring
much luggage on it. If you have merchandize to dispose of in
Melbourne, call on Mr. Germain Nicholson (at one o'clock),
Grocer, Sign of Coffee Pot, Collins Street, Melbourne. You will
be sure to catch him at that time, and he will advise you what
to do for the best.

     This is the last week I shall be at Glendonald. Our new house
at Forest Hill is built, and our furniture is on the road up.
When it arrives I shall go to put it in order and remain there.
I have just come up from Melbourne. I have been there a fortnight making purchases.

     In case you write me another letter before you leave, address
it, Mrs. B. Hepburn, Forest Hill, Post Office, Creswick.
Mr. Ferrars did not leave me a sample of your coffee in Melbourne
as he promised. Try and bring some seeds with you (fruits,
vegetables, flowers, and grain), but please do not bring any
monkeys. Things are coming down in this country. Hay is
reduced to £5 per ton, Potatoes to £6 per ton, and all garden

produce is so low that it will not pay to take it to Market.
The agitators have done this, raising the cry "Throw open the
lands", "let people with little money have it in their power to
buy". It has been done, and the result is a glut in the markets
and the produce sacrificed, and plenty of the small farmers
ruined. This Summer has been a most beautiful one, so much rain,
which is unusual, but we have been very unlucky in getting in
our hay. It is all damaged, and more than half spoiled
altogether.

I have only just heard of my dear Mother's death, seven months
after the melancholy event took place. I know you will grieve
very much that you did not see her once more before she died, but
Almighty God sways events as he pleases, and we his creatures
must bow in submission.

I hope you will be happy here with us. Write me a letter on
the receipt of this telling me whether you are coming and when,
for you very often change your mind. I have nothing else to
communicate to you, and until we meet

Believe me
Dear Tom
Your very affectionate Sister
C.E. Hepburn

162. *Family bereavements - the new house - Tom's request for
a loan*

Ellen Hepburn to F.M. Bassano   Forest Hill
                                                 16 June 1856

My dear Father
    I received your kind letter of the 18th of Feb[ruar]y about
a fortnight since, and the mournful news it contained was quite
heart-rending to me. I had prepared myself to hear of my poor'
Mother's death. I knew I should never see her again when I
parted with her at Gravesend, and Philip had written how feeble
she had become. But my dear Christopher to be cut off in the
prime of life and in a Strange land, with none but Strangers
to close his eyes! This is indeed a grief. Yet it is a mercy
as they were so soon to follow each other that my dear Mother
was spared the deep affliction that the circumstances of his
death would have caused her. Give my love to Walter and Annie,
and tell them not to grieve for their babe.[7] She is taken
"from the evil to come". She is gone to a bright land of bliss.
Let our prayers be that we may join her there, and let our lives

---

7. Charlotte Ellen (1852-4).

be such that through the redeeming blood of Christ we may have a lively hope in that realization. I am sorry to hear that our cousin Jane has so soon lost her husband. She is about 24 years of age, is she not? Is there property to keep her, and has she any family? Thank you for the promise of the Silver Tankard, but you mistook me about the miniature. I did not ask for it now. I think I said would you kindly will it to me.

I wrote you a letter from Melbourne last March when I was there making purchases for our new house, which we are now occupying. We got all our furniture up without damage – a wonder for this country. We have made our fittings more like the home style than is usual in this country. The usual plan is Cedar doors, Skirting, and Mantel pieces, with rambling hearths to burn long logs of wood. We have our doors and skirtings grained, with mantel pieces of marble, and register stoves. Our furniture came to nearly three hundred pounds. The piano is a very nice one, and in a beautiful walnut wood case. It is [a] great amusement to me during the many hours I have to spend entirely alone.

I am sorry poor Tom does not seem to be making any headway after so many years of toil. He would have made his fortune twice over in the time, had he come to this country. He is just the sort of man for this place, rough and ready. He wrote to ask Benjamin to lend him a thousand pounds about six weeks since. But his money is always being turned over and engaged in business, and [he] had not any unemployed or he would have let him have it. I wish he would sell his plantations and come to us. He would be the gainer, I know, but I do not like to persuade him, in case it might not turn out as we expect.

Benjamin is putting up Sale yards at Ballarat for the disposal of Sheep and Cattle. At present there are not any in the Colony except at Melbourne, and country dealers are obliged to go to Melbourne to buy Stock, and drive them up the country, after the Stock has first been driven into Melbourne out of the country. You may suppose this proceeding materially decreases the weight and deteriorates the quality, and it is thought the Speculation about to be entered into will be a great convenience to the various diggings. Ballarat is 14 miles distant from Forest Hill; that is the worst part of the affair, as it will often take him from home.

Love to all,
Yours affec[tionate]ly
C.E.H.

163. *Do you intend going out to Port Phillip?*

Ronald Farrer to Tom Bassano

On board the Caldera
At sea
30 June 1856

My dear Bassano

I write to you quite on the *chance*, as I know not whether the old boy is dead alive at Manantoddy, or on his way to Australasia. I heard from you last when I was in Melbourne after having been two or three days up at Creswick's Creek with your sister & brother-in-law, Mr. & Mrs. Benj[ami]n Hepburn. Your letter was forwarded to me from Singapore. I wrote you a regular twister & open[e]d you a long yarn.

Do you intend going out to *Port Phillip?* It is a fine climate, & with roughing it at first, and assistance such as y[ou]r brother-in-law has promised, you could be sure to get on, I should think - far better than sticking plants into holes, pruning branches, pulling berries, kissing [*illeg.* - name], & wasting life in an out of the way place amongst wild beasts, savages, & jungle fever.

I have been to Singapore, Batavia, Melbourne, the bush in Victoria, Hobar[t]town & the bush in Van Dieman's Land since I wrote to you, and all over the diggings.

I was married on 24th May and had to hurry away most unpleasantly quick a few days after, on board the Caldera w[hic]h left Melbourne for Madras. She is a splendid large sea boat. We were knocked from hell to hackney off & round the Leeuwin, most infernal squall, & gales of wind rendered two thirds of the passage anything but pleasant for a lady. Now, old boy, I write this on board (with the ship rolling about like a dead whale in a gale of wind) because I know I shall have no time to add more than a line when I get to Madras. Write *soon* and tell me how you are and all news worthy of note & what you *are* & *have* been doing & how you are progressing & what y[ou]r plans are for the future. Now, old boy, Adieu. Write sharp & address me to care of Messrs. Arbuthnot & Co., *Madras*.

Very sincerely yours
Ron[a]ld Farrer

P.S. All sequorum - landed on 13th July - am at *Elphinstone Hotel*, Madras. 17 July.

317

164. *Reasons for the refusal of the loan - Benjamin Hepburn's business affairs*

Ellen Hepburn to Tom Bassano

Forest Hill
16 February 1857

My dear Tom
   I am afraid it is a long time since I wrote to you and I
cannot find your last letter to me. The one before that you
dated Oct[obe]r 55, which I answered as soon as I could, after
receiving it. I think it must have been in May or June last,
and your last letter to me would cross it, which was the reason
I did not write immediately, and since that time one thing or
another has prevented. I hope you will excuse me. I will be
more prompt in future.

   I am very sorry that Benjamin could not lend you the money
you asked for. But I explained to you in answer to the first
letter that I received on the subject that his money was always
employed. He has not any funded property. He buys from a
thousand to two thousand Sheep at a time, whenever an advantageous flock offers. He gives a bill of two or three months
which he has to prepare himself to meet at the appointed time.
He has also bought many land allotments, amongst which is that
on which we live, consisting of 140 acres, and the building of
our house and clearing the land of the timber, making yards,
fencing, and other improvements has cost above £3000. All this
I explained in my last letter to you, but in case it did not
reach you, I repeat it.

   He has also been at other great outlays. This is a very
fluctuating country as I have told you before. There has been
great competition lately amongst holders of Stock, which has
reduced the profits so much that it scarcely pays. My husband
was obliged to shut up his Slaughter yard about a year and a
half since and turn his thoughts to something else, which is as
follows. He has bought a plot of ground in Ballarat on which
he has erected [a] yard for the sale of Cattle which are brought
down from all parts of the Country by Stockholders, and sold by
Auction in these yards, for which my husband charges 7½ per cent.
With the exception of Melbourne and Geelong these yards are the
first established in any part of the country. At present they
seem likely to answer, but if the gold mines in Ballarat should
be exhausted I suppose there would not be any cattle brought
into Ballarat. It was the decrease of gold found in Creswick
that drove the population off and consequently made our business
of no value there.

   My husband entered into the business at Ballarat in conjunc-
tion with a partner who was to put £1000 into the concern, and
when the circular was printed in the name of both, and the
property bought, and additions and alterations made, it is

discovered that this Van Hemert cannot produce his thousand
pounds, so it has caused my husband much trouble and anxiety,
and the affair is not settled. There was an Inn on the ground
that Benjamin thought desirable for his yard, which he was
obliged to buy with the ground, so he lets it to another party
at a rental of £200 per annum. The property cost him £1000 and
other expences to make it fit for business £600, so that he
scarcely knows which way [to] turn himself for money sometimes.
I have written on this circular thinking you might like to see
it.[8]

I trust your health is still good as you have represented it
in these last letters. Write me all about yourself and what you
are doing soon again. Is Mr. Ferrers near you? We did not get
the coffee you were so thoughtful to send for us owing to some
carelessness of our agent with whom Mr. Ferrers left it. It
would have been gratifying to me to have tasted the coffee grown
on your plantation. Do you think of going home some day soon?
What changes we shall see in our family and friendly circles if
we ever return again, shall we not? How dull our Xmas would be
now to what it used to be a long time ago when we were al[l]
together. The last that I spent at home was rather painful, poor
Mother crying nearly all the evening. You and Alfred were in
India, and poor Christopher was on the point of starting. Mother
seemed to have a presentiment that she should never see us all
together again. But ours is not the only circle that has been
cut up. We must bear our lot with resignation and prepare ourselves for a world that changes not for ever and ever.

Your affectionate Sister
Charlotte Ellen Hepburn

165. *"Tom said in his last letter that he had given up all idea*
of coming to this colony"

Ellen Hepburn to Philip Bassano   Forest Hill·
                                                   17 July 1857

My dear Philip
    It is a long time since I wrote to you, and longer still since
you wrote to me. I have been expecting a letter by each mail
for some months past, but have been always disappointed. Pray
write to me on receipt of this, and tell me every particular
concerning yourself, also all you know about our other friends ...

    I received a letter from Father dated December/56 in due time,

---

8. Circular of Hepburn & Van Hemert, Commission Agents for the
   sale of Fat Stock, &c.

also the parcel of newspapers favored by Mr. Collin, I got up
the country a few weeks since. Alfred is a most fortunate young
man to have attained to the rank of Captain at his age. Alway[s]
tell me all you know about him, please, for he and I have never
corresponded. What pay is that of a Captain?

I often receive a nice letter from Tom. He asked Benjamin to
lend him a thousand pounds. I was very grieved to have to refuse
but although my husband has made about ten thousand pounds since
he married me, it is all in use. Much of it is laid out on real
property, and a large amount is always required in his business.
Six weeks since he took a long journey in search of Stock. He
was absent three weeks and purchased two thousand fat Sheep for
the Markets, and a Mob of Store Cattle to put on his run to
fatten - the Sheep at 19/- per head, the cattle at £4 per head,
to be paid for in two and four months, so of course he is
obliged to look about him to find money to meet these bills at
the appointed time. So that you see his business is of such a
nature as to be constantly turning over money, and the markets
are very fluctuating and uncertain in this country, so that these
outlays almost may be called speculations.

I am very sorry I did not persuade Tom to come here three
years since. He would have been a richer man than he is had he
done so, but I was afraid of the responsibility in case he might
find things different to what he expected. Benjamin wished it
very much. He would have been of immense service to him in his
business, but I think one of his own brothers will come out to
him now. Tom said in his last letter that he had given up all
idea of coming to this colony.

Captain Hepburn has just married his eldest son, aged 21, to
a very pretty little woman. They were married in Melbourne
while Benjamin was gone up the country, so we could not be at
the marriage.

I am very comfortable in our new house which I think I
described to you in a previous letter. We have been making
improvements here ever since we bought the land. We shall have
a fine garden and orchard in time, but all is new at present,
and it is exceedingly expensive in this country to get the land
cleared of the native trees and made fit for agriculture. Out
of our five hundred and forty acres at Forest Hill we have only
been able at present to put one hundred and twenty acres under
cultivation. It consists, independent of the garden around our
house, of Barley for hay, Oats, Wheat, and potatoes.

I forget whether I explained to you that Benjamin, in con-
junction with a gentleman of the name of Van Hemert, opened
Cattle Yards in Ballarat last October for the sale of Stock, on
the same principle as the Melbourne yards, viz. to put up Stock
to auction belonging to settlers who bring them in mobs from

off their runs to these sale yards. The charge made to those bringing in their stock for sale is at the rate of 7½ per cent. The average number sold in our yards is about 150 head of cattle per week. The price a beast fetches is from £5 to £14 per head according to quality, so you will see it is answering very well at present. Yet the expences attached to the concern is very great, and more of the cares of the business fall on Benjamin than fairly belong to him in consequence of Mr. Van Hemert being too easy with his men, and not energetic enough for the occasion. Benjamin was much deceived in him or he would never have entered into partnership with him. His object in taking a partner was that he being a single man might transact such branches of the business as called him from home. But as he proves himself to be a man of no judgment Benjamin is obliged to do all himself. The consequence is that I am so often left all alone that I feel quite miserable sometimes. I have filled all my letter, so with best love and prosperity to you all, Believe me,

Your affectionate Sister,
C.E. Hepburn

166. *Return from first visit home*

Tom Bassano to Melinda Bassano
        [Bombay]
        2 October [1857]
        [should be November]

My dear Melinda
    Herein enclosed the list of officers &c. alive & well at Lucknow, when relieved by General Havelock.[9] You can fancy how my hart leaped when I got it. We had a champagne dinner in the evening, at my expence & drank dear little Allie's health and success.

    Things are still in a confused state, and troops slow in coming in. A ship load arrived hear a few days ago, which put the fear out of men's minds *here*, as the sepoys are in a dreadfully mutineer state, and will not believe Delhi has fallen.

    I start for Tellicherry in the Morning, having been detained here untill I could get a horse, they being dear and scarce. I expect Phil will have written about the shipment of my goods, by the mail, but shall not get my letters untill I get down, so will write to him from home when I get down. In Mean[time], dearest Linney, give my love to him, Annie, Children, Walter,

---

9. A cutting from the *Telegraph & Courier*, Bombay, dated 26 October 1857. The envelope is postmarked Bombay, 3 Nov. 1857, and London, 30 Nov. 1857.

and dearest Father, and believe to remain

        Your ever affectionate
        Brother
        Tom

    P.S. A Plesent passage out. I feel happy to say [I] am as
strong and well as ever I was in my life. The run home has done
me a world of good. Love to all

            Your Tom.

168. *Back at work*

Tom Bassano to Melinda Bassano   Manantoddy
                                                  26 December 1857

My dear little Lin
    A merry Xmas and happy New Year to you, dear Father, Annie,
Walter, and the *KIDS* "as W[alter] calls them". Having an hour
to spare in my monstrous pile up of business I thought it could
not be better spent than in writing to you, and getting a letter
ready for the next mail to prevent the possibility of my in any
way being prevented, thereby loosing the mail. And knowing the
great anxiety you and all of you have been in for the safety of
our dear Alfred I enclose you the account of what he has gone
through and what the world say of him, or rather the press of
India. What are his wounds their are as yet no knowing. He
has evidently been wounded as you will see by the enclosed,[10]
but recovered. What dreadfull suspence they must have gone
through during the sigh [*sic* - siege], and how thankfull you and
all of us ought to be to *one*, to think that dear Alf should have
been one of the chosen few to escape. Out of one thousand men
and officer[s] only 300 came out *alive*.

    Tell Fan to write me a line, as also little Did[o], and to
tell me in particular how the dear little Bill is. I often look
and laugh at his portrait. The little buster looks like life
sitting with a half sort of independant pout, as much as to say,
it is very fine sticking me upon this table, but there is something wrong. Or like his look when I used to try to [? prison]
him down. Is Harry at School yet? If not, pitch into Walter
like beens, and say I said so. Don't let him turn out a nother
Bassano dunce.

    I wrote to Phill last mail acknowledging Bills of Lading,
which I trust has been received. Also asking you to send out a

---

10. From *The Bangalore Herald.*

opy of my portrait. See that this is complied with, as also
ad's portrait, if you have bounced him to sit for it. With best
ove to all, believe me, dear Lin, your affectionate Brother

T.B. Bassano

P.S. Send me by return of post a 1/6^d map, Abington's
anoramic view map of India, for Capt. Brennen. Don't fail.

P.S. Small seeds (red ones), Wild Ginger, a pretty leaf and
lower. TBB

P.S. Seeds of a splendid creeper. Give to Mrs. Osborn with
ay regards. TBB. *POISON*

P.S. I have just return[e]d from a Xmas feed 32 miles off at
a planter's welcome to my return to India. Merry Xmas to Phill.

P.S. [inside envelope - torn] ... don't be in a fright ...
[Alfred] though wounded ... getting all *RIGHT*.

III

"I THOUGHT I MIGHT AS WELL TAKE A RUN OVER TO SEE TOM"
(Alfred & Tom Bassano, 1858)

168. *"Here I am ... [having] already accomplished thirteen
hundred miles of the distance ..."*

Alfred Bassano to Philip Bassano   Madras Club
                                                    13 May 1858

My dear Phil
    Here I am, not very ill, but with Six Months sick leave in my
pocket to visit the Neilgherry Hills. Our Regiment had got out
of the Fighting, so I thought I might as well take a run over to
see Tom, and have already accomplished thirteen hundred miles of
the distance, having five hundred more to go, which I can do, if
I like, in four or five days. Not a bad idea going eighteen
hundred miles to see a fellow, but Tom is always writing to me
to come & see him, having about as much knowledge of geography
as a Tom Cat, just as if I could get into a Railway train after
breakfast and be set down at his door for dinner, at an expense
of about a sovereign. Instead of which I had to run the
gauntlet of 2000 of the Ennemy under Koor Sing[h],[11] travel day

---

11. Koer Singh, rebel commander, led fresh rising in Bihar in
    April 1858; died of wounds 24 April 1858. He was 80 years
    old.

& night by horse Dawks, bullock carts, river Steamers, boats,
P. & O. Steamer for 700 Miles by sea, Railways for short broken
distances, pitching you out in jungles, horses, foot, &c., &c.,
at an expense of only about something under £100.

I sent Father home one hundred pounds about a Month ago, in
part payment of the debt I owe to you & him. As I don't know
the proportions you and Father gave me, or indeed the total
amount, you must settle it between you whenever I make a
remittance. I have paid Linney by draft on Cox & Co., so that
is settled. Se[e] if he has rec[eive]d it all right. I could
send you home 50£ now, but want to see Tom first, as he wants
money to work the plantation, and says you would have no objection to my giving it to him on your account.

I have paid all my debts in this country, which were pretty
extensive, and only owe £26 in England, barring yourself, and am
expecting another 6 months batta immediately (£100), and *£1500*
prize money for Lucknow. Don't you wish I may get it?

I see they have made me a Major, but I expect Gen. Inglis to
get me something more than that, as I commanded the Regiment for
nearly two Months of the Siege.

Give my love to all at home & tell Fan Fan it is very unkind
of her never to write to me.

Your affectionate brother
Alfred

169. *"I have had my horses posted for him ever so long ... and
by jove he has not come ... I have not a nerve left"*

Tom Bassano to Melinda Bassano   Bleak House
                                               31 May [1858]

My dear Lin
    I send you herewithin enclosed a Maltese lace collar. The
sleavs to match I will send you by the next mail. I also send
you 2 little gold coins. I have no end of coins to add to your
collection if I could but send them. A lot I dug out of the
Catacombs at St. Paul's cave, Malta.

    Little Alf is somewhere near here. He landed in Madras on
the 11th May, Passed through Bangalore on the 18th or 20th,
since which time I have lost sight of him, he being like all the
rest of you too lazey to write, or else like the greater part
of the world seem to live for yourself and any occasionally
passing vanity. He wrote from Calcutta to say he would be with
me as fast as steam and rail would carry him. I have had my

horses posted for him ever so long, one 80 miles away since [the] 11th, the other since the 15th, and a borrow[ed] one also since the 15th. Kept cooking no end of grub, expecting to see him ride in every minute, and by jove, he has not come. I never passed such an anxious fortnight in my life. I have not a nerve left. However, I have now recalled 2 Horse[s] and given him up. I suppose he [is] sight seeing somewhere, quite jolley. Will write you again when I hear from him, or else make him do so.

Death has been thinning out our small community during the last fortnight. Poor Richmond being one of his victims, the man who looked after my property durin[g] my absence, the other Mr. O'Loughlan, an old and worthy planter - the former a great loss to me, being my Neighbour, and my first chum in Wynaad in 1847, a real good fellow. But it is always the case, the good go first.

I wrote Phill on 9th March, & 23rd. Have received his of 16th April. Will answer in a few days. Love to Father and Annie, Walter & children, and believe [me]

Your affection[ate] Brother
Tom

The Medicines from Apotchery [*sic* - Apothecaries] Hall going off well. Sold 620 Rupees worth - stood me in here 749 Rs. Have 500 Rs. on hand.

170. *"I was greatly surprised to find you had been home"*

Ellen Hepburn to Tom Bassano   Forest Hill
                                                17 June 1858

My dear Tom
    I received your affectionate letter written in Jan[uar]y last about three months since. I should have answered it sooner but for a string of misfortunes which have overtaken us. On the second of March, Benjamin was thrown from his horse and broke his leg. He lay six weeks on his back in the same position, and suffered very much part of the time, indeed I may say all the time, for nothing could be more trying to an active man than to be obliged to be so long without being allowed to move. You may be sure I was fully employed all the time, for the first week the leg required being constantly bathed night and day without intercession, and I never went to bed during that period. And all through his illness he kept me so much engaged that I could not find an hour to write to you. And then when he was allowed to get up he of course walked on crutches and was quite helpless, so that I had to go about with him everywhere in his buggy to assist him. Today is the first day I have trusted him by himself,

and I take the opportunity of writing to you.

A few weeks after he met with his accident, some thieves broke into the office belonging to his cattle yards in Ballarat and stole cash box, value three hundred pounds in cash, besides various documents.

On the first day of May our Barn was set fire to, by a good for nothing darkie, a native of Bombay, whom we had had in our employ for some time. Our harvest was in and the wheat and oats threshed and stored in the barn, which was built of sawn timber, and of course soon burnt down with all the grain and two valuable machines. The loss is estimated at about two thousand pounds.

Benjamin has also made many bad debts in the cattle yards, and considers his losses in the last twelve months to amount to £5000.·

The Blackfellow came to us without any engagement and when he was going away Benjamin said to him "there is £7 due to you as a Balance" which was at the rate of £40 a year, besides his food, but he was not satisfied, and said he thought he was working for a pound a week, the same as the other men were getting, but Benjamin told [him] he did not work half his time, and must be paid accordingly, but this did not meet his views, and so he set fire to the barn. He is in custody, and there is strong circum-stantial evidence against him, and it is supposed his sentence will be fourteen years on the roads.

I was greatly surprised to find you had been home. I never received the letter you wrote me before leaving India, and I was wondering why you were so long silent. Everything you wrote me was new to me. I had been watching the papers, and could never meet with anything relative to the 32nd, and after you wrote me about Alfred I dropped upon a slight mention of the regiment once or twice, but I am very much in the dark about it. I have just received a letter from Phil, who mentions that Alfred is a Major and that his regiment will soon be returning home, but he supposes that I have seen all about him in the papers.

Now I should like you to write and give me the whole history of Lucknow from beginning to end, for I cannot make it out. I thought the English were besieged in it, but this Mail's papers talk of the rebels having made good their retreat out of Lucknow.[12]

---

12. Siege of Lucknow 1 July–17 November 1857; garrison evacuated 22 November 1857 and city abandoned to rebels; Lucknow re-captured 21 March 1858.

You seem to be highly pleased with your visit home. How
wonderful it is that Father should not have changed in so many
years. He is still very well, Philip writes word. He has sent
me plenty of news and seems in excellent spirits, and says our
oldest niece Fanny has overtopped her Aunt Melinda. You seem to
be very much pleased with the children. So was poor Chris when
he went home. He wrote me a very nice letter from Scutari just
before his death, and gave me an account of the two eldest, who
seemed to have particularly taken his fancy.

I am glad you talk of coming to see me, but could you not
manage it in less than three years? I should think you might put
affairs in order and set things going, and then run over for a
few months and back again. Try what you can do, will you? I
should be so delighted to see you. Write often please, because
this war in India makes me so fidgety about your safety. I hear
Mr. Farrers has sent his wife to Melbourne, so I suppose he
expects to be in the fight. What a miserable state of things.

Never mind about sending me the coffee. I will wait till you
come and bring it yourself. I trust your consignments, that
Philip speaks of, will turn out profitable. You are going to
open up 50 acres for him too, he tells me. He says you were
looking very well.

I think it must be two years since he has written to me until
the present letter came. So be sure you give me all the home
news whenever you write, for I do not know how long I may have
to wait for another from him. I suppose I must make an end, so
with kind love

Believe me
Dear Tom
Your affectionate Sister
C.E. Hepburn

171. *"I have been laid up in bed for the last ten days ... don't
make arrangements for my coming yet"*

Alfred Bassano to Tom Bassano   Ootacamund
                                                 1 July 1858

My dear Tom,
    I have at last succeeded in getting Dawson to send off 4 cooly
loads of potatoes & one of bacon to your address. The 6 yards of
fine flannel accompanies the bacon. Let me know if the things
arrive all right & whether there is anything else I can send you.
I think the Coolies started the day before yesterday, if not
previously, but I have been laid up in bed for the last ten days
and don't remember exactly. Don't make arrangements for my

coming yet, as I am awfully shaken & fearfully weak & doubled up, but the Doctor seems to think I shall soon pick up again.

It is stated in the papers that the 32nd go home this cold season, in which case I shall bid adieu to India, probably for ever. Even if they do not go I shall, on two years leave, which I am sure to be able to get under present circumstances.

You cannot run up here, I suppose, at present, on account of your numerous plantation duties, but take the first opportunity. I am heartily sick of this place now & should be very glad to get to Manantoddy, but am afraid I shall not be able to move for some time. It is always the same with me; after one really good bout of sickness I like to get away from the place where I was laid up as soon as possible.

Good news today from Bengal: the Gwalior Rajah placed on his throne again & the niggers polished off in all directions by our Brigades.[13]

Goodbye. I am too sick & seedy to write a decent or cheerful letter.

Your affectionate brother
Alfred

P.S. The Doctor has put me on a short allowance of food, stopped all lush but water, & put my pipe out. If that is not enough to make a poor beg[ga]r miserable, I don't know what is. I shall mutiny soon. I don't think you have anything to pay the Coolies, as I told Dawson to settle everything & charge it in my bill, which he promised to do.

172. *"I am now beginning to wind up my affairs in order to pay you a visit"*

Alfred Bassano to Tom Bassano   Ootacamund
                                                  14 July 1858

My dear Tom
    I am all right again & as hearty as a Turk, in fact never was in better health. I am glad you got the bacon & potatoes, but you do not mention the flannel I sent as having arrived safe. I am trying to get you the boots, but have not yet succeeded.

Your news about the Governor made me laugh for hours, altho' of course I am damnably annoyed for Lin's sake, and trust it

---

13. Gwalior was re-captured from the rebels on 20 June 1858.

will not come off.[14]

So, you are going to make a fortune in 3 years. Bravo! Go it, you cripples!

I am now beginning to wind up my affairs in order to pay you a visit, which I hope to be able to do about the latter end of the Month, but will give you positive intelligence in ample time for you to make arrangements about the horses. I am up to my ears in business, as the Calcutta Agency Houses are all shaking & I am trying to avoid losing my little savings during the Campaign, which is in a Calcutta firm. Allan Duffell & Co. have already stopped payment, by which lots of my friends are sufferers, but my banker still holds out shaky.

No news here. Raining like blazes.

Your affectionate brother
Alf Bassano

173. *"Here I am ... only about 80 miles from Tom's place"*

Alfred Bassano to Philip Bassano

Union Hotel
Ootacamund
Neilgherry Hills
18 July 1858

My dear Phil
Here I am, on six Months leave, only about 80 Miles from Tom's place. I have been too seedy to go & see him yet, but think I shall make a start of it next week as I am now as strong as a Bengal tiger, with the appetite of a boa constrictor & if the *Light Infantry* have any more fighting, I think I shall be able to smite niggers to some tune.

How I laughed the other day, when I heard from Tom that the Governor wanted to get married again. It is a delicious joke, and glorious idea, altho' of course I am very much annoyed for Lin's sake & hope it will not come off.

Did Father get the 100£ I sent him some Months ago, & Linney the Tailor £48 - the amount of his bill - also Fan Fan £10 to buy little Alfred a christening cup?

I rec[eive]d your letter of April & sent you a line from

---

14. See Letters 174-6. F.M. Bassano (aged 72) married in late 1858 Susan, the daughter of his first wife's older half-sister and therefore a cousin of the Bassano children.

Madras, which I hope has reached you all right. With regard to Wyndham's[15] business, he does not deserve half the abuse heaped upon him, as he was one of the few at Cawnpore who was not in an awful funk. One Officer of rank retired from the building he was posted in, a very important position which should have been held to the last, because *one round shot* hit the building. And then the Recruits the Authorities have been sending out lately, perfectly undrilled & the damndest set of cowards in creation. I would sooner fight with 50 of my old veterans than five hundred of them. It is a well known fact here that one old Indian Regiment is worth three of your Crimean heroes.

I have been very hardly used, as I commanded the Regiment for the last two Months of the Siege of Lucknow & have got no honor conferred upon me. However, I have written to Gen. Sir J. Inglis on the subject & expect to get something additional yet, as he was pleased to say I com[mande]d the Reg[imen]t as well as he ever wished to see it commanded & showed me a letter to the Duke of Cambridge in which he mentioned me in the most handsome manner

Rumour says the 32nd L[ight] I[nfantry] return home in the cold season, also that we are to get a second Battalion, which will probably give me my full Majority. What excitement and rapid promotion! Depend upon it there is nothing like a bloody war for a poor man. You are either shot, or shot up to the upper grades with great rapidity. If our Reg[imen]t is not to have any more fighting, I shall probably return home the latter end of this year, as I have now won my spurs & think I could live at home on my pay with tolerable comfort.

Love to Lin, Annie, &c. &c.

Your affectionate brother
Alfred

P.S. Remember me to all my kind friends at the C[ommander] in C[hief's] Office, War Office, &c. &c., particularly to Leonard Coleman.

[Written on the inside of the envelope]

These War stories are very long-winded ones & cannot be told in letters. Besides there are so many imbecile old fools of high rank generally implicated in all disasters which makes it dangerous to express opinions, for fear of your friends showing the letters.

---

15. Maj. Gen. Windham who had been defeated by the rebels near Cawnpore, 28 November 1857.

174. *"Fancey dear Alfred being on the Hills and I not yet seen him"*

Tom Bassano to Melinda Bassano

Bleak House
25 July 1858

My dear Lin
    Having an hour to spare I cannot put it to better account than to write to you too cheer you up after the awfull disclosure of Phill's last letter regarding the funney old Governor. What a start for the old boy to take. But I knew he was up to that sort of thing from my first visit home. Don't you know how I told you of his [*illeg.*] in omnibus &c.? Knowing old card, so close with it. Tell Phill to kid him on down to Teddington and their Fortify the home as Admiral Tronion[16] did in Peregrine Pickle. All I can say is kid Anni[e], Walter, the Children &c. &c. on to declare they will cut him, if he gets up to the larks any more, as it won't do. I am sure he or any of us would not be so jolley if the Governor is to play the fool in that sort of way. However, I hope and trust there is no feer now, as Phill says.

    Fancey dear Alfred being on the Hills and I not yet seen him. I send you a few of his letters to cheer you up. Hope to see him heer in a few days.

    Planting and rushing about my severel plantations keeps me pretty well employed, as this is the busy time. I wrote Phill a long letter sending a/c of Estate, &c. Kiss the Children for me and give them my love. Hope they are getting on in their Classes. I wish they would send me a letter now and then. I sometimes think you are all very unkind, but I suppose it is not so, mearly however, the old thing over again; a letter once a year, you all seem to think is enough. I should like a letter once a month, telling me about the Children, their pleasure trips, &c. &c., and how Harry is getting on. Is he going to be a coffee planter, have a nice horse to ride and a splendid country to gallop about in? If so, tell him to get on at school, for he can come out at 14 or 15 year old, in fact, as soon as his Father, the honor'd Wt is willing.

    Remember me to Alfred & Jane Wooster, and how is little Trottey getting on, and the other small fry? Tell Alfred I shall be glad to do business in coffee for him or any of his friends, so send him an estimite.

    Baring Brother & Co. have writ off 10,000£ for Wynaad Coffee, the Man Reed being their Bla[ck]guard agent, the Fellow w[h]o stole my land when over in England. However I think they [*sic*]

---

16. Commodore Trunnion, in *Peregrine Pickle* by Tobias Smollett (1751).

way he is going to work he will, like bigger men have done before him, come to grief. He is surrounded by all the rif[f] raf[f] of the district. Of course, with lots of money to spend [he] cut[s] rather a swell.

Many thanks to you & Annie for sending Portraits, or rather sitting for them. They are jolley, but why [do] you look serious? You should laugh when the portrait is being taken, thinking at the same time you are looking and laughing at the person you are going to send it to.

With love to Annie, Walter, Father, Phill, and all of you, and Believe me ever to remain

Your affectionate
Brother Thom

A Pair of cuffs and gold coins. I must send the copper ones home with Alfred - too heavy to send by letter.

Did you receive my last dated May 30th 1858?

175. *Tom's plan for Melinda to join him, and a proposal to Miss King*

Tom Bassano to Melinda Bassano   Bleak House, Sunday
n.d. [July 1858]

My dear Lin
I have just heard from Phil that the Governor is determined to marry Susan. But surely it is not a proper thing to do? At all events, if he has resolved to do so, let him in God's name. But before doing so make him the following Propositions. That he gives you the outfit of a Ladie, pays your passage out to Cannanore to me; makes you a present of 500£, which you can lend to me at int[e]rest of 10 per cent, and with the said 500 in your pocket to pay on my account ask Miss King, the Eldest, if she will have me for a husband and bring her out with you, also her Brother, the Biggest Boy, that nice Lad the mother was looking about to get out into the world. He shall, if bound to me for 5 Year, get 25£ advanced for his passage out, the same to be deducted out of his pay.

1st Year he shall have 40Rs. per month	A House to live in, a
2 do 40	horse to ride, one
3 do 50	servant, and Horse
4 do 70	expences paid for. He
5 do 80	can live like a gentle-
	man on the named sums,
	would

be living 5 miles away from you and his sister, and could ride in of an evening whenever he liked. I say the 500£ to you to cover all my expences, for my House heer will require making larger, and would cost me 1000Rs. However, Lin, you would at once be settled in the world, but it would make my residence then in India certain for 10 years, in the mean time your 500Rs. [*sic*] would have been repaid you and could be in the shape of a pretty Estate of 50 acres, giving you an independance. Besides, a month's residence in Wynaad would find you a husband. Put this to the Governor, and [I] am sure he will do it for his youngest daughter provided you concur in my propositions, and Miss King &c. If not, your arrangements can stand good, and I will look to you to propose to someone else, or name someone else, but of all the girls I saw in England, Miss King appeared to me the most jolley for a wife.

Remember me to all the children, and best love also [to] Annie, Walter & all friends. How is little Trottey, Woosters little two shoes?

Your affectionate Brother
T.B. Bassano

176. *Melinda's reply to the above*

Melinda Bassano to Tom Bassano   Stamford Villas
                                                    Fulham
                                                    4 February 1859

My dear Tom
    I am no end of letters in your debt, but I will endeavour to be a better correspondent now that I am more comfortable in my mind than I have been from one cause or another for a very long time. I believe I have never thanked you for the pretty Maltese collar & sleeves you were so kind as to send me. I have worn them a good many times, & they have been very much admired.

As to your last letter, I was on a visit to the Gaffneys when I received it, & could not of course do anything in the affair until I returned, & also being very much astonished, I was anxious to consult Philip & Walter before writing to you, as I hardly knew how to act. I very warmly approve of your choice, for Miss King is the nicest girl I know, & if she will accept you, nothing would give me greater pleasure than to have such a sister, but I think the proper thing for you to do would be to write to her yourself. Besides, the offer appears to be dependent on so many other circumstances that I do not quite understand in case I cannot fulfil your money arrangement (& I am quite sure Papa will give me nothing) whether your proposal to Miss King still stands good.

Papa and Susan were married three months ago, of course
greatly to our disgust and annoyance. I packed up everything
of my own & poor Mamma's as soon as the intelligence reached me
& sent them together with my piano to Walter's, where I have been
staying ever since. Philip asked me to live with him at Tedding-
ton, but as we did not expect Papa would get married until March,
Philip had put some[one] into his house to take care of it.
Papa refused to make any settlement of his money upon us. Phil
pressed him to settle a thousand upon us, for me to draw the
interest for Papa's lifetime, but he would not have it at all,
but agreed to make me an allowance of £30 a year. I think he
ought to have given me £50, but of course he is under Susan's
influence, & I don't trouble myself much about it. I parted on
good terms with him, & Annie & I went the day before yesterday to
see him. I thought he was looking rather thin, poor old gentleman. He seemed pleased to see us, & promised to come & give the
children a look.

I have not seen the Kings since I heard from you, & will not
mention it to them until I hear further from you.

I have just seen an official account of Alfred's wound & find
it is much more severe than he led us to suppose. I am afraid
he is lame. Tell me in your next letter whether it is so or not,
& be sure you write by the next mail.

Annie & all the children send their love to you. The younger
ones are growing very fast, Frances not quite so much lately.
She & Dido are going to a party on Monday & Harry is getting on
very nicely at school now. He is going with me this afternoon
to see the Woosters. The baby is a year old today - he is such
a fine little fellow. I don't know if anyone has told you he
is named after our dear Chris, & I am to be his godmother. He
is registered but not christened yet.

Be sure you write directly you receive this, for although I
don't write much it is not that I don't very very often think of
my absent brothers, & long to hear from them - & so with kind
love, believe me dear Tom

Your ever affectionate Sister
Melinda

I have omitted to tell you that Phil & Walter think you
should take time for a little consideration before you propose
to Miss King, as your letter to me seems rather hastily written,
& as it is the first intimation you have given us we are afraid
it might have been a sudden thought on your part, & so you must
write again & tell me if you are still in the same mind.

Ellen Hepburn to Tom Bassano

Forest Hill
10 August 1859

My dear Brother
  I received your kind letter of September 15th. I am ashamed
of having taken so long to answer it, but I have been in such
bad spirits lately that I have not had the heart to set about
anything. Benjamin's business in Ballarat is greatly on the
increase, which takes him from home for four or five days at a
time, then home again for two and three days only, then off again.
It is so very uncomfortable that I have been fretting now for a
long time, and that has impaired my sight and is telling upon me
in other ways.

  I received a letter from Philip in Oct[obe]r last communicating
the intelligence of our old Father's marriage with Susan. I think
it is a very unkind act towards his children, especially to
Melinda, also a great weakness to have allowed an artful and bold
woman to cajole him as she has. Philip said it was probable that
he should take Melinda to keep his house for him.

  I trust you are getting on again and making plenty of money at
Coffee planting. Mind and keep your promise, viz. pay us a visit
as soon as you can put things in the proper order to leave. You
will like Benjamin very much. I know he sees things in very much
the same way as you do, and he can work as hard as you can too.
He has got rid of his Spendthrift partner and carries on the
business of Cattle Commission agent by himself.

  Where is Mr. Far[r]ers now? I heard some time since that he
had sent his wife to Melbourne for the benefit of her health.
The war in Europe has put the inhabitants of this country in a
great state of alarm, for if anything should happen which should
oblige England to take any part against the French Emperor, it is
here thought, that the French fleet stationed at New Caledonia
(an Island not far distant from Australia) would immediately come
down upon us, and we have not the means of defence against them.

  I suppose Alfred has returned home before this. He did not
write to me again after he left you. Do not serve me as I have
served you, but write to me soon telling me all you know from
home, for I have not heard anything these ten months ... I do
not think there is anything more at present to tell you about, so
with best love

                    Believe me
                    Dear Tom
                        Your affec[tiona]te Sister
                        Ellen Hepburn

178. *A hero's return*

Morning Star, Wednesday, September 14th, 1859

Banquet to the Heroes of Lucknow   Dover
                                                    Tuesday evening

   Today the people of Dover did honour to the three hundred
gallant officers and men of the 32nd Regiment, who landed at
Portsmouth a fortnight since, direct from the scene of their
endurance in India, and who were received, as then reported, with
an enthusiasm almost unparalleled in the quiet town of Dover.
The *fête* embraced a dinner to the men ... and a light refection
to the officers ... Among the officers present, who withstood
the siege of Lucknow, were Lieutenant-Colonel Lowe, C.B.;
Brevet-Major Bassano, Brevet-Major Lawrence, Brevet-Major Foster,
Captain Harmar, Dr. Boyd, and Quartermaster Stribling. They
occupied the centre of the table, being faced on the opposite
side by Lieutenant-Colonel Carmichael, who, as senior officer,
is in command of the regiment, and surrounded by their brother
officers, every officer of the regiment, except those on leave,
being present ...

   Colonel Carmichael, C.B., replied as follows: ...

I have been deputed to convey to you the earnest thanks of
Lieut. Colonel Lowe, C.B., of Major Bassano (who both commanded
the regiment during the siege) ...

336

CHAPTER NINE

Success and retirement
(Tom Bassano 1858-76)

In the ten years following his meeting with his brother Alfred, Tom Bassano achieved some success in his business ventures, getting out of coffee before the crash, and setting up as an agent in Tellicherry. He went home in 1862, and six years later, after visiting his sister Ellen in Australia, he left India for the last time, reaching England towards the end of 1868. He was then 47 years old and had lived in India for 24 years - in the Wynaad for 21 years.

After a period of riotous living in London, he went to settle in France where he lived for most of the rest of his life, first in Paris, then Boulogne and Le Havre. He hired a yacht in which he sailed across the channel to visit his family and friends, and if a letter from his nephew Alfred is to be believed, he even sailed to New York. At the same time he kept up his business interests in India.

I

"AN INDIAN MERCHANT PRINCE"
(Tom Bassano 1858-68)

179. *"... here is a go ... 1260£ sterling* [sent] *and no receipt or acknowledgements ..."*

Tom Bassano to Walter Bassano

Bombay
27 October [1860]

Dear Walter

I have written a letter to Phil today, sent via Marseilles to War Office, enclosing Bill to amount of 700£ sterling on Oriental Bank, London, made payable to P.H. Bassano. See if he receives it, and if not, stop payment.

I send also 2nd of Exchange of a Bill for 350£: the 1st of

same tenor and date was sent direct to P.H. Bassano by Oriental Bank. See if he has received it also.

I also sent Alfred 110£, one hundred and ten pounds sterling, by a Bill direct by Bank &c., open in his favour: second was sent to Phil. No acknowledgement yet to hand.

I also sent P.H. Bassano a Bill for 100£ in his favour, 1st of Exchange sent by Oriental Bank Agent Bombay. No receipt has been sent. So here is a go: Alf   110£
                                    Phil   100
                                    Phil   350
                                    Phil   700 now sent
                                    —————
                                    1260£ sterling, and no receipt
or acknowledgements. See to this, and drop me a line.

I am rather seedy, and up here looking for $2\frac{1}{2}$ [? $9\frac{1}{2}$] tons of coffee which is been made away with or something.

Give my love to Annie, who with the kids I trust are well, as also yourself.

Your affectionate Brother
Tom Bassano

180. *Returning to India from home leave*

Tom Bassano to niece Melinda (Dido) Bassano   Off Sicily
                                                     Sunday 2 p.m.
                                                     [1862]

Dear Dido
I write to say we shall be in at Malta at 12 o'clock tonight and away again at 4 in the morning, so you must not look for the lace collars as it will be impossible for me to go on shore so late, and only to find the shops shut, so I must try and remember them on my way home again, which I dare say will be one of these fine days. I am happy to say I am harty and well. The bright sun and pleasant weather has made me quite jolly.

I think I answered your long and interesting letter from Marseilles – am not sure however, and it is in my box in the Hold so cannot refer to it to see if "answered" is written across it or not. I had to write so many letters at Marseilles, sending remittances &c. to India, so don't be surprised at my not remembering if you were included in the correspondence.

I am glad you got the letter and its enclosure from Paris ... I also note what you say about the poor dear baby. Do you really

ean to say Frances pinches her! How very cruel if she does.
you know I have seen it cry sometimes when F[rances] had her.
, but surely it cannot be. Rubbish. You don't mean it.

If the Paris man does not send you the Cart[e], write him,
nd don't neglect to send the 2 copies to Mrs. Steven. Remind
an.

I shall expect you to write me all the news whenever you can
nd half an hour idle and want a little amusement. You ought
have a little desk always at hand and make it an amusement,
t a toil as some young people of my acquaintance do, and always
emember a letter from Home is gratefully received and appreciated.
the same time recollect that a man in Business in India has an
mmense correspondence to keep up, which causes toil & thought
nd does not allow of delay in answering, and should your [letter]
t be answered as soon as you might expect don't let that be an
xcuse for not writing often. I have only myself to write about,
hich would not be amusing. You have your home, England, and lots
f friends, all subjects which would make up a letter at any time,
e mear telling me of them &c.

I wrote your A[u]ntie Melinda from Marseilles, which I hope
e got. Kindly tell her I did not succeed in getting the letter
e mentioned, addressed to the Vectris. I went on board and
nquired for it. The Illustrated I got, but no Punch – the
mperor won't allow them in France.

By all ac[c]ount what severe weather you have had in England.
should not have liked it much, I fear, just as well I got away
en I did. The dreadful gales in the Mediterranean have played
e mischief amongst the shipping, and the French murdered two
ngineers belonging to the Man of War Steamer ... which was
aiting at Marseilles for Lady Elgin, a dreadfull, cowedley
ffair. I could scarcely believe it when I heard the matter, as
e place is so quite [sic] and well conducted as a shipping
rt. I was quite pleased with it. It only shows that notwith-
tanding the outward show of civility, that ill feeling really
xists amongst the Frenchmen towards the English in the parts of
ance away from Paris.

Ask Fanny to write me a letter soon, and in all your letters
t me know how Harry get[s] on. Dwell particularly on the
bject. Also about the little ones. And with love to all

I remain
Your affectionate Uncle
T.B. Bassano

339

Tom Bassano to niece Frances Bassano   Off Aden
                                                17 December 1862

My dear Fan
    I have written two letters this morning and as it is getting
warm I must away on deck, but as I have not written to you since
I left, I cannot think of leaving my pen untill I complete a
small yarn to you, just to tell you I am so well, Fan, really
well, and quite myself again. If I keep in such jolly health
and spirits I don't think I shall be coming home again in a few
months as I had intended. I hope, Fan, you are enjoying yoursel
and having a jolly Xmas, and Happy new year to you and all of
you, and my best love.

    The ship I am on board of is such a beauty, and such nice
people. We manage to get up a dance of an evening and a song.
Everyone seems to be desirious of enjoying themselves and adding
to the enjoyment of others, without which their can be no
pleasure in this life.

    I hope, Fan, you will write me now and again and give me all
the news of home and the kids, how they progress. Also send a
sketch of Alf's now and then to see how he gets on - just one of
the pieces of paper he scribbles on of an evening, without his
knowing you do so. When does he intend despatching his first
letter to me? Keep a memo of post account, all the sixpences,
and make Uncle Bill pay for them. Give him the letters to post
- the best way, as posting letters to India is expensive to the
public, if I am to get many letters, and you all have so many
ways for your little means.

    Remember me kindly to Madamosell and I trust, dear Fan, you
continue to improve in your studies. Hold yourself up, and
cultivate pretty fingers, that I may have the pleasure of
embel[l]ishing them with another pretty ring some of these fine
days.

    Continue to love Miss Brown, and take all she says and does
for your good. How jolly it would be if we could always be
young and have kind friends to guide us for our good. Don't
neglect going to Church under any pretext whatever, once a day
at least, and take one of the little kids with you if opportunity
admits, remembering that the inclination displayed in your little
brothers that way should be fostered, as it will be a comfort to
them in after life. Depend upon it, there is nothing, dear Fan,
more consoling and cheering through life than a moral, religious
feeling instilled into us when young by those old enough to know
the value of it.

    Have you got my portraits yet, and have you sent them to

persons also? Did you send your[s] & Dido['s] to Mrs Stevens?

I had not an opportunity to send you any lace collars from
Malta, as the Ship got there at night and no shops open, so must
bring you some when I come home. Write me for anything you want,
and with Best Love, dear Fan, Believe me,

Your affectionate Uncle
T.B. Bassano

P.S. Kind love to your Mama & Papa, Dido & little ones. TBB

P.S. My kindest regards to the Miss Ramsey of course. Dwell
particularly on it when mentioning it to the one with the Brown
hair - I always forget her name.

182. *Arrival at Bombay*

Tom Bassano to Walter Bassano   Bombay
                                                 26 December 1862

My dear Walter
    I arrived here yesterday at Eleven o'clock and went straight
to Friend Forman, who was delighted to see me back, but [I] got
a great wiggin[g] from Mrs. Forman for not coming back married
- spent a pleasant Xmas with them all, so I did not get my
pudding boiled, as the Baggage was not passed through the custom
house untill today. I start on Monday 29th for [the] Coast, so
will be at sea on the new year's day and will have it boiled
then instead.

I had a most delightful passage out, fine and delightful
weather all the way, and feel quite up to the 5 years stay at
Money Making. All my affairs have been progressing most
satisfactory. Bleak House still [? lett] and all the Estate
work going on well.

I have been at it since 10 oclock, opening and reading
letters - L. & Co. office was full of them - 100 at least, such
a job. I am now [in a] hurry to get home with Forman, so Love
to Annie, who with the girls & kids I trust are well, and love
to all.

Believe me
Dear Walter
Your affec[tiona]te Brother
Tom

Love to Lin. Tell her I have no time to write her by this
mail. TBB.

183. *About a clock belonging to "a very swell native Friend of
mine" sent to London for repair – his coffee estates and
agency business – his "splendid house" at Tellicherry*

Tom Bassano to Walter Bassano   Tellicherry
                                                     25 June 1863

My dear Walter
     I wrote to Bill a couple of months ago, asking him if he would
see to a clock which I had shipped in the Morayshire, the Bill of
Lading of which I handed to Bennett, and took his receipt for it,
which I now enclose you, also a bill I paid them on the same
date. It will make things *more certain*, if they want to
repud[i]ate the signature of Mr. Dean. Now this clock belongs to
a very swell native Friend of mine and I am really ashamed of not
being able to tell him anything about it. The Clock was an old
fashioned box clock, striking the houres and qua[r]ters &c., and
was made by Barraud, Cornhill, about 18 inches high, and 8 broad.
I left written instructions at Bennett's of what I wanted done
to the Clock, and when repaired he was to pack it and ship it to
my address, and draw on me for the money, or else write me and
say the clock was done, bill so much, and I would send him the
amount, and order him to deliver the clock packed to Messrs.
Forbes & Co. for shipment, or give them the Bill of Lading.[1]

     Now Walter, kindly find out what is wrong and write me a line
by next mail just to say "Clock all right and is coming",
"Bennett's have it in hand', or how. John Ryle will find out in
a Minute by applying to Lloyds if the Morayshire arrived in
London, and the Bill of Lading, if not lost, will soon produce
the Clock, or else the owners are liable for its cost. Any
expence you may be put too, charge me with, drawn on Bill for a
few Pounds. But let's have the Clock, or else purchase me
another and send by ship (that is, if the other is really lost).
If you purchase me another, write me first to say the other is
lost, and I will describe the sort of one required. I shall be
much obliged to you if you will promptly attend to this, as I
have a great respect for the owner.

     If the clock has turned up Bennett had to reveneer it, gold
gild the brass bindings and beading work, in fact to fit it up
very well with double gilt work, rosewood veneering &c., &c.,
like a very swell musical Box I got from Paris, which cost me
40£. The bells were to be renewed, if not high toned. One of
them, an iron one, to be replaced with a high toned brass one –
a Glass Cover to Clock, and a Pedistal in Blackwood and velvet.[2]

     Write me something about it. I dare say the ship has been

---

1. There is a small drawing of the clock "value 800Rs".
2. There is a small drawing showing cover and pedestal.

lost, and I do not believe the thing was insured. It will be
necessary to send me the Bill of Lading back here for me to
recover Insurance in Bombay, for I do not know but that Capt.
Forman has insured.

Now to other matters. I am very well and awfully jolly.
Found the Est[at]es all right on my return, and found the young
men disgusted at my returning. Young Smith has murdered the
Berghery Estate, the young sweep; overdrew his account some
hundreds of rupees above his pay, and seduced his writer's
Sister, and I believe he won't shake her off in a hurry. He
ow[e]s me fully 50£, the advance money, which I cannot get out
of him. Wilkins did his work well, and so did [? Minton]. Miny
Ha Ha & Bushey Park cost me in [? Minton's] hands 8000Rs. I
have just sold for 13,000 rupees, so that will pay. Laurie was
well untill Capt. Forman began writing to him, which made him
bumshus, and Forman has handed him over to me disgusted with him,
but of course like all those sort of men they require keeping
in hand or are no use. I am working him into shape again now.
The swell[s] are going ahead in coffee here, but you will [see]
them come down smash, some of them, ere long. I don't think much
of it now. Labour is deer and the Fellows, from the Superintendants to the dog boy, do nothing - all getting too big for
their work. I have only an interest in Altoor Estate now, and I
expect to get that off my hands ere long. However, if not, must
make a bag out of it by cheap superintendance and a big crop or
two, which you can always wring out of an Estate.

I am living a good deal at Tellicherry now, as I am getting
up a sort of Agency business, and beet up the estates once a
month. I purchased a splendid house in a park of several acres
and looking over the coconut trees to the sea - such a splendid
place, cost me 6000Rs. and I must spend 1500 on it to make it
all square. The girls' cart[e]s caused such a sensation out
here that I was at once thinking of getting you to send out Lin,
Tobe [Frances], and Dido. I could get them all married in a
week. I should have to do the swell for a bit, 100£ worth of
[? furnishing]. Mail Phaeton & Pair & Dog Cart I have - could
make a bit of a dash, and all the Cantonment of Cannanore would
go mad. You know the fellows all look upon me as immensely
rich, nothing like mystyfying people. Directly I arrived I
bought this swell home I had had my eye on for years - that
licked them. Of course I had an offer for the other properties,
Miny Ha Ha & Bushey Park, in my pocket that licked them - they
did not know that though at the time - keep the ball rolling,
you know. Such is life. In England, I don't know how it is, I
don't feel myself so much as I do out here, and I don't think I
should care a rap about the place if it was not for your young
'uns. I am expecting to do a good stroke of Business in
purchasing coffee this seson on my own account, so I think I
shall either Claw myself up in a year or so, or else I will
settle down quietly on something good and must either get the

girls & Lin out, or else come home and do a little Continental
tour again with them. South of France took my fancy. Marseilles
was perfectly lovely in November, a most jolly place to stay for
the winter.

Allow me to pay for Annie's & you[r] cart[e]s this fine
weather. Get the dibs from Phil on my account. I want you,
Annie, Alfred and Baby, also a couple of copies more of myself,
and a new cart[e] Book to hold 25. That dreadfull fellow,
Master Theo Clark, has not sent me his Carte yet, although he
promised me faithfully he would do so. What rum busters English
chaps seem to be. Mrs. Sam Clark has not yet sent me hers. She
promised to send it to the girls to be forwarded to me. Stir
them all up, Walter. The winter, I really believe, puts half
London to sleep like so many door rats.

What has got Fan? Is she getting lazey or what? No letter
from her since I have been out. Or is it the winter again, or
am I getting old and forgetfull. I don't remember one for ever
such a heap of a while. I hear[d] from Dido, a delightful
letter. Was not in my good spirits when I answered it, as I was
busy making up accounts and have been sitting at it for a whole
week, so apologise if it was a dull affair. Try something
better in my next. I was glad to hear Harry was getting on so
well at school. Give him a sovereign with my love out of the
tips you get from Phill. Tell him to go ahead with his book,
for 'pon my word, in the race of life a chap with a decent
education can do anything - a Chap with a good one, no end.

Kind love to Annie, children, and yourself
Your affect[ionate] brother
T.B. Bassano

184. *About the missing clock*

E.D. Fernandes to T.B. Bassano (Pally Koonoo)   Tellicherry
22 June 1863

Sir
    As ordered I called on Coonby Packey, shewn him the receipt
& explained him all about the Clock. He says that he would wait
till the result of your inquiries with your Brother is known, &
he would then tell you the value of Clock, & would *only* receive
a Clock in lieu thereof, but shall not receive its price.

I remain,
Sir,
Y[ou]r obed[ien]t servant
E.D. Fernandes

P.S. I return you the enclosed receipts. [These are from ohn Bennet and Geo. Dean, 65 Cheapside, 16 October 1862.]

P.S. I know the Clock belonged to Mr. Vaughn, late Provincial udge, and was purchased by Coonby Packey in Auction, and altho' t cost that gentleman some hundreds, yet I do not think it was ·urchased for any thing above a hundred Rs. or so. I hope you ·ill consider this as private. E.D.F.

85. " ... *if it were not for you and the kids ... I do not think I should be in a hurry to come home again.*"

om Bassano to Walter Bassano   [? C[a]noot] Estate
                                                9 July 1863

ly dear Walter
     I have not written to you, but to Lin and the Girls. How is
.t you have not been informed of it and my love to you properly
■elivered? Really, it is too bad. I suppose you think I am
'orgetting all about you, as you say.

     I am working up a close of accounts, which cannot be done in
ın hour. These things take time, and I find there is no hurry
ıbout it as I am in as good health here as I was at home, and
.f it were not for you and the kids, who I like to be among, I
lo not think I should be in a hurry to come home again. I should
■like to see the Governor again, poor old *deluded* gentleman. I
ıope to see him again as I think he is good for many years yet.
ʒetting childish with his brooches. Susan is a knowing one and
ɔlays her cards well. Do you consider all womankind on average
ıs knowing? By jove, I should like a good coloured portrait of
·the Governor. Get it done, if you keep it at home for me.

     I am glad Lin has got settled at Lalum.[3] She must not go
■teaching any more. It is rot and compleatly spoils girls. A
ʒood looking girl like her ought to have kidded on some chap to
ɔave spliced her long ago. If you hear Tobe [Frances] talk
ıbout going as a governess please scold her, and say I told you
▪to do so. Tell them to look about them and be kind, good
▪tempered and amiable - these are point[s] to study. And think
ɔf suppressing the irritable bumps and develop the good bumps,
not by a screw as the man did in one of Marryatt's novels, but by
▪thinking and doing good daily and hourly. Get a good husband
ɪand draw on me for *100£* to help to furnish her house (refer to
this). The same to Did[o], but there is no fear of her. It is
ɔnly Tobe that I think is not studying this most important point
ɔf gettin[g] married. I am sorry to hear Toby has left school.

---

3. Laleham - home of Philip.

Another year would have been better for her. However your pocket, perhaps, won't stand it. Don't let her be Idle. Have her Educated in Water Colour drawing immediately by a Master, or someone. I will pay the score. I want her to paint from Nature as my Friend the Doctor's Wife does. Don't let Annie laugh at this, as I cought it for not bringing the Bonnets.

The Prince of Wales' marry was a jolly affair. We have been watching the events with great int[e]rest, and Did[o] wrote me all about it. She is a good girl and write[s] a most interestin letter. She might perhaps curtail the slang a little. I know it is becoming fashionable. All serene. How are her poor feet? Just fancy Tom Scott going on at such capers, running up to Town every fortnight, like his cheek. Just tell him so with my salam next time you see him.

I have been so busy that the segars have not been sent. You don't want any? Did I promise you some? If so, I had forgott all about it. I am so delighted to hear Harry is getting on at school. Really, without a good Education a man starves now-a-days. The no. of young Gentlemen knocking about here looking for berths is dreadfull. I shall have no chance for sending for young King, I fear, as I have sold almost all my Estates, and reduced to the management of this, which in the event of leaving should have to hand over to a good man. So tell Harry he must push ahead.

Dear little Alf. I wish you could send him to school with Harry. I suppose it is that your increase of pay has not come, or something. I should be delighted [to] come to the rescue if I could, but as I am trying to get a Bag out at int[e]rest first, I don't like being too liberal as sickness may at any moment compell me to return, and then a poor devil without an income to mix and assosiate with his friends is a perfect nuisance.

Old Lovel is a jolly old card. I hope you were pleased with him. I wrote you a week ago. It is funny you should have dropped down on my post after my having written. Tell the girls I will be home amongst them as soon as I can come home and be of any use. England is no place without lots of Cash. If I don't come home I shall give them a trip as promised to Germany under your and Annie's guardianship next summer. So keep them at the German. If I can, I will meet you all there on my way home, or just on a flying visit.

I wrote Dido a few days ago from Tellicherry, same date I wrote you. So with love to Annie, Cris, Baby, &c., &c., yourself, and believe me

your affection[ate] Brother
T.B. Bassano

346

Your address is all right via Bombay, when Bombay is going
out - Madras, when Madras mail is going out.

186. *"I shall not be able to run home this year ... I dropped
2000Rs a little time since ..."*

Tom Bassano to niece Frances Bassano   Tellicherry
                                                        24 June 1864

My dear Fan
    Your letter of the (no date) to hand, and for which many
thanks. I do not understand you saying you have not received
any letter from me since I came out, as I have written dozens to
the whole family or you, collectively and individually, and
scarce got a word from any of you. Now this of yours puts me
quite in a state. What can be coming of my letters?

    I am glad you have been enjoying yourself at Lalum [Laleham].
The steeple chase must have been very pretty. I am glad to hear
Mrs. Scott and children are well ... I sent Jimmy a Box of
coffee through your uncle Phill. I hope it will come to hand.

    A sad end to poor Wooster. A sad thing to see a young Man go
so suddingly, who seem[e]d to be so apparently happy and well to
do when I was at home the first time.

    Dido said she was looking out for a house and that the family
found it so difficult to get one that you all anticipate taking
to the Workhouse for a time. I am glad to hear you have not been
turned out of the one you are now in, as somehow I like the
situation amazingly, and I should not like to see you all in the
workhouse.

    I hear now and again from your A[u]nt Ellen. She is well and
is always asking me to come and see her, and I have promised to
go by the first opportunity, so suppose in consequence I shall
not be able to run home this year to take you all on the Rhine.
I dropped 2000Rs. a little time since foolishly in speculating,
so am working up the deficit this year, instead of coming home.
I am trying to Establish a house[4] here so that when I want to
run away I can do so and leave all going on in my absence. So
I have added t[w]o more Europeans to my Establishment, a Mr.
Algar and [*illeg.*] who do the Low country work, and myself and
the young gentlemen the Estate work above the Ghauts.

    I am sorry to say my papers go astray and arrive very late at

---

4. A business House.

time[s], my address being Tellicherry, not Manantoddy. So Fan
Fan sent them on a long travel, so it is very likely that your
other letter went adrift some how. So, Fan, write me monthly,
ther[e's] a good niece, and I shall be sure to catch some of them.

So, poor little Janey Vernon is also gone. I have heard her
spoken of as such an amiable little person that A[u]nt Melinda
must miss her much. I am glad to hear so good account of the
boys. Master Alfred has not sent me that letter he was going to
write me by every mail when I was at home. However, tell him I
should like to have a line from him just to see how he writes
and how he can get up a letter unaided by anyone. He must be a
big fellow by this. Harry must be growing also, and I hope it
will be as you say that he will succeed in getting a prize or
two this seson. It will be a great day when he can look down on
Dido ... [more in the same vein]

I cannot say when I shall be with you all. I wish it was
close at hand. I cannot say when it will be. Soon I hope, and
with kind love to your Mamma and Papa and all of you, and many
thanks for your entertaining letter,

I remain, Dear Fan, your affectionate Uncle
T.B. Bassano

187. *About Tom's visit to Ellen in Australia*

F.M. Bassano to Walter Bassano   53 Camden Grove
                                              Peckham
                                              25 May 1868

Dear Walter
    Last night I received a letter from Ellen, dated 28th March.
She says that Tom started by the Feb[ruar]y mail to India, and
thinks that, after paying us all another visit, he will ultimately return to Ballarat and settle in the Colony as the Climate
appeared to him very suitable for his present delicate constitu-
tion. She trusts that your children are all restored to health.
I have sent to Melinda this news regarding Tom.

My visit to you on Sunday gratified me much and improved my
health which continues better than usual.

With love to Annie and the bairns,

I remain
Your ever affect[ionat]e Father
F.M. Bassano

88. *Back in India*

M. Bassano to Tom Bassano

53 Camden Grove
Peckham
15 June 1868

ᵧ dear Tom
  Your aff[ectionat]e letter of 30th March reached on the 5th
ₑ this month and it was a great relief to my anxious thoughts
ₒr your welfare. I immediately sent its contents to Walter and
ₑlinda who were very glad to hear of you. Thank God we are all
ₑll, altho' the infirmities of age are telling upon me.

  I was at Walter's last month and found them all in perfect
ₑalth. I have long read the Gazettes and am now gratified to
ₐnd that Alfred was promoted on the 12th instant to the rank of
ₒlonel under the Royal Warrant of 3d February 1866.

  I am very unworthy of the comforts which the success of my
ₕildren afford me and pray that thro' the mediation of our
ₐviour the Almighty will bestow his ever lasting blessing upon
ₕem.

  It being now Post time I am obliged to conclude hastily with
ₕe best love and wishes of your ever affectionate Father

F.M. Bassano

  P.S. I am very grateful for the kind reception of your
ₒother-in-law Hepburn and am sure it will afford a lasting
ₒomfort to Ellen and yourself that you have secured the friend-
ₕip of so worthy a man. [addressed to Tellicherry]

89. *Settling affairs at Tellicherry*

ᵧ.M. Bassano to Melinda Bassano

53 Camden Grove
Peckham
4 July 1868

ᵊear Melinda
  I am very glad you anticipated my anxiety to hear again of
ᵧom, as my answer to his last letter would not have reached him
ₙ May. I pray the Almighty to bestow upon him his Grace and
ₑerciful facilities towards a good and speedy settlement of his
ₐffairs at Tellicherry, and that his seperation from us may not
ₑe much longer delayed. I am also gratified to hear of Colonel
ₒolls's visit to Laleham, and hope that the result of it will
ₑnable you to tell me further news as to Alfred's prospects –
ᵣesulting from his late promotion.

Give my love to Tom when you write and say we all pray for hi improved health and that the good time of again seeing him is coming ...

Your ever affectionate Father
F.M.B.

II

"THANK GOD I HAVE MADE A START TO LIVE WITHIN MY MEANS"
(Tom Bassano 1869-76)

190. *"I really must settle down quietly as soon as I can"*

Tom Bassano to Walter Bassano   Hotel de Rouen
                                     13 Rue Notre-Dames-des-Victoires
                                     Paris
                                     n.d. [September 1869]

Dear Walter
    I got here all right on Tuesday at 7 o'clock and have located myself in the above hotel, a nice quiet place, and am getting on pretty well considering I cannot speak French.

    I enclose you an advertisement that I cut out of a paper before leaving. Like a good fellow write a note to the young fellow and see what you could engage him for as a clark and interpreter. I must make up the Closson accounts[5] and so he might be just the thing for me. It is a question of expence, how much a year would he want, he living at his own expence and coming to me at my lodgings or hotel daily as desired, to go out with me or sit at home and write, also to give lessons in French &c., in fact make himself generally usefull. He is not proud, as he says in his advert as a porter, so he could run on any errands I wanted.

    I really must settle down quietly as soon as I can, for it will not do spending money as I have been for the last year, in fact 2 years and a half since I have been running about all over the world, out of which time I have only been 15 days at my house in Malabar.

    I called to see you on Monday ev[en]ing, but missed you.

---

5. Tellicherry business.

350

th love to all at home I remain

Your affectionate brother
Tom

1. " ... *don't bully a poor devil who has not got a nerve left ...*"

m Bassano to Walter Bassano   Hotel [Paris]
                                               n.d. [postmark
                                               18 September 1869]

y dear Walter
    Your note to hand. I want the lad to come to me in Paris and
ill pay him a second class passage here and back if he does not
iit me. I do not see my way to employing one here, not talking
ie language make[s] my operations difficult. I dare say 50£ or
2£ a year will be what he will take, and I would take him for 3
nths certain and a year if he suits, or 6 months. It will all
pend on the best bargain you can make for me, if you can
range for the best, dropping me a line of what you can do and
iat he will take, before settling with him.

    I write Phil asking him for a letter to his friend, but I do
ot care about knowing any one at present, if I can get my own
an, and as you say the Advertisement reads well. I dare say
ie youngster will be best for me. If not, I can fall back on
iil's friend. But go in for the young man at once, there is a
od fellow. Don't bully a poor devil who has not got a nerve
ft. I did not like Mrs. Nancy to call on you, and it was like
er cheak. I said, or me[a]nt to say in my letter, send in my
ccount, and I would then send my nephew to pay her.

    I told you about her fuss and went to your cub [? club] to
scape it. I hate bother and think I may say I have cut out a
ine of policy which is going to answer. I don't think Mrs.
ancy knows anything about the young person. As for bolting at
o'clock, I went to Victoria to katch the morning express, and
s the old lady was not there to give me my bill, I was not
bliged to wait.

    I note what you say about a Paris winter, but if I have an
nterpreter (to go anywhere mind, Paris, Spain, or Italy, or
ermany) to help me to go farther South if necessary, I can pick
y climate.

    My little friend is everything I can wish and our room costs
e 4 franks a day, table dote, dinner, a good one including wine,
 Franks each, breakfast one Frank, so for 12 franks a day I am
iving jolly - a few Franks a day at a Caffee, and all is told.

351

Thank God I have made a start to live within my means, for I do not want to over-run the constable and be a beggar like poor John R. in my old age. I know the world too well for that to have to look forward to anything of the sort. I have had to work hard in India to get a little togather for retirement, and so wish to take care of it now that I have no need to return.

You give me a lively picture of your position. I hope it is not what you say. If so, all I can say is, you ought to gird up your loins and go in for the economics and square yourself, for in London it seems to me a man can live how he pleases without anyone taking the slightest notice of him, if in the position you are, with a wife. With me it was different. A man from India is expected to be a gordous [gorgeous] swell and to live with a woman seems to [be] simply ruin, as nothing seems to controul them in their eagerness to have everything they see. I should have gone to the bad if I had not left, and now I must keep a light hand and recover myself, and I see nothing at present to prevent me. Write me soon regarding the lad, but there is no violent hurry to settle, as I am getting on better every day and am really as happy as a sand boy, and my companion, as far as I can see, the best little thing that could be.

I enclose a note to Phil, and have asked him to give the needful to Harry to go and pay the Bill. Also tell Harry to battle the watch about the Week['s] worning, if you think it right, for I agreed with the lady at 4£ a week 25 instead of 21, upon the understanding I was to go when I liked as my movements were uncertain, and I have been in her home for upwards of 6 months, I think. Of course pay her, if it is right.

I am glad to hear all are well at home. I quite agree with Annie regarding "Formosa". It is not a nice one for a young lad to go and see. I have not been to a theatre yet. We dordle about in the Gardens in the day time, and the Bolovards at night getting home to bed at 10 to eleven o'clock. So you will say, "Ah, don't you wish you may get it," I suppose. It is the truth at all events.

Your affection[ate] broth[er]
Tom

P.S. Keep a memo of any little expences on letter &c. and I will settle it. In haste to save post. TBB

192. *A new apartment*

Tom Bassano to Walter Bassano

12 Rue Montaigne
Champs Elysee
[Paris]
11 October 1869

Dear Walter
  I wrote you I was going to move. Volai [voilà] my new
address - such a nice place, 2 minutes walk from the Grand
Promenade, Fountains, flowers, &c., &c. My Apartments consist
of Kitchen, SalarManga [salle à manger] sitting room and Bedroom,
and cost me 140 F. a month, a servant finding herself, 30 more,
so I am glad to say I am comfortable and do not mean to move at
present. Untill I have got my accounts made up and all things
square of course, Paris to me is all on a par with any large city
as far as amus[emen]ts go, for I do not care, or did I ever care,
about knocking about at night. What I like at Paris is it is so
nice a climate, and one can loaf about in the gardens all day
without chance of getting wet, sit down at a Caffee when tired
... Diu mon aimi [adieu, mon ami].

> Your affectionate Brother
> Tom

193. *"I have not yet turned too at my accounts"*

Tom Bassano to Walter Bassano

Paris
9 November 1869

Dear Walter
  Just a line to say I received your note of 2nd, for which many
thanks. I was not luckee enough to get hold of a Saturday *Times*
- should like to read the account. See if you can get an old
paper and cut out the piece. I should like to see all about it
though I know the facts ...

So Downing is to be in town for a few days [and] Phil going to
come to town and lodge at the Gaffneys. Ah, ah! Set Melinda
not to let him be kidded on to marry one of them. There are no
fools like old fools. I am glad to hear you are all well, and
trust little Tom is again all serene. We have had some cold
weather here, but the rooms I have are snug and so I don't feel
it. However, I have given notice to quit on 9th of Dec[embe]r
so that if I prefer going away further south I can do so, if not,
go on again for the winter in the same place.

I have not yet turned too at my accounts, as I want the last
a/c of sales of coffee from Forbes & Co. & Day & Algar's last
accounts ...

With kindest love to all
I remain
Your affect[ion]ate brother
Tom

194. " ... *after my 30 years hard work, a many years as a mean
labourer, I have a nice kettle of fish brewing up around
me ...* "

Tom Bassano to Walter Bassano   Paris
13 December 1869

Dear Walter
    Your letter to hand. I got all the paper & letter all serene.
You surprise me regarding Melinda. Phil told me his residing in
town would make no difference to Melinda, so cannot understand
what you say. The money her Papa left her will keep her going
in clothes a long time, so she must not be allowed to go to
service. The idea is monstrous. As I bettered my prospects in
India I considered it my duty to try and better the prospects
of my family. The thing was easy at that time. Since that,
failing health compelled me to sacrifice a valuable position
which might have been retained in the Family, all for the want
of a little co-operation of my brother & sister. I am now what
I cannot like, spending capital ... but living under 30£ a
month, instead of 100£ I was in London. But untill I have made
up lost way and worked up my accounts and made out my [? posi-
tion] I cannot promise anything. Alfred won't pay me. Cheeks
me by telling me if I like to drive him to sell his commission
he will do so. Phil is riled with me because I don't pay him a
little bill Alf drew on me of 250£. So after my 30 years hard
work, a many years as a mean labourer, I have a nice kettle of
fish brewing up around me and bad helf [health] to rebut it with.
And in this my first stay in Europe for so many years I must be
excused for any little extravagance hitherto. I have now pulled
up and sit at home from weeks end to weeks end quite happy of an
evening, and if I had not so much to pay in shape of house rent
would live under 20£ a month till I get square. So I want
breathing time. Phil must go on with his trust which I feel
sure he wishes to do. I will, I hope, be able to come in for my
share in due course. She has never been forgotten by me since
Father married in event of anything happening to me.

    Many thank[s] re lithograph. Keep them for me, bar one send
me by post wrapped round a piece of wood. Get Annie one Framed
on my a/c. I promised it her, like the Frame of those of her &
Melinda.

    Enclosed a letter from Ellen. Give it to Melinda and ask her
to write Ellen about her friends. I don't know one of them.

hat re Father will seem strange.[6] The letter had better be
anded to Phil. I am sorry to hear your two youngest are poorly,
ut hope they will soon be all right again. Make one of the big
irls take them out as a rule for a long walk every fine day. It
as been cold here, but warm for the last few days, more blowing
nd windy tonight. I am thinking of running down south in a few
ays, but go on sending my letters as I shall make arrangements
e them.

With love to Annie, yourself and kids, also Melinda, I remain

Your affection[ate] Brother
Tom

95. *"I broke out with the old complaint"*

om Bassano to Walter Bassano

Paris
15 December 1869

)ear Walter
    Will you kindly send me Bow Bells, a weekly Journal, one
)en[n]y a number, postage I suppose Book post, 1½ or so postage.
▌ have the 1st Number for Dec[embe]r 1st 1869.

    I have been awfully bad with R[he]umatics for [the] last few
days since the frost. The medicine I suppose I have been taking
in for the last year without any good that I can see - for a
nonth after I came over to Paris I broke out with the old
complaint more than ever, and it is only by dint of the greatest
denial of stimulants and steadily living on [*illeg.*] that I have
again checked it. And it seems inclined to go away again now.
▌ am thinking of going to Paw for the sake of [the] Baths, but
am not certain. It is such a bother travelling, and [I] am as
it were comfortably settled in my present lodgings.

    I have not been for any of Eastee's letters yet,[7] but will go
in the morning. I am not in a hurry for any Epistle for [from]
him, as they will only be cheakey and wanting money.

My love to you all,

Your affect[io]n[a]te Brother
Tom

P.S. Kindly send enclose[d] to Messr[s] Day & Algar,[8] by
Marseilles. TBB

---

6. F.M. Bassano had died the previous June (1869).
7 and 8. These refer to his Indian business.

196. *"I worked a many year to get a Xmas at home ... and now feel ... not excited on the subject"*

Tom Bassano to Walter Bassano   [Paris]
                                                 17 [December 1869]

Dear Walter
    Your letter to hand. I fear I shall not be able to [? buck]
you up this Xmas. I worked a many year to get a Xmas at home
and succeeded in the end, and now feel the same as I have been
used to do in India, not excited on the subject. The cold is
crip[p]ling me so [I] can't move. Got a bad toe, the old toe
again, the gout, a chilblain and the nail going into it.
R[he]umatics in the leg and S[c]iatica in the hip, swelling up.

    Melinda need not go to service if it is only to invest money
in the funds. If anything happen[s] to me she will be well
provided for and I suppose in a few years I shall, if I live, be
able to allow her money. Ever since Father married, she has
been my first thought, so Danial or no Danial, I have some plans
in life, although I write rubbish according to your account. So
please tell Melinda in some way that I set my face against her
going out as a Governess. I wonder if she had any thought really
to do so. She did not write me or consult Phil on the subject
of her ways and means. I don't know her affairs. It would be no
harm if our youngest sister consulted her brothers a bit as to
her position. Poor C[h]ris left her money. Has she spent all
this? Phil said something to me one day about her selling out
stock before Father's death, and that she was extravagant. Mind,
this is between you and me. I dare say you know all about these
things, so let me know anything further you may know on the
subject.

    I pity poor Annie the prospect of her Xmas week with Kit &
Alf to worry her. Give old The[ophilus] Clark a Xmas box for me.
I think one for his nob will do him, or a good one in the wind,
saying at the same time "Tom sent you that". I hope he is
lively, and with love to all

                    Your affect[io]n[a]te brother
                              Tom

197. *"This is coffee in Malabar"*

Tom Bassano to Walter Bassano   [Paris]
                                                 [21 December 1869]

Dear Walter
    A merry Xmas and happy New Year to You and Yours. I got your
note and Eastee's card. Have got no letter from him, so perhaps

e did not write. He can wait untill I can get Malabar a/c and offee sales squared up when account can be made up. In the eantime they are no worse off than poor Mrs. Palmer, who put in 00£ and got 50, and Price, who put in 800£ and got back about 00£. This is coffee in Malabar under men like Closson and Co. ince 1858. Phil did not thank me for getting him out of it. e ought to have got into a speck with the men who brought the hing down.

I see you have had some cold weather. It has been cold here or a couple of days, but fine since.

Post the two enclosed letters as French Indian postage is ear and I fear uncertain. Give my love to Melinda - hope she s all serene. I am lazy or would write her. Love to Annie and 11 your kids.

>   I am, Your affect[iona]te brother
>   Tom

98. *Written inside an envelope flap*

om Bassano to Walter Bassano   [Paris]
                                                [28 December 1869]

Compliments of se[a]son to you & yours & happy new year. BB.

Dear Walter, Post enclosed. I don't feel sure with French osts. Via Marseilles & Bombay. Messrs. Day & Algar, Telli-herry, Malabar, India.

99. *"I am coming to London ... provided I don't get scragged in the Revolution"*

om Bassano to Walter Bassano   [Paris]
                                                13 January 1870

Dear Walter
    I cannot read the administrater['s] name. You can do it for ne by assistance of your red book, then kindly put in his name and send it to him.

The letterbook duly to hand, for which my thanks. The book you mention I can get here, but they charge a lot more money for them and then irregular in getting them, so have ordered them. I am coming to London in a week or two for a few days, provided I don't get scragged in the Revolution. Such going[s] on you never saw. The excitement is awfull here ...

The weather is getting so beautifull, days drawing out, so the winter seem[s] to be passing away, with only the 5 days cold a week ago.

> Your affect[io]n[ate] brother
> Tom

P.S. Love to all.

200. *"I think the Revolution business has blown over now"*

Tom Bassano to Walter Bassano   [Paris]
                                                 28 January 1870

Dear Walter
    I have not had a letter from you since the 14th Inst. Have you any letter for me? If so, please send them by return of pos♦ I am in expectation of some important ones, now a week overdue.

    I shall not leave Paris yet, as I see by the English papers that you are having fog in London. Here delightful sun, and clear. I have a game leg which keeps me awake all night. It is s[c]iatica or neuralgia. Never[the]less it is one prolonged pain. I cannot get sleep when taking 2 opium pills at bedtime.

    It was a mistake not sending the Administrater['s] letter to you, which I intended doing, but I made the mistake.

    I think the Revolution business has blown over now. If you could get a week's leave and pay 1£ passage, 2nd Class, via Newhaven, you would find me here glad to see you, and would cost me nothing. I have a spare bed and I could show you Paris. My lodgin[g]s I intend giving up on the 9th next month, intending to go south. So if you would like to come across, do so and see Paris. I will take you the rounds, as well as my game leg will let you [*sic* - me].

> Your affect[iona]te Brother
> Tom

201. *"Keep my address dark"*

Tom Bassano to Walter Bassano

No. 1, Osbourn Street
Summers Road
Portsea
Portsmouth
[24 June 1870]

Dear Walter
    If you have any letters for me send them to the above address.
I am making up my accounts like a house on fire, so untill I
have all compiled keep my address dark. In posting letters to
me drop them in the Charing X post office yourself.

    I hope all is going on well at my diggin[g]s at Hammersmith,
and that Annie, yourself and family are all well.

                    Yours affectionately
                        T.B. Bassano

    P.S. Is Miss Purkis name Purkis or Perkins? I don't think I
ever knew.

202. *"I certainly do enjoy any place except England"*

Tom Bassano to Melinda Bassano

149, Rue Royale
Boulogne
n.d. [early 1872]

My dear sister
    Your two notes to hand. I am glad to hear you are enjoying
yourself and that you are having fine weather at Eastbourne.
I am quite well, I am glad to say, and joggin[g] along quietly
in my pet place, as you call it. I certainly do enjoy any place
except England, for English people as a rule are such false,
backbiting humbugs. The more they are shut up in their English
homes as they call them, the worst they become. I suppose it is,
as an English judge told me the other day here, it is a mere
matter of liver. People feed heavily in England on butcher's
meat & strong tea. All other nations south of England use more
vegetable diet, and consequently their liver[s] are more active,
and the fine climates induce more outdoor exercise, consequently
a greater amount of ozone is enhaled. The English Thanksgiving
day seems to have been a great success. I was too indolent to
go to it - read all about it in your rag. I am surprised to
hear Walter cannot find a house to suit him - there seems to be
no end advertised.

Phil went away[9] without telling me what was to become of my letters. I am anxiously looking for one which is 2 month[s] overdue. I hope he will be home soon.

Your affectionate brother
Tom

P.S. How do you like the Great Titchbourn trial ... I believe if his friends back him and he can go in for an appeal he will get it yet.

203. *Tom's health*

Melinda Bassano to niece Annie Frances Bassano

45 Terminus Road
Eastbourne
26 February [1872]

My dear Tob
...I have not heard from your Uncle Tom again. He said he had been very ill since he had been to London, that Gas & heavy living did not agree with him. I asked him to write to me again, but he has not done so yet. I don't suppose it is anything more than one of his liver attacks ...

Your's affectionately
Auntie Lin

204. *Alfred's debt of £200 repaid, and given to Melinda*

Tom Bassano to Melinda Bassano   [20 April 1872]

Dear Melinda
    Herewith a letter from Alf. I want you to do something for yourself which will answer as well in your old age as the present moment. My Idear is that you can purchase or rent a house at Eastbourne and take my furniture out of store and live down there altogether. When you have no lodgers I could come

---

9. Philip went on a Cook's tour to Italy in January 1872. Diary of the tour survives.

and stay a month or so. It would make a home for me. You also could have Dido down and give her a change at times. She wants sea bathing, fresh air, or you will be losing her next, which will never do. If to purchase a house at Eastbourne now is the time, as you can have the 200£ Alfred has given me, the balance purchase money I will lend you in some way on the deeds, or any way for [the] best. I don't want to thrust too much money into your hands and so make you careless. Not that you will ever be that. Still, it is so nice to do the Lardedardy in givin[g] away, if one has it to give. However, see if you can enter into my ideas in any way. Write to me to Boulogne and I will come over again and talk the matter over. This is just a general idea for you to better if you can.

Enclosed a note to Phil to pay you the money. Send it through Al's Master, and tell him to purchase you four of the 5 per cent Turkish loan which will be about 210£, the ten pounds I can send you a check for. This will give you 20£ a year about, and I can give you the balance making up the 25. This is only an arrangement which will stand untill you have written me re your Idear of the house, when you can sell out your Turkish and pay for your house. The purch[as]ing will give Al's Master a bon from Philip &c., and do you & I do no harm. I cannot write more at present, so will no[w] wait your news, but don't disappoint me in the investment. I want to find out something about Turkish bonds and thus my request about them. I have marked the one. I request you to purchase them [like] a good little Lin.

Your affection[ate] Brother
Tom

I return to France tomorrow morning or this evening.

P.S. I have spent a pleasant week and which has done me a great deal of good. I have been suffering of late. The fact is a quiet life does not suit me, London gas is worse, so if you think my life is worth coaxing a little b[u]y a house and let me be a Lodger now and then with you when I am seedy.

Your affect[io]n[a]te Tom

P.S. Enclose Phil note and address it. TBB.

205. *Enclosures in the above*

Alfred Bassano to Tom Bassano   Laleham
                                                 17 April 1872

Dear Tom
    I had made arrangements with Phil before receiving your

361

letter, for the payment of the £200. He has the money and will credit you with the amount. Thanks for not pressing me sooner.

Yours affectionately,
Alf Bassano

Tom Bassano to Philip Bassano   20 April [1872]

Dear Phil
    Will you kindly hand the 200£ to Melinda, as I have asked her to invest it in her name as something for her to fall back upon in case of anything happening to me.

Your affect[io]n[a]te brother
Tom

206. *Philip's comment on Tom's suggestion to Melinda*

Philip Bassano to Melinda Bassano   Laleham
                                                     24 April 1872

Dear Lin
    I really cannot advise you to do what Tom recommends as even to furnish and let a house, as I think it requires a deal of vigilance to prevent being swindled. You must also recollect that although Tom has a good deal of nice sitting-room furniture, there is scarcely any for Bedrooms, as he took the greater part of what little he had away with him, so that if you furnished you would have to lay out a good deal of money in Bedding &c.

    Am I to understand that I am to send the £200 to Walter for him to take to whoever young Al has been placed with and invest it in Turkish bonds? ...

Yours very affectionately
P.H. Bassano

207. *Melinda's comment on Tom's scheme*

Melinda Bassano to Annie Frances Bassano   Eastbourne
                                                            28 April [1872]

Dear Frances

362

..I fear indeed my proposition to visit Eastbourne must seem
dull by the side of your Uncle Tom's proposed excursion to Malta.
Still, perhaps a visit down here under my care would be a good
preparation for the Maltese trip ...

I dare say your Uncle's scheme seemed a very good one, but
you know he does not propose it as *well* as the 25£ a year he
allows me, & I do not think a *small* house to let *entire* would
answer down here, & a large one would involve more risk than I
am plucky enough to undertake. You know your Uncle stripped the
house at Hammersmith of a good many things, so that I do not
exactly know what he has, & it would probably take more than the
£200 he offers me to furnish it in a way that would be remuner-
ative. House rent here is not low, a house two doors off of us,
not much larger than this, & not half so pretty, lets for £80,
& the situation is not one in my opinion that would let well.
So that I fear if I were to contemplate it, the rent of a house
in a good situation would be too high for a safe speculation.
If it didn't answer, & I could not get it off my hands, it would
probably swallow up the little I have in the Bank, & you know
how I should worry myself for fear it should not pay. You say
I am on the spot, but you know October will soon be here, & then
see what a journey it would be to see after it. Mrs. Ryle's
cottage at Laleham would be quite a different thing, the rent is
so small, & the distance from London so trifling, that I could
easily see after it, & so scarce as places are on the Thames
near London, it is a *certainty* that it would let. I only wish I
could get hold of it. As I said before, this scheme of your
Uncle's is *instead* of the allowance he makes me, & I really
think I prefer the allowance. I may make something by my teaching after all, & I certainly am running no risks ...

                    Yours very affectionately
                         Auntie Lin

208. *Investing in Turkish bonds*

Tom Bassano to Melinda Bassano   149 [Rue Royale]
                                        [Boulogne] France
                                        30 April 1872

Dear Lin
    Your note to hand. I enclose you a check for 20£, your
quarter and balance on a/c of the Turkish loan. Alfred's
Master is a Mr. Duncan through whom you can invest, and the
loan papers will be handed to you. Interest will be payable

½ Yearly, I presume. This you will find out in due course.
That is right. Get everyone's views re the Turkish bonds. All
people always call everyone else sillies, either to keep one out
of a good thing or else out of jealousy because they have not
got the cash to invest in it themselves.

Keep a little Dr. & Cr. account re the loan when you invest,
and if you get early dividends put it down to your yearly
allowance from me, and if nothing comes in before next quarter
I will pay your allowance as heretofore. I dare say you will
be wiser in a few months, and then we can sell Turks and invest
in something else. Alfred, as he says, will be able to give us
the straight tip as he calls it. Not that I know what he means,
but I know what I mean. I want to know a little about English
stockbroking and then I can go deaper in ...

I see you don't consider it quite the thing doing the House
or lodging business, so I must apologise. The fact is, I am so
green, having been brought up in such a humble manner.

[incomplete letter ends here]

209. " ... *the very thought of again making money sends a
thrill through me like an old war horse at the sound of
cannon*"

Tom Bassano to Melinda Bassano   Le Havre
                                                 13 September 1872

Dear Lin
    Your note to hand for which many thanks. Let me know when
you go to London.

    Your little account is quite nice. You are quite a woman of
business. I shall have to send you, or give you, one Pound in
Nov[embe]r, I suppose, and that will pay you another quarter.

    You said something about wanting a trunk. I have bought you
a nice one. Do you want it sent to your present diggin[g]s or
sent to Walter's to await your arrival? Let me know by return
of post.

    Your description of the Eastbourne people put me in mind of
the old saying of the Early bird gets the worm. They let their
houses for the se[a]son and thus live rent free for 9 months in
the year. Clever Idear. Very likely go to some London cheap
lodgin[g] when London is empty, and lodgin[g]s cheap, and amuse
themselves of the Exhibition &c. as best they can. Always some

wrincle to be picked up. I shall let my house next se[a]son and
go to Isle of Skey or some other place unknown – realise 300£ by
the transaction. I have been Idle so long that the very thought
of again making money sends a thrill through me like an old War
horse at the sound of Cannon.

My trip to Rouen with little Alf quite knocked me up. I have
been suffering from liver so very much ever since, the heat was
terrific.

Your affect[ion]ate Brother
Tom

210. " ... *my first start in life was some 300£ Phil lent me* ... "

Tom Bassano to Melinda Bassano   36 Rue Just Viel
                                         Havre, France
                                         [21 October 1872]

Dear Melinda
Your letter duly to hand. I am glad to hear you are still
well and jolly, as you appear to be by the tone of your letter.
You need not frett for your dear old dearty London and its
humbuggin[g] ways. I never seem to be so well as when away from
it as I feel I am away from the sins of the world.

Your Mrs. Davies seems to have a head on her shoulders.
Lettin[g] her house seems to pay her or she would not go on
doing so. What a little duffer you are. Why did you not think
of the Pupil dodge when I could have lent you the Furniture?
It is all over here now. I often thought of the thing and have
been going to speak about it, but my Idear was to have got you
to form a partnership with Dido or Fan, but your objection of
[? separating] the girls from their Father deter[r]ed me. We
are all full of objection[s], but my experience of life is that
one person cannot conduct a business as well as two. Sickness
and a little low spirits do not stop the waggon, as one person
rallies as the other droops, and so the ship floats. But I
see in everything in England, perticually in ladies' society,
that there is so much doubt and little confidence. If I say I
see, I mean my Idear is so, but then it is only my opinion, and
so is worth nothing except to those who are of similar opinion.

Would it be worth while you thinking over it and letting me
know when we meet at Xmas. For I should like to see you doing
something better than teaching little kids at 25£ a year, if it
seem only possible.

For you must always bear in mind my first start in life was
some 300£ Phil lent me and which I returned to him in the shape

of 800£ to 1000, I forget which, in some 2 or 3 years. But
without Phil's lift I should still be perhaps nothing, or dead
of dissapointment. Of course when a person gets a lift and
cannot turn it to advantage he must be lazey or dafftey, as
little Kit would say. The only road to success is hard work,
and it surprises me to see in England the way some men walk
ruff [rough] shod over others, and the quiet lazey way in which
others drag a miserable existance of doing nothing but talking
rot from day to day, weak to week, & year to year, until they
seem so used to it that they try to pretend to all around them
that they are as happy as Crickets – the shams of life in the
year 1872 as we read of in the Bible before Christ.

I shall be home to Xmas, so trust to meet you in good health,
and in the meantime I am glad to say I am quite recovered from
my liver & my R[he]umatic ...

I remain your affectionate Brother
Tom

P.S. I was delighted to hear Dido had returned from Scotland
quite recovered from her late attack of low spirits or liver or
what men call "Blues" and which Poor Alfred seems to be drifting
into, by all accounts. TBB.

P.S. I have not heard from Ellen for an age. By all means
keep one of your cart[e]s for me. I really have not got a
decent Photo of yours. The old one of Collins is quite faded.
TBB.

211. *Description of Tom Bassano's life at Le Havre by his*
    nephew, young Alfred, just thirteen years old

Alfred E. Bassano to his aunt Melinda Bassano   Rue Just Viel 36
                                                 Hâvre, France
                                                 [October 1873]

My dear Aunt Lin
    Many thanks for your kind letter and still kinder intimation
of "presents". Would you believe it your letter and Edith's,
which came with yours, took me quite by surprise. At first I
could not understand what you were driving at, for I had let
the day go by without so much as thinking about birthdays, but
as I read on it dawned upon me that it ought to have been a
case of "lucky boy" on Sunday, instead of constitutional and
afternoon promenading. I am sure that I shall appreciate
anything that the fair fingers of my beloved Aunt Lin have
operated on, whether it consists of the festive "list" or the
lordly worsted such as those which you have sent over to Uncle.
He is not very much struck with the splendour of the pattern,

ɔut he seems to set great store by them and is talking about having high heels put on them "comme ça". [Here is a drawing of a high heeled slipper.] I am trying to dissuade him from it, for I think it will look rather silly for a man of his years, but as he seems bent on it I shall offer no more opposition.

He has chartered a small yacht of 60 tons, such a "clipper", schooner rigged, and has a crew of 2 men & a boy, which crew he bullies like mad when we are out in her of a day. I amuse myself by firing of a small cannon she carries, whilst he abuses the men and kicks the boy whilst we are coasting about of a day. He tells me to inform you that you need not go to the expense of coming across, but that he will go over & fetch you and the Davis family the first time we have a bit of a breeze from the right quarter. It is very enjoyable sailing about on such fine days as we have been having lately and I am as brown as a berry.

The temperature today in the sun is 110 Fath^r and I have been hard at work this afternoon making a chicken house for a new lot of "Mealy Chittagongs" which he bought yesterday in the market. It takes me half the day to attend to the pets. There are now 16 fowls, inclusive of the new lot, 9 canaries, 2 gold-finches, 2 linnets, 2 dogs, 14 pigeons, and an Alderney Cow, the last a recent acquisition, but one which is a very valuable one, for we can supply the whole of the Rue Just Viel and make it pay.

I had a dreadful accident with a saw in sawing a piece of wood just now. In fact it is that which makes me write so badly. I cut almost through the 2nd finger of my left hand and it is extremely painful yet. When you cut through the nail from side to side you know how bad it is. But by the bye, you did not know that I was over here. Well, I am, and I wish you would just pull your blind down when you dress in the morning, for I distinctly saw you as I passed Eastbourne at 9 o'c[lock] on Friday morning, and I was much shocked. I had a very strong glass and tried to attract your attention, but could not.

Uncle Tom sends his love, thanking you for the slippers, but will write himself. Thanking you myself very much for your kindness, believe me, your aff[ectionate] nephew, Alfred.

212. *"Uncle Tom is blooming"*

Alfred E. Bassano to Melinda Bassano

Rue Just Viel 36
Hâvre, France
30 October 1873

My dear Aunt Lin
    I am really almost ashamed to begin to answer your kind

letter of the 7th after so long a delay, but I can assure you that I have been so busy, and time slips away with me at such an alarming rate that it really is utterly impossible for me to realize the fact of my receiving an epistle until at least a fortnight after I get one. However, better late than never, so here goes.

First and foremost, Uncle Tom is blooming bar a slight affection of the Bronchial tubes which keep him constantly coughing, but I think his Rheumatism is entirely gone. Anyhow we must see how the cold though bright weather we are now having will affect him before predicting as to its utter evacuation of territory. Talking of evacuation of territory, it is more than likely that France will now indulge in a slight Civil War to keep herself warm this winter. I mean, between the Republicans & Monarchists. The people of Hâvre are very loud in their determination to die on the household stove (they have no hearths) and mingle their blood with the daily "Bouille" rather than again submit to a rule of Jesuits and a Papal King. It is difficult to imagine how it will all end. I might wake up tomorrow morning & hear the cries of "Vive Henri Cinq" or the roar of the Cannon singing death to the multitude ... I induced Uncle to buy an old edition of the Spectator in 8 volumes the other day: and as we only gave 13 francs for it I consider it cheap, especially as it is in very good condition, and tolerably well bound ... And now I am afraid I must shut up, so with best love in which Uncle joins believe me

Your affec[tionat]e nephew,
Alfred

P.S. Uncle is off on a cruise to New York in a day or two.

213. *Tom Bassano in 1874 and death of Melinda*

Extracts from Edith Bassano's pocket diary

Sunday, 29 March 1874. Pa [Walter Bassano], Uncle Tom & Mr. Scott went to Twickenham ...

Tuesday, 31 March 1874. ... Uncle Tom came.

Wednesday, 1 April 1874. ... Uncle Tom came ...

Sunday, 5 April 1874. ... Uncle Tom came.

Friday, 10 April 1874. ... Mr. Lemon & Sam Clark came, Uncle Tom [came] ...

Sunday, 17 May 1874. Lizzie & Ede and Uncle Tom in the evening ...

Tuesday, 7 July 1874. Uncle Tom came to town, brought a little Pomeranium dog for Alf ...

Wednesday, 8 July 1874. ... The little dog was given away.

Thursday, 9 July 1874. ... Madame Rickette called about ... Uncle Tom.

Saturday, 11 July 1874. ... Ma, Pa, & Uncle Tom went to Walton, Hampton Court & Sunbury ...

Wednesday, 15 July 1874. Uncle Tom came up.

Friday, 17 July 1874. Uncle Tom went home.

Saturday, 25 July 1874. Auntie [Melinda] came home from Eastbourne very ill. Dr. D. came to see her in the eve ...

Thursday, 30 July 1874. Papa went to Hâvre ...

Friday, 31 July 1874. Auntie Lin died at ½ past 3 A.M. ...

Saturday, 1 August 1874. Pa & Uncle Tom came back ...

Tuesday, 4 August 1874. Auntie was buried – Uncle Tom came in eve, not well.

Thursday, 6 August 1874. ... Uncle Tom came ...

Friday, 7 August 1874. ... Uncle Tom & Pa started for Hâvre ...

Saturday, 19 December 1874. ... Uncle Tom came up ...

Tuesday, 22 December 1874. ... Uncle Tom ill ...

Friday, 25 December 1874. Christmas Day ... Uncle Tom & Willie to dinner ...

Sunday, 27 December 1874. ... Uncle Tom to dinner.

214. *"I have done what I never did before in my life, past the most of a week in bed and the house"*

Tom Bassano to niece Melinda [Dido] Bassano   Hâvre
                                                1 November 1874
Dear Dido
    Your note of the 8th Ultimo duly to hand with its enclosed.
I hope Fan returned with a big loote of old bottles, rags,
scraps of carpet, apples, empty flowerpots &c. and has ere this
set up an old bone & rag shop, and finds it pays.

    You should have sold your Turks when on the rise at 71 & 72.
It never pays to wait untill dividend is paid. They always drop
twice as much as the dividend gives you. Get rid of them on the
rise now going on, and settle it up yourselves.

    The weather is so nice the last few days that it has done me
good and I begin to feel quite myself again. I should have
answered your letter sooner but have been so poorly that I have
done what I never did before in my life, past the most of a week
in bed and the house. These European climates are beastly, no
mistake ...

    Give my love to all at home and much love, I remain,

                  Your affection[ate] Uncle
                          Tom

215. *" ... the niece of a C.B. and Indian merchant prince ..."*

Tom Bassano to niece Melinda [Dido] Bassano   Hâvre
                                             8 November [should
                                           be December] 1875
My dear Dido
    Your note of the 25th to hand. I hear from Tom [Dido's
fiancé] a few days since. He writes in the happiest mood as to
the coming event. What on earth made you think I should wish to
interfere in any way with his or your arrangem[en]ts? I mearly
asked you in confidence if any trust arrangement had been made
or mentioned. You should not call yourself a pennyless girl.
The niece of a C.B.[10] and Indian Merchant prince are as good as
untold gold amongst the slumbering native[s] of Scotland. I
hope and trust you are not still ruffelled at my letter for you
know it is the last thing in the world I could do to be cross
with you, particularly on such a happy occasion ... I ment it
to act as a tonic, do you all the good in the world. I am under
tonic medicine myself, in the shape of Turks rising, and so
trust to be able to give you some pretty present on your marriage

10. Maj. Gen. Alfred Bassano was made a C.B. in 1873.

370

than a silver thimble which was floating before my eyes under
the Dooms of Turkish Palaces and Ottoman Bonds.

I will try to be home at Xmas. It must be warmer than it is
here the last week. The glass has been standing at 20 and snow
18 inches thick, ice 4 to 6 inches thick. I am quite well I am
glad to say, and with love to you and all at home

                    I remain
                 Your affectionate Uncle
                         Tom

[Tom Bassano died on 9 February 1876, in his 55th year.]

KASHMIR

Peshawar ● ●Attock ●Srinagar

✕
Gujrat ●
Wazirabad ●

Cheniote ●
●Amritsar
LAHORE ●Jullundur
Ferozepore ● ●Simla
✕ Kussowlie ●
Multan ● ●Mussoorie
Ambala ●

●Meerut
DELHI ●

●Aligarh
Agra ●
Cawnpore ●Lucknow
Gwalior ●

SIKKIM

NEPAL
Darjeeling ●
BHUT

●Dinapore
Allahabad ● ●Benares

●Karachi

Chinsura ●
●Dum Dum
CALCUTTA ●

BOMBAY ●

Mangalore ● ●Bangalore ●MADRAS

Cannanore ●
Tellicherry ● ●Manantoddy
Calicut ● ●Ootacamund

CEYLON

GLOSSARY
(spelling as in text)

adjutant (adjatent) - very
large scavenging bird
anna (anner) - one sixteenth
of a rupee
bahin - sister
bannia (baneeah, banyan) -
merchant, trader, shopkeeper
batta - allowance
bearer - carrier, personal
servant
bhai (bihe) - brother
bheestee (bistee, beastie) -
water carrier
boat achcha - very good
to bone - to take, to steal
Bones - Surgeon
burra - big
burra adamies - great men
butchas (batchas) -
young ones, children
carte - photograph on stiff
card
chahti - a pot
chit - a note
chockree - little girl
chota - little
to clap on the darbies -
to put on the handcuffs
coolie - porter, day labourer
to cut - to run away, to desert
daguerreotype - a precursor
of the photograph
dak (dawk) - post
dibs - money
dobie - washerman
doolie - a litter
dowsing the glims - putting
out the lights
faquirs (fakirs) - religious
mendicants
Feringhee - European
garbling (of coffee) -
sifting, sorting
garry - carriage
ghat (ghaut, guat) -
a landing place, steps on
the river bank, the E. & W.
mountain ranges of India

gora loge - white men
(pale-faced people)
hackeries - ox carts
khana - dinner
khitmutgar (kitmutgar) -
table servant
khubur - news
kopra - clothing
a mill - a fight
mofussilite - an upcountry
resident
a muff - a silly fellow
mutwala - drunk
nautch - dance
nullah - dry canal
palanquin (palankeen) - a
covered litter, or long box,
on poles, carried by a team
of from four to eight
bearers
palki (polkies) - palanquin(s)
palki gari - palanquin on
wheels
pice - small coin, one
quarter of an anna
puckah (pucka) - first rate,
genuine
punkah (punkers) - fan(s)
rot roj - every day
rupee - standard E.I.C. coin
worth two shillings (or
10p.) at this time
Sawbones - surgeon
scragged - killed
screwed - drunk
sepoy - Indian soldier
serdar (sirdar) - military
chief, courtesy title used
in addressing a Sikh
a shallop - a fishing boat
syce - groom
talwar (tulwar) - sword
tank - reservoir
tat - pony
tiffin - lunch
tin - money
tope - grove
wallahs (wallars) - fellows

373

[The references are to *items*, not pages, except
when preceded by "p."]

378

LINNEY, George, cont.
104, 146, 158, 168, 173
---- bill of, 41
Liverpool, 42, 104
LLOYD'S of London, 183
London, Intro., pp.2-6 *passim*,
p.19, p.31, pp.39-40
LONSDALE, Mr., War Office, 5
looting, after fall of
Multan, 32, 33
LOVELL, "Old", 185
LOWE, Capt. (Major, Lt. Col.),
32nd Regt.
---- before Multan, 31
---- at siege of Lucknow, 157
---- at banquet, 178
Lucknow, Intro., pp.29-31
---- C.B.B. visits, 88
---- march to by A.B., 150
---- after Chinhut, 155
---- siege of, 150, 154, 157,
158, 166, 167, 168, 170,
173, 178

McANDREW, Dr., Staff Surgeon,
Army Med. Dept., 100
MACAULAY, Dr., Hon. Artillery,
24
McGRIGOR, Sir James,
Director-General, Army Med.
Dept., 45, 46, 47, 68, 71
---- retirement of, 76, 80
---- portrait of, 97
MACKENZIE, "Ould", 114
McNEILL, Sir John, 136, 137,
140
MADDEN, Mrs., gives birth at
sea, 51
Madeira, 2, 51
---- voyage to, 5
---- Letter from, 5
MADOCKS, - , 98th Regt., 27
Madras, 100, 106, 118, 121,
161, 163, 169, 173, 185
---- Letter from, 168
Madras juggler, performance
by, 26
MAHONEY, Mrs., gives birth at
sea, 51
Malabar, 106, 116, 190
---- coffee failure in, 197

Malta, 142, 169, 180, 181,
207
Manantoddy, 17, 18, 163, 171,
186
---- Letters from, 94, 106,
127, 128, 169, 174, 175
Mangalore, 94, 125
MARKHAM, Col. Frederick,
32nd Regt., 28, 59, 68
---- shot in leg, 30
---- "laughingly reproves"
A.B., 30
---- leads attack at Multan,
31
---- Letter from, 56
Marseilles, 135, 179, 180,
183, 195
MARTELLI, Mr., 37
Masonic Ball, at Meerut, 83
MATHESON, Mr., 15
---- *see also* JARDINE &
MATHESON
MATTHEWS, Mr., Army Med.
Dept., 40, 61, 68
MAUNSELL, Lieut., 32nd Regt.,
wounded at Multan, 33
medical supplies, deficiency
of, 38, 80
Meerut, Intro. pp.21-3, 36-8;
p.73
---- 57, 58, 73, 74, 76, 77,
93
---- march to, 20, 21
---- descriptions of, 22, 83,
84
---- drill at, 24
---- life at, 21-27, 80, 83
---- military executions at,
24
---- St. Patrick's Day at, 21
---- C.B.B. at, 80-87
Melbourne, 90, 91, 108, 110,
118, 119, 120, 131, 159,
160, 161, 162, 163, 164,
165, 170, 177
---- Ellen's arrival at, 83
---- cost of living at, 91,
102, 108, 118
---- Letter from, 96
MENZIES, Dr., 141
Meurice's Hotel, Paris, 137
Middlesbrough, coaling
voyage to, 6